Westminster Aids to the Study of the Scriptures

THE WESTMINSTER HISTORICAL ATLAS TO THE BIBLE

WESTMINSTER AIDS
TO THE STUDY OF THE SCRIPTURES

THE WESTMINSTER DICTIONARY OF THE BIBLE

Edited by John D. Davis

Fifth edition revised and rewritten by Henry S. Gehman

THE WESTMINSTER HISTORICAL ATLAS
TO THE BIBLE

Edited by G. Ernest Wright and Floyd V. Filson

(OTHER TITLES IN PREPARATION)

THE WESTMINSTER
HISTORICAL ATLAS
TO THE BIBLE

Edited by

GEORGE ERNEST WRIGHT

Associate Professor of Old Testament, McCormick Theological Seminary

AND

FLOYD VIVIAN FILSON

Professor of New Testament Literature and History
McCormick Theological Seminary

WITH AN INTRODUCTORY ARTICLE BY
WILLIAM FOXWELL ALBRIGHT
Professor of Semitic Languages, Johns Hopkins University

PHILADELPHIA

The Westminster Press

1946

PRINTED IN THE UNITED STATES OF AMERICA
THE LAKESIDE PRESS, R. R. DONNELLEY & SONS COMPANY
CHICAGO, ILLINOIS, AND CRAWFORDSVILLE, INDIANA

PREFACE

THE study of geography cannot give the ultimate explanation of human life. Nevertheless, life has a geographical basis which the study of history cannot neglect. For example, the peculiar conditions within Palestine and its setting in the Near East provided a background for a people who lived in the world, yet were never quite united with the world. They enjoyed enough detachment to preserve and develop their gifts, but in their constant contact with the stream of significant events they faced the deepest and most vital problems of life.

Careful study of the historical geography of Biblical lands is imperative for two reasons. First, these regions have exercised an immense influence upon our Western World. Indeed, the foundations of modern civilization are to be found in the heritage which the ancient civilizations of the Mediterranean area have left to us. This is true not only in such details as the alphabet, pen and ink, metallurgy, astronomy, medicine, and mathematics, but more basically in the heritage of the Judaeo-Christian religion, Greek philosophy, and Roman law. Hence he who would understand the major factors which have shaped our faith, thought, and life cannot neglect the historical geography of Biblical lands.

Second, the study of geography is necessary for understanding the Bible. The Scripture is not a treatise on philosophy or theology, nor does it present a manual of abstract ethics. It is primarily a historical literature, which tells how God confronted men at particular times and places. Geography, history, and religion are so inextricably bound together in it that the religious message cannot be truly understood without attention to the setting and conditions of the revelation. In this respect the Bible is unique among the world's scriptures; it is the only one for whose comprehension the study of historical geography is basic.

I. GEOGRAPHICAL INFLUENCE ON BIBLICAL HISTORY

The focal center of Biblical history is the small land of Palestine, and the geographical influence upon the Judaeo-Christian movement may be suggested by a brief discussion of four facts about this country's situation:

A. The basic cultural ties of Palestine were with Syria and the rest of the Fertile Crescent. From this region, which lay along the great Arabian Desert, came the dominant factors in the cultural life of Palestine. No permanent or thorough shaping of Palestinian life ever came from the west. Moreover, it was separated from Egypt by the barren coastal desert and the wilderness of Sinai. This does not mean that there were no contacts between Egypt and Palestine. The influence of Egypt on her northern neighbor was constant; in nearly every excavation of ancient Palestinian ruins, objects imported from Egypt have been found. Yet that influence was always superficial; it did not affect the basic elements of the native culture.

The conceptual life and material civilization of Palestine were oriented mainly toward the Fertile Crescent on the north and northeast. When we examine the Israelite beliefs about life after death, about the essentially anthropomorphic rather than theriomorphic nature of God, about man as created for the service of the Divine, and about the divine requirements concerning both the ritualistic and the moral law, it becomes clear that the closest kinship of these beliefs is with the conceptual life of the Fertile Crescent. In Egypt, on the other hand, as indeed also in Greece, the fundamental doctrines about human and divine life were very different. Similarly, the arts and crafts, architecture, agriculture, metallurgy, and ceramics of Palestine were dependent upon Syria. It was in the latter country that new inventions, new styles, and new fashions originated. From Syria they gradually filtered down into Palestine, where, however, they never possessed the same brilliance. In material culture Palestine was the borrower and imitator, rarely the originator.

This culturally dependent region of Palestine was never a center of wealth. It was comparatively poor in natural resources, and as a result was not fought for with quite the same intensity as were the richer portions of the ancient Near East. None of the world's large cities were located within its borders. A sophisticated urban culture, of a type common in such centers as Tyre, Byblos, Ugarit, and Babylon, did not exist in Palestine except as a weak reflection or imitation of the cultured and wealthy north. Here, therefore, was the providentially provided setting, in which the prophetic minds of Israel could understand that the real purpose and blessing of God for his people were not to be found in riches, political power, and cultural distinction. The prophets reacted against contemporary culture because of its pagan character and the easygoing, compromising tolerance which it promoted.

B. Proximity to the Arabian Desert was a second noteworthy feature of the geographical situation of Palestine. Between that land and the Desert to the east there was no barrier. Hence here, as in the other countries of the Fertile Crescent, there was the eternal struggle between the nomadic and the settled peoples.

The struggle between the Desert and the Sown seems to be a perpetual one. The moment that the central political authority weakens or is destroyed, that moment the Bedouins sweep in . . . . Like the waters of the ocean, the Bedouins may be held in check, but the moment the barriers are weakened, in they sweep with a destructive force that cannot be stemmed. . . . They can always retreat into the desert whither few can follow, and they are always prepared to break into the fertile lands at the first appearance of weakness there.*

Before Israel invaded Palestine, the comparative poverty and culturally dependent nature of the country meant that there was no real political strength and no deeply seated urban culture which could successfully resist nomadic invasion and influence. The incoming Israelite hosts constituted a nomadic group with the typical patriarchal organization of Arabia, and in later times they continued to look back upon this organization as the ideal one. In addition, later Israel preserved the relatively high moral purity and austerity of the patriarchal, nomadic religion, so that when the people settled down to agriculture and became increasingly urbanized, the family God of the Fathers did not become another nature or weather deity. The close relation of God and people, as symbolized in the covenant, was Israel's nomadic heritage, and the most important factor in saving her from idolatry. These basic elements of patriarchal religious life were idealized in later Israel and always remained as a purifying agent, not only among such extremists as the Nazirites and Rechabites, but among the great prophets as well.

This does not mean, however, that we can explain away Israel's unique conception of God simply by reference to the Arabian Desert or nomadic life. Before the days of Mohammed, Arabs were polytheists. Geography may explain the conditions of divine revelation, but cannot provide a substitute for it. What can safely be said, however, is that the patriarchal influence upon Israel remained dominant throughout her struggle with Canaanite polytheism. The ideal background of her religion lay in the desert, not in the scenes of urban civilization, and to that background the prophets constantly appealed.

C. A third important geographical fact about Palestine was its situation on two of the most vital trade routes of the ancient world: one between Egypt and Asia, and the other running west from Arabia to reach the coastal plain and there branch off to Egypt or Syria. By reason of this involvement in the economic life of the world, Palestine inevitably was drawn into world affairs. The period of Biblical history was the first great epoch of empire-building. It witnessed the impressive rise and rule of such mighty empires as Egypt, Assyria, Babylonia, Persia, Macedonia, and Rome. Each in succession reached out to seize and dominate the trade routes which passed through Palestine. This little country was thus inescapably forced within the bounds of each succeeding kingdom. It is not surprising, therefore, that the prophets deal with the international situa-

*Glueck, Nelson, *The Other Side of the Jordan* (New Haven, 1940), pp. 6 f.

tion and see the far reach of the power of God. Nor is it strange that along the many lines of trade and travel Jews moved out from their homeland until in the early days of the Christian movement, settlements of Jews were found in every important city of the known world.

D. The geographical features of Palestine and the character of its borders offered its inhabitants the possibility of a definitely limited but nevertheless real detachment. It would be easy to exaggerate that detachment; indeed, this has often been done. Palestine was too much involved in the currents of the ancient world to live in "splendid isolation" at any period of its history, and the study of its life always requires attention to the surrounding world. In spite of this immensely significant fact, however, Palestine was set apart from every neighboring region. On the south and east were uninviting wilderness and desert. The almost unbroken shore line of the Mediterranean Sea severely limited maritime contacts with lands to the west. On the north the massive heights of the Lebanons and Hermon rendered complete identification with the life of Syria impossible.

Thus on every side the borders of Palestine marked it as destined to have its own peculiar history. This provision for detachment was further effected by the lack of geographical unity within the country itself. Galilee was separated from Samaria; the hills were distinct from the plains; Transjordan was divided from western Palestine by the deep cleft of the Jordan Valley. Thus when the Canaanites were in control, no unified state ever came into being. Instead, there were numerous city-states. Even the deities became localized and pluralized, so that we hear of Baals and Ashtoreths, although in the official religion Baal and Ashtoreth were a single god and goddess. The basic geography of the country, therefore, created divisive forces which naturally tended to separate people into groups.

When Israel entered the country, she possessed a common religious and historical tradition, but throughout her existence she had to struggle against the geographical factors which divided north from south and east from west. Yet the partial isolation of the country as a whole provided sufficient detachment to enable Israel to develop a unique spiritual heritage. In Judaism this detachment was magnified into a national and religious exclusiveness. So basic did this element become that it continued to shape the lives of Jews even when they moved out into Gentile lands, and the Jews as a strong religious and cultural group continued to exist even when deprived of homeland and political independence. Under the stimulus of Hellenistic influence and Roman rule, however, the setting was created in the first century for a fuller revelation of the world scope of God's purpose. The days when detachment could be creative and fruitful were past; it was the time for Israel to give her gifts to the world.

II. THE PLAN OF THE ATLAS

In this volume the Editors and Publisher have sought to supply a series of maps which will set forth clearly and vividly the geographical setting of the Biblical story. The explanatory chapters which accompany the maps attempt to provide the essential facts needed to comprehend the historical and geographical framework of Scripture. Carefully selected photographs supplement the maps and text.

A new Biblical atlas is urgently needed. In recent decades extensive exploration has added greatly to our geographical knowledge of the Biblical lands. The last generation has seen an epoch-making advance in the methods and achievements of archaeological work. A new degree of mastery of the languages of the ancient Near East, a hitherto unattained correlation of the discoveries in the Mediterranean and Near East, and the development of adequate methods of excavation have all combined to make this advance possible.

The volume begins with an introductory article on the methods that have been employed in the rediscovery of the Biblical world. Professor W. F. Albright, the acknowledged authority in this field, has been kind enough to supply it. Following this article is a table of dates for convenient reference; it places the persons and events of the Biblical story in the full setting of the ancient world.

In the main body of the book each map plate is accompanied by an explanatory discussion. Chapter I deals with the general geography of Palestine. Chapters II-VII are primarily historical, and cover the period beginning with the world of the Patriarchs and ending with Judah in Nehemiah's time. At this point the historical maps are interrupted to give enlarged section maps of Palestine and their accompanying geographical discussion in Chapters VIII-X. Chapter XI, with its four section maps, continues the historical discussion, dealing with the great empires between the ninth and second centuries B.C. Chapters XII-XVI carry the story to the fourth century A.D., discussions of Palestine alternating with discussions of the Mediterranean world into which Christianity spread. Chapter XVII traces the history of Jerusalem; and Chapter XVIII surveys the archaeological excavations in Palestine during the past century.

It is hoped that the Index of Sites at the close of the volume will prove to be one of the most useful features of the work. It is not limited to the sites that appear on the maps, but is enlarged to provide a geographical index to the Bible (the spelling used is generally that of the A.V.). It gives directions for finding any site shown on the maps, and in the case of other places gives the approximate location, if it can be determined. With the expert aid of Professor Albright, an attempt has also been made to present the accurate spelling of the modern Arabic names of the places with which the ancient Palestinian sites are identified.

The Editors have divided responsibilities as much as possible. In general, Professor Wright's work extended through the Old Testament period. Professor Filson was responsible for the later period, beginning with the time of Alexander the Great. Plates I-VII, XI: A-C, XVII:A, and XVIII, together with Chapters II-VII, X, XVIII, and portions of Chapters XI and XVII have been done by Professor Wright. Professor Filson edited Plates XI:D, XII-XVI, and XVII: B-D, and prepared Chapters VIII, XII-XVI, and parts of Chapters XI and XVII. They collaborated on Plates VIII-X and Chapters I and IX.

The Editors are greatly indebted to their advisory committee, consisting of Professors W. F. Albright, of Johns Hopkins University; Millar Burrows, of Yale University; and O. R. Sellers, of McCormick Theological Seminary. These scholars gave generously of their time and interest in examining the material in the volume and making many suggestions. To Professor Albright in particular we owe a great debt for his sympathetic counsel and advice at every stage of the work. Professors George Cameron and I. J. Gelb, of the Oriental Institute of the University of Chicago; and Professor A. A. Hays, of McCormick Theological Seminary, also gave scholarly aid in connection with the preparation of Plates II, III, XI, and XVI.

Constant aid has come from the Rev. L. J. Trinterud and Mr. John Ribble, of The Westminster Press, and from Mr. W. R. Bowes and the technical staff of the R. R. Donnelley and Sons Company in Chicago. The interest of these men went far beyond the usual function of publisher and printer, and the results of their expert and patient counsel appear on every page. To them is due also the revolutionary method of map making, developed especially for use in this atlas. It provides skillful reproduction of complicated geographical factors and beauty of appearance, and makes possible the publication of the atlas at a price within the reach of the student.

Dr. Georges Barrois, of Princeton Theological Seminary, drew the relief map of Palestine which was used on Plates I, IV, VI, VIII-X, XII, XIV, and XVIII. He began work on the relief map of the Mediterranean world, but pressure of other duties prevented him from completing it. Mr. Hal Arbo, of Chicago, completed this map, which is used on Plates II, III, XI, XIII, XV, XVI; he also prepared the special maps used on Plates V, VII, and XVII. Mrs. Jean Arbo prepared the maps for the engravers by lettering sites, drawing in roads and boundaries, et cetera, on the basis of original copy supplied by the Editors. To these artists we express our sincere appreciation for their painstaking and highly competent work.

G. ERNEST WRIGHT.
FLOYD V. FILSON.

McCormick Theological Seminary
August 31, 1944.

TABLE OF CONTENTS

TABLE OF ILLUSTRATIONS

ACKNOWLEDGMENTS *We gratefully give credit to the following sources for the illustrations used in this volume:*

Oriental Institute, University of Chicago, Figures 1 (Aerial Survey of the Oriental Institute), 3, 5, 10, 11 (Painting by M. Bardin after Unger), 12 (Cast in Oriental Institute), 16, 17, 18, 20 (Cast in Oriental Institute), 28, 29, 32 (Cast in Oriental Institute), 49 (Cast in Oriental Institute), 51 (Painting by M. Bardin after Unger).

Ewing Galloway, ©, Figures 2, 4, 6, 8, 13, 15, 34, 35, 38, 39, 40, 42, 54, 57, 58, 59, 60, 61, 65, 67, 68 71, 72, 73.

Philip Gendreau, ©, Figures 7, 36, 37, 50, 56, 62, 63.

Lepsius, *Denkmaeler*, Part 2, Pl. 133, and Part 3, Pl. 40, Figures 9, 22.

Petrie, Sir W. M. F., *Hyksos and Israelite Cities* (Bernard Quaritch Press), Pl. IVa, Figure 14.

Boreux, *La Sculpture égyptienne au Musée du Louvre*, Pl. XXVIII, Figure 19.

Syria, Vol. 17, Pl. XXI, Photograph by C. F. A. Schaeffer, for the French expedition to Ugarit, Figure 21.

Wilson and Palmer, *Ordnance Survey of the Peninsula of Sinai*, Photographs, Vol. I, Numbers 48–50, Figure 23.

American Schools of Oriental Research, Figures 24, 25, 43, 44, 45, 47, 76; Figures 25 and 47 being by courtesy of the Air Officer Commanding, Royal Air Force, Middle East.

H. G. May, Figures 26, 27, 30, 55.

Watzinger, *Denkmaeler Palaestinas*, Vol. I, Pl. 16, Figure 31.

Wellcome-Marston Archaeological Research Expedition to the Near East, Figure 33.

G. Ernest Wright, Figures 41, 46, 52, 69.

O. R. Sellers, Figure 53 (from the Beth-zur Excavation; courtesy, Royal Air Force Official, Crown Copyright Reserved).

Oxford University Press, Figures 64 (from Sukenik, *Ancient Synagogues in Palestine and Greece*, British Academy, Pl. XVI:A) and 70 (from Rostovtzeff, *Dura-Europos and Its Art*, Pl. II).

W. A. McDonald, Figure 66.

Illustrated London News, ©, Figure 74.

University Museum, Philadelphia, Figure 75.

Palestine Institute, Pacific School of Religion, Figure 77.

THE REDISCOVERY OF THE BIBLICAL WORLD

WILLIAM FOXWELL ALBRIGHT

I. INTRODUCTORY CONSIDERATIONS

THERE are few fields where the progress of discovery makes constant revision of handbooks and other aids to study more necessary than in Biblical research. This is not easy, even for scholars, to realize, since one instinctively feels that old books are more useful as guides to the study of old subjects than new books. On the other hand, there is danger in seeking new discoveries and novel points of view at the expense of more solid earlier work. This is particularly true in fields like Biblical archaeology and geography, where mastery of tools and of methods of investigation is so arduous that there is always a temptation to neglect sound method, substituting clever combinations and brilliant guesses for slower and more systematic work.

Since it is only in our generation that the progress of research has made real synthesis possible, all standard books appearing earlier are in imperative need of revision, often of complete rewriting. Moreover, many of the latest books and articles have been written by men who are not really competent. The reader who is not a specialist is naturally helpless in selecting a reliable authority to follow. The mere fact that an author occupies a distinguished academic position or has made some remarkable discoveries in the field or museum does not prove his scholarly competence. Hence the value of such an organization as the American Schools of Oriental Research, which is not tied to any one university or organization but gathers the best skills and selects only the most reliable scholars to present the results of excavation, exploration, and interpretation to the educated public.

In evaluating the information contained in standard Biblical handbooks, it is well to compare the dates of their publication with the dates of the most significant archaeological discoveries. To begin with standard English works of conservative character, Clarke's great *Commentary*, which is still used by many, appeared in 1810–1826; Kitto's famous *Cyclopaedia* came out in 1843–1845. If we consider fundamental German works, Eichhorn's *Introduction* (with which the history of the so-called higher criticism really begins) was published in 1783, while the first scientific Hebrew dictionary and grammar were brought out by Gesenius in 1810–1813. The most important developments in literary criticism of the Old Testament came in 1805

with De Wette's contention that Deuteronomy was composed in the reign of Josiah, in 1853 with Hupfeld's successful revival of Ilgen's view that there were three documents instead of two in Genesis, and in 1876 with Wellhausen's consolidation of the Graf-Kuenen view that the Priestly Code was the latest of the four documents of the Pentateuch.

Turning to compare the most important dates in the history of modern Biblical archaeology, we note that the Egyptian hieroglyphics were not deciphered until the years 1822–1841 and that Assyrian cuneiform was not decoded until 1845–1851. Systematic excavations were not begun in Assyria until 1843 and in Egypt until 1850; the first scientific excavations from our present point of view were undertaken by Flinders Petrie in Egypt (since 1883) and Palestine (1890). But it was not until 1887 that the Amarna Tablets (see p. 35) were found, while the Elephantine Papyri did not become available to scholars until 1911. The great Hittite archives of Boghazköy were unearthed in 1907, but it was not until the middle twenties that enough material became available to make synthesis possible. The long-lost Canaanite religious literature has been excavated only since 1929, while successful interpretation of its remains cannot be said to have begun until 1932. Scarcely any original Sumerian literature from the third millennium was available for scholarly research until S. N. Kramer began to publish in 1938. It was not until 1939 that the present writer felt that the time had come to begin the preparation of real syntheses of ancient Near-Eastern history and civilization. During the preceding decade our knowledge of archaeological chronology had increased so rapidly that it was then possible for the first time to date events and cultural phenomena in different lands correctly in relation to one another.

This tremendous improvement in knowledge and method applies not only to the broad field of ancient civilization but at the same time to such special aspects as geography and topography, with which this book is primarily concerned. Even in the field of map making there has been great advance since Robinson began his epochal researches in 1837. At that time few points in the entire Near East had been precisely located in latitude and longitude, while details were left to be roughly sketched in by cartographers who utilized naval observations and explorers' records of distance and direction.

FIG. 1. The Behistun "Rock" in Iran (Plate III, E-3). On the jagged face of this mountain the Persian monarch Darius I (522–486 B.C.) carved an inscription, twenty-five feet high and fifty feet wide, to commemorate his first victories. It was written in the three most important languages of the eastern portion of his realm, Old Persian, Babylonian, and Elamite. An English army officer, Sir Henry Rawlinson, copied the three versions of the inscription between 1835 and 1847. The monument is three hundred feet above the plain, and Rawlinson's deed was a most difficult one. Yet it was by this means that Babylonian was deciphered. The inscription cannot be seen on the photograph, but it is located on the left side of the vertical fissure in the center of the photograph, just above the road.

The Holy Land was the first country of southwestern Asia to be systematically surveyed, yet the Survey of Western Palestine was not undertaken until 1865 and was not finished until 1877. Schumacher's much sketchier survey of northern Transjordan, begun in 1885, was not finished until 1914. The region of Moab and Edom has never been properly mapped. In recent years considerable progress has been made with the detailed cadastral survey of Palestine, and a number of sheets are now available. Moreover, a century ago nothing was known about geological formation, and little about soils and water supply, rainfall and temperature, etc. Above all, however, from our present standpoint, we have learned how to use archaeological data to locate, date, and often identify ancient sites. How this is done will be concisely explained below.

II. HOW WE EXCAVATE IN THE NEAR EAST

It is often supposed that the archaeologist digs merely for the purpose of unearthing monuments and finding museum objects in the buildings or tombs which he excavates. It is true that much excavation of the nineteenth century was undertaken for these ends; the outstanding example of it is Mariette's work in Egypt from 1850 to 1880. Fortunately, however, not nearly so much harm could be done in Egypt as in Mesopotamia by such rough-and-ready methods, since there was almost no stratification in the temples and tombs of the Nile Valley which Mariette cleared of their silt and sand. From the very beginning of the work of Botta and Layard in Assyria, about a century ago, much more care was devoted to the recording of the finds as they were made, to the planning of excavated buildings, and to the prompt publication of the principal objects discovered. Yet scientific archaeology cannot be said to have commenced until 1890, when Flinders Petrie dug for six weeks at *Tell el-Ḥesī* in southern Judah (Plate XVIII, B-5). At that time he was able to demonstrate once for all that most important ancient sites of southwestern Asia consist of more or less regular, superimposed layers of debris, and that it is possible to date them by the artifacts (objects made by man) which each layer contains. The most valuable artifacts for dating are pieces of pottery, whole or broken. These broken pieces are found in enormous numbers on these ancient sites. Pottery was fragile and seldom was usable for any great while. Moreover, pottery styles changed rapidly. In his brief season in Palestine, preceded and followed by many years of excavation in Egypt, Petrie showed that archaeological chronology could be based on a careful study of the relation of objects to one another in the light of the deposits in which they occur, as well as on equally systematic study of the evolution of pottery forms or styles (sequence dating). The study of the physical relationship of artifacts in the light of the strata in which they are found is called "stratigraphy," and the study of the relation between the forms of objects is called "typology." All scientific modern archaeology is based on the application of these two basic principles, to which we shall return presently.

The best recent archaeological method is associated with the name of George Andrew Reisner, a native of Indianapolis, who became the foremost excavator of modern times. Reisner combined the methods employed by the leading German excavators, who stressed the architectural and engineering side of archaeology, with the stratigraphy and typology of the Petrie school, employing both with the aid of American filing cabinets and recording systems. Fortunately, Reisner was always supplied with adequate funds to provide for assistants and apparatus, so he was able to set an example of comprehensive and accurate recording of his work in the field.

Today archaeological treasure hunts are no longer permitted in the Near East. In all the countries of this region, whether independent nations or mandatories, there are organized departments of antiquities, headed by Government appointees who are generally scholars of distinction. The directors of antiquities are assisted by staffs of trained archaeologists, who care for the archaeological museum or museums, inspect ancient monuments and see that they are protected against injury, watch over the trade in antiquities and prevent illicit digging and smuggling as far as practicable, and control the excava-

tions carried on by native and foreign institutions. In Palestine the officials of the Department of Antiquities are British in the higher grades and Jewish or Arab in the lower grades; there is also an international archaeological advisory board consisting of representatives of domestic and foreign archaeological interests. There are detailed ordinances which control archaeological matters affecting governmental organization and the rights of individuals. For the best recent approach to a uniform archaeological system in the Near East, we may refer to the text of the resolutions of the archaeological conference in Jerusalem, July, 1943, as published in the *Bulletin of the American Schools of Oriental Research*, October, 1943.

The excavator of today is expected to undertake his work with an adequate staff of assistants, who are provided with all necessary equipment, such as surveying instruments, photographic apparatus, drawing tools, picks, hoes, baskets, and sieves. In large sites light railways and cranes may be required. The work of the native diggers, who are generally untrained, must be supervised directly by the members of the excavating staff or by trained native foremen, whose own supervisory activity is carefully controlled by the director of the expedition. The site and its environs are surveyed first, if possible, and a survey grid, composed as a rule of squares twenty meters on a side, is prepared. All excavated remains are recorded on this grid as exactly as possible, in order to avoid errors. All artifacts found during the excavation are labeled with the number of the room or other locus where they were found. If desirable, the exact spot, as well as the precise level above the floor, is noted. Many photographs are taken to show the exact appearance of the ruins as they are cleared, and especially to record the relation of objects to one another as well as to the adjacent walls. The levels of the excavated ruins are also duly recorded, attention being concentrated mainly on tops of walls in each locus, floor levels, and foundation levels. When this task is finished and the excavator has taken careful notes on details, such as peculiarities of construction and indications of repair or reoccupation, the entire stratum may be removed down to its foundations and the next stratum below may be cleared in the same way. Sometimes, of course, there was so much reuse of older walls and so much partial reconstruction that it is not practicable to remove any walls until the excavator has cleared a sufficient number of superimposed foundations to make a systematic analysis of their relation to one another possible.

All significant objects of human manufacture found should be recorded summarily, with brief descriptions and identifying drawings or photographs, on cards or in a record book, the objects themselves being correspondingly labeled. When possible, objects are restored and cleaned, though final cleaning and restoration are generally left to be done in the museums where they are later deposited. It is particularly important, moreover, that pottery be cleaned and put together on the spot, since it is all of chronological interest and since most broken pottery is discarded after the close of an excavation. Accurate outline drawings and clear photographs are prepared on the spot as far as possible, so that errors and losses may be averted. Chemical treatment of objects and detailed technical study of them must nearly always be left until later, since few expeditions possess the necessary facilities or technologically trained staff.

In interpreting his finds as sources of historical information the archaeologist must be particularly careful not to allow his judgment to be biased by preconceived ideas. In other words, he must remember that archaeology is primarily an inductive science, and that the careful use of factual data precedes all deductive reasoning. Hence the importance of distinguishing throughout between stratigraphy and typology, which we have defined above. First of all, he must be sure of the limits and relations of his strata and must determine whether any unique piece from a given stratum really belongs there or is an intrusion from above or below. Strata are not always level, and later pieces were sometimes washed down from a higher level on a site, or earlier pieces were dropped on the surface after being brought up from an ancient pit, excavated for a cistern or silo. The trained excavator has little trouble with such intrusions, but care

FIG. 2. The Sphinx and Pyramids at *Gîzeh*, Egypt (Plate v, C-3). The great age of pyramid-building in Egypt was during the Old Kingdom between the twenty-seventh and the twenty-second centuries B.C. The pyramids are the most spectacular and tremendous tombs ever built by man. The Sphinx, while possessing the body of a lion, is actually the portrait head of Pharaoh Khafre, the builder of the pyramid behind it. The great Pyramid of Khufu stands just to the right of the photograph.

is obviously required in making deductions from the appearance of a singular object in a given stratum. Unwritten objects, such as pottery, must first be dated relatively to other comparable objects which recur in higher or lower deposits. Then one can give them a date in absolute chronology (B.C. or A.D.) by noting what kind of datable objects (inscriptions, scarabs, coins, etc.) are found with them or in known relation to them. For such evidence we may have to turn to another site, where identical objects may occur together with intrinsically datable remains. Typology is of the greatest importance in fixing chronology, since it enables the scholar to group archaeological objects into classes and species, to identify given types wherever they may recur—sometimes hundreds of miles apart—and to trace the evolution of a given form. When the successive steps of evolution of form are once known, it is possible, for instance, to assign approximate dates to objects which are a little later in type than objects found in a given datable stratum and a little earlier in type than corresponding objects found in the next stratum above. By the combination of inductive reasoning from stratigraphy and deduction from typological indications the archaeologist gradually builds up a coherent chronological system. After such a system has been built up it may be rectified and adjusted by reference to formal historic chronology (see below, section IV).

Once the excavator has accurately described and interpreted his data, they can be used for a great many historical purposes. Particularly significant, of course, are written objects and documents, since they enable the scholar to reconstruct the life of religion, politics, and commerce. But other remains have great and steadily increasing significance. Through them we learn about the arts and crafts of antiquity, how men built and where they lived, how they made pottery, practiced metallurgy, what crops and animals they possessed. Through them we also learn to follow the history of human settlement. Once the archaeologist has determined the pottery chronology of a given region by excavating a number of sites, he can proceed to date all other occupied sites of antiquity by the potsherds with which they are strewn. The outstanding illustration of the successful application of this principle is Nelson Glueck's archaeological survey of Transjordan, in which he has examined and described more than 1,500 ancient sites, dating them by their sherds.

III. HOW WRITTEN DOCUMENTS ARE INTERPRETED

As stated above, written documents form by far the most important single body of material discovered by archaeologists. Hence it is extremely important to gain a clear idea of their character and of our ability to interpret them. Just as in all archaeological work, the question of method takes first place. It must be remembered that every single script employed in the ancient Near East has had to be deciphered in modern times. Curiously enough, for every ancient script to be deciphered two new ones seem to be discovered. We have deciphered Assyro-Babylonian cuneiform and various other independent cuneiform scripts, three principal varieties of Egyptian hieroglyphics, and many other alphabetic and syllabic scripts, but an even greater number remain to be interpreted, and new ones turn up every few years.

As a characteristic example of the nature of our task, we may point to the cuneiform alphabet of Ugarit. First discovered in 1929, many hundreds of tablets in this script have been excavated by C. F. A. Schaeffer at *Râs Shamrah* (Ugarit) on the Syrian coast opposite Cyprus (Plate II, E-2). The first fragmentary tablets were published by Virolleaud in 1930 and almost immediately deciphered by Bauer and Dhorme, both of whom were distinguished as Semitic philologians and as cipher experts. First Bauer correctly identified over half the letters, then Dhorme added five more, after which Bauer made various corrections in his own system, raising the total number of letters identified by himself to nineteen. Subsequently, on the basis of a vastly increased body of texts, Virolleaud and others added six more characters, making thirty in all. However, decipherment was here again only the beginning, and it is characteristic of the difference in the type of skills required that neither Bauer nor Dhorme, in spite of their outstanding ability as Semitists, contributed much to the task of interpretation as such. The next step required schooled imagination, held constantly under control by a rigid sense of grammatical form. Many scholars now entered the field; outstanding among them was H. L. Ginsberg, whose keen grammatical instinct had been cultivated by a thorough training in Semitic philology. Thanks to Gordon's *Ugaritic Grammar*, which appeared in 1940, we now have a solid grammatical basis for further work. Students of Ugaritic are

FIG. 3. The ruins of Persepolis, the magnificent capital of the Persian Empire begun by Darius I (522–486 B.C.) and completed by his successors. The low building in the center is the royal treasury, which has been reconstructed as the expedition headquarters of modern excavators. Columns of the royal palaces can be seen as they were left standing by Alexander the Great, who wantonly set fire to the beautiful capital.

now concentrating on the explanation of passages in the texts hither-to published, with special attention to the meaning of words.

We must distinguish sharply between the earlier and the more recent periods of philological research in our field, since the translations of documents written in different languages depend for accuracy on the progress of grammatical and lexical knowledge. Thus it is unsafe to rely on any translations of Egyptian historical texts which appeared before Breasted's *Ancient Records* (1906), since Breasted was the first historian to take full advantage of the tremendous progress in the knowledge of Egyptian achieved by Erman and Sethe after 1880. It is equally unsafe to depend on any translations of Egyptian religious texts made before about 1925, since that year marked the publication of the first volume of the great Berlin dictionary of Egyptian, while the year 1927 saw the appearance of Gardiner's monumental *Egyptian Grammar*. The first reliable English translations of Egyptian religious texts appeared in Blackman's *Literature of the Ancient Egyptians* (1927) and Breasted's *Dawn of Conscience* (1933). Turning to Mesopotamia we find ourselves in a worse situation, since no English translations of cuneiform texts adequately represent the great progress in scientific philology marked by the brilliant work of Landsberger and his pupils since about 1923. Luckenbill's *Ancient Records of Assyria and Babylonia* (1926–1927) was far below the standard set twenty years earlier by Breasted in the corresponding Egyptian field. Scarcely any Accadian (Semitic-Babylonian) religious text of importance is now available in an up-to-date English translation. The student who does not wish to be misled by antiquated renderings must, accordingly, study recent German work, though even in German no comprehensive translations from the past fifteen years are available. Assyriologists are handicapped by the lack of a comprehensive and up-to-date Assyrian dictionary, the latest lexicon being the sketchy and antiquated glossary of Bezold, edited by Goetze in 1926. The field of Sumerian took a forward step in 1923, when Poebel's grammar was published. Fortunately the publication of the valuable Sumerian religious literature from the temple library at Nippur (Plate II, F-3) in Babylonia is in the hands of Poebel's gifted student, S. N. Kramer, who in 1938 began to edit and translate reconstructed Sumerian epics from the third millennium. Since this is the oldest body of narrative literature in the world, and since it influenced much of the religious literature of the Semites of later times, its importance can scarcely be overestimated.

Our understanding of cuneiform Hittite is now abreast of our knowledge of Sumerian, in spite of the fact that cuneiform Hittite was not deciphered until 1915 and that workers are few. On the other hand, decipherment of hieroglyphic Hittite was brought to an abrupt stop by the outbreak of the current world war after a decade of steady progress. We are still unable to translate a single inscription in hieroglyphic Hittite satisfactorily, though most of the phonetic characters and many ideograms can be read and a good deal is understood about the grammar. At present Ignace Gelb, of the University of Chicago, is the leader in this elusive field. The study of Horite (Hurrian), though begun more than fifty years ago after the publication of the first cuneiform tablets in that language, is still hampered by the small number of texts, which come from half a dozen different excavations, in Egypt, Syria, Mesopotamia, and Asia Minor. E. A. Speiser's excellent *Introduction to Hurrian* (1941) represents the high-water mark in this field.

IV. HOW ANCIENT DATES ARE FIXED

Since chronology is the backbone of history and since it is impossible to get a clear idea of the relationship of events and movements unless we know their dates, it is extremely important for the thoughtful student of the past to get a clear idea how dates are fixed. Since 1938, Mesopotamian chronology has gradually become stabilized until it is probably correct to within half a century as far back as the twenty-fifth century B.C. Egyptian dates for the Old Kingdom have had to be rather drastically reduced to agree with the lower Mesopotamian chronology, and the archaeological chronology of Syria and Palestine has been adjusted to harmonize with the concurrent evidence from both sides. For the first time since the beginning of excavations we are, accordingly, in a position to validate our chronology of the ancient Near East. On what basis can we make this affirmation?

Assyrian chronology is now fixed back toward the middle of the second millennium B.C., thanks to the publication by Arno Poebel, in 1942–1943, of the so-called Khorsabad List of Assyrian kings, which begins in the late third millennium and ends in the eighth century B.C. Moreover, the latter part of this list overlaps other lists of annual magistrates, or eponyms, which are preserved intact from the early ninth century to the middle of the seventh. Part of the period is also covered by a terse chronicle, giving each eponym with the outstanding events of his year. Under one year a solar eclipse is recorded, thus enabling the astronomer to compute the precise date —763 B.C. In this way it is possible to fix the precise date of all the dated events recorded in the Babylonian Chronicle, covering the years from 745 to 667 B.C.—and the accessions of the kings of Babylon agree throughout to the year with the data of the Ptolemaic canon, compiled from Babylonian sources by the famous Greek astronomer of the second century A.D.! Further, thanks to many thousands of dated business documents, we are able to control practically all intercalary months employed in the Neo-Babylonian and Persian periods to adjust the calendar. With the aid of exact astronomical data, it thus becomes possible to give the Julian equivalents of nearly all dates in Mesopotamian records of the first millennium B.C. This means that we have invaluable pegs on which to hang our Biblical chronology from the ninth to the fifth century B.C.

Thanks to the agreement of the Khorsabad List (checked and controlled by numerous other Assyrian sources) with the astronomically fixed chronology of the New Kingdom in Egypt, we can be sure of our approximate dates back to the reign of Asshur-uballit (c. 1362–1327), who came to the throne not long before the death of Amenophis IV (c. 1377–1360). Dead reckoning on the basis of the Khorsabad List brings us to about the middle of the eighteenth century for Shamshi-Adad I, the older Assyrian contemporary of the great Hammurabi of Babylon. The contemporaneity of these outstanding figures in ancient history was not discovered until 1937, with the sensational find of the Mari tablets, which flooded the age in question with historical illumination (see p. 24). Since lists of the annual events by which years were then dated in Babylonia have been recovered—confirmed by many thousand dated business documents of the age—we possess a record of the chronology of Babylonia from the beginning of the Third Dynasty of Ur to the end of the First Dynasty of Babylon, a period of over five centuries, so we can now fix the chronological position of every year in this series with reference to the Khorsabad List within thirty years or so. Moreover, in 1912 the German scholar F. X. Kugler discovered that a cuneiform table of movements of the planet Venus had originally been drawn up under King Ammiṣaduqa of Babylon, as proved by a date formula from that king's reign. This table makes it possible for the astronomer to calculate possible alternative dates for the reign of Ammiṣaduqa, and it becomes easy to show that only one of them fits the data provided by the Khorsabad List and the Mari documents. Employing this astronomically calculated date, the reign of Hammurabi falls between 1728 and 1686 B.C. and the beginning of the Third Dynasty of Ur between 2070 and 2050 B.C.

Turning from Mesopotamia to Egypt, we find one great advantage in the existence of the Sothic cycle, a period equivalent to 1,460 Julian years. When the Egyptian calendar was formally regularized, perhaps about 2780 B.C., it opened each year with the first day on which the star Sirius was visible on the eastern horizon before sunrise, which then coincided roughly with the appearance of the annual Nile inundation in Lower Egypt. But since there were only 365 days in the Egyptian civil (vague) year, each year the calendar fell behind about a quarter of a day. In the course of 1,461 vague years the date of any astronomically fixed event in the calendar returned to its original place in this calendar, so 1,461 vague years = 1,460 Julian years of 365¼ days each. Since the Egyptians celebrated the festival of the heliacal rising of Sirius every year, to the accompaniment of elaborate ritual and mythology, they could not help becoming aware of this discrepancy and its cyclic character. Fortunately for us, we have a definite, though not entirely clear, statement about the end of a Sothic cycle in the second century A.D. in Censorinus, and a probable allusion to the commencement of the same cycle in the monuments of Sethos I, toward the end of the fourteenth century B.C. These fixed dates, combined with new moons and other data, enable us to give fairly exact dates for the kings of the Twelfth Dynasty, between c. 1989 and 1776 B.C., for Amenophis I of the Eighteenth Dynasty, c. 1546 B.C., and for Tuthmosis III, c. 1490 B.C. (These dates follow the correlation of Borchardt, corrected in part by Edgerton, and may have to be moved up or down a few years.) For years many scholars fought the "low chronology" of Borchardt, Meyer, and Breasted, until overwhelmed by the weight of new evidence. I know of no competent ancient historian today who places the beginning of the Middle Kingdom before 2000 B.C. Thanks to the corroboratory evidence of Mesopotamian chronology, there can be no doubt about the substantial correctness of Borchardt's date.

All our chronology of the lands of the Aegean, including Crete, as well as of Palestine and Phoenicia during the Bronze Age, depends upon direct or cultural synchronisms between these regions and Egypt. The archaeological chronology of the entire Bronze Age in Palestine is based on Egyptian. The results are so reasonable throughout and are now so beautifully confirmed by Mesopotamian evidence (through Syria) that they cannot be changed more than a century or two in the future. Since our Palestinian dates depend largely on pottery, they are generally somewhat fluid, but even so they remain fixed within narrow limits. Before 3000 we are again reduced to conjecture on the basis of cultural periods and geochronology.

V. HOW ANCIENT SITES ARE IDENTIFIED

Few scholarly matters have been as cavalierly handled as the identification of ancient sites. Owing to the intense interest of pilgrims and travelers in the Holy Land, well-meaning clergy and helpful guides have made many hasty identifications, generally on the flimsiest pretexts. Moreover, few of the modern scholars who have identified Biblical sites have possessed the necessary scholarly training. Most of what has been written on the subject of Palestinian topography since the seventeenth century is now virtually worthless. However, here and there are some outstanding names of men who made valuable contributions to our knowledge of the topography of the Holy Land. In 1714, Adrian Reland published a careful and comprehensive account of Palestine and its ancient towns, compiled from all available ancient literary sources—the Bible, Graeco-Roman literature, and the Talmud. In 1837, Edward Robinson undertook his epoch-making trip to Palestine, in the course of which he vastly

FIG. 4. A cedar of Lebanon. The cedar forests of the Lebanon range are now greatly diminished in size, but they were once extensive and the most important source of excellent furniture and building wood in the ancient East. Egyptian, Mesopotamian, Canaanite, and Israelite monarchs drew heavily from these forests for their luxurious palaces.

improved existing maps and located hundreds of modern sites, besides identifying for the first time scores of Biblical towns whose location was completely unknown. Dozens of Western scholars followed his footsteps during the following half century, but few of their identifications have stood the test of sound method. In 1865–1877 Conder, Kitchener, and others carried out the great Survey of Western Palestine, followed by an abortive American expedition and later by a successful one-man German undertaking (see above). In 1894, George Adam Smith published his *Historical Geography of the Holy Land*, which became astonishingly popular and passed through many editions. From the scholarly point of view it was abreast of the times when it first appeared, but it has become more and more antiquated with the progress of investigation. The next important step forward came in 1902, when the German Evangelical Institute for the Archaeology of the Holy Land was founded under the direction of Gustav Dalman. He and his pupils introduced much greater precision in their treatment of the material, observing the physical facts as accurately as possible, reproducing modern Arabic names correctly, and dealing with the literary and documentary sources as exhaustively and critically as possible. The German school added some good identifications and discarded many bad ones, as may be seen most conveniently from the *Atlas* of Hermann Guthe (latest edition: 1926). Dalman was succeeded in 1922 by Albrecht Alt, who has improved Dalman's method by utilizing inscriptions and results of archaeological excavations and surface explorations. Since 1922 the American Schools of Oriental Research has taken the lead in surface exploration, dating sites by the potsherds with which they are strewn. The high-water mark of its investigations is marked by the explorations of Nelson Glueck, who began a systematic examination of all ancient sites in Transjordan in 1932, and has continued it ever since with occasional interruptions. No such thorough archaeological survey has ever been made in any other comparable area in the Near East. For the first time we can analyze the fluctuations of population in Transjordan, from period to period, and delimit the boundaries of Edom, Moab, and Ammon on purely archaeological grounds.

The topographical student of today can begin with an admirable French work, Father Abel's *Géographie de la Palestine* (two volumes, 1933–1938). But he will soon find that this is only a convenient starting point for further research, especially on the basis of the rapidly accumulating archaeological and inscriptional material. The serious investigator must consider the following aspects of his problem: (1) criticism of the written sources in which ancient place names occur; (2) approximate location of sites from documentary indications; (3) toponymy, or the analysis of place names and their linguistic transmission; (4) archaeological indications; (5) the evidence of tradition.

The first requirement boils down to a very simple yet often neglected principle: all ancient literary works must be edited with the greatest possible exactness, after a methodical comparison of all preserved manuscripts (whose variant readings must be recorded); all inscriptions must be accessible in photographs or in good copies by scholars of recognized competence and precision. In the case of important places, such scientific editing of passages where they are mentioned frequently gives a clearer idea of their relation to other places in the neighborhood. In the case of less important places, it is well to know the most reliable form of their names before proceeding to locate them. Textual criticism becomes a matter of primary value in dealing with long lists of names such as we have in Joshua, where the Greek translation of the third or second century B.C. often corrects the Hebrew Bible, though it is sometimes not possible to restore the original Greek reading with any degree of confidence. The topographer is thus heavily dependent on the laborious work of textual critics of the Greek Bible. As one out of many possible illustrations we select Josh. 19:45, in a list of towns of Dan. The Hebrew text reads, "And Jehud, and Bene-berak," whereas the oldest Greek manuscript, from the fourth century A.D., offers, "And

(I)azor and Banaibakat." The Taylor Prism of Sennacherib, in its account of the campaign of 701 B.C. against Hezekiah, offers, "Azuru and Banai-barqa." Today we find the two Arab villages of *Yazûr* and *Ibn-ibrâq*, with ancient names, only a mile and a half apart, thus proving the correctness of the Iazor of the oldest Greek text against the Jehud of the much younger Hebrew text of the Masoretic Bible (see Plate IX, C-4, where the traditional name Jehud is placed at modern *Yazûr*).

Our second approach depends more upon knowledge of the country, ancient and modern, as well as upon common sense, than upon any other considerations. The topographer must analyze accounts of journeys and campaigns, comparing routes and lists of different periods with one another; he must be able to select the most suitable location for an ancient town on the basis of terrain, communications, water supply, etc. If he can find different references to a place, he can often locate it approximately by the simple method of drawing lines or circles and noting where they intersect. The greatest danger here is that the scholar will content himself with the application of this method and perhaps the third one, without taking other approaches into consideration.

The third approach to topographic problems begins by comparing ancient place names with modern. Since this method is the most obvious of all, it has been sorely abused by amateur topographers, as well as by many scholars who should know better. Thus Palmer proposed the identification of Zephath (Hormah in the south) with modern *Isbeitā* (*Subaita*), though all Semitic vowels and consonants are different (Plate XVIII, B–7). It is quite true that both vowels and consonants shift in the course of history (thus Hebrew *g* becomes Arabic *j*), but these shifts are subject to regular phonetic laws, which can never be stated arbitrarily but must always be worked out inductively by first collecting all certain examples of correspondences between ancient and modern names. It is also true that popular etymology often modifies an ancient name slightly: e.g., ancient Shefar'am in Galilee is now called *Shefa'amr*, which means, "Healing of 'Amr." Note, however, that even here all the consonants and vowels are kept; the only change is in transposing two consonants. There is little excuse save ignorance for the frequent disregard of sound linguistic method by topographers, especially by archaeologists without any philological training, since Kampffmeyer published an admirable—now slightly antiquated—monograph on the subject as far back as 1892.

The fourth approach consists in utilizing the results of surface exploration and excavation for identifying sites. Thus, for instance, Palmer's identification of Zephath was disproved by the results of the Colt expedition ten years ago. No pottery or other remains from the Israelite period were discovered either at *Isbeitā* (*Subaita*) itself or in the vicinity, thus confirming the objections to the identification previously made by philologians and territorial geographers, who considered the site as much too far south of the mountains of Judah and the arable lands of the tribe of Simeon. An increasing number of identifications have been made on an archaeological basis and subsequently confirmed from other sources: e.g., *Tell ed-Duweir* as the site of Lachish (Plate XVIII, B-5). The archaeological method may be used together with territorial geography: if a town can be limited to a certain district, an exhaustive examination of all possible sites in the area in question often yields the correct identification without any further ado. In this way Garstang discovered the site of Hazor in Galilee (Plate XVIII, D-2).

Our final approach is that of tradition, which can be very valuable but must be employed with great caution. Modern "traditions" are often worthless: e.g., Masterman identified ancient Tarichaea on the Sea of Galilee with modern *Khirbet Kerak* (Plate XVIII, D–3) because the Jewish colonists of Chinnereth—established in the nineteenth century—told him that their ancestors had pickled fish there. Naturally the facts are that the colonists had learned about this once popular but quite erroneous identification from travelers or teachers!

cloud upon the mount" in Ex. 19:16 are interpreted as evidence of an active volcano. In this case the Hebrews would have journeyed across Sinai to Ezion-geber along the present Mohammedan pilgrim route to Mecca (v, D-F 4); but the stages of the journey as described in Exodus hardly fit this route.

On Plate v the stations of the Israelite journey which can be identified with the most probability along the traditional route have been designated. The first source of water on the ancient road to the Sinai mines is *'Ain Hawârah*. This, therefore, is probably Marah, the first station of the Israelite journey which was reached after three waterless days in the wilderness (v, D-4; Ex. 15:22 ff.). The next oasis to the south is in the *Wâdī Gharandel*, which corresponds to the Biblical Elim where twelve springs and seventy palm trees are said to have existed (v, D-4; Ex. 16:1; Num. 33:9). The next stages of the journey took them along the Red Sea, and thence inland to the Wilderness of Sin and to Dophkah (Num. 33:10-12). The exact route at this point depends upon the location of Dophkah. From its etymological meaning in Hebrew we should judge that this name was probably connected with smelting operations. If so, then the best identification of the site is with the Egyptian mining center of *Serâbît el-Khâdim* (v, E-5). The Wilderness of Sin would then be the plain along the edge of the Sinai plateau called *Debbet er-Ramleh*. From this point a series of valleys lead directly to *Jebel Mûsā* past Rephidim (*Wâdī Refâyid;* v, E-5). While various mountains in the neighborhood have been identified with the Biblical Mount Sinai, the most probable location is the range designated at v, F-5 (see Fig. 23), of which the chief peak is called *Jebel Mûsā*, "Mountain of Moses."

After spending a year at Mount Sinai, Israel left it and journeyed through the Wilderness of Paran (v, F-4; Num. 10:11, 12). None of the stations along the way which are listed in Num. 33:16-35 can be identified with any degree of certainty except Hazeroth (v, F-5) and Ezion-geber (v, G-4). From the latter the itinerary led to Kadesh-barnea in the Wilderness of Zin (v, F-3). Judging from the implications of the narrative as it now stands, the purpose of the Hebrews was to storm Canaan from the south. The pessimistic report of the spies (Num., ch. 13) and the defeat at Hormah (v, F-2; Num. 14:39 ff.) so weakened their morale, however, that they were forced to live in the area of Kadesh-barnea (for description see pp. 63 f.) until the older generation had been replaced by a new one.

THE CONQUEST OF CANAAN

After considerable time had passed, Moses led the new generation of Israelites from Kadesh-barnea with the purpose of going through Transjordan to storm Canaan from the east instead of from the south (Num. 20:22 ff.). The exact route which was taken is somewhat obscure, partly because the location of Mount Hor is uncertain. Apparently they circled northward in order to descend into the Arabah (v, F-G 3-4). According to Deut. 2:1 ff. they continued south in the Arabah to Ezion-geber (v, G-4) in order to traverse the King's Highway (v, G 2-4, and Fig. 25), though Num., ch. 33, says nothing about this journey. In any event, the king of Edom refused permission for them to traverse the highway, and no attempt was made to force the matter (Num. 20:14 ff.). Instead, Moses led the people northward in the Arabah past the mining center of Punon (v, G-3; Num. 33:42; see p. 65) and the spring at Oboth (v, G-3), crossing eastward at the northern border of Edom along the Brook Zered (v, G-3). Ije-abarim on the border of Moab (Num. 33:44) cannot be located with certainty at present, but there is no doubt that the itinerary as shown on Plate v is at least approximately correct.

Likewise unwilling to join battle with Moab, the people circled its territory to the east, and crossing the River Arnon they found themselves at the border of the Amorite Kingdom of Sihon (v, G 1-2 and IV, D 4-5; Num. 21:10 ff.). The latter was defeated in the battle of Jahaz (IX, I-6), the first great triumph of Israelite arms (Num. 21:21 ff.). Then followed the defeat of the giant king Og, whose kingdom north of the Jabbok had capitals at Edrei and Ashtaroth (IV, E-3; Num. 21:33 ff.) Thus ended the first phase of the conquest, with Israel in possession of the territory of Transjordan between Bashan

and the River Arnon. The kingdoms of Ammon, Moab, and Edom were left unchallenged (cf. Plates IV and VI; for description see pp. 36, 65 f.).

The second phase of the conquest, led by Joshua, is described as beginning with Jericho (Josh., chs. 2 to 6), continuing with the capture of Ai, the Gibeonite alliance (see p. 36), the defeat of the five Judean kings, and the conquest of Judah (Josh., chs. 7 to 10). A third campaign was directed against Galilee in the north, and resulted in the capture of the chief city of that area, Hazor (IV, D-2; Josh., ch. 11).

It is peculiar that not a word is said about a conquest of central Palestine, where the Joseph tribes, Ephraim and Manasseh, settled (see Plate VI). The capital of this region at the time was Shechem (IV, C-4), situated between Mount Ebal and Mount Gerizim, and known from excavations to have been a very strong city. While nothing is said about its capture, yet in Josh., ch. 24, it was the scene of the gathering of all the tribes for the renewal of the covenant. It is possible that friends or relatives of Israel were already in control of this region, so that all Joshua had to do was to make a treaty or covenant with them. Most scholars believe that this was the case. In control of Shechem, it is thought, were Hebrews who had never been in Egypt, or more probably had come out of Egypt at an earlier time, some perhaps at the expulsion of the Hyksos (see p. 29), and some, just possibly, at the burial of Jacob (Gen. 50:7 ff.). The *Tell el-Amarna* letters of Canaanite kings to the Egyptian court in the early fourteenth century indicate that Shechem and the region around it to the north and south were at that time in control of a rebel who showed by his actions little respect for the Egyptian Pharaoh (see p. 35). It is possible also that the story about Simeon and Levi in Gen., ch. 34, may reflect certain early tribal disputes at Shechem. In any event, the city was an early Israelite center (see Judg., chs. 6 to 9, and Josh., ch. 24), which Joshua did not have to conquer.

The best-known story connected with the conquest is the stirring account of the fall of Jericho (v, G-2; Josh., ch. 6). Yet this story furnishes the major problem in the reconstruction of the history of the Exodus. Excavations at the site (see p. 105) have revealed that the Canaanite city suffered two violent destructions during the final century or century and a half of its existence. The first probably occurred in the fifteenth century and the second in the fourteenth. After the latter the site was abandoned until Israelites rebuilt it during the tenth and ninth centuries (cf. I Kings 16:34). Some scholars have held that on the basis of this evidence from Jericho the entrance of Israel into Canaan must be placed during the late fifteenth or early fourteenth century. Other facts, however, appear to indicate that Moses and Joshua lived in the thirteenth century. In this case Joshua could not have captured Jericho because the city was not then in existence. These facts may be listed as follows: (1) As noted on p. 35, the city-state system of early fourteenth-century Canaan was not the same as

FIG. 24. The small *Wâdī Qudeirât* in which was possibly located the site of Hazar-addar (Plate v, F-3 and p. 64). This valley is watered by the largest spring in the area of Kadesh-barnea. The neighboring spring, *'Ain Qedeis*, where Kadesh-barnea is located on Plate v is very small, and the Israelites during their long stay in this area probably made use of *'Ain Qudeirât* as well.

FIG. 25. A section of the King's Highway (Num. 20:17; 21:22) as it runs north along a valley to cross the Brook Zered in the background (Plate V, G 2-4). This was the old road through Transjordan used by the four invading kings in Gen., ch. 14. It is here so clearly marked because it was paved by the Romans and is still used. Today it is being constructed anew by the Government of Transjordan. Note the ruins of an ancient watchtower beside it.

it was in the time of Joshua. The Canaan described in The Book of Joshua is later than the *Tell el-Amarna* period of the early fourteenth century. (2) Explorations in Transjordan have shown that the kingdoms of Edom, Moab, and Ammon were not founded until the thirteenth century. This conclusion is based upon the careful archaeological examination of hundreds of sites in which the people of these kingdoms once lived. Some have argued that the Edomites, Moabites, and Ammonites may well have been in the country about 1400 B.C., though living a nomadic life. Numbers, ch. 21, however, mentions a number of towns in which the people were living when Israel traversed this territory, and this presupposes a period when nomadic life had been abandoned. (3) The Egyptian cities of Pithom and Rameses which Israel built for the Pharaoh must have been constructed after c. 1319 B.C. (see above). (4) Finally, as will be noted below, Joshua's Judean campaign took place after 1250 B.C. according to the archaeological data.

Thus the evidence for Joshua's date in the thirteenth century appears strong, while the evidence for the final fall and abandonment of Jericho in the previous century is conclusive. At the present there is no final solution of this discrepancy, and we must await further study and excavation before indulging in too much speculation. For the moment, however, we are led to the conclusion that Jericho fell, not to Joshua, but to relatives of Israel, perhaps from the Shechem area, during the disturbances of the fourteenth century. According to this view, the conquest was a gradual one, covering a considerable period, though the climax came in the thirteenth century when the army under Joshua entered the country from the east.

Any invaders of the hill country from the Jericho area would first be forced to seize a foothold in the region of Bethel and Ai, rather than around Jerusalem, because the valleys leading from the Jordan give easy access to the former, but not to the latter (cf. IX, G 5-6). Consequently, when Josh., chs. 7; 8, describes the capture of Ai, it is describing the first great victory over the Canaanites in the hill country. From excavations it is known that the city involved was not Ai, but rather Bethel (see p. 105), the ruins of which bear eloquent testi-

mony to a violent destruction sometime during the first half of the thirteenth century.

In the tenth chapter of Joshua the itinerary of the conquest of the southern hill country is described. After the defeat of the five Canaanite kings in the Valley of Aijalon (IX, D-E 5), Joshua turned south into the Shephelah or Lowlands (I, B 5-6), carefully avoiding the strong fortress of Gezer, which did not come into Israelite hands until the time of Solomon (V, F-2; IX, D-5; I Kings 9:16). He first captured Makkedah (Josh. 10:28), a city near Beth-shemesh and Azekah (IX, D-6) but one which cannot be located with certainty. Next, he took Libnah at the head of the Valley of Elah (where David was later to fight Goliath; V, F-2; IX, D-6). A small excavation was made at this site in 1898-1899, and while it was found to have been occupied during this period, the precise date of its fall to Israel was not determined. The next Canaanite royal city to the south of Libnah was Lachish (V, F-2; IX, D-7). From excavations this exceedingly strong fortress is known to have been violently destroyed about 1230 B.C., and the conflagration is certainly to be attributed to Israel (Josh. 10:31 ff.). Joshua then proceeded to Eglon, seven miles southwest of Lachish (V, F-2; IX, C-7). The evidence gained from excavations indicates that this city was also destroyed about the same age, though the date of its conflagration cannot be as precisely determined as that of Lachish.

Now in control of the most important fortresses guarding the passes to the later Judean capital at Hebron, Israel turned upon Hebron itself, presumably following the pass by Mareshah (see the road drawn on Plates IV and VI, B-C 5-6). When Hebron was captured, it was a simple matter to take the remaining frontier fortress of Debir (V, F-2; IX, D-8; Josh. 10:38, 39), the Canaanite name of which was Kirjath-sepher. Excavations at this site show that it too was violently destroyed at approximately the same period as Lachish.

From this evidence two things are to be noted. One is that the campaign was carried out during the third quarter of the thirteenth century (c. 1250-1225 B.C.). That Israel was in Palestine at that time is shown by an Egyptian monument of Pharaoh Merenptah (c. 1235-1227 B.C.) who claims to have defeated "the people of Israel" in Palestine during the fifth year of his reign. This event is not mentioned in the Old Testament; it certainly was of minor significance and without lasting effect, for the Egyptian control of Canaan was then very weak. The reference does show, however, that Israel was already established in its later home by 1230 B.C.

A second feature of Joshua's campaign is the evidence of sound military strategy which it exhibits. In conquering Palestine Israel did not waste its strength on the strongest military fortresses at Jerusalem and Gezer (see pp. 44, 97). The strategy employed was the same as that used by the Assyrians and Babylonians later on. That was to conquer first the string of fortresses in the Shephelah which guarded the approaches to the Judean hill country. After that was accomplished the capture of the hill country was a comparatively simple operation.

In Judg., ch. 1, further information in detail is given which at first glance appears to conflict with that of Josh., ch. 10. There we are told that Othniel took Debir (Judg. 1:11 ff.) and Caleb, Hebron (v. 20). The implication is that instead of one great campaign the various tribal groups completed the conquest unaided by others. After the days of Joshua, this was certainly true (see pp. 43 ff.); but these passages are not necessarily in direct conflict with each other if it is assumed that the original plan was Joshua's.

By way of conclusion it should be stated, however, that these chronological problems must not obscure the central facts: namely, that at least some Israelites suffered slavery in Egypt, that they were freed in a wonderful deliverance, and that they were led victoriously into the Promised Land after years of murmuring and faintheartedness. In these remarkable events the Israelites saw the hand of their God, a gracious God who had taken pity on their afflictions, and saved them for his providential purpose.

The Lost Mountain

In the wake of Israel's tough, little army, a task force of scholars and pilgrims may invade the Sinai peninsula. Their objective: to find Mount Sinai, lost in the desert drifts of history.

Four Possibilities. Ever since the six-day blitz against Egypt, Israel's Minister of Religion, Dr. Samuel Cahane, has been snowed in by cables and letters from would-be pilgrims hoping to see the holy mountain while Israel still held the peninsula (Jewish travelers had been discouraged by the Egyptians). "It seems as if all the Jews in the world want to go to Mount Sinai," said Dr. Cahane. But nobody knows where Sinai is. Modern archaeologists and ancient traditions recognize four main possibilities:

¶ Oldest Christian tradition identifies Sinai with Jebel Serbal, an inaccessible 6,750-ft. peak with an oasis, well watered but perhaps too small to have supplied the Israelites.

¶ Other scholars think Sinai is in the volcanic Mount Seir range in southern Israel, which would account for the "thunders and lightenings, and a thick cloud upon the mount" of *Exodus 19:16*, but the route there would not jibe with Biblical accounts.

¶ Most popular theory is that Sinai is Jebel Musa (Mount of Moses), an impressive 8,000-ft. of granite in the southern end of the Sinai peninsula. Part of the Greek monastery of St. Catherine there dates back to 330 A.D., indicating how old the tradition is. But to get to Jebel Musa, Moses would have had to lead his people through the Egyptian copper and turquoise mines in the area.

¶ Most recent theory is that in their Exodus the Israelites did not follow the southern route traced by tradition but the sandy northern road along the Mediterranean coast (*see map*). In that case Mount Sinai should be that unimpressive mound known as Jebel Hillel, 30 miles south of El Arish, and rising a mere 2,000 ft. from the alluvial plain.

Majestic Moment. Foremost supporter of Jebel Hillel is Dr. Benjamin Mazar, Archaeologist President of Tel-Aviv's Hebrew University. To get to Jebel Hillel, he points out, the Israelites would have had to cross a marshland sometimes known as the Sea of Reeds, which might well have been that Red Sea whose waters parted to let the Children of Israel through. Dr. Cahane backs up Dr. Mazar's theory: according to legend, he says, Sinai was not a high but a low mountain—evidence of Jehovah's willingness to descend to man's level.

Last week, after a conference with 100 rabbis, Minister Cahane and Scholar Mazar were planning an expedition into the Sinai peninsula to seek evidence that would back up their theory. But the Israeli army was in no mood to wait for the archaeologist's word. Last week a jeep-borne band of soldiers barreled down from their base in the Sinai peninsula to Jebel Musa. There they climbed the 737 steps in the sheer rock to plant the Israeli flag where they were sure that Moses talked to God. At the nearby monastery of St. Catherine they picked the soldier with the best handwriting, and he wrote in the visitor's book: "We are the first unit of the Israel Army to stand on top of our holy Mount of Moses. We have made history. This moment has majesty for us all."

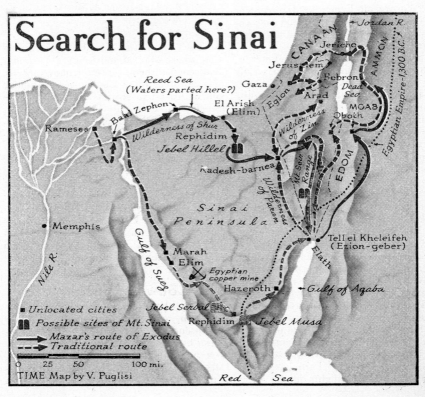

Search for Sinai

Reed Sea (Waters parted here?)
Jordan R.
CANAAN
Jericho
Jerusalem
Gaza
Hebron
Dead Sea
El Arish (Elim)
Eglon
Arad
MOAB
Rameses
Baal Zephon
Wilderness of Shur
Rephidim
Jebel Hillel
Wilderness of Zin
Oboth
AMMON
Egyptian Empire 1300 B.C.
Kadesh-barnea
Mt. Seir Range
Wilderness of Paran
EDOM
Sinai Peninsula
Memphis
Gulf of Suez
Marah
Elim
Egyptian copper mine
Hazeroth
Elath
Tell el Kheleifeh (Ezion-geber)
Gulf of Aqaba
Nile R.
Jebel Serbal
Rephidim
Jebel Musa

■ Unlocated cities
▮▮ Possible sites of Mt. Sinai
→ Mazar's route of Exodus
--→ Traditional route

0   25   50   100 mi.
TIME Map by V. Puglisi
Red Sea

xtraordinary Adventure

Pundits Joseph and Stewart Alsop, who
ve criticized the Administration's Mid-
e East policy and defended the Franco-
ritish attack on Egypt, last week goaded
d Socialist Norman Thomas into un-
onted words of praise for the Eisen-
wer Administration. In a letter to 21
the papers that carry the Alsops' col-
nn, Thomas marveled at the Alsops'
xtraordinary adventure in support of
e blundering Eden and the sorry social-
, Mollet." Said Thomas: "Suppose (as
e Alsops would have it) that the U.N.,
th the President's approval, had put off
cease-fire in the Middle East. We might
ready have been caught in the first
ages of that new world war which there
still hope of avoiding."

Thomas, who has frequently criticized
e Administration's foreign policy, urged
pport of "Eisenhower's effort to use the
.N. as the world's main hope of avoid-
g World War III." He blamed Truman
d Acheson for "failure to turn truce
to peace before Russia [could achieve
e] strength to interfere so ominously
the Middle East." Concluded Thomas:
he President, however, and the Ameri-
n people, who must deal with things as
ey now are, can only be hurt by the
nd of pontificating [exemplified by] the
sop effort."

ast Man In

At the steelworks south of Budapest, a
my note was slipped surreptitiously last
ek into the hand of the last American
wsman left in Hungary, United Press
rrespondent Russell Jones. The note,
dressed to a relative in New York,
ad: "We are all living. Louis." Added
nes, in a telephoned file: "I did not see
m, only his hand, but there is his mes-
ge, and God bless him."

In the past three weeks U.P. Veteran
nes has received "dozens and dozens" of
milar messages. They have been slipped
der his dinner plate, tucked into his
r, pressed into his hand on the street.
ometimes," he wrote last week, "they
nt you to get word to relatives in
nerica. Or perhaps it's just a message to
erybody in the U.S." To Jones they
ve become a symbol of his own "con-
uous feeling of inadequacy, both as an
merican and a reporter who helplessly
tched the murder of an entire people."

Black-Market Beat. Minnesotan Russ
nes, 38, arrived in Budapest six days
ore Soviet troops and tanks roared in
crush the rebellion, decided to stay on
en some 150 Western correspondents
led out of Budapest. Other Western
ss representatives who stayed: Asso-
ted Press Staffer Endre Marton, a na-
e Hungarian who had recently been re-
sed from prison by the Communists;
rton's wife, U.P. Correspondent Ilona
ilas (who had also been imprisoned);
uters Reporter Ronald Farquhar.
After spending two nights in the U.S.

legation at the height of the battle, Jones
moved back to his unheated fourth-floor
room in the shell-pocked Duna Hotel.
Phone service was disrupted, but the
Western correspondents were able to file
brief pooled dispatches on the only Tele-
type circuit to Vienna left intact. To get
out the full, running narrative of Hungary's deathwatch, Jones ran off five carbon copies of his stories, sent them out
with acquaintances, passers-by and an
Austrian black-marketeer. So effective
was their improvisation that the first big
convoy of correspondents who arrived in
Austria with eyewitness accounts of the

United Press

REPORTER JONES IN BUDAPEST
A message to everybody.

Soviet counterattack in Budapest found
that Jones, Marton and Reuters' Farquhar
had scooped them. Since telephone service
was restored, Jones has managed to phone
out at least two stories a day in calls to
Stockholm, Frankfurt or Vienna.

Russ Jones has been on hot spots before. He was in Prague when A.P. Correspondent William Oatis was jailed on a
phony charge of spying (TIME, July 16,
1951 et seq.). After ignoring repeated
warnings from the State Department that
it would only be a matter of time before
he was arrested, Jones was finally in-
veigled to Frankfurt by the U.P. for a
"conference," was not permitted to go
back. Said a U.P. colleague: "He's just a
guy who likes to stay where things are
happening."

The Cobweb Curtain

At the height of Princess Margaret's
off-again, on-again romance with Peter
Townsend last year, Britain's *Sunday Pic-
torial* burst out with a Page One headline:
FOR PETE'S SAKE, PUT HIM OUT OF HIS
MISERY. Last week the British Press
Council roundly deplored such instances

PLATE V

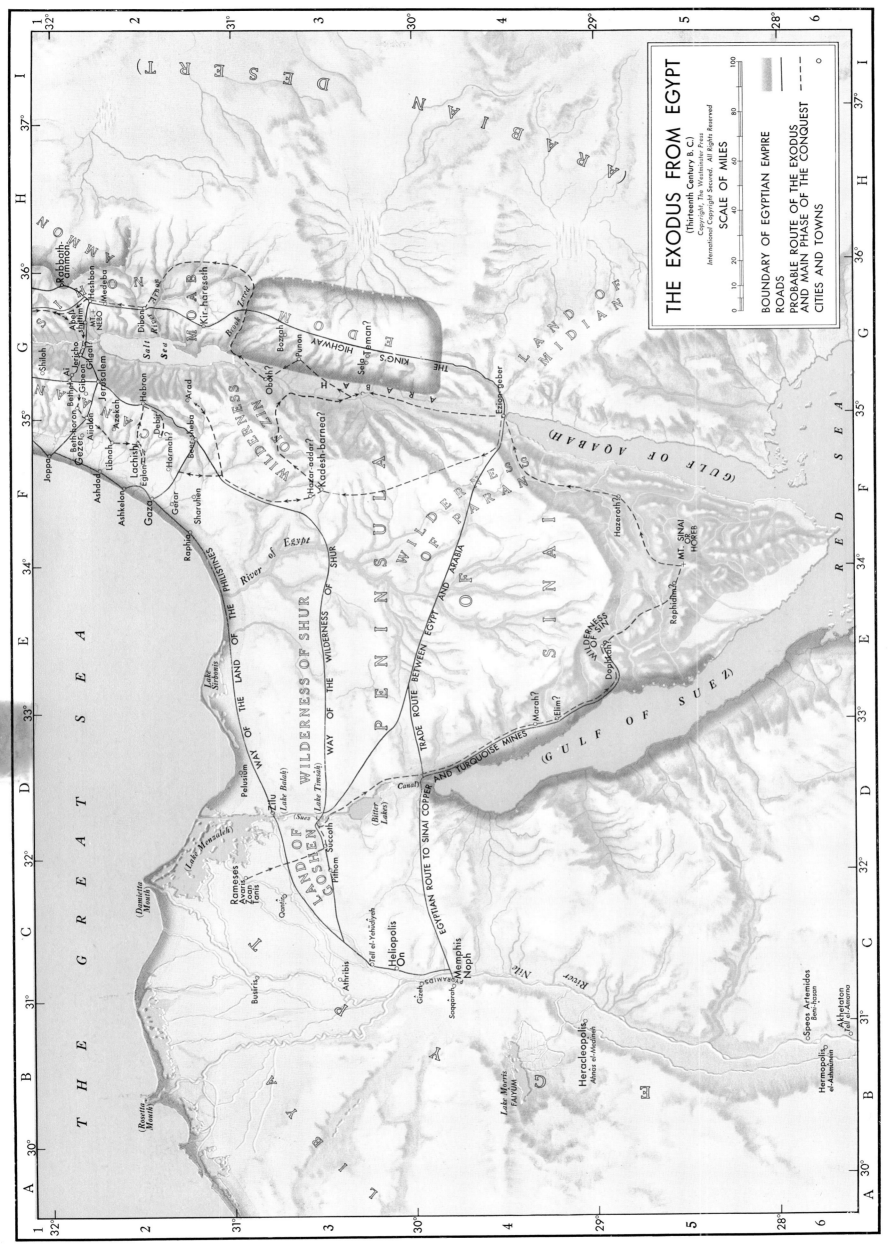

THE EXODUS FROM EGYPT

(Thirteenth Century B.C.)

Copyright, The Westminster Press
International Copyright Secured. All Rights Reserved

SCALE OF MILES

BOUNDARY OF EGYPTIAN EMPIRE
ROADS
PROBABLE ROUTE OF THE EXODUS
AND MAIN PHASE OF THE CONQUEST
CITIES AND TOWNS

PLATE VI

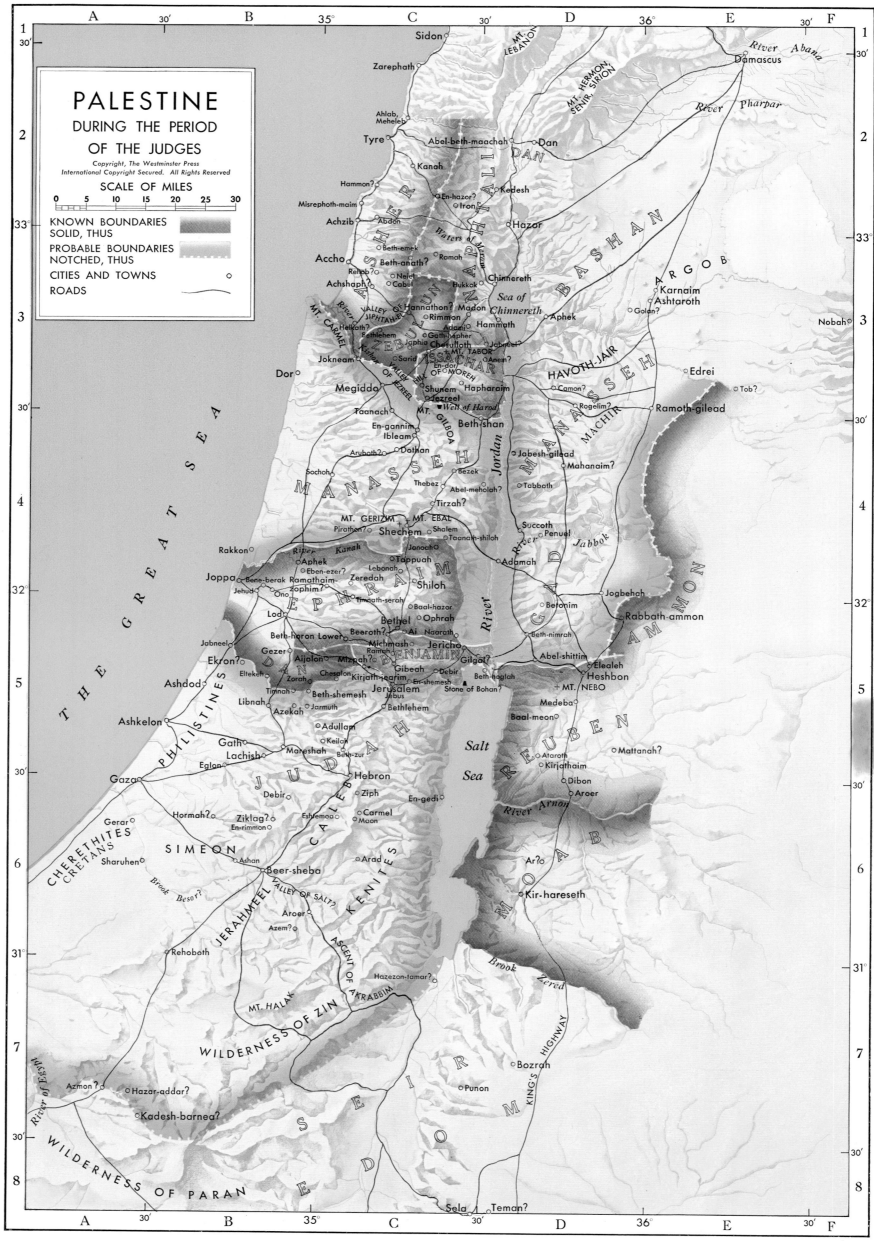

PALESTINE
DURING THE PERIOD
OF THE JUDGES

PALESTINE DURING THE PERIOD OF THE JUDGES

(C. 1200–1020 B.C.)

PLATE VI

THE settlement of the Israelite tribes in their newly won territory is described in Josh., chs. 13 to 19. Israelite society was patriarchal in structure; that is, it was composed of families, each headed by a patriarchal head or father. A number of related families made up a clan, and a varying number of clans made up a tribe. During and at the conclusion of the conquest, the country was parceled out among the eleven tribes, while the tribe of Levi, which was to attend to religious matters, was distributed among the others by the allotment to it of specific towns (Josh., ch. 21). In each tribal area the land was further subdivided among the clans and families. The process by which the distribution east of the Jordan was effected is described as a drawing by lot. Reuben, Gad, and one half of Manasseh (of which the chief clan was Machir) were given the territory of Sihon and Og (Num., ch. 32; Josh., ch. 13). West of the Jordan the house of Joseph, composed of Ephraim and Manasseh, was settled first (Josh., chs. 16; 17), after which the rest of the country was divided at an assembly in Shiloh (Plate VI, C-4). The land thus allotted became the ancestral property of each family, and laws were made to protect the inheritance. The well-known story of Ahab and Naboth's vineyard makes it plain that not even the later kings of Israel had the right to confiscate family property. Naboth was quite within his legal rights when he exclaimed to King Ahab: "The Lord forbid it me, that I should give the inheritance of my fathers unto thee" (I Kings 21:3).

In recent years a great advance has been made in the accuracy with which the tribal boundaries can be traced. This is due primarily to the work of archaeologists in locating the places where the ancient towns once stood (see pp. 13, 14). On Plate VI the tribal districts are shown as they can now be located.

THE SETTLEMENT OF TRANSJORDAN

South, east, and northeast of the Dead Sea were the kingdoms of Edom, Moab, and Ammon, which Israel made no attempt to conquer at this time. The plateau of Edom proper lay directly south of the Brook Zered (VI, D-7; see X, H-J 5-7), although the Arabah (X, G-H 5-6) and some of the wilderness west of it were probably also under Edomite control. Moab at this time was confined between

the Brook Zered and the River Arnon, while Ammon lay east of the River Jabbok as the latter turned in a wide loop southward to the capital at Rabbath-ammon (VI, D-5). The tribes of Reuben and Gad were situated in the territory formerly ruled by King Sihon (cf. Plates IV and VI, D 4-5). The northern boundary of Reuben was the *Wâdī Hesbân*, a valley leading to the Jordan from Heshbon (VI, D-5). To the south Reuben bordered on Moab at the River Arnon. Gad extended from the *Wâdī Hesbân* to a point north of the River Jabbok near Mahanaim (VI, D-4), but we cannot establish the boundary precisely. These two tribes were located in a precarious position, since Moab and Ammon were always a threat to their independence. During the ninth century Moab took over all of Reuben's territory, and that tribe disappeared from history (see Plate VII:C). Similarly, Gad was pressed by the Ammonites, who as early as the eleventh century were in position to threaten the Israelite territory as far west as Jabesh-gilead (VI, D-4; I Sam., ch. 11).

To the north the half tribe of Manasseh occupied the kingdom of Og (cf. IV and VI, D-E 3-4) with its strong cities of Ramoth-gilead, Edrei, Ashtaroth, and Karnaim (VI, E-3). The northern boundary is not shown on Plate VI because it cannot be precisely located, but Argob (VI, E-3), Nobah (VI, F-3), and Salcah (VII:A, D-4) were included (Num. 32:42; Deut. 3:14; Josh. 13:11 ff.). During the ninth and eighth centuries this region became a battleground between Israel and the Aramean kingdom of Damascus, while the Ammonites pressed against it on the southeast (see Plate VII:B). King Ahab was mortally wounded in battle at Ramoth-gilead (I Kings 22:29 ff.; VI, E-3).

THE SETTLEMENT OF WESTERN PALESTINE

For the tribal settlement of the country west of the Jordan more information is available, and the core of the documentary lists in Josh., chs. 15 to 19, is very old. Thus among the towns of Simeon, Sharuhen (VI, A-6) is listed (Josh. 19:6). We know from the excavations at the site that it was destroyed shortly after 900 B.C. and not reoccupied for four centuries. Consequently, a list of villages containing this town must date before 900 B.C. Similarly, we are told that the tribe of Ephraim did not drive out "the Canaanites that dwelt in

FIG. 26. The pass of Megiddo, on the main highway from the Plain of Sharon across Mount Carmel to the Valley of Jezreel (Esdraelon). This highway is the main road between Syria and Egypt. Along it armies and caravans have moved for millennia. This view, looking toward the southwest, is taken at the point where a side road branches off at the left to Taanach (VI, C-3).

FIG. 27. The small plain of Lebonah (modern *Lubban*) in the hill country of Ephraim near Shiloh (VI, C-4). The road shown is the highway from Jerusalem through the hill country to Nazareth in Galilee. In the background at the foot of the hill is the modern village on the approximate site of ancient Lebonah (Judg. 21:19).

Gezer [VI, B-5]: but the Canaanites dwell in the midst of Ephraim unto this day, and are become servants to do taskwork" (Josh. 16:10). This verse must certainly have been written in the time of David or Solomon in the tenth century. Not only did Gezer first come under Israelite control at that time (I Kings 9:16), but it was only then that Israel was strong enough to place the Canaanites in labor battalions as slaves (I Kings 9:21). Gezer was destroyed and abandoned at the end of the tenth century and the verse must date, therefore, before that period. We may be confident from these and similar reasons that we are dealing here with old lists upon which much reliance can be placed.

At first glance Plate VI would indicate that during the period of the Judges (c. 1200-1020 B.C.) the Israelites were in control of the whole country. Yet a careful reading of Joshua and Judg., ch. 1, indicates that this was not the case. While the tribal lists divided up the land and Israel laid claim to all of it, there were portions which could not be subdued. As mentioned above, Gezer was not conquered until the time of Solomon, and Jerusalem was first taken by David (Judg. 1:21; II Sam. 5:6 ff.). Judges 1:19 states that Judah occupied the hill country, but "he could not drive out the inhabitants of the valley, because they had chariots of iron." This refers primarily to the coastal plain from Gaza to Ekron and extending inland as far as Gath (VI, A-B 5-6). Similarly, the tribe of Manasseh failed to subdue a string of Canaanite fortresses along its northern boundary, and these separated it from the tribes in Galilee (Judg. 1:27). Chief among them were Beth-shan, Ibleam, Taanach, Megiddo, and Dor (VI, B-C 3-4). From the excavations it appears likely that Megiddo, a strong city guarding the main pass from the Plain of Sharon (Plate I, and VI, B-C 3-4) to the north (see Figs. 5 and 26) fell to Israel at least temporarily either c. 1150 or 1100 B.C. After each of the destructions at these dates, the town was deserted for a period of years. During one of the periods of desertion the battle between the forces of Barak and Sisera as described in the Song of Deborah (Judg., ch. 5) probably took place. The location of the battle was "in Taanach by the waters of Megiddo" (v. 19). These waters are those of the River Kishon (VI, C-3), the sources of which were at Megiddo. Since, however, the town which is mentioned to give the general location was not Megiddo but Taanach some distance away, we may infer that the former was not in existence at that time. Beth-shan (see Fig. 75) continued in Canaanite and Philistine hands and was not destroyed until the time of David, judging from the evidence found in the ruins (cf. also I Sam. 31:10; the temple there mentioned has been excavated).

It is evident, therefore, that the Israelites during the period of the Judges were not in possession of the whole country but chiefly of the central ridge, while Canaanites continued to live around them—a situation that was little altered until the great conquests of David.

THE "JUDGES" OF ISRAEL

There was a striking difference between the political organization of Israel and that of the surrounding peoples during this period. The latter were highly organized. Edom, Moab, and Ammon to the east and southeast were monarchies, controlling numerous cities and with capitals at Sela (see Fig. 46) or Teman (VI, C-D 8), Kir-hareseth (VI, D-6), and Rabbath-ammon (VI, D-5) respectively. The Canaanites continued their old city-state organization (see pp. 34 ff.), each major city possessing its own ruler (for example, Jerusalem, Gezer, Megiddo, Beth-shan, Dor, Sidon, etc.). There was no great power to interfere in the local struggles; effective Egyptian control was at an end (see pp. 29, 30), and the Assyrian Empire had not yet extended its power this far. Assyria, about 1100 B.C., conquered northern Syria, but the success was ephemeral and scarcely affected Palestine.

In contrast to her strongly organized neighbors, Israel was only a loose federation of tribes. These were held together, not by a central political figure who exercised dictatorial control, but solely by a common tradition and a religious bond or "covenant." The visible symbol of the bond was the "Ark of the Covenant," which during most of the period of the Judges rested in the central sanctuary at Shiloh (VI, C-4). With no central government we should expect the tribes to be in constant danger of attack from raiders and "oppressors" on every hand, unless the Israelite sense of religious unity were kept so strong that danger to one tribe would immediately cause all tribes to come to its defense. But according to The Book of Judges the people in settling down to an agricultural life succumbed in large measure to the seductive nature worship which was the religion of Canaan (see p. 36). Whenever they did this, we are told, God sent "oppressors" to afflict them (Judg., ch. 2). In other words, the more paganism they adopted, the weaker the covenant bond between them became, and the more each tribe tended to live by and for itself, isolated from the other tribes. This disunity made subjugation and oppression by outsiders relatively easy.

Several of these oppressors are mentioned: Moabites (Judg. 3:12 ff.), Canaanites (Judg., chs. 4; 5), Midianites from Arabia (Judg., chs. 6; 7; V, G 4-5), Ammonites (Judg., ch. 11), and Philistines (Judg. 3:31; chs. 13 ff.; I Sam., chs. 4 ff.). As previously indicated, the Moabites and Ammonites were peoples of Transjordan whom Israel had not conquered. During this period they took advantage of the separatist tendencies of the tribes and tried to gain control over Transjordan. Apart from the Philistine oppression (see below) the most dangerous threats to Israel were from the Canaanites and Midianites. A formidable Canaanite army was assembled in the Valley of Jezreel (I, C-3) under the leadership of one Sisera from the village of Harosheth (IV, C-3). A call to arms was issued to the tribes of Israel by the prophetess Deborah. Six of the tribes responded and an army was assembled at Mount Tabor (VI, C-3) under the leadership of Barak from Kedesh-naphtali (VI, D-2; Judg. 4:6 ff.). The subsequent defeat of the Canaanites in a battle near Megiddo (VI, C-3) was celebrated by the remarkable poem, composed by an eyewitness, which is preserved in Judg., ch. 5. The Midianite oppression was also exceedingly serious, since it was an invasion from the Arabian Desert of Bedouins who for the first time were using domesticated camels on a large scale. This use of the camel made the Midianites dangerous; they could travel long distances with comparative rapidity without concern for water supply. The story of their defeat by Gideon in the valley leading from Jezreel to the Jordan, between Mount Gilboa and the Hill of Moreh (VI, C-3), is well known.

Complete disaster for Israel in these crises was avoided by spontaneous leaders who were called "judges." These figures have been called "charismatic" leaders, because they were believed to possess some special gift of God's grace. They were set apart from others by special abilities, such as military prowess, wisdom, honesty, and natural capacities for leadership. In disputes between individuals and families, it was only natural that the cases be taken before such leaders for decision. In this way the name "judges" was given them, though for the most part in the stories about them they appear as military leaders. The charismatic nature of the leadership during this period is a remarkable feature of Israel, and distinguishes its history sharply from that of the surrounding peoples.

ARCHAEOLOGY AND THE PERIOD OF THE JUDGES

During the period of the Judges considerable difference can be observed between the material civilization and wealth of Israelite towns and those of the neighbors who were not driven out. Canaanite cities which have been excavated, such as Beth-shan (VI, C-4), Megiddo (VI, C-3), and Salmonah (the probable name of modern *Tell Abū Hawâm*, IV, C-3), show a considerable degree of wealth. Houses were well built, and their contents indicate that an active trade with Syria and Cyprus was carried on. Occasionally objects of art from Egypt are found. At Beth-shan, after Egyptian control came to an end, the temples of the Canaanite deities Dagon and Ashtaroth were built (I Sam. 31:10; I Chron. 10:10); and in their precincts were placed numerous coveted objects, including three Egyptian stelae (monumental stones) set up by the Pharaohs Seti I and Rameses II some two hundred years before.

At Megiddo during the early twelfth century was an elaborate palace of the local king, in all probability as large as the palace which Solomon later built for himself in Jerusalem. In its basement was the treasure room which had been looted of its finest objects when the city was destroyed by some enemy about 1150 B.C. Left on the floor in a confused mass were a large number of gold, ivory, and alabaster objects, which while unimportant to the looters are of great value to us, since they so vividly illustrate the wealth and culture of the Canaanite king (Figs. 28, 29).

In contrast to the wealth of these Canaanite towns the Israelites were extremely poor. Between 1200 and 1000 B.C. the hill country, for the first time, became dotted with towns, indicating an increase in the population and witnessing to the Israelite settlement. Several of these towns have been excavated (see Plate XVIII), and their ruins testify to a civilization very different from that of the Canaanites. Everywhere there is evidence of poverty. House walls are crude and ill-planned. Art is exceedingly primitive. Before about 1050 B.C. there is no evidence of trade with foreign peoples other than with the immediate neighbors. City fortifications, when constructed, were poorly built and scarcely capable of withstanding serious attack. All this was to change during the period of David and Solomon after 1000 B.C., when strong government and military success brought an economic revolution to Israel.

THE PHILISTINES

Shortly after 1200 B.C. there appeared in the southern coastal plain a people called "Philistines" (VI, B-5), from whom the name "Palestine" was later derived. The Philistines were one group of a large number of sea peoples from the Greek islands and particularly from Crete (Caphtor; see Amos 9:7). This we know, not only from references in the Bible and in Egyptian records, but from the characteristic pottery which they made in Palestine. The shapes of the vessels were quite unlike the traditional forms of Canaan, but were patterned after styles well known in the Greek world whence the people came.

While attempting to invade Egypt the sea peoples suffered a severe defeat at the hands of Pharaoh Rameses III (c. 1195-1164 B.C.), and some at least fell back on Palestine (see Fig. 16). One group settled at Dor in the Plain of Sharon (VI, B-3), though we hear about them, not from the Old Testament, but from the Egyptian story of a certain Wenamon, an Egyptian emissary who stopped there on his way to

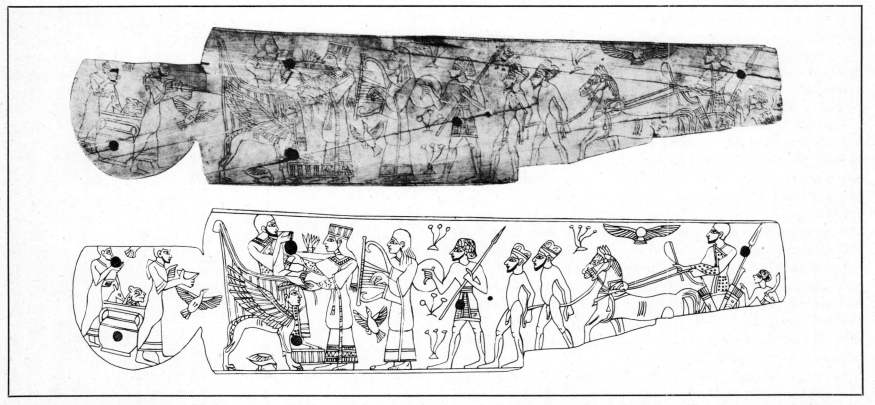

FIG. 28. One of the ivories from the collection of the king of Megiddo, dating c. 1200 B.C. A Canaanite ruler is shown sitting on his throne, drinking from a small bowl. Before him are an official and a musician plucking the strings of a lyre. The latter reminds us of David playing the lyre (not the "harp") before the moody Saul (I Sam. 16:23). The king's throne is supported by winged lions with human heads. These are the imaginary, composite beings which the Israelites called "cherubim" (which were not the small winged children that appear as "cherubs" in modern art). In Solomon's Temple there were two large figures of this type in the Holy of Holies, on which Jehovah was believed to be enthroned, though invisibly, precisely as Canaanite kings such as this were enthroned (see p. 48; cf. I Sam. 4:4).

Syria for cedar. South of Gerar was another group called the "Cherethites" (VI, A-6), but we know nothing about them apart from three references in the Old Testament (I Sam. 30:14; Ezek. 25:16; Zeph. 2:5).

By far the most important of the sea peoples in Palestine was the Philistine group, which was organized around five cities: Gaza (VI, A-5), Ashkelon, Ashdod, Ekron, and Gath (VI, B-5). Each city, with the area it controlled, was ruled by a "lord," who, though independent, co-operated with the others in important matters. Thus in political and military affairs the people were able to act as a united group. As a result they proved to be the most serious threat to the independence of Israel during the period of the Judges. Most disastrous was the battle at Eben-ezer and Aphek (VI, B-4) about 1050 B.C., when the Israelite Ark was captured and taken to Ashdod (I Sam., ch. 4). After the trouble it caused in the Temple of Dagon, it was sent to Ekron, and from there up the Valley of Sorek past Beth-shemesh to Kirjath-jearim (VI, C-5; see also IX, C-E 5-6). The primary interest of the writer of this story was to tell about the Ark, and we are left to infer what happened to Israel politically. From archaeological investigation we know that Israel's central sanctuary, Shiloh (VI, C-4), where the Ark had been kept, was violently destroyed at this time, making the reference of Jeremiah to its destruction quite clear (Jer. 7:12 ff.; 26:6 ff.). Later we hear of Philistine garrisons in the hill country itself (I Sam. 13:3), and also in possession of such a far-away city as Beth-shan (VI, C-4), on the wall of which was hung the body of Saul after his defeat at Mount Gilboa (VI, C-4; I Sam., ch. 31). This means that between c. 1050 and 1020 B.C. the Philistines were able to dominate Israel politically, and it is small wonder that the people of Israel came to Samuel demanding a king who would organize them and drive off the oppressor.

One direct consequence of the Philistine pressure was the fact that the small tribe of Dan was forced to leave the territory originally assigned to it (Josh. 19:47; Judg., ch. 18). This tribe had been allotted an area from Beth-shemesh, Zorah, and Aijalon (VI, B-5), to Ekron (VI, B-5), Jehud, Bene-berak, and Rakkon (VI, B-4; Josh. 19:40 ff.). Philistine power drove the Danites from the plains, whereupon they traveled to the foot of Mount Hermon and settled there, after taking a Canaanite city called Laish and renaming it for themselves (VI, D-2; Judg. 18:27-29).

The period of the Judges marks the beginning of the Iron Age; that is, the time when iron came into common use. The metal used for tools and weapons since 4000 B.C. had been copper, though since the Hyksos period (pp. 27 f.) it had been common practice to introduce tin into the copper to produce a harder product, bronze. Before 1200 B.C. iron appears to have been a magic product in Western Asia, valued almost as much as gold and silver. This was not because of the scarcity of the ore, but because the secrets of the rather complicated smelting process seem to have been jealously guarded by the Hittites.

Throughout the period of the Judges the Israelites, who were poor in material possessions, were thwarted time and again because of their lack of this important metal for agricultural implements, nails, and weapons. They were unable to drive out the Canaanites from the plains because these people owned iron chariots (Josh. 17:16; Judg. 1:19; 4: 2, 3).

From excavations in Philistine territory it has been learned that the Philistines possessed iron weapons and jewelry, while the Israelites appear to have had none. It is very probable, therefore, that the metal was introduced into common use in Palestine by the Philistines who had learned about it in the north. They held a "corner" on the iron market, however, and closely guarded the trade secrets of its production. This we infer from the excavations and also from the interesting passage in I Sam. 13:19-22.

Once the Philistine power was broken by the first kings of Israel, Saul and David, the secret of the iron-smelting process became public property, and the metal came into use in Israel. This promptly resulted in an economic revolution and higher standard of living for the common man. The war with the Philistines was one of survival for Israel. Small wonder that it was celebrated in song and story, since it furnished the occasion for great exploits, notably those of Samson (Judg., chs. 13 to 16) and of David against Goliath (I Sam., ch. 17).

ISRAEL'S NORTHERN NEIGHBORS

During the period of the Judges the people of Israel were not troubled by oppressors from Syria. Yet to the north and northeast Phoenician and Aramean states were in process of formation which were to influence greatly the course of events in Palestine.

The coast line of Syria apparently suffered severely in the twelfth century from the depredations of the invading sea peoples. The great city of Ugarit (III, C-2), and probably Tyre (VI, C-2) also, was destroyed and abandoned at this time. Yet by the time of David and Solomon in the tenth century the Canaanites in the Tyre-Sidon (VI, C 1-2) area had been united into a strong state with its capital at Tyre. This Phoenician state came into being during the period of the Judges and was apparently quite unique among the world's kingdoms. Instead of concentrating its energies on expanding its territory by force of arms, it spread its influence, its raw materials, and its artisans throughout the Mediterranean by trade and treaties. We are unable to trace its boundaries at any one period or to determine how much territory it comprised. The tribe of Asher, following the conquest, laid claim to the whole coast from Mount Carmel well into Syria (VI, C 2-3), but it is improbable that Israelites ever really controlled this area (see Judg. 1: 31, 32). By the time of Solomon the tribe had virtually ceased to exist, having become a dependency of Phoenicia (VII:A, B-C 2-3).

East of the Syrian mountains to the north and south of Damascus new invaders from Arabia were settling down during the period of the Judges. These were the Aramaeans (a name which is translated "Syrians" in the A.V. and R.V.). Towns were founded by them throughout this area as far south as the Yarmuk (I, D-3), so that by the end of the tenth century the whole of Bashan and eastern Syria was under Aramean control (VII: A-B). By 1000 B.C. the Aramean kingdom of Zobah had extended its frontiers to the Euphrates and was conquering Assyrian territory there, but this was stopped by the Davidic conquest of Zobah (p. 47). During the ninth and eighth centuries the Aramaeans were a formidable enemy of Israel. Even after their subjugation by the Assyrians in 733-732 they continued to be great traders who by commercial means became as influential in Western Asia as Phoenicia was in the Mediterranean.

FIG. 29. A Canaanite maiden, as restored from a Megiddo ivory. Note the long hair and flowing robe which were characteristic of the Canaanite fashions of the day.

Fɪɢ. 30. Esdraelon or Valley of Jezreel as seen from the hills west of Nazareth. In the background is Mount Carmel, a spur of the hill country of Samaria which pushes out to the Mediterranean. North of Carmel, at Haifa, the British have developed a safe though small harbor.

THE POLITICAL HISTORY OF ISRAEL AND JUDAH

Pʟᴀᴛᴇ VII

FOLLOWING the golden age of the empire in the time of David, the territory controlled by the Hebrew people was gradually diminished in extent until in the fifth century it was but a tiny province in the Fifth Satrapy of the vast Persian Empire. Excavations in Israelite and Judean towns reveal the progressive weakening and impoverishment of the people, owing to bad politics, bad economics, civil and international war.

Plates VII and XII, supplemented by Plates XI, XIII, and XIV, picture the political fortunes of the Israelite-Jewish people from the time of David to the period of Paul. Plate VII shows the state of affairs in Palestine during the tenth, ninth, eighth, and fifth centuries B.C.

THE EMPIRE OF DAVID AND SOLOMON

A centralized state with a monarchy apparently became a necessity during the period of the Judges to avoid permanent subjection to the Philistines (pp. 45 f.). We gather that there was opposition to it, as we should expect, since human kingship ran counter to Israel's traditional belief that Jehovah was the true King of his people (cf. I Sam., chs. 8 and 12). The problem was partially solved by considering the king the "anointed" (messiah) of the Lord (I Sam., ch. 10), who was to rule his people under the dictates of God's will as it was revealed to him by God's spokesmen. Thus when Saul was anointed as the first king, Samuel was the spokesman who was to make God's will known to him. An innate instability on the part of Saul and an inflexibility on the part of Samuel, however, soon brought a rupture in their relations. This fact, coupled with Saul's largely irrational jealousy of David, weakened his efficiency as king. Yet his reign was Israel's political salvation. The Philistines were expelled from the hill country following the battle of Michmash (ɪx, F-5), and the Ammonites were thrown back from Jabesh-gilead (ɪx, H-2; I Sam., chs. 11 and 14 ff.). Saul's fortress at Gibeah (ɪx, F-6) has been excavated. It was of rustic simplicity in size and construction; yet nevertheless it was evidence of a good beginning in the political and military strengthening of a divided people.

At the death of Saul (c. 1004 B.C.) his kingdom split into its northern and southern parts. David was made king over Judah at Hebron (VII: A, C-5; II Sam. 2:1-4), while Ishbosheth (Ishbaal), Saul's son, reigned over Israel. Seven and one half years later, after the murder of Ishbosheth (II Sam. 5:5), David was made king over the united people and began an illustrious reign, thirty-three years in duration (ending c. 965 B.C.). During that period the centralization of power in the throne was vastly increased and strongly supported by a large standing army of sworn loyalty to the king.

David's first acts exhibited a high degree of political sagacity. Jerusalem, which had never been conquered by Israel, was captured and made the political center of the state (II Sam. 5:6 ff.). Due to its strategic position between the northern and southern groups, its choice prevented charges of favoritism from arising against David. The Ark of the Covenant was then brought to Jerusalem and placed under the royal protection, so that the court became not only the center of political unity but the symbol of religious unity as well (II Sam., ch. 6).

A brief summary of the remarkable conquests of David is found in II Sam., chs. 8; 10; 12:26 ff. First, he confined the Philistines to a small area on the coast (VII:A, B-5) and dominated them economically. The kingdoms of Edom, Moab, and Ammon across the Jordan were next subjugated and their inhabitants made to work on royal projects. The road to the Red Sea and the trade routes between Arabia and Syria were now in David's control. His greatest military triumph, however, was his conquest of Aram ("Syria"; VII:A-B, D-E 2-3). The Aramaeans in this region (see p. 46) had come to the assistance of the Ammonites during David's siege of their capital at Rabbah (VII:A, D-5), but they had been defeated. Now he seized Damascus and also subdued Zobah (VII:A, D 2-3), the leading Aramean kingdom. Assyrian records indicate that the state of Zobah had become sufficiently powerful to begin the conquest of Assyrian territory along the upper Euphrates. It is part of the irony of history that David's subjugation of this kingdom may have saved Assyria and made it possible for her to rise rapidly to power and during the subsequent centuries to conquer the whole of the Fertile Crescent.

Just where David finally fixed the northern boundary of his empire is not recorded in II Samuel. It is known only that his empire bordered on the state of Hamath (ch. 8:9 ff.; VII:A, D-1). Numbers 34:7 ff. and Ezek., ch. 48, however, describe the ideal northern border of Israel as extending from Hazar-enan and Zedad to "the entrance of Hamath" (in the area of Riblah and Kadesh; VII:A, D-2). From

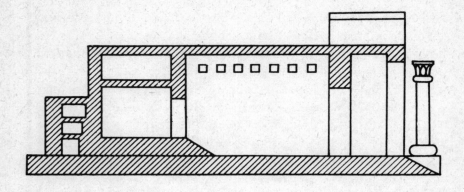

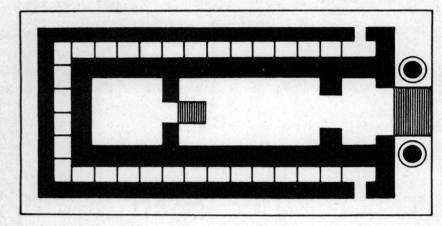

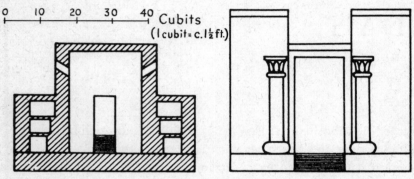

FIG. 31. A reconstruction of the Temple of Solomon modeled on the specifications given in the Old Testament and on what has been learned through archaeological study of similar edifices. The Temple itself was built according to Phoenician designs and was notable, not for its size, but for its beauty and artistic workmanship.

that point it would have descended the valley along the eastern side of the Lebanons. This description probably reflects the actual northern extent of the Davidic empire. Otherwise we should be at a loss to explain how the tradition could have arisen that this was Israel's true boundary.

After Edom had been subjugated, David had nothing to fear from the south, because Egypt at that time was unable to interfere in Asia. Treaties were made with the states of Hamath and Tyre to the north, so that the borders of the empire were now firmly established and remained so through most of the days of Solomon. The reign of David was thus one of great political and economic prosperity. Population increased; and the introduction of iron into common use after the breaking of the Philistine control over it (see p. 46) brought an economic revolution to the country.

Solomon (c. 965-926 B.C.) did not add to the Davidic conquests, but instead devoted his reign to the cultural and economic development of his empire. Political ties with the smaller countries and with Egypt were strengthened by the addition to his harem of numerous princesses, chief among whom was the daughter of the Egyptian Pharaoh. He set out on a vast building program, remains of which have been recovered in various parts of the country, notably at Megiddo (VI, C-3), Gezer (VI, B-5), and Eglon (VI, B-5; I Kings 9:15 ff.). Most notable were his palace and administrative buildings and the Temple in Jerusalem.

The erection of the Temple is described in I Kings, chs. 6; 7, and additional data are preserved in Ezek., ch. 40 ff. With this information and with a wealth of archaeological data it is possible to reconstruct the building with a fair degree of accuracy, even though remains of it in Jerusalem have never been found (see p. 97). It was a comparatively small building, slightly more than 100 feet long and

c. 30 feet wide in the interior (see Fig. 31). It was probably built entirely with stone but lined on the inside with cedar and highly decorated. In the rear room ("Holy of Holies") were two olivewood cherubim, standing c. 15 feet high and overlaid with gold leaf, under whose outstretched wings the Ark was placed (cf. Fig. 28). In the vacant place above them Jehovah was believed to be invisibly enthroned. In the exterior court were the large altar of burnt offering, the lavers, and the bronze "sea." The latter was a tremendous bronze bowl, c. 15 feet in diameter and 7½ feet high, which was cast in the clay beds of the Jordan Valley at Adamah (VII:A, C-4). The "sea" and the bronze pillars placed in front of the Temple (I Kings 7:15 ff.) were so large that we marvel at the genius of the artisan Hiram who cast them.

To obtain both material and artists for the work Solomon had a trading agreement with the Phoenician, Hiram of Tyre (I Kings, ch. 5). At the end of twenty years Solomon had accumulated a serious deficit and had to cede to Hiram twenty Galilean cities in the vicinity of Cabul (I Kings 9:10 ff.; VII:A, C-4). To finance this elaborate building program and to support his great court Solomon entered into numerous business ventures. With Hiram's aid he built a fleet of ships for the Red Sea trade (I Kings 10:22), with port at Ezion-geber (VII:A, B-7). This site has been excavated, and has revealed a totally new phase of Solomon's activity. Here the king had built a huge smelter, the largest ever found in the ancient Near East, in which to smelt the ores obtained from the Arabah mines (see p. 65). Another phase of his commercial activity is revealed by I Kings 10:28, 29, which though long regarded as untranslatable, can now be rendered as follows: "And Solomon's horses were exported from Cilicia [XI:B, B-2]: the merchants of the king procured them from Cilicia at the current price; and a chariot was exported from Egypt at the rate of 600 shekels of silver and a horse from Cilicia at the rate of 150; and thus [at this rate] they delivered them by their agency to all the kings of the Hittites and the kings of Aram."

Another interesting phase of Solomon's career was his division of Israel into administrative districts for taxation purposes (see I Kings 4:7 ff.). Over each district was placed a governor, for whom were provided (judging from the excavations at Megiddo, Beth-shemesh, and Lachish) a palace and large, thick-walled storehouses in which the grain, oil, et cetera, collected in taxes could be stored. In a general way the provinces followed the old tribal districts (cf. VII:A and VI), though certain exceptions are to be noticed. The Plain of Sharon in the area of Dor was made a separate district; Zebulun had disappeared and in its place was a district of which a chief city was Megiddo; Reuben and Gad were joined as one province, while Manasseh across the Jordan was divided into two. The areas as outlined on Plate VII:A are given numbers which represent the order in which the districts are listed in I Kings 4:7 ff. How the province of Judah was administered is not clear, since little information on the subject is preserved. It is evident, however, that the old tribal system was giving way before the needs of a centralized and commercialized state.

The fame of Solomon spread far beyond the borders of his realm. Yet by the end of his reign the country was rocked by disaffection, caused by the heavy taxes, the forced labor on royal projects, and the traditional jealousy between north and south. A new dynasty, the Twenty-second, had come to power in Egypt, headed by the Libyan Shishak. As a result, the political tie between the two countries was broken, and Egypt now became a haven for political refugees who were able to plot in safety against the Israelite monarch.

THE EARLY DIVIDED MONARCHY

On the death of Solomon the northern and southern groups of his kingdom immediately separated, as they had on the death of Saul. This time, however, they remained permanently separated. Jeroboam, one of the political refugees in Egypt, returned to become king over Israel, while Rehoboam, Solomon's son, retained the throne of Judah. During the fifth year of the latter's reign, Shishak of Egypt raided the country and destroyed numerous cities, not only in Judah, but also in Israel and in Edom (I Kings 14:25). While the purpose of the raid may have been to revive an Egyptian empire in Asia, it achieved no lasting results since no attempt was made to reorganize the country into subject provinces.

In the years which followed, the strength of the two Hebrew kingdoms was weakened by conflict between them. The tribal district of Benjamin and a portion of that originally allotted to Dan (VI, B-C 5) were included in Judah, but the northern boundary was disputed. The tremendously strong fortifications at *Tell en-Naṣbeh* (XVIII, C-5) were erected at this time, and their great size (Fig. 77) illustrates the bitterness with which the civil war was fought.

About 882 B.C. the throne of Israel was seized by an army officer named Omri (I Kings 16:15 ff.), who became one of the most illustrious rulers of Israel, in spite of the fact that he reigned only twelve years. He was so well known that for more than a century the official name for Samaria in the Assyrian records was "House of Omri," even though his dynasty was swept from the throne in the Elijah-Elisha revolution c. 845 B.C. His greatest act was to build a new and powerfully fortified capital at Samaria (VII:B, C-4). This city has been excavated, and the elaborate palace and a portion of the strong fortifications which he built have been recovered (see pp. 104 f.).

Following the policy of David and Solomon, close commercial relations were established between Israel and Phoenicia, and they were strengthened by the political marriage of Ahab, Omri's son, with Jezebel, the daughter of the king of Tyre. Ahab is pictured in I Kings as a weak character, completely dominated by Jezebel. The latter was an extremely forceful person, who attempted to impose her own religion and the totalitarian methods of Tyre upon Israel. The reaction to her was led by the prophets Elijah and Elisha, who did not rest until every vestige of the dynasty of Omri had been swept from the throne and a new dynasty formed under an army leader named Jehu (II Kings, chs. 9; 10).

Plate VII:B shows the state of affairs at this time. Aram or Syria, having secured its independence during the days of Solomon, was now a formidable kingdom with its capital at Damascus. By the time of Ahab this kingdom was Israel's most potent enemy, and a succession of battles was fought as far south as Ramoth-gilead, an Israelite city which was now on the frontier (VII:B, D-4). Israel and Aram composed their differences long enough to unite in defeating the Assyrian king Shalmaneser III in a great battle in Syria in 853 B.C. (see p. 68). However, war between them broke out anew once the danger was past. Israel was aided in this warfare by Jehoshaphat, king of Judah, with whom the dynasty of Omri had made a treaty of mutual assistance, thus ending the state of hostilities between the two kingdoms. By 840 B.C. both Moab and Edom had rebelled against Israel and Judah respectively (II Kings 3:4 ff.; 8: 20 ff.) and become independent. Mesha, the king of Moab, commemorated his triumph by erecting a stele or monumental stone in Dibon (VII:B, C-5; see Fig. 32). The comparative weakness of Israel during the third quarter of the ninth century is further illustrated by the "Black Obelisk" of Shalmaneser III (Fig. 49), on which a large tribute of gold and silver from Jehu is shown as it was presented to the Assyrian monarch.

ISRAEL AND JUDAH DURING THE EIGHTH CENTURY B.C.

The power of Assyria now became the chief political factor which troubled the small kingdoms of Palestine-Syria. Both Israel and Judah were ultimately to come under Assyrian control, but between c. 825 and 745 B.C. internal troubles in Assyria gave the western peoples a breathing space, of which Israel and Judah took full advantage during the long reigns of Jeroboam II in Israel and Uzziah (or Azariah) in Judah. Excavations reveal that Jeroboam refortified Samaria with a double wall, which in the most vulnerable part of the city was nearly 33 feet wide, fortifications so strong that it took the Assyrian army three years to conquer the city in 724-721 B.C. (II Kings 17:5). Most astonishing was Jeroboam's defeat of Aram and the restoration of the northern Davidic border in Syria (II Kings 14:25; cf. Plate VII:A). During the latter part of his reign (c. 760-750), Amos prophesied in Bethel. The prophet denounced vigorously the

false sense of security which these favorable events had caused in Israel and the social iniquities that accompanied them. Judah likewise prospered, having reconquered Edom (II Kings 14:7) and the copper and iron mines which the latter owned, and for the first time subjugated completely the coastal plain of Philistia (II Chron. 26:6 ff.).

As Amos had foreseen, however, this prosperity was only temporary. He with Hosea and Isaiah shared a belief in impending crisis and doom—a belief which events fully justified. In 745 B.C. the Assyrian advance began again when the great king Tiglath-pileser III came to the throne. The latter inaugurated a new policy of conquering small states, deporting their populations, and turning them into Assyrian provinces, usually governed by Assyrian officials. In 733-732 B.C. he conquered Damascus, Gilead, Galilee, and the Plain of Sharon, turning them into six provinces (Sharon ruled from Dor, and Galilee from Megiddo—Plate VII:C; II Kings 15:29 ff.). To throw back the attack, Rezin, king of Damascus, and Pekah, king of Israel, had formed an alliance into which they attempted to force Judah. Judah, however, refused to join it and was attacked by the others, but the approach of the Assyrian army prevented her overthrow (II Kings 16:5 ff.; Isa., ch. 7). As a result of this first Assyrian conquest in Palestine, Israel was confined to a small area in the hill country of Samaria, saved from further reduction only by paying a heavy tribute together with Philistia, Judah, Ammon, Moab, and Edom.

A few years later, however, as a result of refusal to pay tribute, Shalmaneser V, the successor of Tiglath-pileser III, laid siege to Samaria. He died before the city was captured, but Sargon II (722-705 B.C.) completed the task in the first months of 721 B.C. According to his own statement, he carried 27,290 Israelites (presumably all the political leaders, the elders, the artisans, and the well-to-do) into exile, settling them in the region of "Gozan, and in the cities of the Medes" (II Kings 17:6; XI:A, C-2 and D-2). In their place new

FIG. 32. A replica of the stele or monumental stone of Mesha, king of Moab. It was set up by him in Dibon (IX, I-8) to commemorate his victory over Israel shortly after the middle of the ninth century, which for the first time in a century and a half made his country independent.

Fig. 33. A reconstruction of the Judean fortress-city of Lachish (VII: A-D, B-5). Note the double fortification walls, the strongly protected city gate, and the palace of the local Judean governor in the midst of the city—all probably erected by the command of Rehoboam (II Chron. 11:9). A group of letters written by the officer in charge of a near-by outpost to the commandant of Lachish were found in the ruins of the gate. They date from c. 589 or 588 B.C., before Nebuchadnezzar's subjection of Judah in 588–587 B.C.

settlers were brought from Babylonia, Elam, and Syria by Sargon and his successors. Thus, what the prophets had foretold came to pass; the Kingdom of Israel was ended. The central interest of the Biblical story now shifts to Judah.

Plate VII:C shows the state of affairs in Palestine about 700 B.C., several years after the fall of Israel. Judah had barely escaped the fate of Israel in 701 B.C. when Sennacherib had attacked the country (II Kings, chs. 18; 19; Isa., chs. 36; 37). Hezekiah, against the advice of Isaiah, had entered into a defensive alliance with the Philistine cities, after having secured the promise of Egyptian help. Among his preparations for the battle was the digging of the Siloam Tunnel in Jerusalem to insure the water supply in case of siege (see p. 98, and Plate XVII:A). Isaiah denounced these acts in strong terms (chs. 22; 30:1-4; 31:1-3); yet the revolt was carried out. Sennacherib crushed it severely, destroying, he says, forty-six Judean cities, chief among which was Lachish (VII:C, B-5; Fig. 33). Jerusalem was saved by payment of a heavy tribute (II Kings 18:13 ff.). The Kingdom of Judah was thus left in a weak condition, controlling only its hill country, the lowlands (Shephelah), and part of the barren wasteland (Negeb) to the south of Beer-sheba, where the boundary with Edom was not clearly defined because the wilderness contained no natural resources in which either state was interested.

THE LAST DAYS OF JUDAH (c. 700–587 B.C.)

For the better part of the seventh century Judah continued as a vassal of Assyria, paying regular tribute. But new hope welled in the hearts of the subject peoples when, after 625 B.C., the Assyrian Empire began to totter (see p. 68). Josiah was king of Judah at this time, and he was quick to take advantage of the situation, expanding his kingdom northward in the attempt to re-establish a united Israel. In 621 B.C. he carried out a great religious reform (II Kings, chs. 22; 23) under the influence of an old law book (Deuteronomy or some portion of it) found during repair work in the Temple. Worship at the shrines and high places about the country was prohibited by royal decree. Sacrificial offerings could now be made only in Jerusalem where pagan excesses could be kept under control.

Josiah lost his life in 609 B.C. in the attempt to prevent the Egyptian army under Pharaoh Necho from going to the aid of the Assyrians at Haran (II Kings 23:29, 30; the phrasing of this passage gives the impression that Necho was on his way to fight against Assyria; but Mesopotamian records reveal that just the opposite was the case). The hopes that had arisen with the fall of Assyria were soon dashed, for Babylonia now rapidly took over the former empire (Plate XI:B), following much the same policies.

The dominant prophetic figure of this period was Jeremiah, who warned the Judeans against the disaster which would surely come if their current policies were not altered. His advice, however, was unheeded. Thinking themselves strong enough with Egyptian promises of aid, they revolted, only to be promptly subjugated in 598 B.C. by Nebuchadnezzar (II Kings 24:10 ff.), who carried the youthful King

Jehoiachin into exile together with numerous officials and artisans. Yet the lesson was not learned, and nine years later the country revolted again. This time Nebuchadnezzar utterly laid waste every important town of Judah, destroying Jerusalem and the Temple in 587 B.C. after a siege which lasted a year and a half (II Kings, ch. 25; Jer., ch. 39). The devastation was so complete that town after town was never reinhabited, and it was centuries before the country recovered. Lachish (VII:C, B-5; Fig. 33) has evidence of both destructions. In the ruins of the final devastation of the city gate were found a group of letters written by the commander of a neighboring outpost to his superior in the city, revealing the same state of tension and excitement in the country as does The Book of Jeremiah.

Thousands of Judeans were now scattered in the Babylonian Empire, among them Ezekiel. The poor who were left in Judah were prey to the hostile neighbors. Edom in particular was never forgotten because of the cruelty of her raids upon Judah, and because her people rapidly took over complete control of the southern part of the country (cf. Ps. 137:7; Ezek., ch. 35; Obadiah).

POST-EXILIC JUDAH

Immediately after the Persian conquest of the Babylonian Empire (cf. p. 69) permission was given for the exiles to return to Judah (c. 538 B.C.), and over a period of years a considerable company did so (Ezra, ch. 1 ff.). Plate VII:D shows the approximate size of Judah during this age. It was a tiny province in the Fifth Persian Satrapy, extending from Bethel to Beth-zur. To the north and east were the provinces of Samaria and Ammon, whose governors hindered the returned Jews in every way they could. To the south was the province of Idumaea (or Edom), which by the middle of the fifth century was composed largely of Arabian tribes (cf. Neh. 2:19; 6:1) who had invaded the ancient Edom and brought it to an end, as was prophesied in Jer. 49:7 ff. This province appears to have been controlled from Lachish, where the large palace of the Persian official has been excavated.

The first group of those who returned was led by one Sheshbazzar, who immediately laid the foundations for a new Temple on the site of the one which had been destroyed (Ezra 5:16). He was unable to complete it, however, because of the interference of the hostile neighbors and of "the people of the land" (Judeans who had not been in Exile). When Darius I came to the throne in 522 B.C. he appointed Zerubbabel, the grandson of King Jehoiachin (Jechoniah; Matt. 1:12), as governor of the province. Zerubbabel returned from Babylon with a considerable company of priests and Levites (Neh. 12:1), and with the help of the high priest Joshua and with the encouragement of the prophets Haggai and Zechariah completed the Temple between 520 and 516 B.C. The obstacles in the meantime had been partially cleared away by decree of Darius (Ezra, chs. 5; 6).

During the reign of Artaxerxes I (465-424 B.C.) two additional groups of exiles returned to Judah. The first was led by Ezra (c. 458 B.C.), who carried with him a letter from the king, authorizing him to take the leadership in the reform of the religious life of the community. One of his most important acts was the publication of the Pentateuch (Genesis to Deuteronomy) and the organization of the people's life in accordance with the laws it contained. His intense desire to guard the community from contamination with the surrounding people led to a religious exclusivism which alienated many, in particular the people of Samaria. As a result the Samaritan schism was made complete (see pp. 57 f.).

In 445-444 B.C. an additional group returned under the leadership of Nehemiah, who had been appointed governor with permission to rebuild the walls of Jerusalem (Neh., chs. 1 ff.). This task was brought to completion against the strong opposition of the neighbors and even of several of the nobles of Judah. No enlargement of the city was made, since the new fortifications followed the line of those destroyed by the Babylonians (see Plate XVII:A). Thus a century and a half after Jerusalem's destruction, its rebuilding had been completed and it again became the center and focus of the Jewish national and religious life, both in Judah and throughout the Dispersion.

and took over the whole of the west to the border of Egypt. The new hopes which the fall of Assyria had raised among the subject peoples were dashed. Babylon was substituted for Nineveh.

We do not possess detailed information about the conquests of Nebuchadnezzar, because he followed the Babylonian tradition of writing chiefly about his religious and architectural activity, rather than about military exploits. Yet he was certainly the central figure of his time. Syria and Palestine remained vassal territory because there was no great leader to establish a coalition against him. Only Jehoiakim of Judah, with Egyptian encouragement, offered trouble. Judah was promptly besieged in 598 B.C., and the young king Jehoiachin, who had just succeeded his father, was carried into captivity (II Kings, ch. 24). A decade later Judah again rebelled, in spite of strong protests by Jeremiah. This time the country was utterly devastated, and Jerusalem with the Temple was destroyed (II Kings, ch. 25).

Meanwhile most people in Judah still considered the captive Jehoiachin as their legitimate king, and expected his return at any time (Jer. 28:1-4). Documents found at Babylon in the basement of the Palace of Nebuchadnezzar list Jehoiachin, his five sons, and numerous other Judeans, along with people from Philistia, Egypt, and Phoenicia, as receiving regular provisions from the royal storehouse.

Apart from his wars, the chief work of Nebuchadnezzar was the enlargement and beautification of Babylon, which now surpassed Nineveh in architectural glory. He repaired the great Temple of Marduk, the Tower of Babel (see Fig. 11, and p. 24), and erected a vast imperial palace, on top of which, rising terrace upon terrace, was a garden. This place was called "The House at Which Men Marvel," and the "Hanging Gardens" were listed by the Greeks among the Seven Wonders of the World (Figs. 50 and 51).

Commerce, literature, art, and science flourished during this age. The Chaldeans were the founders of astronomy as a science. Careful astronomical observations were continuously kept for over 360 years, and these calculations form the longest series ever made. One great Chaldean astronomer, living shortly after the completion of this period of observation, was able to calculate the length of the year as 365 days, 6 hrs., 15 mins., and 41 secs.—a measurement which the modern telescope has shown to be only 26 mins., 26 secs. too long! His calculations on the diameter of the face of the moon were far more accurate than those of Copernicus. Certain measurements of celestial motions by another Chaldean astronomer actually surpass in accuracy the figures long in practical use among modern astronomers.

THE PERSIAN EMPIRE

During the days of Nebuchadnezzar two powerful empires, the Median and Lydian, existed to the east, north, and northwest of Babylon. By a treaty the boundary between them had been fixed at the Halys River in Asia Minor (Plate XI:B). The Medes, who had captured Asshur in 614 B.C. and assisted the Babylonians in destroying Nineveh in 612 B.C., had their capital at Achmetha (Ecbatana; XI:C, C-2). By 549 B.C. a Persian named Cyrus had united the people of his land and defeated the Median king. The attention of the west was now focused on the career of this extraordinary individual. A Judean prophet rightly interpreted the signs of the times, and saw in Cyrus one anointed of the Lord, who "giveth nations before him, and maketh him rule over kings" (Isa. 41:2; 44:28; 45:1). By 546 B.C. Sepharad or Sardis, the capital of Lydia (XI:C, A-2), had fallen to Cyrus, and Croesus, its king, was a prisoner. Cyrus was then ready to strike at Babylonia; in 539 B.C. he easily defeated the Chaldean army (led by the crown prince Belshazzar? Cf. Dan., ch. 5) and entered Babylon without opposition.

Thus just seventy years after the final Assyrian defeat at Haran in 609 B.C., the days of the Semitic empires were past. The Persian, Greek, and Roman empires were ruled by Indo-Europeans or Aryans. In 525 B.C. Egypt was added to the Persian Empire by Cyrus' son. In the space of twenty-five years the whole civilized east as far as India was brought under the firm control of Persia (Plate XI:C). Repeated

FIG. 50. Ruins of the Ishtar Gate of Babylon. The animals shown were made of highly colored glazed tile. For a reconstruction see Fig. 51.

attempts were made to add Greece (XI:C, A-2) to this empire. One was led by Darius the Great, who was defeated by the Greeks at Marathon in 490 B.C.; another, ten years later, was led by Xerxes, who was defeated in a naval battle off Salamis. Unable to subdue Greece, the Persians nevertheless held a firm hold over Asia for almost two centuries.

The organization of the great empire was a colossal task, brought to completion by Darius the Great (522-486 B.C.). While ruling Egypt and Babylonia directly as actual king, he divided the rest of the empire into twenty "satrapies" or provinces, each under a governor or "satrap"—a development of the earlier Assyrian provincial system. Aramaic, the language of Aramean ("Syrian") traders, which by this time had become the commercial tongue of the Fertile Crescent, was made the official language of government. Stamped coinage, an idea borrowed from Greece, was introduced throughout the empire as a convenience for business and government alike. A fleet was organized, and to provide a sea route from Egypt to Persia, a canal was dug between the Nile and the Red Sea.

Babylon and Susa (Shushan; XI:C, C-3) were used as royal residences. Cyrus had built a palace at Pasargadae, and there he was buried (XI:C, D-3). Darius, however, erected a magnificent palace with attendant buildings at Persepolis (XI:C, D-3), structures which surpassed in grandeur even the work of Nebuchadnezzar in Babylon. It is most unfortunate that Alexander the Great saw fit in 330 B.C. to burn them, leaving only the ruins for the modern excavator to uncover (Fig. 3).

The Assyrian and Babylonian policy of deporting subject peoples was reversed by the Persians, whose enlightened policies won a measure of gratitude from subject peoples. The exiled Jews benefited from this policy, and quite a large number of them returned to the area of Jerusalem, building a new Temple between 520 and 516 B.C. (Ezra, chs. 5; 6), and rebuilding the walls of Jerusalem under Nehemiah's leadership after 445 B.C. (Neh., chs. 2 to 6).

The best of the Persian monarchs felt obligated to rule justly and righteously. Their acts and words set them apart from Assyrian kings

FIG. 51. A reconstruction of ancient Babylon in the time of Nebuchadnezzar, showing a royal procession passing through the Ishtar Gate on its way to the palace. The latter had on its roof the famous "Hanging Gardens," shown in the upper right. In the distant background is the Tower of Babel (see Fig. 11).

in this regard, and the reason is probably to be sought in their religion. Darius and his immediate successors, at least, were followers of Zoroaster, a Median religious reformer who lived about 600 B.C. Zoroaster saw life as a ceaseless struggle between the forces of good and evil. The good, the light, he believed, was a supreme being, named Ahura Mazda. Opposed to him and the helpers he created were the evil spirits; but the good Ahura Mazda would ultimately prevail over them. Zoroaster called men to take their stand on the side of the good, and worship "the righteous Master of Righteousness." The influence of this religion spread widely, and even Judaism by the second century B.C. had borrowed certain conceptions from it.

THE HELLENISTIC EMPIRES

In the fourth century B.C. the center of political power moved westward and Greek culture made a strong though largely futile attempt to penetrate eastward. Culturally, Greece had long been important. Its brilliant cluster of city-states had generated a vitality and originality still unsurpassed. Particularly at Athens (XI:D, A-2) political vigor, expressed in civic interest, extensive sea power, and outreaching colonies, had joined with intellectual and artistic genius to create a permanently stimulating heritage.

An eastward movement of Greek influence may appear strange. Greek colonies and trade had previously been limited to the Mediterranean and the Black Sea (Plate XI:B). Two factors, however, directed attention eastward. The Greek cities in Asia Minor were inevitably bound up with trends farther east. Moreover, the competing city-states of Greece recognized that Persia, which at Marathon and Salamis had tried to conquer the Greeks, was still a threat.

These divided city-states found unity and protection, but only through unwilling subjection to Macedonia (XI:D, A 1-2). Philip of Macedon (359-336 B.C.), whose capital was at Pella (XI:D, A-1), extended his power southward until a decisive battle in 338 B.C. gave him control of all Greece except Sparta (XI:D, A-2).

It fell to Philip's son, Alexander the Great (336-323 B.C.), to carry

out the war Philip had planned against Persia. This brilliant pupil of Aristotle, a provincial governor at sixteen, able general at eighteen, and king at twenty, swiftly won loyalty in Macedonia and Greece. In 334 B.C. he crossed the Hellespont into Asia Minor to challenge Persia. A victory at the River Granicus (XI:D, A-2) opened Asia Minor to conquest. The next spring, he passed through the Cilician Gates (XI:D, B-2; Fig. 48) and decisively defeated the Persian army of Darius at Issus (XI:D, B-2). Turning south, he subdued Syria, Palestine, and Egypt (XI:D, B 2-4). At the western mouth of the Nile he founded the famous city of Alexandria (XI:D, A-3). Returning northward, he crossed the Euphrates at Thapsacus (XI:D, B-2), moved east, and in 331 B.C., at Gaugamela, near Arbela (XI:D, C-2), he crushed the remaining forces of Darius and was master of the Persian Empire.

Alexander continued eastward. His route took him through Babylon (XI:D, C-3), Susa (XI:D, C-3), Persepolis (XI:D, D-3), Ecbatana (XI:D, C-2), and Zadracarta (XI:D, D-2). At Prophthasia, in Drangiana (XI:D, E-3), when it had become apparent that he wanted to unite East and West in one great brotherhood, revolt was brewing among his followers, but he crushed it, and moved on into Bactria (XI:D, E-1), Sogdiana (XI:D, E-1), and India. There his troops mutinied and refused to go further. He returned westward, moving his troops partly by sea and partly by a land route through Gedrosia (XI:D, E-3) and Carmania (XI:D, D-3). At Babylon death ended his plan to create a world brotherhood with a culture prevailingly Greek (323 B.C.). He had proved a military genius; he had planted Greek cities and Greek influence in a wide area. But he made no deep and lasting imprint on the eastern regions which he had conquered. His work and the later Roman conquest did, however, determine the direction in which Judaism and Christianity were later to spread.

At his death there was no logical successor to hold the empire intact, and Alexander's generals fell to fighting among themselves. One of the many rivals, Ptolemy Lagi, emerged with secure possession of Egypt. Seleucus, another general, was able in 312 B.C. to establish the Seleucid dynasty in Syria and the east. The battle of Ipsus (XI:D, B-2) in 301 B.C. finally excluded from Asia the Antigonid dynasty, which henceforth contented itself with Macedonia. By 275 B.C. the situation shown on Plate XI:D had resulted. Three great empires existed, and they continued in essentially the same form until the eastern expansion of Rome absorbed them one by one. In Macedonia, Antigonus Gonatas ruled (283-239 B.C.). He was not able, however, to bring Greece under his control. In Egypt the Ptolemaic dynasty was firmly established, and Ptolemy II Philadelphus (285-246 B.C.) ruled also Cyrene, the southern part of the Aegean Sea, Lycia, Cyprus, and Palestine.

The dry climate of Egypt has permitted the survival of thousands of papyri, and from these records much of our knowledge of ancient life and history is derived. Tradition dates the translation of the Pentateuch from Hebrew into Greek in the reign of Ptolemy Philadelphus. The number of Greek-speaking Jews in Egypt, especially in Alexandria, was increasing, and they needed a Greek translation of their Scriptures.

The greater part of Alexander's empire, however, was in the hand of the Seleucid Antiochus I (280-262 B.C.), whose capital was at Antioch in Syria (XI:D, B-2). Northern Asia Minor, including Bithynia under Nicomedes (XI:D, B-1), Pontus under Mithridates (XI:D, B-1), and Galatia (XI:D, B-2), where the invading Gauls had just settled, was outside his control. But his empire extended from Thrace in Europe to the borders of India, although the effectiveness of his control over the eastern provinces is open to doubt. These eastern areas were soon to be lost, and Parthia (XI:D, D-2) was soon to begin its rise to power.

At this time Palestine was fulfilling its usual role of border region. Ptolemy Lagi had obtained control of it when Alexander's empire began to break up, and Ptolemaic control, though challenged more than once by the Seleucids, continued until 198 B.C., when Antiochus III added Palestine to the Seleucid empire. From that time until the coming of the Romans in 63 B.C. the history of Palestine was closely linked with that of Syria (see pp. 73 ff.).

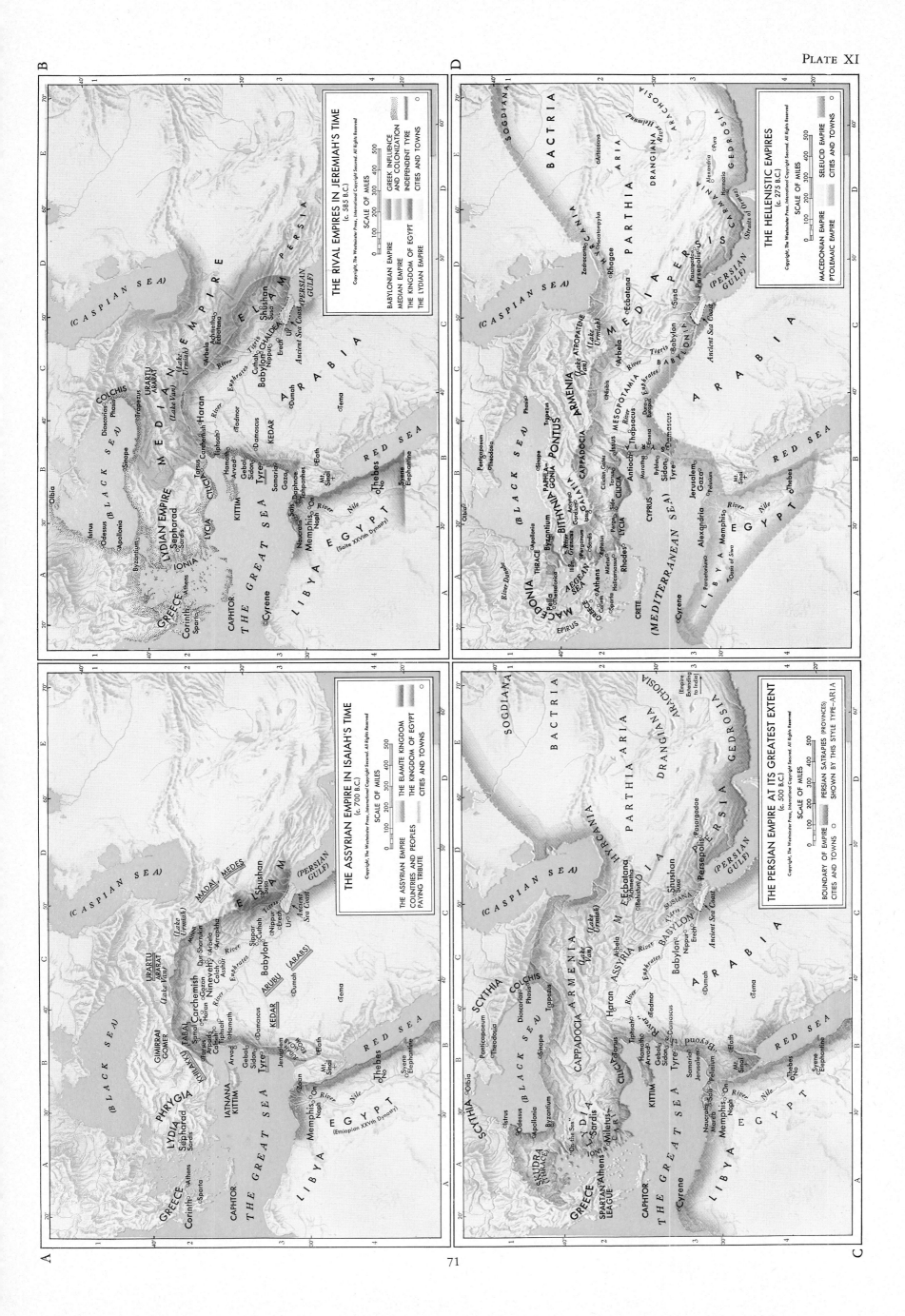

PLATE XI

Plate XII

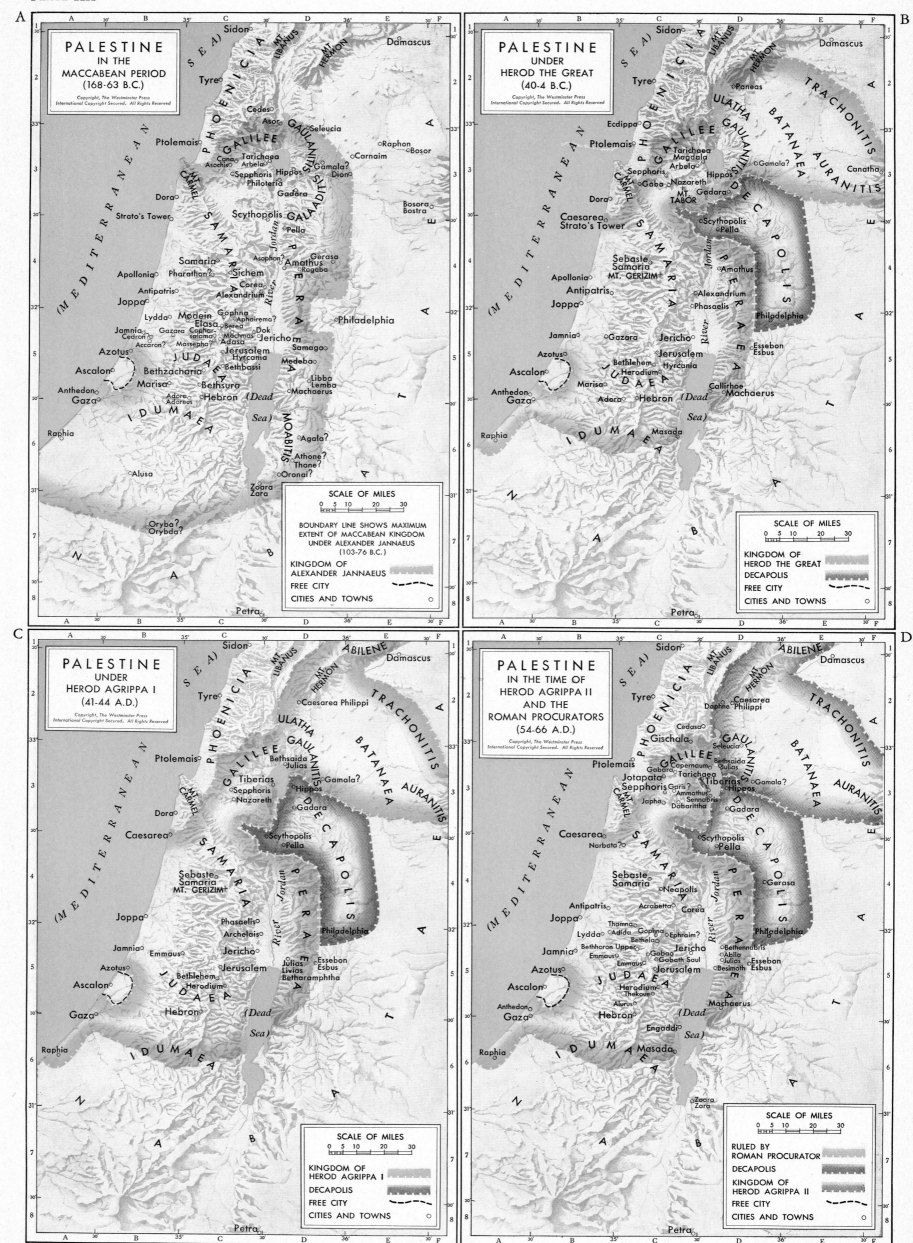

PALESTINE IN THE MACCABEAN PERIOD (168-63 B.C.)
Copyright, The Westminster Press
International Copyright Secured. All Rights Reserved

SCALE OF MILES
0 5 10 20 30

BOUNDARY LINE SHOWS MAXIMUM EXTENT OF MACCABEAN KINGDOM UNDER ALEXANDER JANNAEUS (103-76 B.C.)

KINGDOM OF ALEXANDER JANNAEUS
FREE CITY
CITIES AND TOWNS

PALESTINE UNDER HEROD THE GREAT (40-4 B.C.)
Copyright, The Westminster Press
International Copyright Secured. All Rights Reserved

SCALE OF MILES
0 5 10 20 30

KINGDOM OF HEROD THE GREAT
DECAPOLIS
FREE CITY
CITIES AND TOWNS

PALESTINE UNDER HEROD AGRIPPA I (41-44 A.D.)
Copyright, The Westminster Press
International Copyright Secured. All Rights Reserved

SCALE OF MILES
0 5 10 20 30

KINGDOM OF HEROD AGRIPPA I
DECAPOLIS
FREE CITY
CITIES AND TOWNS

PALESTINE IN THE TIME OF HEROD AGRIPPA II AND THE ROMAN PROCURATORS (54-66 A.D.)
Copyright, The Westminster Press
International Copyright Secured. All Rights Reserved

SCALE OF MILES
0 5 10 20 30

RULED BY ROMAN PROCURATOR
DECAPOLIS
KINGDOM OF HEROD AGRIPPA II
FREE CITY
CITIES AND TOWNS

MACCABEAN AND HERODIAN PALESTINE

PLATE XII

TO GRASP the importance of studying the history of Maccabean and Herodian Palestine, one need only review the outstanding religious developments of the period. At least one Old Testament book, Daniel, was written. Formation of the Hebrew canon of the Old Testament was practically completed. The Pharisee sect arose, and the rabbis developed much of the oral tradition which still gives orthodox Judaism its basic character. Above all, the Christian movement appeared and entered upon its missionary career. Obviously neither Judaism nor Christianity can be understood without careful study of the history of this significant period.

PALESTINE UNDER SYRIA

During the decades preceding the Maccabean period, the struggle between Syria and Egypt for the control of Palestine came to a decisive issue (see p. 70). For over a century after Alexander the Great's empire had been divided among his generals, Egypt dominated Palestine. Syria, however, was constantly seeking to extend its power southward, and under Antiochus III (223-187 B.C.) finally succeeded. His first effort, to be sure, was thwarted when in 217 B.C. he was beaten in battle at Raphia (Plate XII:A, A-6). In 198 B.C., however, he defeated the Egyptian forces at Paneas (XII:B, D-2) and became master of Palestine.

The policy of the Syrian rulers was to promote the influences which would effect unity of culture in their territory. Hence they looked with disapproval upon the strangely different Jewish religion, and were ready to further any steps which would strengthen Hellenistic culture in Palestine. In this effort they found many allies among the Jewish people themselves. Even some of the younger priests at Jerusalem took up the Greek language, athletic sports, and manner of dress. The Jews were split over the issue.

THE MACCABEAN REVOLT

This was the situation when Antiochus IV, called Epiphanes or "(God-) Manifest" (175-163 B.C.), became impatient with the stubborn opponents of his policy and determined to stamp out the Jewish religion. In 168 or 167 B.C. he desecrated the Jewish Temple at Jerusalem, prohibited the sacrifices, and made possession of a copy of the Law, keeping of the Sabbath, and the practice of circumcision crimes for which the penalty was death. Representatives of the king erected heathen altars in various places and tested the loyalty of the Jews by requiring them to offer pagan sacrifice.

Obviously this was a life-and-death struggle for Judaism, and resistance soon appeared. The revolt began at the little town of Modein (XII:A, C-5), in the hill country northwest of Jerusalem. Here lived the aged Mattathias, a priest of the Hasmonean house. When summoned to sacrifice he refused, killed a Jew who was willing to abandon his ancestral faith, and also slew the Syrian officer. Then, with his five sons, he fled into the hills, where he was joined by many who were ready to die rather than give up their faith.

Such loyal Jews were in a difficult position. They faced civil war with other Jews, and they were in revolt against the king. Mattathias was too old to lead the movement; on his deathbed, shortly after the revolt began, he appointed his son Judas to captain the rebel forces. From the title given Judas comes the name Maccabean; Judas was called Maccabaeus, which is usually explained to mean "Hammerer" and to refer to his sudden, heavy blows against the enemy. But it would be quite wrong to think of Judas as the general of a large and disciplined army. The Syrian forces controlled most of Palestine, and Judas depended much upon sudden thrusts and brilliant surprise attacks. Yet the desperation of the Jews, who were fighting not only

for their lives but also for their faith, made them the equal of an army many times their number.

The campaign of Judas took place mainly in the region of Judaea. Employing the methods of guerrilla warfare, he won victories at Beth-horon, Emmaus (XII:D, C-5), and Bethsura (XII:A, C-5). When the Syrian leaders withdrew to Antioch to prepare greater forces for the war, Judas led his forces to Jerusalem, and although the Syrians still held the Citadel, he cleansed the Temple of pagan objects, rebuilt the altar, and resumed the sacrifices in December, 164 B.C. Since that time the Jews have observed the Feast of Dedication, or Hanukkah, in memory of this occasion. The profanation of the Temple and the struggle of the Maccabeans to rescue it from the control of the Gentiles is the background of The Book of Daniel (c. 166 B.C.).

Judas and his brothers next made expeditions to Gilead, Galilee, and Idumaea to rescue loyal Jews. In other words, for a brief time the band of loyal Jews was limited to the central part of Judaea, and did not constitute the whole of the population even in that small area. Judas, however, after bringing to safety Jews in other regions who were in danger from the Gentiles or more often from their own countrymen, had to meet the armies of the Syrian king, who was now determined to crush the growing rebellion. His general, Lysias, forced Judas to withdraw from battle at Bethzacharia (XII:A, C-5), where Eleazar, the brother of Judas, lost his life. Bethsura (Fig. 53), an important military center which changed hands several times in these decades, had to surrender to the Syrians. Then, however, news of a rival claimant to the rule of Syria forced Lysias to make peace with Judas and grant religious freedom to the Jews.

FIG. 52. The *Sîq* and *el-Khazneh* at Petra. The approach to this site of rugged grandeur and great defensive strength is through the *Wâdī Mûsâ*, which for a mile and a quarter forms a narrow gorge, the *Sîq*, with side walls 100 to 160 feet high. At a final turn there comes into view the *Khazneh*, or "Treasury" of Pharaoh, as the Arabs call it. This famous temple, whose front is carved in the red sandstone side of the valley, is over ninety feet high. It is dated in the second century A. D. or earlier.

THE FIGHT FOR POLITICAL FREEDOM

This marked the achievement of the aim with which the revolt began. However, it did not satisfy the Maccabean leaders. They began to work for political independence. One thing which they undertook was to gain support from the Romans; to this end they concluded a league of friendship with the Romans about 161 B.C. This league, however, was of no immediate benefit to the Jews; the Romans did not intervene in Palestine until they were ready to take it over and control it (63 B.C.). The immediate future held in store more conflict with the Syrians, who were called in by the pro-Syrian party of the Jews to fight against Judas. After an indecisive fight at Capharsalama (XII:A, C-5), the Syrians were defeated and their general Nicanor killed at Adasa (XII:A, C-5). But the forces of Judas had been hard hit. When Bacchides came down from Syria with another army and met Judas at Elasa (XII:A, C-5), few Jews rallied to the battle. Judas was killed and his army crushed (160 B.C.).

His brother Jonathan assumed the leadership, but had pitifully few soldiers to support him. He was, indeed, almost a fugitive, and at first could wage only furtive guerrilla warfare. For a time he dwelt at Machmas, i.e., Michmash (XII:A, C-5). His first successes were due not so much to Jewish military prowess as to Syria's internal troubles, which so occupied the Syrians that Jonathan was able to get control of all Jerusalem except the Citadel. Hard-pressed by their troubles at home, the Syrians also evacuated many of their strongholds in Judaea, although they did not give up the important fortress at Bethsura. Jonathan took Joppa (XII:A, B-4), won a victory near Azotus (XII:A, B-5), and was given Accaron, i.e., Ekron (XII:A, B-5). In an attempt to strengthen his political position, he renewed the alliance of the Jews with Rome.

Emboldened by success, Jonathan went to meet the Syrian general Trypho at Scythopolis (XII:A, D-4). Trypho, however, avoided battle; instead he enticed Jonathan to a parley at Ptolemais (XII:A, C-3), and treacherously took him prisoner. He then began to move against Jerusalem, using his captive as a hostage. Jonathan's brother Simon, however, assumed command of the Jews, and Trypho, finding himself balked, finally put Jonathan to death (142 B.C.).

Simon gained from one of the rival claimants to the Syrian throne the grant of political freedom (142 B.C.), and the Jews dated a new era from this year. Nevertheless, as soon as Syria's internal affairs permitted, her leaders resumed attempts to subjugate the Jews. In the meantime, however, Simon won noteworthy successes. He finally forced the Syrian garrison out of the Citadel at Jerusalem. He took Gazara (XII:A, B-5), Joppa, and Bethsura, and is said to have made Joppa a port for Jewish use. At Joppa he defeated the Syrian general Cendebaeus, who attempted to re-establish the Syrian rule of

Palestine. His successful career was soon cut short (134 B.C.) by the treachery of his son-in-law Ptolemy, who murdered Simon and two of his sons at Dok (XII:A, C-5), near Jericho, and sent agents to murder Simon's other son, John Hyrcanus, who was at Gazara. John, however, learned of the plot, and by hastening to Jerusalem gained control of that city before Ptolemy's supporters reached it. He was promptly recognized as the rightful successor of his father, and became both ruler and high priest.

THE PERIOD OF TERRITORIAL EXPANSION

John Hyrcanus had a long and successful reign (134-104 B.C.). In its early years he was forced to admit the control of the Syrian king for a time, but he later renounced this control and extended the range of Jewish power. For instance, he gained the mastery of Medeba (XII:A, D-5), east of the Jordan. He broke the resistance of the region of Samaria, and captured Sichem (XII:A, C-4). After seizing the Samaritan temple on Mount Gerizim, he destroyed this bitter rival of the Temple in Jerusalem (cf. John 4:20). He took the city of Samaria (XII:A, C-4) and razed it He also captured Scythopolis and successfully asserted control over the Plain of Jezreel.

His son and successor Aristobulus I ruled but a year (104-103 B.C.). He extended Jewish control northward to Galilee, which Judas had abandoned to the Gentiles. Josephus states that Aristobulus was the first Maccabean to assume the title of king.

In the reign of Alexander Jannaeus (103-76 B.C.) the territory under Maccabean control reached its maximum extent, approximately that shown on Plate XII:A. His reign was by no means without its conflicts. When he attacked Ptolemais, that city appealed to Ptolemy of Egypt for help. Ptolemy saw a chance to extend his power to the north, and undertook against Alexander Jannaeus a futile campaign which included battles at Asochis (XII:A, C-3) in Galilee and Asophon (XII:A, D-4) in the Jordan Valley. Alexander was able to take Gadara (XII:A, D-3) and Amathus (XII:A, D-4) on the east side of the Jordan. In the southwestern corner of Judaea he took Raphia, Anthedon, and Gaza (XII:A, A 5-6). By this time, however, the worldly character of Maccabean ambitions and methods had grown until Alexander was using foreign mercenary soldiers to aid him in his warfare. The movement which started out to protect religious freedom had become so secular and nationalistic that many of his devout countrymen supported the Syrian ruler against him. He almost lost his power in a battle with the Syrian Demetrius at Sichem, but was saved by last-minute support from some Jews who at first fought against him.

Further difficulty for Alexander arose when the Syrian ruler came boldly into Palestine to meet Aretas, the Nabatean king, in battle. The latter defeated and killed the Syrian king, and later overcame

FIG. 53. Beth-zur (Bethsura). Air view while the 1931 excavation was in progress. Particularly during the Maccabean period this isolated hill was an important military stronghold. Note the hilly character of the Judean upland, and the way the rocks are cleared from the field and used in soil conservation.

JESUS IN JERUSALEM

Jerusalem was the scene of comparatively little of Jesus' ministry, but his dramatic and momentous experiences there merit careful attention. His visit to Jerusalem when twelve years of age (Luke 2:42) recalls the fact that great throngs went there for the three great festivals of the Jewish year. It also reminds us that pilgrimages and religious devotion gave Jerusalem much of its economic support.

Of places mentioned in the Gospels, the Pool of Siloam is certainly known (XVII:B, D-6). The Pool of Bethesda is probably not the Pool of Israel (XVII:D, D-E 3) or the Virgin's Spring (Gihon) or the Pool of Siloam, but the pool, now many feet below the surface, near the present Church of St. Anne (XVII:B, D-3). Solomon's Porch, where Jesus walked in December for protection from wintry winds (John 10:23), was the east portico.

In the triumphal entry Jesus used a gate located approximately where the walled-up Golden Gate now stands (XVII:D, E-4). When he cleansed the Temple he drove traders and money-changers from the Court of the Gentiles; only this part of the Temple area was a "house of prayer for all the nations" (Mark 11:17). The place of the Last Supper is not certainly known; strong ancient tradition fixes the site at the modern Coenaculum (XVII:D, C-6). The modern Grotto of the Agony and the Gethsemane Church (XVII:D, E 3-4) show approximately where Jesus withdrew for prayer on his last night (Mark 14: 26, 32). Dubious tradition locates the house of Caiaphas just north of the Coenaculum (XVII:D, C-6).

The Praetorium where Jesus stood before Pilate was probably in the Palace of Herod rather than in the barracks at Antonia. If this is so, the traditional Via Dolorosa (XVII:D, C-D 3-4) cannot have been the path from Pilate's residence to the crucifixion. To take Jesus to Herod Antipas (Luke 23:7), then, the guard would have taken Jesus from the Palace of Herod to the Palace of the Hasmonaeans.

The traditional site of the crucifixion, continuously identified as such since the time of Constantine (C.A.D. 325), is where the Church of the Holy Sepulcher now stands (XVII:D, C-4). A recent rival claim for a hillock called Gordon's Calvary (XVII:D, C-3) has little strength, and the "Garden Tomb" near by, in which some hold that Jesus was buried, probably dates several centuries later than the first.

THE FIRST-CENTURY WALLS

Discussion of the site of the crucifixion requires a study of the walls of first-century Jerusalem. On the south, the wall ran approximately as seen on Plate XVII:C. Later, however, the south wall, as excavations show, ran northeast to the Temple area along the line JKLMN, leaving the southern Tyropoeon and the ancient City of David outside the wall. Another later course followed much the line of the modern wall.

On the north were at least four ancient walls. The earliest ran eastward from the Palace of Herod to the Temple area. The second north wall is discussed below. Herod Agrippa I began a third wall about A.D. 42; it enclosed the hill Bezetha and other sections north of the

second wall. This third wall was long thought identical in course with the present north wall. A century ago, however, traces of it were found much farther north, and in the last twenty years nearly 800 yards of it have been discovered. The rest of its course can be plotted with little error by noting the elevation of the land. The tower of Psephinus, at its northwest corner, was probably on the edge of high ground northwest of the city.

Ancient remains along the course of the present north wall are proved by recent soundings to be from a wall built by Hadrian about A.D. 135. Before that date there was no wall along this line.

The second north wall began at the Gate Gennath, which was probably between the towers Hippicus and Phasael, encircled a section north of the first wall, and ended at Antonia. Four courses for it have been suggested. The circular course indicated by the letters ABCDP is unlikely; some evidence indicates this wall ran west, not north, from Antonia. The course AEFH encloses too small an area, and places the Gate Gennath too far east. Prevailing tradition favors the course AEFGP. Some debated remains of walls and a line of ancient cisterns appear to support this view. This, however, is a queer course for a city wall. Walls were built for defense; yet this line runs on low ground as compared with the ground outside it. Moreover, the traditional view assumes that the wall left a hill, Golgotha, just outside. Military judgment would have dictated the inclusion of such a hillock within the wall. On the whole, and with considerable hesitation, one may conjecture that the wall which ran west from Antonia and north from Phasael followed more nearly the line marked AEGP. If so, the traditional site of Golgotha cannot be authentic, and we do not know where Jesus was crucified and buried.

EARLY CHRISTIAN JERUSALEM

Apostolic Christianity was closely linked with Jerusalem and the Temple. The disciples met in Solomon's Porch; Peter and John went up to the Temple at the hour of prayer; they healed the lame man at the Beautiful Gate; even Paul the Apostle to the Gentiles was fulfilling a vow in the Temple when his enemies started a riot, dragged him out of the inner court, and caused the Roman guards to rush down from the Tower of Antonia and arrest him. From the stairs leading to the tower he addressed the crowd. Later he was confined in Antonia until sent to Caesarea. It was not until the Jewish revolt began in A.D. 66 that the Christian group, prompted by an oracle, left the city and moved to Pella, east of the Jordan. In A.D. 70 Jerusalem with its Temple was destroyed by the Romans. It was later rebuilt as a pagan city by the Romans, who renamed it Aelia Capitolina.

The Christian emperor Constantine gave the city new prestige as a Christian center and began the building of great churches to commemorate events in the life of Christ. From the seventh century to the First World War, with a few interludes, such as the Crusades, when Palestine was held by Christian armies, Jerusalem was under Mohammedan rulers and the Temple area was a possession, as it still is, of Moslem worshipers. For the last twenty-five years the British, with a mandate over Palestine, have controlled the rest of the city.

FIG. 73. Dome of the Rock, Jerusalem. The sacred rock under the dome is probably the site of the ancient Jewish altar of burnt offering. The beautiful octagonal structure, built late in the seventh century, stands on a raised platform some ten feet above the surrounding area. Just to the right of the Dome of the Rock is the Dome of the Chain. Mount Scopus is seen north and northeast of Jerusalem.

FIG. 74. Panorama of Jerusalem and vicinity, made in 1938, looking northeast. The present walls were built in 1542 by Sultan Suleiman the Magnificent. Within the walls the most striking feature is the *Haram esh-Sherif*, now under strict control of the Moslems, but occupying the site of the ancient Temple area. On an elevated platform in the center stands the Dome of the Rock (Fig. 73), sometimes wrongly called the Mosque of Omar. It was built at the end of the seventh century over the sacred rock where probably was located the Jewish altar of burnt offering. Jerusalem's four quarters reflect the religious faiths of the residents. The Moslems occupy the northeast quarter, the Jews are in the south center, the Armenians in the southwest section, and other Christian groups in the north-west quarter. In the latter section is the Church of the Holy Sepulcher (Fig. 71), on the spot where according to prevailing Christian tradition Jesus was crucified and buried. The tower at the northwest corner of the *Haram* marks the approximate site of Herod's Tower of Antonia. Thence the traditional *Via Dolorosa*, or road which

Christ trod on his way to the cross, runs west toward the Church of the Holy Sepulcher. It is very uncertain, how-ever, that this traditional route was the true one; it is also uncertain that the Church of the Holy Sepulcher marks the spot of Jesus' death and burial (see p. 99).

In recent decades the city has spread north and west. Important business and government buildings cluster near the northwest corner of the city wall. The railroad station is at the bottom, left of center. The Y.M.C.A. and King David Hotel, west of the old city, are recent structures. The American School of Oriental Research, in the top center, is the hub of American archaeological study in Palestine. The splendid new Museum is near the north-east corner of the city wall.

To bring in as many features as possible, the artist has distorted perspective at the extreme upper and lower right. Nevertheless, the panorama is valuable because it shows so many sites and is such a graphic visual aid.

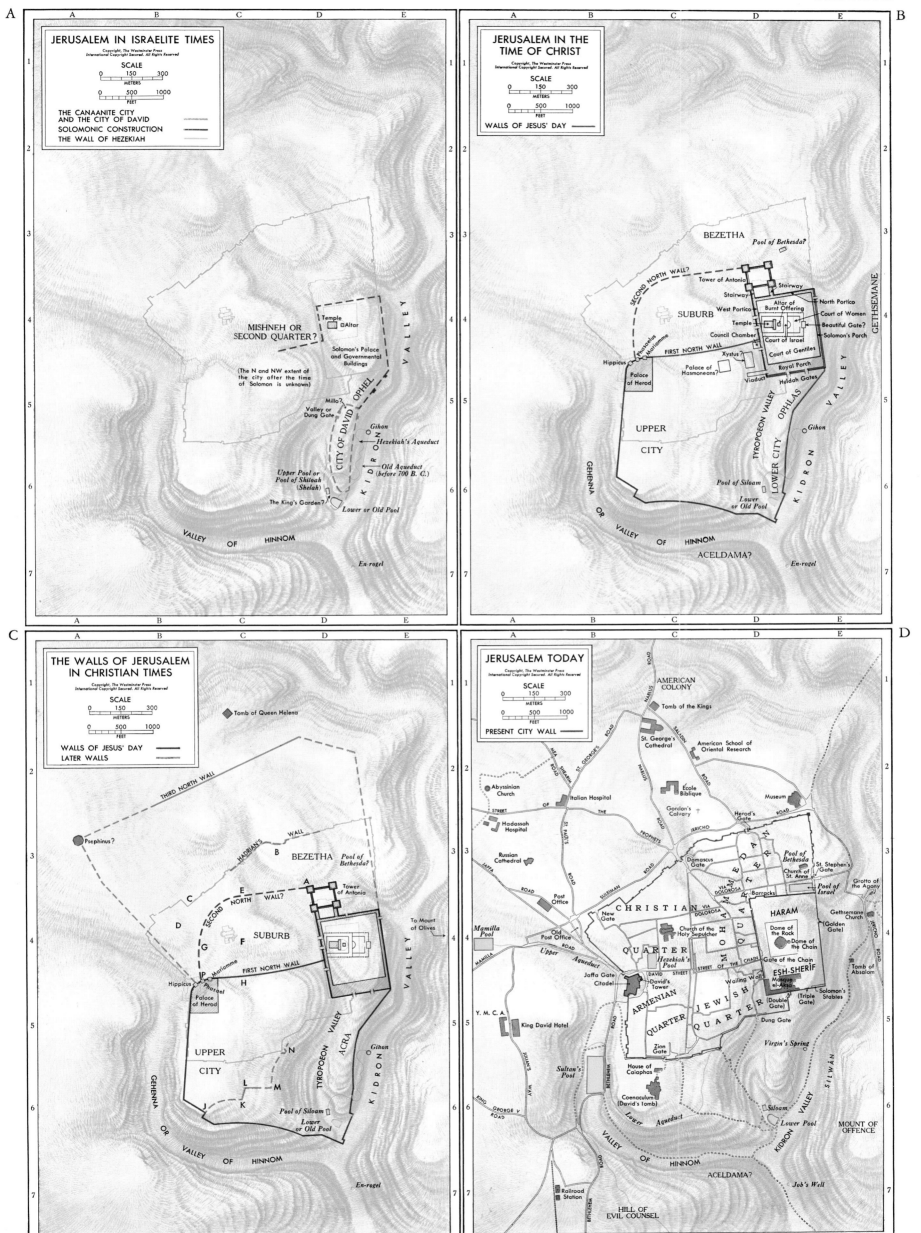

PLATE XVII

A — JERUSALEM IN ISRAELITE TIMES

Copyright, The Westminster Press
International Copyright Secured. All Rights Reserved

SCALE

THE CANAANITE CITY
AND THE CITY OF DAVID
SOLOMONIC CONSTRUCTION
THE WALL OF HEZEKIAH

MISHNEH OR
SECOND QUARTER?

Temple □ Altar

Solomon's Palace and Governmental Buildings

(The N and NW extent of the city after the time of Solomon is unknown)

Millo?
Valley or Dung Gate

CITY OF DAVID

OPHEL

KIDRON VALLEY

Gihon
Hezekiah's Aqueduct

Old Aqueduct (before 700 B. C.)

Upper Pool or Pool of Shiloah (Shelah)

The King's Garden?
Lower or Old Pool

VALLEY OF HINNOM

En-rogel

B — JERUSALEM IN THE TIME OF CHRIST

Copyright, The Westminster Press
International Copyright Secured. All Rights Reserved

SCALE

WALLS OF JESUS' DAY

BEZETHA
Pool of Bethesda?

SECOND NORTH WALL?

Tower of Antonia
Stairway
Stairway
Altar of Burnt Offering
North Portico
Court of Women
Beautiful Gate?
Solomon's Porch

SUBURB

West Portico
Temple
Court of Israel
Court of Gentiles

Phasaelus
Mariamne
Council Chamber

FIRST NORTH WALL

Hippicus
Palace of Herod
Palace of Hasmoneans?
Xystus
Viaduct
Royal Porch
Huldah Gates

UPPER CITY
TYROPOEON VALLEY
LOWER CITY
OPHLAS
Gihon
KIDRON VALLEY

GEHENNA OR VALLEY OF HINNOM

Pool of Siloam
Lower or Old Pool

ACELDAMA?

En-rogel

GETHSEMANE

C — THE WALLS OF JERUSALEM IN CHRISTIAN TIMES

Copyright, The Westminster Press
International Copyright Secured. All Rights Reserved

SCALE

WALLS OF JESUS' DAY
LATER WALLS

Tomb of Queen Helena

THIRD NORTH WALL

HADRIAN'S WALL

Psephinus?

BEZETHA
Pool of Bethesda?

C
E
D
A
G
F

SECOND NORTH WALL?

Tower of Antonia

SUBURB

To Mount of Olives

Mariamne
FIRST NORTH WALL

Hippicus
Phasael
Palace of Herod

VALLEY

UPPER CITY

TYROPOEON VALLEY
ACRA

Gihon
KIDRON

N
L
M
J
K

Pool of Siloam
Lower or Old Pool

GEHENNA OR VALLEY OF HINNOM

En-rogel

D — JERUSALEM TODAY

Copyright, The Westminster Press
International Copyright Secured. All Rights Reserved

SCALE

PRESENT CITY WALL

AMERICAN COLONY
Tomb of the Kings

St. George's Cathedral
American School of Oriental Research

Abyssinian Church
Italian Hospital
Ecole Biblique
Museum

Hadassah Hospital
Gordon's Calvary
Herod's Gate

Russian Cathedral

Damascus Gate
Pool of Bethesda
St. Stephen's Gate
Church of St. Anne
Grotto of the Agony

Post Office
Pool of Israel
Gethsemane Church

New Gate
CHRISTIAN QUARTER
VIA DOLOROSA
Barracks

Mamilla Pool
Church of the Holy Sepulcher
HARAM
Dome of the Rock
(Golden Gate)

Old Post Office
Upper Aqueduct
Hezekiah's Pool
Dome of the Chain
Gate of the Chain

Jaffa Gate
Citadel
DAVID STREET
ESH-SHERIF
Mosque el-Aqsa
Tomb of Absalom

Y. M. C. A.
Wailing Wall
(Double Gate)
Solomon's Stables
(Triple Gate)

King David Hotel
ARMENIAN QUARTER
JEWISH QUARTER
Dung Gate

Zion Gate
Virgin's Spring

House of Caiaphas
SILWAN

Sultan's Pool
Coenaculum (David's Tomb)
Siloam
Lower Pool

MOUNT OF OFFENCE

Lower Aqueduct

VALLEY OF HINNOM
Railroad Station
ACELDAMA?
Job's Well

HILL OF EVIL COUNSEL

PLATE XVIII

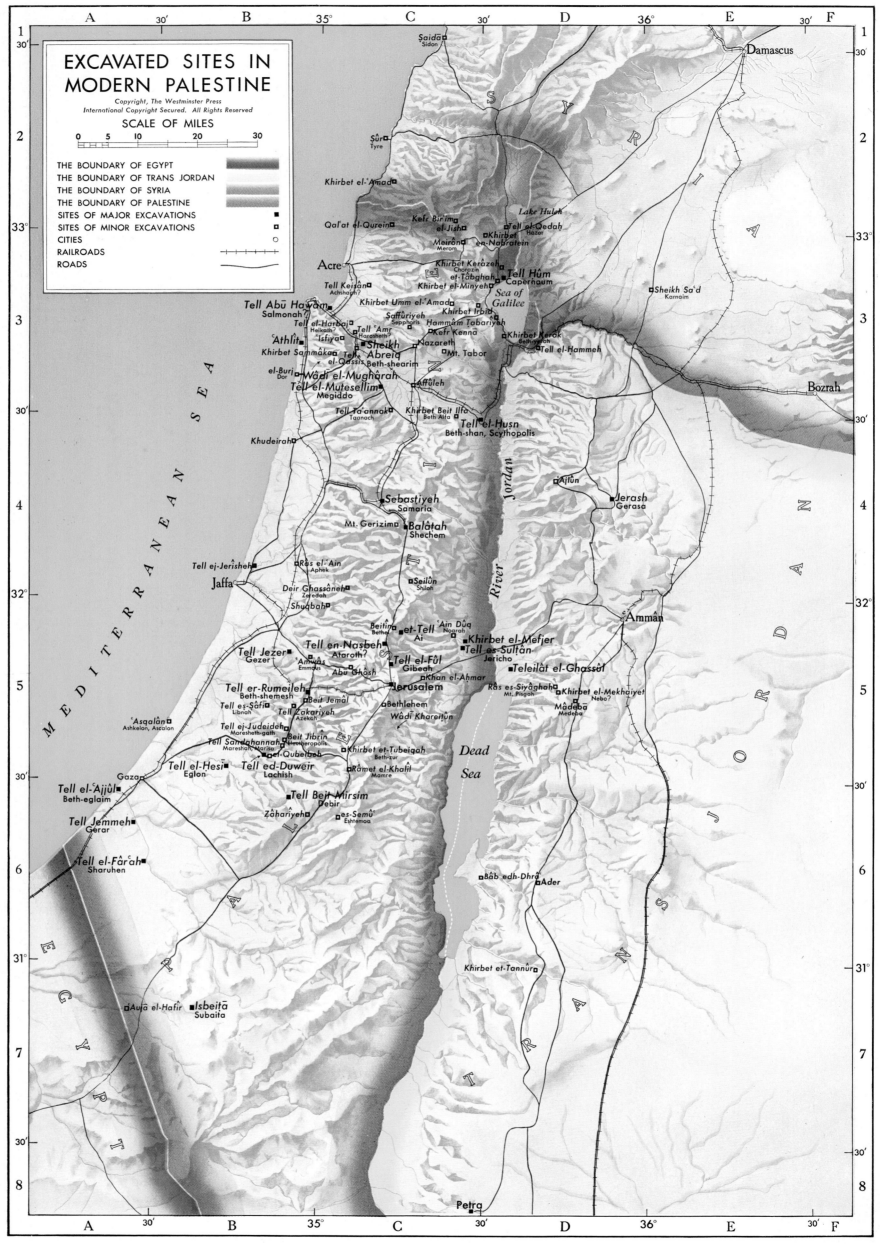

EXCAVATED SITES IN
MODERN PALESTINE

Copyright, The Westminster Press
International Copyright Secured. All Rights Reserved
SCALE OF MILES

0   5   10   20   30

THE BOUNDARY OF EGYPT
THE BOUNDARY OF TRANS JORDAN
THE BOUNDARY OF SYRIA
THE BOUNDARY OF PALESTINE
SITES OF MAJOR EXCAVATIONS
SITES OF MINOR EXCAVATIONS
CITIES
RAILROADS
ROADS

FIG. 75. *Tell el-Husn*, the mound containing the ruins of ancient Beth-shan. In the Roman-Byzantine period the town, then called Scy-thopolis, was situated on level ground mainly to the south (right) of the *tell*, but the cathedral was constructed on top of the mound over the ruins of a long series of earlier pagan temples.

EXCAVATIONS IN MODERN PALESTINE

PLATE XVIII

A LARGE part of what has been written in the pages of this *Atlas* could not have been written, nor could the maps themselves have been prepared, had it not been for the many years of intensive exploration in the Holy Land by scores of devoted students of the Bible. On Plate XVIII may be found the places where excavations have been conducted to determine the nature and history of the ancient towns, though the mere listing of the sites does not tell the complete story, nor does it give any inkling of the problems that have been solved or of the reasons for solving them. Chief among these problems are: how to locate and identify the ancient sites, how to dig the ruins properly, and how to date what is found. These matters have been discussed by Professor Albright on pp. 9-14. Here we need only mention that the journeys of Edward Robinson in 1838 and 1852 and the Survey of Western Palestine by the Palestine Exploration Fund between 1872 and 1878 were the first great achievements in Palestinian archaeology, achievements which formed the basis of all later topographical work.

Between 1920 and 1940 a number of well-trained scholars have studied and traveled extensively through the country and have arrived at a point far beyond that reached by their predecessors. Modern explorers like Albright and Glueck have been able to advance beyond their forerunners, in large part because they have developed new and refined methods for checking conclusions and for dating the ruins explored. For example, Num. 33:49 tells us that the Israelites after the conquest of Transjordan "encamped by the Jordan, from Beth-jeshimoth even unto Abel-shittim in the plains of Moab." Study of the places where these towns had been located by former explorers now reveals that the ruins could not be those of the Israelite period because they date from Roman times. The earlier sites have been discovered a little farther back in the hills along the same valleys (IX, H 5-6; the names Besimoth and Abila of the New Testament period are given to the later ruins). When peace prevailed under a stable government, the people moved their towns out into the plain near their crops; but before that they had to live in the hills near good springs at sites which possessed natural features to aid in fortification and defense even though they were some distance from the fields.

EARLY EXCAVATIONS

The ability to date the ancient ruins is the result of years of excavation. It is comparatively easy to recognize the typical site where an ancient city once stood in western Asia. It is in the shape of a truncated cone, possessing a flat top and steep, sloping sides (Fig. 75). This shape is preserved because the stumps of old city walls remain in the slopes and prevent erosion. The name which the Arabs use for such a mound is *tell*, a word which is very old, occurring not only in the Old Testament but in Babylonian literature as well. The Authorized Version of Josh. 11:13 reads as follows: "But as for the cities that stood still in their strength, Israel burned none of them, save Hazor only." The word here translated "strength" is really *tell*, and the words should be translated, "the cities that stood on their *tells*" (cf. R.V.).

When one digs into an ancient *tell*, he usually finds the ruins arranged in layers or strata, one above another. The reason for this is that the typical city was repeatedly destroyed and rebuilt through the centuries of its history. *Tell el-Husn* ("Mound of the Fortress"), on which ancient Beth-shan was located, contains eighteen different strata of debris and ruined houses, accumulated during the four thousand years of its intermittent occupation (XVIII, C-4). The depth of the debris from the topmost layer to virgin soil was about seventy-nine feet. The smaller Judaean mound of *Tell Beit Mirsim* (XVIII, B-6), occupied for some two thousand years, has about twenty feet of debris and ten strata.

It is not surprising that the translators of the Authorized Version did not understand the significance of a *tell*. Neither Edward Robinson nor the Survey of Western Palestine understood its full significance. The first demonstration of its true nature came in 1872-1874 with the excavations conducted by Schliemann at Troy (II, D-2). Even so, many years passed before the archaeological world as a whole was convinced. Lacking, therefore, a knowledge of the nature of a mound, and, more important, lacking an ability to date the ruins uncovered, early excavations were little more than treasure hunts. The "Tomb of the Kings" in Jerusalem, for instance, was so com-

FIG. 76. The American School of Oriental Research in Jerusalem. For its location in the city, see XVII: D, C-2.

pletely misinterpreted that, while actually dating from the first century A.D., it was thought to be the mausoleum of the kings of Judah (XVII:D, C-1)! Excavations around the walls of Jerusalem by Warren (1867-1870) were carried out with great vigor, but the information gained was scarcely commensurate with the effort required.

The year 1890 was a turning point in archaeological work, for in that year W. M. Flinders Petrie made a small excavation at *Tell el-Hesi* (XVIII, B-5). Here he showed that the pottery varied greatly in the different levels and that it was possible to set up a chronological scheme by means of it. This was the key needed to determine the date of excavated ruins. In a poor country like Palestine where monumental inscriptions are few, and the moist climate destroys papyrus documents, some other means of dating must be found. In the fifty years since Petrie's work the study of Palestinian pottery has been greatly advanced; and today, given a representative collection of broken fragments, it is usually possible for the expert to date them within a century, though the pottery styles of some periods are better known than others.

Between 1890 and 1914 there were a number of important excavations. In 1891-1893 an American named Frederick Jones Bliss continued Petrie's work at *Tell el-Hesi* for the Palestine Exploration Fund, clearing one third of the mound to bedrock. So little money was available for the publication of the discoveries, however, that neither they nor their stratification were adequately described. Between 1894 and 1897, Bliss conducted excavations in the southern part of Jerusalem to determine the line of the ancient walls and the extent of the city. Ruined fortifications along the southern edge of both the western and the eastern hills were unearthed (XVII:C, B-D 6), but their date was not precisely determined. Those which he found on the western hill probably do not go back to the time of Christ, as many have thought. They date chiefly from the Byzantine and Crusader periods, though they may follow the lines of earlier walls.

In 1898, Bliss was joined by R. A. S. Macalister, a young English archaeologist, and together they examined four tells in the Judaean Shephelah: *Tell eṣ-Ṣafi, Tell Zakarîyeh, Tell ej-Judeideh,* and *Tell Sandahannah* (XVIII, B-5). Judaean ruins were found in the first three; the most important was a strongly walled citadel at *Tell Zakarîyeh* (Azekah) which may have been built by Rehoboam (II Chron. 11:9), though the exact date was not determined. At *Tell Sandahannah* the best preserved Hellenistic town yet found in Palestine was unearthed. None of the discoveries were adequately published, however, and little can be said about them.

Macalister then undertook the first major excavation of a mound at *Tell Jezer* (XVIII, B-5). Most of the site was cleared in five campaigns between 1902 and 1909. This was a great achievement, the more so because Macalister directed the work alone, with no assistance except that of an able Arab foreman. He divided the mound into north-south strips, each forty feet wide, and dug the strips one at a time. At first he was able to keep check on the strata and the objects found in each. As time went on, however, he found it in-

creasingly difficult to correlate the strata of one strip with those of other strips near by and to observe and record accurately the precise level from which the objects came. Hence, the value of his energetic work is largely dissipated. In general terms we can now recount the history of the site and its fortifications, but we cannot be precise. The most interesting discovery was that of a Canaanite sacred area in which there were a number of large, upright stones (Hebrew *maṣṣēbôth*). Similar installations have been found elsewhere, particularly in Transjordan, but their religious function, whether as symbols of deities or memorials erected for ancestors, is not yet clear.

The accomplishments of German archaeologists between 1901 and 1905 at Taanach and Megiddo (XVIII, C-3) were far less even than that of Macalister. They destroyed far more evidence than they recovered. At Taanach the most important discovery was a Canaanite structure which contained a few cuneiform tablets dating about a century earlier than the Amarna period. The meaning of the seemingly chaotic results of the Megiddo expedition has been clarified only in part by recent excavations (see below). Interesting objects were discovered, among which was the official seal of "Shema, servant of Jeroboam." This individual is not mentioned in the Old Testament, but the Jeroboam of the seal was undoubtedly the king who reigned in Israel during the early part of the eighth century. The expression "servant" on this and other similar seals means "royal official."

German work at Jericho (1907-1909) was a great improvement over previous excavations, because for the first time the importance of an adequate trained staff was realized. This was the second major excavation before the First World War, and considerable information was gained about the houses and fortifications of Jericho, though some of the strata were misdated by several centuries (see further below).

The third major excavation of this period, and by far the most important, was the work of Harvard University at Samaria (XVIII, C-4), directed by the Americans George A. Reisner and Clarence S. Fisher between 1908 and 1910. Important discoveries were made, including a magnificent temple built by Herod the Great, under which were the ruins of the palace of the Israelite kings (see further below). Equally important was the development by these excavators of the method of excavation now in use throughout the Near East (see p. 10).

EXCAVATIONS BETWEEN 1920 AND 1940

In the story of Palestinian excavations the period before 1920 must be considered largely as one of preparation for what was to come. There were significant discoveries, but none were so important as the knowledge of how to dig and how to date what was found. Consequently, when excavations began again after the war, far more valuable results were obtained. In addition, a number of organizations now entered the field whose co-operative endeavor and sharing of information made advance more rapid. One of the most significant events occurred in 1920, when the Department of Antiquities in Palestine was established by the British Government. Digging by unauthorized and untrained persons was now forbidden, but the work of trained and well-equipped expeditions was greatly encouraged. Before the war the latter were hampered by a corrupt Turkish Government and oppressive laws.

Another significant organization was the American School of Oriental Research in Jerusalem, which has done much to encourage co-operation between national and religious groups and institutions, serving as a clearing house for information, and providing a place where students can study (Fig. 76). Likewise important was the interest taken by the Rockefeller Foundation, which gave to the Government of Palestine $2,000,000 for the establishment of the Palestine Archaeological Museum. In addition, numerous educational institutions have taken a direct interest in the work on a scale far greater than before 1914.

The largest and most elaborate excavation ever planned in Palestine was that at Megiddo (XVIII, C-3; and Fig. 5) by the Oriental Institute of the University of Chicago. The entire site was purchased so that it could be completely dug as a model excavation for the whole of the Near East. The work began in 1925, and during the following decade the first four strata were entirely removed. These dated from the fourth back to the tenth century B.C. The first stratum contained the scattered ruins of the Babylonian and Persian periods, including the walls of an exceedingly strong building that must have been the palace of the district officer. Stratum II contained the ruins of the palaces used by the Assyrians when they ruled the province of Galilee from this site (Plate VII:C). Strata III and IV were Israelite; the earliest phase of IV dated from the time of Solomon, who made the city the capital of his fifth administrative district in Israel (Plate VII:A). Royal stables for horses (cf. I Kings 9:15 ff.) and the palace built for Baana, the district governor (I Kings 4:12), are among the most interesting discoveries.

After some ten years of work the comprehensiveness of the excavation's plan had to be abandoned. Between 1935 and 1938 sections were dug to bedrock which showed that the city had been founded about 3500 B.C. and throughout its history had been one of the strongest and most important in Palestine. During the time of the Patriarchs, about 1900 B.C., three temples with a large adjoining altar for burnt offerings were erected. The main altar in ancient temple enclosures always stood in an open court (cf. II Chron. 7:7), but this is the first large one yet found intact in Palestine. A later temple and the elaborate palace of the local king during the time of Joshua have also been recovered (Figs. 28 and 29).

Next in importance must be placed the excavation of Beth-shan (XVIII, C-4; Fig. 75) between 1921 and 1933 by the University Museum of Philadelphia. The major discoveries were a Byzantine Church and monastery, a Hellenistic temple of the third century B.C., and a series of Canaanite temples dating between the fourteenth and tenth centuries B.C. The Hellenistic structure is a good illustration of the general type of Phoenician temple plan and is similar in its main features to the Solomonic Temple (Fig. 31). The Canaanite temples and their contents are our most important source of information regarding the material equipment of Canaanite religion. Two of them, the "houses" of Ashtoreth and Dagon, are mentioned in the Old Testament (I Sam. 31:10; I Chron. 10:10), and were probably destroyed by David. In any event, the city was laid waste shortly after 1000 B.C. and remained virtually unoccupied for centuries. Between the fifteenth and early twelfth centuries an Egyptian garrison was stationed there, and at least three Pharaohs left their stelae (monumental inscriptions) in the temple area.

Numerous other excavations vie with each other to be mentioned next. *Tell Beit Mirsim* (XVIII, B-6), dug by the American School of Oriental Research in Jerusalem and the Xenia (now Pittsburgh-Xenia) Theological Seminary, under the direction of W. F. Albright, has become a type site because of the many well-preserved strata and the excellence of the excavation. Few spectacular objects were found, but the detailed history of the site and the significance of its various features as reconstructed by the excavator are a most important addition to our knowledge of ancient Palestine.

Of particular interest to students of the Old Testament have been the English excavations at Jericho (XVIII, C-5) between 1930 and 1936, directed by John Garstang. German excavations before the First World War (see above) had already revealed something of the city's history. Garstang's results have greatly clarified and amplified this information. The center of interest naturally lies in the Canaanite city, the fall of which is described in Josh., ch. 6. About 1500 B.C. the city was provided with a strong double fortification of brick (see p. 36). The evidence of violent destruction was clear. The walls had toppled over down the sides of the mound. The base of the outer wall had shifted, and the debris gave evidence of a terrific conflagration and earthquake. Houses were filled with the burned remains, including charred roofing beams, onions, bread, wheat, barley, oats, and dates. There has been considerable debate over the date of this destruction, but it is now certain that it was some time before 1300 B.C.

The city then remained virtually uninhabited until the tenth-ninth centuries (cf. Josh. 6:26 and I Kings 16:34). Since other evidence points to a thirteenth century date for Joshua, this information concerning the final fall of Canaanite Jericho furnishes the major problem in the historical reconstruction of the Exodus and the Conquest (see pp. 39 f.).

Similarly, the excavation of Ai (XVIII, C-5) in 1933-1934 by Mme. Krause-Marquet furnishes an interesting problem. The name of the site in Hebrew means "The Ruin"; its conquest is described in Josh., chs. 7; 8. The excavator found that it was one of the great cities of Palestine during the third millennium B.C., but that it was destroyed c. 2200 B.C. and never again occupied, except for a small Israelite settlement dating after the twelfth century. An excavation by W. F. Albright in 1934 at Bethel (XVIII, C-5), 1½ miles away showed that it was established to take the place of Ai. The ruins of Bethel bore vivid marks of a violent destruction during the course of the thirteenth century (cf. Judg. 1:22 ff.). The simplest explanation of the situation is that the story of the capture of Bethel was transferred to Ai in The Book of Joshua. When Israelite writers recorded the story, they knew of the great ruin near Bethel, and naturally ascribed its capture to Joshua.

Between 1931 and 1935 excavation was resumed at Samaria (XVIII, C-4) under the direction of the English archaeologist J. W. Crowfoot. The results have necessitated a slight revision in the dating of the strata as proposed by Reisner and Fisher. The first phase, consisting of an elaborate palace and strong fortifications, was undoubtedly begun by Omri as previously thought, though almost certainly not completed until the reign of Ahab. The second phase, consisting of the "ostraca house" and a double (casemate) wall which in the most vulnerable part of the city was nearly 33 feet wide, is now known to have been built, not by Ahab, but by one of the kings of the Jehu dynasty, presumably either Joash or Jeroboam II. These fortifications were so strong that it took the Assyrian army three years to conquer the city in 724-721 B.C. (II Kings 17:5). A number of beautifully carved ivories, probably from Ahab's "ivory house" (I Kings 22:39), and the pool where Ahab's chariot was presumably washed after bearing the king's body from Ramoth-gilead (I Kings 22:38) have been found also.

From 1932 to 1938 exceedingly important work was done at Lachish (XVIII, B-5) by the Wellcome-Marston Archaeological Research Expedition, directed by J. L. Starkey before his tragic murder by Arab brigands early in 1938. Among the discoveries were a Canaanite temple, a strong double fortification with protecting gateway built by Rehoboam (Fig. 33; II Chron. 11:9), a group of letters from the time of Jeremiah, and a Persian palace and temple. The letters were by far the most astonishing find, since they are the first

FIG. 77. A reconstruction of the fortifications of *Tell en-Naṣbeh* (XVIII, C-5). The high wall, some 26 feet wide, was built c. 900 B.C. during the civil war between Israel and Judah. It is a good example of ancient fortifications: see also Figs. 18 and 33.

intro

(Appendix D) is perhaps *the* most inclusive dictionary of mountain bike technical terms in existence. Appendix E lists the tightening specifications of almost every bolt on the bike. Appendix F reveals which clip-in pedals work with which cleats, and vice versa; knowing which pedals your cleats work in can save you a ton of time switching pedals when trading bikes around with friends or trying demo bikes. Appendix G is a listing of the illustrations in the book, if you want to quickly find what something is supposed to look like.

THE MOUNTAIN BIKE

This is the creature to whom this book is devoted (Fig i.1). All of its parts are illustrated and labeled here. Take a minute to familiarize yourself with these now and then refer back to diagram i.1 whenever necessary.

The mountain bike comes in a variety of forms, from models with rigid frames and forks to models with high-zoot front and rear suspension systems. A mountain bike generally comes

i.3 **fully suspended**

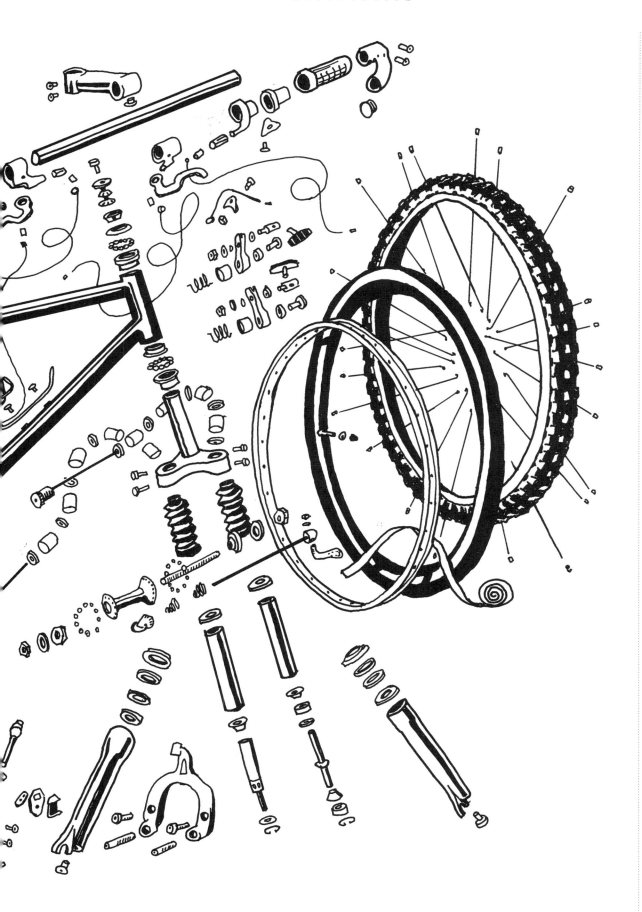

with 26-inch knobby tires. Tire variations are abundant and include everything from studded snow tires to smooth street tires.

I believe that by clearly spelling out the steps necessary to properly maintain and repair a bicycle, even those who see themselves as having no mechanical skills will be able to tackle problems as they arise. With a little bit of practice and a willingness to learn, your bike will suddenly transform itself from a mysterious black box, too complicated to tamper with, to a simple, very understandable machine that is a delight to work on. Just allow yourself the opportunity and the dignity to follow along, rather than deciding in advance that you will

never be able to do this. All you have to do is follow the instructions and trust yourself.

So, set aside your self image as someone who is "not mechanically oriented" (and any other factors that may stand in the way of you making your mountain bike ride like a dream), and let's start playing with your bike!

1.5 hybrid

tools

"Behold, we lay a tool here and on the morrow it is gone."

— *THE BOOK OF MORMON*

You can't do much work on a bike without tools. Still, it's not always clear exactly which tools to buy. This chapter gives a clear idea of exactly what tools you should consider owning, based on your level of mechanical experience and interest.

As I mentioned in the introduction, the maintenance and repair procedures in this book are classified by their degree of difficulty. All repairs mentioned are classified as Level 1, unless otherwise indicated. The tools for Levels 1, 2 and 3 are pictured and described on the following pages. In addition, a list of the tools needed in each chapter are shown in the margin at the beginning of each chapter.

For the uninitiated, there is no need to rush out and buy a large number of bike-specific tools. With only a few exceptions, the "Level 1 Tool Kit" consists of standard metric tools. In a more compact and lightweight form, this is the same collection of tools I recommend carrying with you on long rides. The Level 2 Tool Kit" contains several bike-specific tools, allowing you to do more complex work on the bike. "Level 3" tools are extensive (and expensive), and ensure that your riding buddies will show up not only to ask your sage advice, but to borrow your tools as well. If you are one to loan tools, you might consider marking your collection, so as to help recover those items that might otherwise take a long time finding their way back to your workshop.

I-I: LEVEL I TOOL KIT

Level I repairs are the simplest and do not require a workshop, although it is nice to have a good space to work. You will need the following tools (Fig. 1.2):

◆ **Tire pump** with a gauge and a valve head to match your tubes (either Presta or Schrader valves; see Fig. 1.1).

◆ **Standard screwdrivers**: one small, medium and large.

◆ **Phillips-head screwdrivers**: one small and one medium.

◆ Set of three plastic **tire levers**.

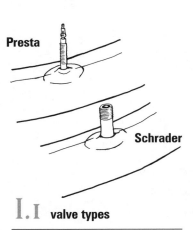

Presta

Schrader

1.1 valve types

◆ At least two **spare tubes** of the same size and valve type as those on your bike.

◆ Container of regular **baby powder**. It works well for coating tubes and the inner casings of tires. Do not inhale this stuff; it's bad for the lungs

◆ **Patch kit**. Choose one that comes with sandpaper instead of a metal scratcher. At least every 18 months, check that the glue has not dried up, whether open or not.

◆ One **6-inch adjustable wrench** (a.k.a., "Crescent wrench").

◆ **Pliers**: regular and needle-nose.

◆ Set of **metric Allen wrenches** (or hex keys) that includes 2.5mm, 3mm, 4mm, 5mm, and 8mm sizes. Folding sets are available and work nicely to keep your wrenches organized. I also recommend buying extras of the 4mm, 5mm, and 6mm sizes.

◆ Set of **metric open-end wrenches** that includes 7mm, 8mm, 9mm, 10mm, 13mm, 14mm, 15mm and 17mm sizes.

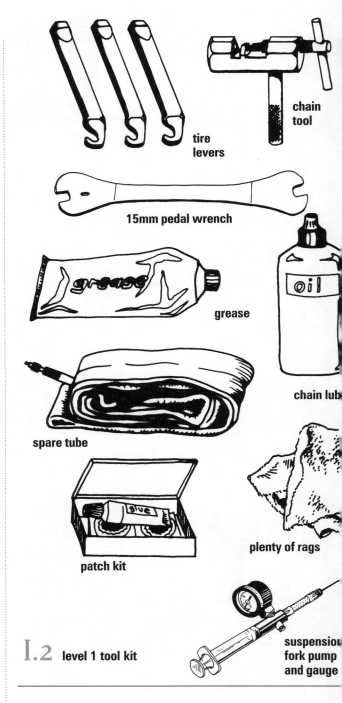

tire levers

chain tool

15mm pedal wrench

grease

oil

chain lube

spare tube

patch kit

plenty of rags

1.2 level 1 tool kit

suspension fork pump and gauge

◆ **15mm pedal wrench**. This is thinner and longer than a standard 15mm wrench but thicker than a cone wrench.

◆ **Chain tool** for breaking and reassembling chains.

◆ **Spoke wrench** to match the size of nipples used on your wheels.

◆ **Tube or jar of grease**. I recommend using grease designed specifically for bicycles;

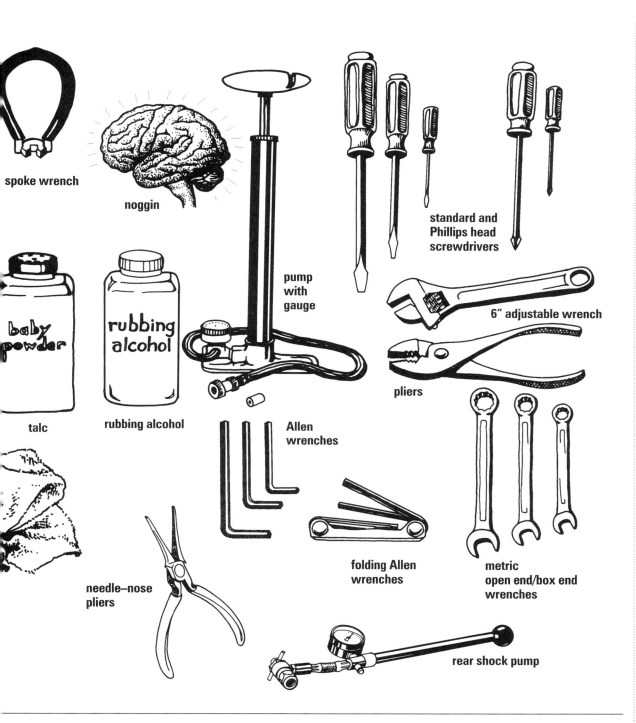

spoke wrench

noggin

talc

rubbing alcohol

needle–nose pliers

pump with gauge

Allen wrenches

folding Allen wrenches

standard and Phillips head screwdrivers

6″ adjustable wrench

pliers

metric open end/box end wrenches

rear shock pump

however, standard automotive grease is okay.

◆ Drip bottle or can of **chain lubricant**. Please choose a non-aerosol; it is easier to control, uses less packaging, and wastes less in overspray.

◆ **Rubbing alcohol** for removing and installing handlebar grips

◆ A lot of **rags**!

OTHER:

◆ Most air/oil suspension forks and rear shocks come with a **small air pump** equipped with the appropriate head and gauge. If you have such a system, the pump needs to be part of your basic tool set.

I-2: LEVEL 2 TOOL KIT

Level 2 repairs are a bit more complex, and I recommend that you use a well-organized work space with a shop bench. Keeping your workspace well organized is probably the best way to make maintenance and repair easy and quick. You will need the entire Level 1 Tool Kit (Fig. 1.2) plus the following tools (Fig. 1.3):

▲ **Portable bike stand.** Be sure that the stand is sturdy enough to remain stable when you're really cranking on the wrenches.

▲ **Shop apron** (this is to keep your nice duds nice).

▲ **Hacksaw** with a fine-toothed blade.

▲ Set of **razor blades** or a sharp shop knife.

▲ **Files**: one round and one flat.

▲ **Cable cutter** for cutting brake and shifter cables without fraying the ends.

▲ **Cable-housing cutter** for cutting coaxial-indexed cable housing. If you purchase a Shimano, Park or Wrench Force housing cutter, you won't need to buy a separate cable cutter, since either of these cleanly cuts both cables and housings.

▲ Set of **metric socket wrenches** that includes 7mm, 8mm, 9mm, 10mm, 13mm, 14mm and 15mm sizes.

▲ **Crank puller** for removing crank arms.

▲ Medium **ball-peen hammer**.

▲ **Two headset wrenches**. Be sure to check the size of your headset before buying these. This purchase is unnecessary if you have a threadless headset and plan only to work on your own bike.

▲ Medium **bench vise**.

▲ **Cassette cog lockring tool** for removing cogs from the rear hub.

▲ **Chain whip** for holding cogs while loosening

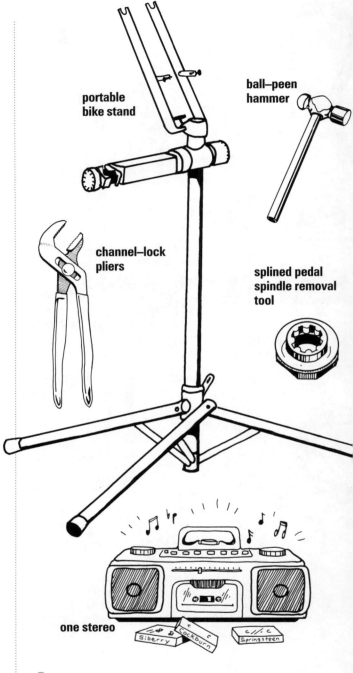

1.3 level 2 tool kit

the cassette lockring.

▲ **Bottom bracket tools.** For Shimano cartridge bottom brackets or other brands with splined cups, you'll need the splined tool for this type of bottom bracket. For cup-and-cone bottom brackets, you'll need a lockring spanner and a

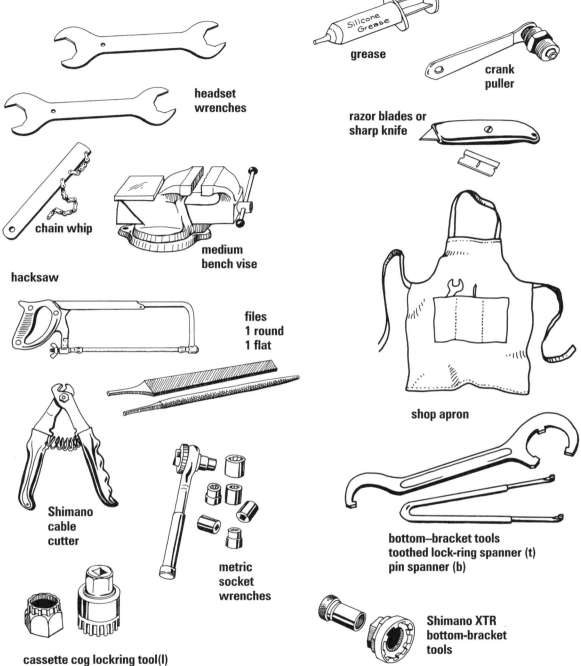

headset
wrenches

chain whip

hacksaw

medium
bench vise

files
1 round
1 flat

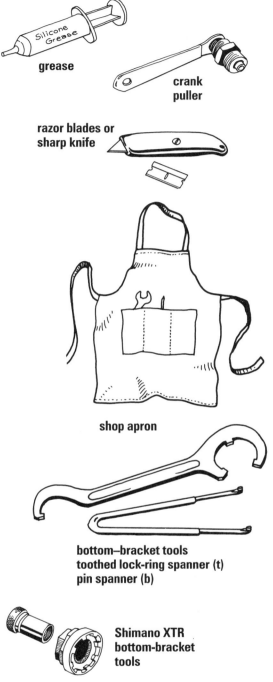

grease

crank
puller

razor blades or
sharp knife

shop apron

Shimano
cable
cutter

metric
socket
wrenches

cassette cog lockring tool(l)
sealed–bottom–bracket tool (r)

bottom–bracket tools
toothed lock-ring spanner (t)
pin spanner (b)

Shimano XTR
bottom-bracket
tools

tools

level
2

pin spanner to fit your bottom bracket.

▲ **Channel-lock pliers**.

▲ **Splined pedal spindle removal tool**.

▲ Tube of **silicone-based grease** if you have
Grip Shift and other non-lithium grease for
suspension forks.

▲ One **stereo** with good tunes. This
is especially important if you plan
on spending a lot of time working
on your bike.

I-3: LEVEL 3 TOOL KIT

If you are an accomplished Level 3 mechanic, you are now completely independent of your local bike shop's service department. This even includes building up brand-new frames. By now, you have a well-organized separate space intended just for working on your bike. Some elements of the Level 3 kit (Fig. 1.4) are obviously heavier-duty replacements for parts of the Level 2 kit.

▶ **Parts washing tank**. Please use an environmentally safe degreaser. But choosing the right kind of degreaser is not enough. You need to dispose of used solvent responsibly, so check with your local environmental safety office.

▶ **Fixed bike stand**. Be sure it comes with a clamp designed to fit any size frame tube.

▶ Large **bench-mounted vise** to free stuck parts.

▶ **Headset press** used to install headset bearing cups. The press should fit all three cup sizes. Chris King headsets need a press that does not contact the pressed-in bearing. King sells inserts for regular headset presses to install his headsets.

▶ **Fork crown race punch** (a.k.a., slide hammer) of the appropriate diameter for your steering tube. This tool installs the fork-crown headset race. (Thin Shimano or Chris King crown races require a second support tool to protect the crown race during installation.)

▶ **Headset cup remover**.

▶ **Star-nut installation tool** for threadless headsets.

▶ An **additional chain whip**. A second whip is handy for disassembling freewheels or old-style cassettes.

▶ **Freewheel removers**. Removers for Shimano, Sachs and Suntour freewheels are almost as obsolete as freewheels but are still some-

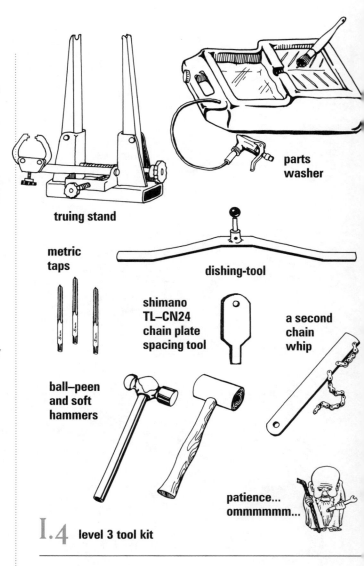

truing stand

parts washer

metric taps

dishing-tool

shimano TL–CN24 chain plate spacing tool

a second chain whip

ball–peen and soft hammers

patience... ommmmmm...

1.4 **level 3 tool kit**

times needed.

▶ **Large ball-peen hammer.**

▶ **Soft hammer**. Choose a rubber, plastic or wooden mallet to prevent damage to parts.

▶ **Torque wrench**. Torque wrenches are great for checking proper bolt tightness. There are many manufacturers who recommend using one when installing their components. I'll be honest, I don't use them all that often. Still, if you want to be thorough, it may be a good idea to pick one up at an automotive supply store.

▶ Set of **metric taps** that includes 5mm x 0.8, 6mm x 1 and 10mm x 1. These work for threading bottle bosses, cantilever bosses,

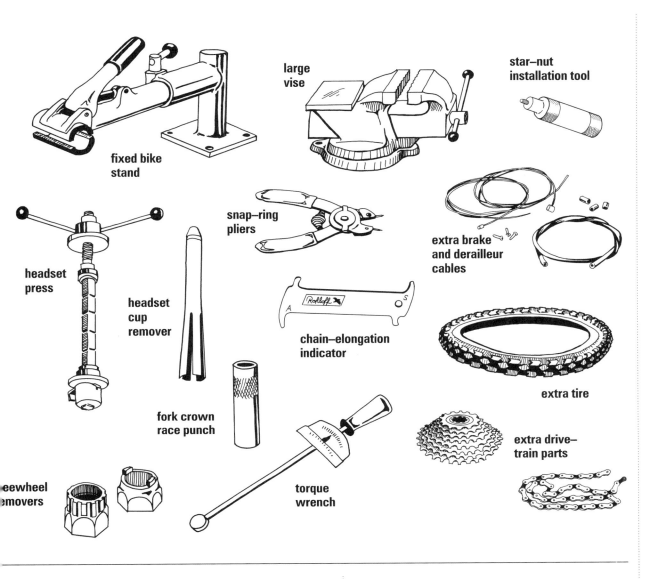

binder bolts, derailleur hangers, etc.

▶ Pair of **snap-ring pliers** for removing snap rings from suspension forks, derailleurs and other parts.

▶ **Chain elongation gauge**. This handy little item helps you quickly determine if a chain needs replacing. An accurate 12-inch ruler can work nicely.

▶ Shimano TL-CN24 **chain plate spacing tool**,

▶ **Truing stand** for truing and building wheels.

▶ **Dishing tool** for checking if that set of wheels you just built is properly centered.

▶ One healthy dose of **patience**, and an equal willingness to work and re-work jobs until they have been properly finished.

OTHER:

▶ **Spare parts.** This will save you from having to make a lot of last-minute runs to the bike shop for commonly used spare parts. Any well-equipped shop really requires several sizes of ball bearings, spare cables, cable housing, and a life-time supply of those little cable-end caps. You should also have a good supply of spare tires, tubes, chains and cogsets. If you expect to be working on suspension forks, be sure to have the proper lubricants and a few spare elastomers on hand.

I-4: NOW, IF YOU REALLY WANT A WELL-STOCKED SHOP:

The following tools (Fig. 1.5) are not even part of the Level 3 kit, and are not often needed for bike repairs. That said, they sure do come in handy when you need them.

▼ **English-threaded bottom bracket tap set**. This simultaneously cuts threads on both sides of the bottom bracket while keeping them in proper alignment.

▼ **Head tube reamer/facer**. This tool keeps both ends of the head tube perfectly parallel.

▼ **Bottom bracket shell facer**. This tool cuts the faces of the bottom bracket shell to ensure that both sides are parallel to one another.

▼ **Electric drill** with drill bit set for customizing.

▼ **Dropout alignment tools** (a.k.a., tip adjusters).

▼ **Derailleur-hanger alignment tool** to straighten the hanger after shifting the derailleur into the spokes or crashing.

▼ **Cog wear indicator gauge** to determine if cogs are worn out.

▼ **A full collection of spoke wrenches**, and don't forget Spline Drive nipples.

▼ **Hydraulic oil** or **automatic transmission fluid** (ATF) for overhauling hydraulic suspension systems.

I-5: SETTING UP YOUR HOME SHOP

I recommend keeping this area clean and very well organized. Make it comfortable to work in and easy to find the tools you need. Hanging tools on peg-board or slat-board or placing them in bins or trays are all effective ways to maintain an organized work area. Being able to find the tools you need will increase the enjoyment of working on a bike immensely. It is harder to do a

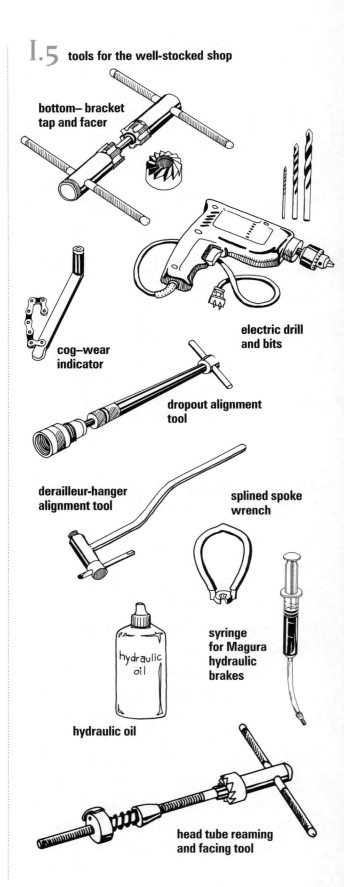

1.5 tools for the well-stocked shop

bottom– bracket tap and facer

electric drill and bits

cog–wear indicator

dropout alignment tool

derailleur-hanger alignment tool

splined spoke wrench

hydraulic oil

syringe for Magura hydraulic brakes

head tube reaming and facing tool

job with love if you're frustrated about not being able to find the cable cutter. Placing small parts in one of those bench-top organizers with several rows of little drawers is another good way to keep chaos from taking over.

I-6: TOOLS TO CARRY WITH YOU WHILE RIDING

A. For most riding:

Keep all of this stuff (Fig. 1.6) in a bag under your seat or somehow attached to your bike. Some people may prefer to keep it in a hydration (a.k.a. Camelbak) pack or a fanny pack. The operative words here are light and serviceable. Many of these tools are combined into some of the popular "multi-tools." Make sure you try all the tools at home before depending on them on the trail.

❖ **Spare tube.** This is a no-brainer. Make sure the valve matches the ones on your bike. If rarely needed, keep it in a plastic bag to prevent deterioration.

❖ **Tire pump/CO$_2$ cartridge**. The bigger the better. Mini-pumps are okay, but they're slow. Make sure the pump is set up for your type of valves.

❖ At least two plastic **tire levers**, preferably three.

❖ **Patch kit**. You'll need something after you've used your spare tube. Check it at least every 18 months to make sure the glue is not dried up.

❖ **Chain tool**. Get a light one that works.

❖ **Spare chain links** from your chain. If you're using a Shimano chain bring at least two "subpin" rivets.

❖ Small **screwdriver** for adjusting derailleurs and other parts.

❖ Compact set of **Allen wrenches** that includes 2.5mm, 3mm, 4mm, 5mm and 6mm sizes. (Some of you might need to bring along an 8mm too.)

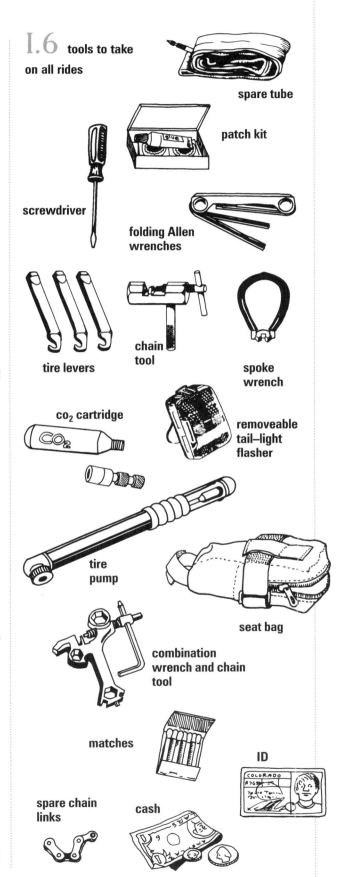

I.6 **tools to take on all rides**

spare tube

patch kit

screwdriver

folding Allen wrenches

tire levers

chain tool

spoke wrench

co$_2$ cartridge

removeable tail–light flasher

tire pump

seat bag

combination wrench and chain tool

matches

ID

spare chain links

cash

- 8mm and 10 mm **open-end wrenches**.
- Properly sized **spoke wrench**.
- **Matches**, because you never know when you can be stranded overnight.
- **Identification**.
- **Cash** for food, phone calls and to boot sidewall cuts in tires.

B. For long or multi-day trips:

The items in Fig. 1.7 are, of course, in addition to proper amounts of food, water, and extra clothes.

- **Spare spokes**. Innovations in Cycling sells a really cool folding spoke made from Kevlar. It's worth getting one or two for emergency repairs on a long ride.
- Small plastic bottle of **chain lube**.
- Small tube of **grease**.
- **Compact 15mm pedal wrench**. Be sure to get one with a headset wrench on the other end.
- **Money**, or its plastic equivalent, which can get you out of lots of scrapes.
- A lightweight aluminized folding **emergency blanket**.
- **Rain gear**.

N O T E

Read Chapter 3 on emergency repairs before embarking on a lengthy trip.

If you are planning a bike-centered vacation, be sure to bring along a "Level 1" tool kit, some headset wrenches and incidentals like duct tape and sandpaper.

1.7 tools for extended trips in the back country

compact headset and pedal tool

Kevlar spoke

grease

chain lube

rain gear

spare spoke

emergency blanket

cash

spoke wrench

basic stuff

pre—ride inspection, wheel removal and general cleaning

"Everything should be made as simple as possible, but not simpler" — *ALBERT EINSTEIN*

This chapter covers three very basic, but important, maintenance procedures. It is a good idea to get in the habit of checking your bike *before* heading out on a ride.

Performing this inspection regularly could help you avoid delays due to parts failure. I won't even mention the injury risks you face by riding a poorly maintained bike. There are folks who just don't want to tamper with anything on their bikes. However, learning how to properly remove and reinstall a wheel is essential if you want to effectively deal with minor annoyances like flat tires or jammed chains. If you do absolutely nothing else to your bike, keeping your chain clean will enhance the enjoyment of riding.

II-1: PRE-RIDE INSPECTION

1. Check to be sure that the quick-release levers or axle nuts (the ones that secure the hub axle to the dropouts) are tight.

2. Check the brake pads for excessive or uneven wear.

3. Grab and twist the brake pads and brake arms to make sure the bolts are tight.

4. Squeeze the brake levers. This should bring the pads flat against the rims (or slightly toed-in) without hitting the tires. Make certain that you cannot squeeze the levers all of the way to the handlebars. If you can, see Section VII-4 in Chapter 7 on brake adjustment.

5. Spin the wheels. Check for wobbles while sighting on the rims, not the tires. (If a tire wobbles excessively on a straight rim, it may not be fully seated in the rim; check it all of the way

around on both sides.) Make sure that the rims do not rub on the brake pads.

6. Check the tire pressure. On most mountain bike tires, the proper pressure is between 35 and 60 pounds per square inch (psi). Look to see that there are no foreign objects sticking in the tire. If there are, you may have to pull the tube out and repair or replace it. For some, it might be worth your time to look at the section on tire sealants (the goop inside the tube that fills any small holes you may get) in Chapter 6, Section VI-7.

7. Check the tires for excessive wear, cracking or gashes.

8. Be certain that the handlebar and stem are tight and that the stem is lined up with the front tire.

9. Check that the gears shift smoothly and the chain does not skip or shift by itself. Ensure that indexed (or "click") shifting moves the chain one cog, starting with the first click.

Make sure that the chain does not overshift

the smallest or biggest rear cog or the smallest or biggest front chainring.

10. Check the chain for rust, dirt, stiff links or noticeable signs of wear. It should be clean and lubricated. (Be cautious about overdoing it, though. Over-lubricated, gooey chains pick up a lot of dirt, particularly in dry climates.) The chain should be replaced on a mountain bike about every 500 to 1000 miles of off-road riding or every 2000 miles of paved riding.

11. Apply the front brake and push the bike forward and back. The headset should be tight and make no "clunking" noises or allow the fork any fore-aft play.

12. If all this checks out, go ride your bike! If not, check the table of contents, go to the appropriate chapter and fix the problems before you go out and ride.

II-2: REMOVING THE FRONT WHEEL

You can't transport your mountain bike easily if you can't remove the front wheel. This is generally required for most roof racks, and for jamming a mountain bike inside your car. As outlined in the following sections, wheel removal involves releasing the brake and opening the hub quick-release or bolt-on skewer, or the axle nuts on the low-end models.

II-3: RELEASING THE BRAKE

Most brakes have a mechanism to release the brake arms so that they spring away from the rim (Fig. 2.1), allowing the tire to pass between the pads. **V-brakes** are released by pulling the end of the curved cable guide tube (a.k.a. the "noodle") out of the horizontal link atop one of the brake arms while squeezing the pads against the rim with the other hand. Most **cantilevers** and **U-**

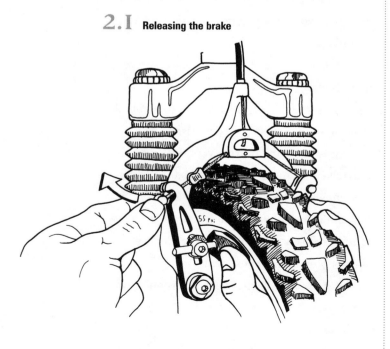

2.1 **Releasing the brake**

2.2 opening quick–release skewer

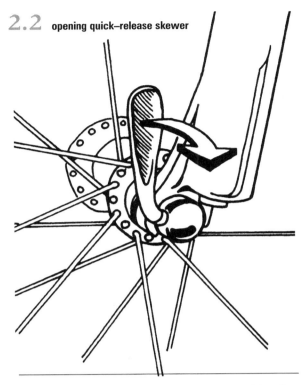

brakes are released by pulling the enlarged head of the straddle cable out of a notch in the top of the brake arm while holding the pads against the rim with the other hand (Fig. 2.1).

Roller-cam brakes are released by pulling the cam down and out from between the two rollers while holding the pads against the rim. Many **linkage brakes** are released like V-brakes or cantilevers. Hydraulic rim brakes usually require detaching the U-shaped brake booster that connects the piston cylinders together, if installed, followed by unscrewing or quick-releasing one wheel cylinder. Most disc brakes allow the disc to fall away without releasing the pads. The **Dia Compe disc brake** requires opening a latch under the caliper securing it to the fork. The entire caliper can then be swung up and forward, allowing the wheel to come out.

II-4: DETACHING A WHEEL WITH A QUICK-RELEASE SKEWER

This is easy and you don't need a tool for this one.

1. Pull the lever out to open it (Fig 2.2).

2. After opening the quick-release lever, unscrew the nut on the opposite end of the quick-release skewer's shaft until it clears the fork's wheel retention tabs.

3. Pull the wheel off.

N O T E

Some bikes have non-quick-release superlight titanium bolt-on skewers (Fig. 2.3). The wheel is removed by unscrewing the skewer with a 5mm Allen wrench.

II-5: DETACHING A WHEEL WITH AXLE NUTS

1. Unscrew the nuts on the axle ends (usually with a 15 mm wrench) until they allow the wheel to fall out (Fig. 2.4).

2. Most mountain bikes have some type of wheel-retention system consisting of nubs or bent tabs on the fork ends (also known as "dropouts"), or an axle washer with a bent tooth hooked into a hole in the fork end. These sys-

2.3 bolt-on skewer

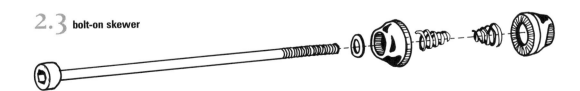

tems prevent the wheel from falling out if the axle nuts loosen. Loosen the nuts enough to clear the retention tabs on the fork ends.

3. Pull the wheel out.

II-6: INSTALLING THE FRONT WHEEL

Leave the brake open and lower the fork onto the wheel so that the bike's weight pushes the dropouts down onto the hub axle. This will seat the axle fully into the fork and center the rim between the brake pads. If your fork or wheel are misaligned, you will need to hold the rim centered between the brake pads when securing the hub. Continue with the appropriate hub-securing step.

II-7: TIGHTENING THE QUICK-RELEASE SKEWER

The quick-release skewer is not a glorified wing nut and should not be treated as such.

1. Hold the quick release-lever in the "open" position.

2. Tighten the opposite end nut until it snugs up against the face of the dropout.

3. Push the lever over (Fig. 2.5) to the "closed" position (it should now be at a 90-degree angle to the axle). It should take a good amount of hand pressure to close the quick-release lever properly; the lever should leave its imprint on your palm for a few seconds.

4. If the quick-release lever does not close tightly, open the lever again, tighten the end nut 1/4 turn and close the lever again. Repeat until tight.

5. If, on the other hand, the lever cannot be pushed down perpendicular to the axle, then the nut is too tight. Open the quick-release lever, unscrew the end nut 1/4 turn or so, and try clos-

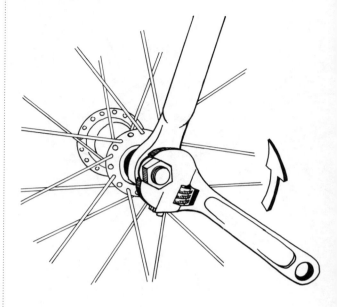

ing the lever again. Repeat this procedure until the quick-release lever is fully closed and snug.

When you are done, it is important to have the lever pointing straight up or toward the back of the bike (Figs 2.2 and 2.5) so that it cannot hook on obstacles and be accidentally opened.

6. Check that the axle is tightened into the fork by trying to pull the wheel out.

II-8: TIGHTENING BOLT-ON SKEWERS (FIG. 2.3)

Hold the end nut with one hand and tighten the skewer with a 5mm Allen wrench. Control Tech recommends 65 inch-pounds of torque for its steel bolt-on skewers and 85 in-lbs for the titanium versions. You can come close to applying the right amount of torque by using a short Allen wrench and tightening as tightly as you can with your fingers. It is easy to over-tighten these skewers so try to avoid that by approximating

front
wheel
installation

2.5 tightening the quick release

the pressure a quick-release skewer applies and do not go higher than that.

II-9: TIGHTENING AXLE NUTS (MASS-MERCHANT BIKES)

Snug up the nuts clockwise (opposite direction of Fig. 2.4) with a wrench (usually 15mm) a little from each side until they are quite tight.

II-10: CLOSING THE BRAKES

1. With a cantilever or U-brake, hold the brake pads against the rim with one hand and hook the enlarged end of the straddle cable back into the end of the brake arm with your other hand (Fig. 2.1 in reverse). The steps required to close the brakes are the reverse of what you did to release them.

2. Check that the brake cables are connected securely by squeezing the levers. Lift the front end of the bike and spin the front wheel, gently apply-

ing the brakes several times. Check that the pads are not dragging, and re-center the wheel (or adjust the brakes as described in Chapter 7, under your type of brake). If everything is reconnected and centered properly, you're done. Go ride your bike.

II-11: REMOVING THE REAR WHEEL

Removing the rear wheel is just like removing the front, with the added complication of the chain and cogs.

1. Shift the chain onto the smallest cog. Do this by lifting the rear wheel off of the ground, turning the cranks and shifting.

2. To release the wheel from the rear dropouts and the brakes, follow the same procedure as with the front wheel. When you push the wheel out, you will need to move the chain out of the way. This is usually a matter of grabbing the rear derailleur, pulling it back so the jockey wheels (pulley wheels) move out of the way,

rear
wheel
removal

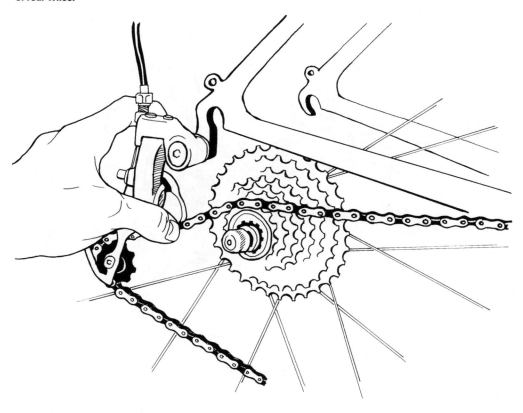

while pushing forward on the quick release or axle nuts with your thumbs, and letting the wheel fall as you hold the bike up (Fig. 2.6). If the bottom half of the chain catches the wheel as it falls, lift the wheel and jiggle it upward to free it.

II-12: INSTALLING THE REAR WHEEL

1. Check to make sure that the rear derailleur is shifted to its outermost position (over the smallest cog).

2. Slip the wheel up between the seatstays and maneuver the upper section of chain onto the smallest cog (Fig. 2.6).

3. Set the bike down on the rear wheel.

4. As you let the bike drop down, pull the rear derailleur back with your right hand and pull the axle ends back into the dropouts with your index fingers. Your thumbs push forward on the rear dropouts, which should now slide over the axle ends. If the axle does not slip into the dropouts, you may need to spread the dropouts apart or squeeze them toward each other to get them to clear the axle ends.

5. Check that the axle is fully seated in the dropouts, which should mean that the wheel is centered between the brake pads. If it is not, hold the rim in a centered position as you secure the axle.

6. Tighten the quick-release skewer, bolt-on skewer, or axle nuts the same way as explained for the front wheel.

7. Reconnect the rear brake the same way as

II

2.7 **wiping down chain**

dowel

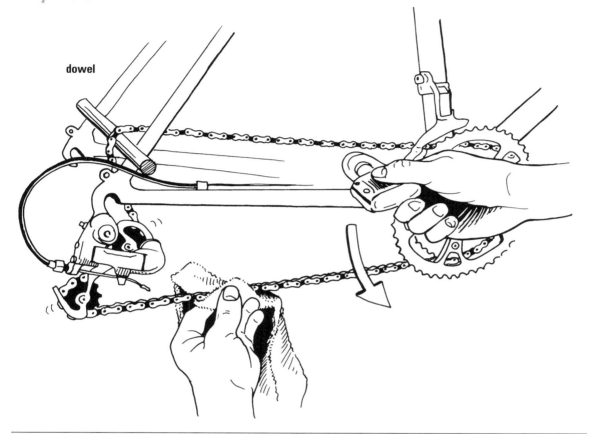

you did on the front wheel.

You're done. Go ride your bike.

II-13: CLEANING THE BICYCLE

Most cleaning can be done with soap, water and a brush. Soap and water are easier on you and the earth than stronger solvents, which are generally only needed for the drivetrain, if at all. Avoid using the high-pressure sprayers you find at pay car washes to clean your bike. The soaps are often very corrosive, and the high pressure forces them into bearings, pivots, and frame tubes, causing extensive damage over time.

A bike stand is highly recommended when scrubbing the bike. In the absence of a bike stand, the bike can be hung from a garage ceiling with rope, or it can be stood upside down on the saddle and handlebars, or on the front of the fork and the bars with the front wheel removed.

1. The wheels can be cleaned easily while on the bike. Remove the wheels to clean the frame, fork, and components.

2. If the bike has a chain hanger (a little nub attached to the inner side of the right seatstay, a few centimeters above the dropout), hook the chain over it. If not, pull the chain back over a dowel stick (Fig. 2.7) or old rear hub secured into the dropouts.

3. Fill a bucket with hot water and dish soap. Using a stiff nylon-bristle scrub brush, scrub the entire bike and wheels. Leave the chain, cogs, chainrings and derailleurs for last.

general
cleaning

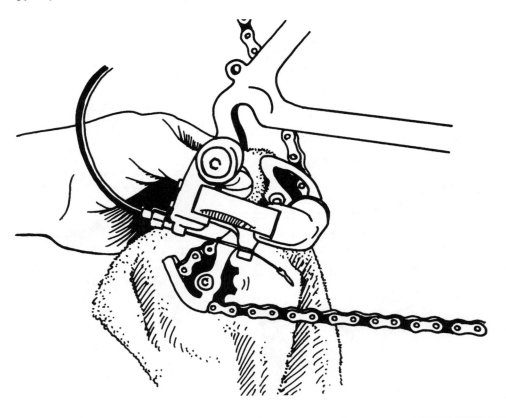

4. Rinse the bike with water (low pressure!), either by hosing it off or by wiping it with a wet rag.

Avoid getting water in the bearings of the bottom bracket, headset, pedals or hubs. Also avoid getting water into the lip seals of suspension forks, as well as any pivots or shock seals on rear-suspension systems. Most frames and rigid forks have vent holes in the tubes to allow expanding hot gases to escape during welding. The holes are often open to the outside on the seatstays, fork legs, chainstays, and seatstay and chainstay bridges. Avoid getting water in these holes. This is especially true when using high-pressure car washes. Taping over the vent holes, even when riding, is a good idea.

II-14: CLEANING DRIVETRAIN

The drivetrain consists of an oil-covered chain running over gears and derailleurs. It is all exposed to the elements, so it picks up lots of dirt. Since the drivetrain is what transfers your energy into the bike's forward motion, it should move freely. Frequent cleaning and lubrication keep it rolling well, and extend the life of your bike.

The drivetrain can often be cleaned sufficiently by using a rag and wiping down the chain, derailleur jockey wheels and chainrings.

1. To wipe the chain, turn the cranks while holding a rag in your hand and grabbing the chain (Fig. 2.7).

2. Holding a rag, squeeze the teeth of the jockey wheels in between your index finger and thumb, as you turn the cranks (Fig. 2.8). This will remove almost any buildup on the jockey wheels.

3. Slip a rag in between cogs of the freewheel

2.9 **cogset cleaning**

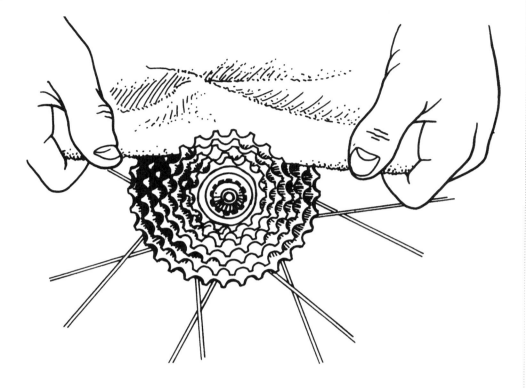

and work it back and forth to clean each cog (Fig. 2.9).

4. Wipe down the derailleurs and the front chainrings with the rag.

Your chain will last much longer if you perform this sort of quick cleaning regularly, followed by dripping chain lube on the chain and another light wipe down. You will also be able to skip those heavy duty solvent cleanings that are necessary when a chain gets really grungy.

You can also remove packed-up mud from derailleurs and cogs with the soapy water and scrub brush. The soap will not dissolve the dirty lubricant that is all over the drivetrain; rather the brush will smear it all over the bike if you're not careful. Use a different brush than the one you use for cleaning the frame. Follow it with a cloth wipe down.

II-15: SOLVENT CLEANING THE CHAIN

If you use chain lube sparingly by putting lube only on the rollers where it is needed, rather than all over the chain, you can minimize the need for solvent cleaning with its associated disposal and toxicity problems. If you determine that using a solvent is necessary, work in a well-ventilated area, use as little solvent as necessary, and pick an environmentally friendly one. Using one of the many citrus solvents on the market will minimize the danger of breathing the stuff or getting it onto and into your skin, and it will reduce a major disposal problem. If you are using a lot of solvents, organic ones like diesel fuel can be recycled, which may be a preferable solution to using citrus solvents, as long as you protect yourself from the fumes with a respirator.

Since all solvents suck the oils out of your

chain
cleaning

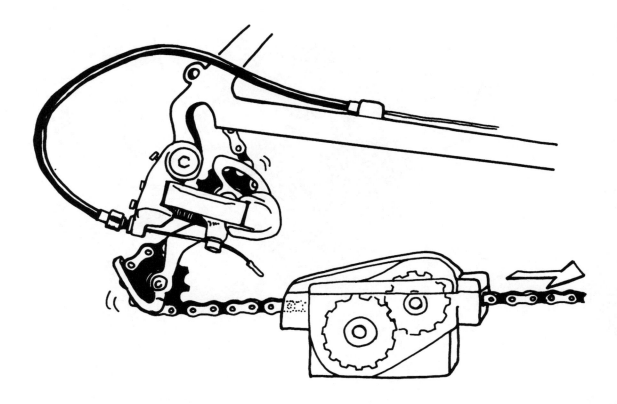

skin, I recommend using rubber gloves, even with "green" solvents. A self-contained chain cleaner with internal brushes and a solvent bath is a quick and convenient way to clean a chain (Fig. 2.10), but it does not clean well deep inside the rollers. A nylon brush or an old toothbrush dipped in solvent is good for cleaning cogs, pulleys and chainrings, and can be used for a quick clean of the chain as well.

A way to thoroughly clean the chain is to remove it and put it in a solvent bath.

1. Follow the directions in Chapter 4, Section IV-7 for removing the chain.

2. Put the chain in an old water bottle about 1/4 full of solvent.

3. Shake the bottle vigorously to clean the chain. Do this close to the ground, in case the water bottle leaks.

4. Hang the chain up to dry completely, especially inside the rollers.

5. Install the chain on the bike, following the directions in Chapter 4, Sections IV-8 to IV-11.

6. Drip chain lubricant into each of the chain's links and rollers.

7. Lightly wipe down the chain with a rag.

You can re-use much of the solvent by allowing it to settle in a clear container over a period of days or weeks. Decant and save the clear stuff and dispose of the sludge.

A clean bike invites you to jump on it, and it will feel faster. Corrosion problems are minimized, and you can see problems as they arise.

A clean bike is a happy bike.

II-16: GENERAL GUIDE TO PERFORMING MECHANICAL WORK

1. Threaded Parts

A. All threads must be prepped before tightening. Depending on the bolt in question, prep with lubricant, thread-lock compound, or an anti-seize compound. Clean off excess thread-prepping compound to minimize dirt attraction.

1. Lubricated threads: Most threads should be lubricated with grease or oil. If a bolt is already installed, you can back it out and drip a little chain lube on it, and tighten it back down. Lube items like crank bolts, pedal axles, cleat bolts on shoes, derailleur- and brake-cable-anchor bolts, and control-lever mounting bolts.

2. Locked threads: Some threads need to be locked in order to prevent them from vibrating loose; these are bolts that need to stay in place but are not tightened down fully for some reason or other. Examples of this are: derailleur limit screws, jockey wheel center bolts, brake mounting bolts, and spokes. Use Loctite, Finish Line Threadlock, or the equivalent; use Wheelsmith Spoke-Prep or the equivalent on spokes.

3. Anti-seize threads: Some threads have a tendency to bind up and gall, making full tightening as well as extraction problematic. They need anti-seize compound on them to prevent galling. Examples of this are: any steel or aluminum bolt threaded into a titanium part (this includes any parts mounted to titanium frames, like bottom bracket cups), and any titanium bolt threaded into a steel or aluminum part. Use Finish Line Ti-Prep or the equivalent.

CAUTIONARY NOTE:

Never thread a titanium bolt into a titanium part; even with anti-seize, these will almost certainly gall and rip apart when you try to remove them.

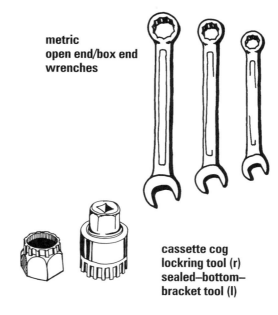

metric open end/box end wrenches

cassette cog lockring tool (r) sealed–bottom– bracket tool (l)

headset wrench

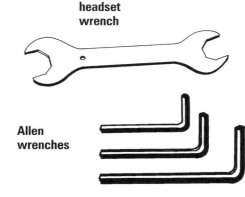

Allen wrenches

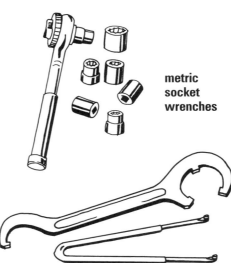

metric socket wrenches

bottom–bracket tools toothed lock-ring spanner (t) pin spanner (b)

basic stuff

general guide to mechanical work

B. Wrenches must be fully engaged before tightening or loosening. (Fig.2.11)

1. Allen keys must be fully inserted into the bolt head, or the wrench and/or bolt hex hole will round off. A good example is a shoe cleat bolt.

2. Open-end, box-end, and socket wrenches must be properly seated around a hex bolt, or it will round off. A good example is an aluminum headset nut.

3. Splined wrenches must be fully engaged or the splines will be damaged or the tool will snap. A good example is a cassette lockring.

4. Toothed-lockring spanners need to stay lined up on the lockring; if they slide off, they will not only tear up the lockring, they will also damage the frame paint. A good example is a bottom bracket adjustable cup lockring.

5. Pin spanners need to be fully seated in the holes to prevent slipping out and damaging the holes in the part. Good examples are bottom bracket adjustable cups and crank bolt collars.

C. Tightening torque: a full list of specific tightening torques is in Appendix E.

Generally, tightness can be classified in three levels:

1. Snug (10-30 inch-pounds): Small set screws (like Grip Shift mounting screw), bearing preload bolts (like on Aheadset top cap), and screws going into plastic parts need to be snug.

2. Firmly tightened (30-80 inch-pounds): Cable anchor bolts, shoe cleat bolts, and brake mounting bolts need to be firmly tightened.

3. Really tight (300-600 inch-pounds): Crank arm bolts, cassette lockring bolts and bottom bracket cups need to be really tight.

II. Cleanliness

A. Do not expect parts to work by just squirting or slathering lubricant on them (meanwhile patting yourself on the back for maintaining your bike). The lube will pick up lots of dirt and get very gunky.

B. Do not expect parts to work by washing them and not lubricating them. They will get dry and squeaky.

III. Test Riding

Always test ride the bike after adjusting in the bike stand. Parts behave differently under load.

emergency
repairs

**how to get
home when
something big
breaks
or you get lost
or hurt**

"Always carry a flagon of whiskey in case of a snake bite,

and furthermore, always carry a small snake" — W. C. FIELDS

This chapter is included so you do not face disaster if you have a mechanical problem on the trail. If you ride your bike out in the boonies, sooner or later you will encounter a mechanical problem that has the potential to turn into an emergency. The best way to avoid such an emergency is to plan ahead and be prepared before it happens. Proper planning involves steps as simple as bringing along a few tools, spare tubes and a little knowledge.

If you have something break on the trail, there are procedures in this chapter to deal with most "emergencies," whether you have all of the tools that you need or not. You always have the option of walking, but this chapter is designed to get you home pedaling.

Finally, you may find yourself with a perfectly functioning bicycle and still be in dire straits because you're either lost, bonking (your body has run out of fuel) or injured on the trail. Carefully read the final portion of this chapter for pointers on how to avoid getting lost or injured and what to do if the worst does happen.

If this chapter does nothing other than alert you to all of the dangers facing you out in the back country, then hopefully you'll prepare for them, and this chapter will have accomplished its purpose.

III-1: RECOMMENDED TOOLS

The take-along tool kit for your seat bag is described in Chapter 1, Section I-6. If you're going to be a long way from civilization, take along the extra tools recommended for longer trips.

III-2: FLAT TIRE PREVENTION

Flat tires can be prevented with the use of some tire sealants; "Slime" is one that works well. The stuff is a viscous liquid with chopped fibers in it that plug holes in the tube as they happen (use of Slime is covered in Chapter 6, Section VI-7); it can be injected into your tube, or you can purchase tubes with sealant already inside.

If you have Slime or another tire sealant in your tube and your tire gets low (this is most likely to happen when you stop riding for a while), put more air in and spin the wheel or ride for a couple of miles to get the sealant to flow out to the hole. A large hole will not be filled, although amazingly big holes can be plugged enough to get

you home if you locate where the sealant is squirting out through the tire. Rotate the wheel so that spot is at the bottom and wait. The sealant may pool up enough there to plug the hole. Add more air and continue.

I recommend against plastic tire liners that go between the tire and tube. They are so stiff that they decrease traction and cornering ability. They can also slip sideways and cut into the tube.

There is, however, a new generation of liners made from Kevlar. These liners are considerably lighter than their stiff plastic counterparts. They are pretty expensive, though. A pair of "Spin Skins" for mountain bike tires can run around $33.

III-3: FIXING FLAT TIRES
A. If you have a spare or a patch kit
Simple flat tires are easy to deal with. The first

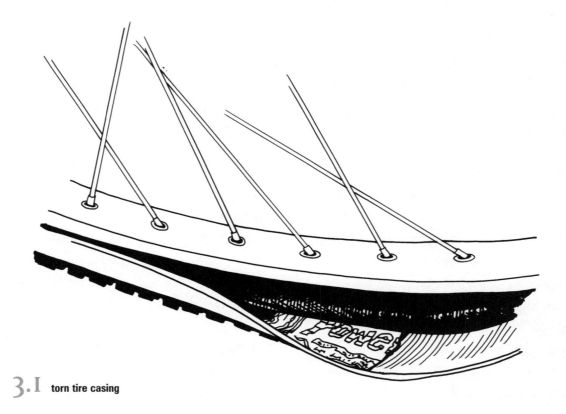

3.1 **torn tire casing**

flats

flat you get on a ride is most easily fixed by installing your spare tube (Chapter 6, Section VI-5). Make sure you remove all thorns from the tire and feel around the inside of the tire for any other sharp objects. Check the rim to see that your flat wasn't caused by a protruding spoke or nipple, a metal shard from the rim, or the edge of a spoke hole protruding through a worn rim strip. Many rim strips are totally inadequate, being either too narrow or prone to cracking or tearing. Also, metal hunks left from the drilling of rims during manufacture can work their way out into the tube. Try to eliminate these problems before leaving on a back-country ride by shaking out any metal fragments and using good rim strips or a couple of layers of fiberglass packing tape (with those lengthwise super-strong fibers inside) as rim strips. If the hole in the tube is on the rim side, tire sealant will not fill the hole, since the liquid will be thrown to the outside when the wheel turns.

After you run out of spare tubes, additional flats must be patched (also covered in Chapter 6, Section VI-2).

B. Torn sidewall

Rocks and glass can cut tire sidewalls. The likelihood of sidewall problems is reduced if you do not venture into the back-country on old tires with rotten and weakened sidewall cords. If your tire's sidewall is torn or cut, the tube will stick out. Just patching or replacing the tube isn't going to solve the problem. Without reinforcement, your tube will blow out again very soon. First, you have to look for something to reinforce the sidewall (Fig. 3.1). Dollar bills work surprisingly well as tire boots. The paper is pretty tough and should hold for the rest of the ride if you are careful. (I told you that cash will get you out of

bad situations. Just don't try putting a credit card in there; tire cuts don't take American Express or Visa!) Business cards are a bit small but work better than nothing. You might even try an energy bar wrapper. A small piece of a tire liner cut in an oval might be a good addition to your patch kit for this purpose. You get the idea.

1. Lay the cash or whatever inside the tire over the gash, or wrap it around the tube at that spot. Place several layers between the tire and tube to support the tube and prevent it from bulging out through the hole in the side wall.

2. Put a little air in the tube to hold the makeshift reinforcement in place.

3. Mount the tire bead on the rim. You may need to let a little air out of the tube to do so.

4. After making sure that the tire is seated and the boot is still in place, inflate the tube to about 40 psi, if you are good at estimating without a gauge. Much less than 40 psi will allow the boot to move around and may also lead to a pinch flat if you're riding on rocky terrain. This is not a perfect solution, so you will need to check the boot periodically to make certain that the tube is not bulging out again.

C. No more spare tubes or patches

Now comes the frustrating part: You have run out of spare tubes, and have used up all of your patches (or your CO_2 cartridge is empty and you don't have a pump), and still you have a flat tire. The solution is obvious. You are going to have to ride home without air in your tire. Riding a flat for a long way will trash your tire and will probably damage your rim. Still, there are ways to minimize that damage. Try filling the space in the tire with grass, leaves or similar materials. Pack it in tightly and then remount the tire on the rim. This should make the ride a little less dangerous,

torn
sidewall

35

by minimizing the flat tire's tendency to roll out from under the bike during a turn.

III-4: CHAIN JAMMED BETWEEN THE CHAINRING AND CHAINSTAY

If your chain gets jammed between the chainrings and chainstay, it may be hard to get out if the clearance is tight. You may find that you tug and tug on the chain, and it won't come out. Well, chainrings flex, and if you apply some mechanical advantage, the chain will come free quite easily. Just insert a screwdriver or similar thin lever between the chainring and the chainstay, and pry the space open while pulling the chain out (Fig. 3.2). You will probably be amazed at how easy this is, especially in light of how much hard tugging would not free the chain.

If you still cannot free the chain, disassemble the chain with a chain tool (Chapter 4, Section IV-7), pull it out, and put it back together (Section IV-9 through IV-11).

III-5: BROKEN CHAIN

Chains break quite often when mountain-bike riding, usually while shifting the front derailleur under load. The side force of the derailleur on the chain coupled with the high tension can pop a chain plate off the end of a rivet. As the chain rips apart, it can cause collateral damage as well. The open chain plate can snag the front derailleur cage, bending it or tearing it off, or it can jam into the rear dropout.

When a chain breaks, the end link is certainly shot, and some others in the area may be as well.

1. Remove the damaged links with the chain tool. (You or your riding partner did remember to bring a chain tool, right?) Again, the proce-

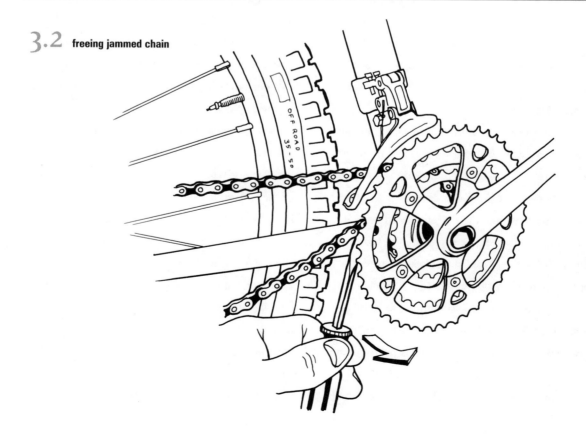

3.2 **freeing jammed chain**

dures for removing the damaged links and reinstalling the chain are covered in Chapter 4, Section IV-7 through IV-11.

2. If you have brought along extra chain links, replace the same number you remove. If not, you'll need to use the chain in its shortened state; it will still work.

3. Join the ends and connect the chain (Fig. 3.3); procedure is in Chapter 4, Sections IV-9 and 10. Some lightweight chain tools and multi tools are more difficult to use than a shop chain tool. Some flex so badly that it is hard to keep the push rod lined up with the rivet. Others pinch the plates so tightly that the chain link binds up. It's a good idea to find these things out before you perform repairs on the trail. Try the tool out at home or at your local bike shop. This way you know what you're getting into before you reach the trailhead.

III-6: BENT WHEEL

level 2

If the rim is banging against the brake pads, or worse yet the frame or fork, pedaling becomes very difficult. It can happen due to either a loose or broken spoke, or due to a badly bent or even broken rim.

III-7: LOOSE SPOKES

If you have a loose spoke or two, the rim will wobble all over the place.

1. Find the loose spoke (or spokes) by feeling all of them. The really loose ones, which would cause a wobble of large magnitude, will be obvious. If you find a broken spoke, skip to the next section (III-8). If you have no loose or broken spokes, skip ahead to section III-10.

2. Get out the spoke wrench that you carry for such an eventuality. If you don't have one, skip

emergency

bent wheel

3.3 **fixing broken chain**

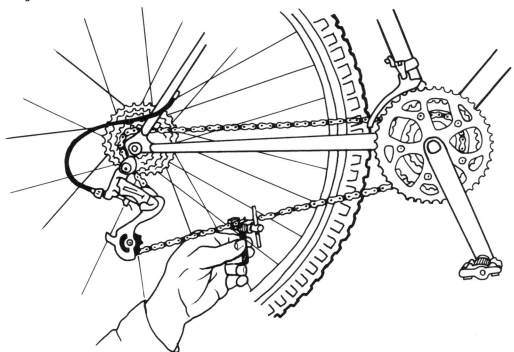

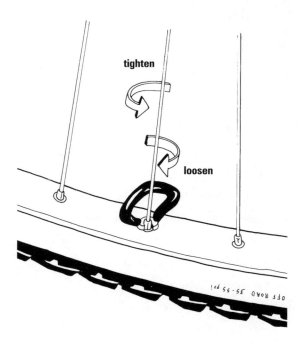

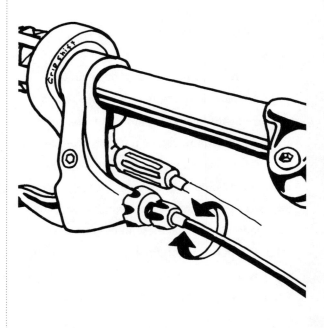

to section III-9 below.

3. Mark the loose spokes by tying blades of grass, sandwich bag twist-ties, tape or the like around them.

4. Tighten the loose spokes (Fig. 3.4), and true the wheel, following the procedures in Chapter 6, Section VI-8.

III-8: BROKEN SPOKES

If you broke a spoke, the wheel will wobble wildly.

1. Locate the broken spoke.

2. Remove the remainder of the spoke, both the piece going through the hub, and the piece threaded into the nipple. If the broken spoke is on the freewheel side of the rear wheel, you may not be able to remove it from the hub, since it will be behind the cogs. If so, skip to step 6 after wrapping

it around neighboring spokes to prevent it from slapping around (Fig. 3.6).

3. Get out your spoke wrench. If you have no spoke wrench, skip to section III-9 below.

4. If you brought a spare spoke of the right length or the Kevlar replacement spoke mentioned in Chapter 1, Section I-6B, you're in business. If not, skip to step 6. Put the new spoke through the hub hole, weave it through the other spokes the same way the old one was, and thread it into the spoke nipple that is still sticking out of the rim. Mark it with a pen or a blade of grass tied around it. With the Kevlar spoke, thread the Kevlar through the hub hole, attach the ends to the enclosed stub of spoke, adjust the ends to length, tie them off, and tighten the spoke nipple.

5. Tighten the nipple on the new spoke with a

3.6 **wrapping broken spoke**

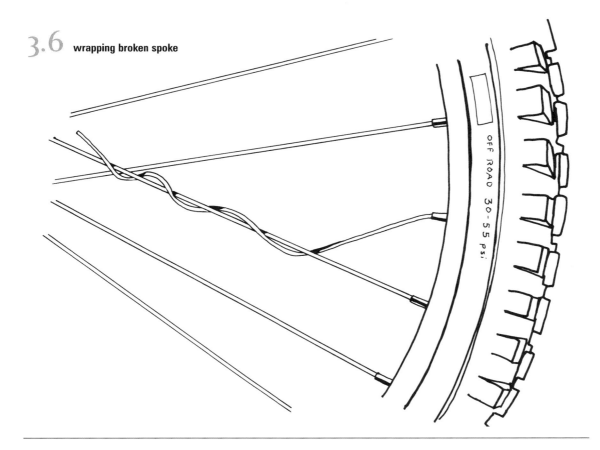

OFF ROAD 30-55 psi.

emergency

spoke wrench (Fig. 3.4), checking the rim clearance with the brake pad as you go. Stop when the rim is straight, and finish your ride.

6. If you can't replace the spoke and you do have a spoke wrench, bring the wheel into rideable trueness by loosening the spoke on either side of the broken one. These two spokes come from the opposite side of the hub and will let the rim move toward the side with the broken spoke as they are loosened. A spoke nipple loosens clockwise when viewed from its top. Ride home, conservatively, as this wheel will rapidly get worse.

7. Once at home, replace the spoke, following the procedure in Chapter 6, Section VI-9, or take it to a bike shop for repair. After you have had a broken spoke more than once on a wheel, it should be re-laced with new spokes, and the rim

may need replacement as well.

III-9: NO SPOKE WRENCH

If the rim is banging the brake pads, but the tire is not hitting the chainstays or fork legs, just open the brake so that you can get home.

1. Loosen the brake cable tension by screwing in (clockwise) the barrel adjuster on the brake lever (Fig. 3.5). Remember that braking on that wheel is greatly reduced or non-existent, so ride slowly and carefully.

2. If the rim is still banging the brakes, and you have a wrench to loosen the brake cable (usually 5mm Allen), do so, and then clamp it back down. You now have no brake on this wheel; ride carefully.

3. If this still does not cut it, or you have

no spoke
wrench

bent rim

hydraulic brakes, you can remove both brake arms from the cantilever posts, put them in your pocket, and pedal home slowly. You will usually need a 5mm Allen wrench for this. Do not attempt to ride a bike with brakes still attached to the frame or fork but disconnected from the cable. The brake arms will flap around as you ride and may get caught in the spokes, which could crack your seatstay or fork, not to mention your head, in a heartbeat.

If you want to straighten the wheel without using a spoke wrench, follow the next procedures for dealing with a bent rim, section III-10. Recognize that if you bend the rim by smacking it on the ground to correct for a loose or broken spoke, you will permanently deform the rim. Try to get home without resorting to this, since you will have to replace the rim.

III-10: BENT RIM

level 2 If your rim is only mildly out of true, and you brought your spoke wrench, you can fix it. The procedure for truing a wheel is explained in Chapter 6, Section VI-8.

If the wheel is really whacked out, spoke truing won't do much. To get it to clear the brakes so that you can pedal home, follow the steps under: III.9: No spoke wrench.

If the wheel is bent to the point that it won't turn, even when the brake is removed, you can beat it straight as long as the rim is not broken.

1. Find the area that is bent outward the most and mark it.

2. Leaving the tire on and inflated, hold the wheel by its sides with the bent part at the top facing away from you.

3. Smack the bent section of the rim against

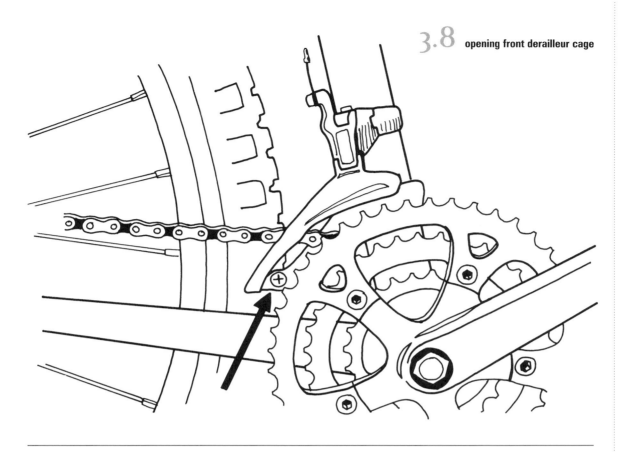

3.8 **opening front derailleur cage**

the flat ground (Fig. 3.7).

4. Put the wheel back in the frame or fork, and see if anything has changed.

5. Repeat the process until the wheel is rideable. You may be surprised how straight you can get a wheel this way.

III-11: DAMAGED FRONT DERAILLEUR

If the front derailleur is mildly bent, straighten it with your hands or leave it until you get home.

If it has simply rotated around the seat tube (the chain, your foot, or a pants leg can catch it and turn it), reposition it so the cage is just above, and parallel to, the chainrings, then tighten the derailleur in place with a 5mm Allen wrench. If the derailleur is broken or so bent that you can't ride, you will need to remove it or route the chain around it as described below.

A. With only a screwdriver:

1. Get the chain out of the derailleur cage. To do this, open the derailleur cage by removing the screw at its tail (Fig. 3.8).

2. Bypass the derailleur by putting the chain on a chainring that does not interfere with it (either shift the derailleur to the inside and put the chain on the big chainring, or vice versa).

B. With Allen wrenches and a screwdriver (or a chain tool):

1. Remove the derailleur from the seat tube, usually with a 5mm Allen wrench.

2. Remove the screw at the tail of the derailleur cage with a screwdriver

3. Pry open the cage, and separate it from the chain. You could also disassemble the chain, pull it out of the derailleur, and reconnect it (Chapter 4, Section IV-7- 11).

4. Manually put the chain on whichever chain-

damaged
rear
derailleur

ring is most appropriate for the ride home. If in doubt, put it on the middle one.

5. Tie the cable up so it won't catch in your wheel.

6. Stuff the derailleur in your pocket and ride home.

III-12: DAMAGED REAR DERAILLEUR

If the derailleur just gets bent a bit, you can probably straighten it with your hands enough to get home. If the rear derailleur gets really bent or broken, or one of the jockey wheels falls off, then you will not be able to continue with the chain routed through it. You will need to route the chain around the derailleur, effectively turning your bike into a single-speed for the duration of your ride (Fig. 3.9).

1. Open the chain with a chain tool (Chapter 4, Section IV-7) and pull it out of the derailleur.

2. Pick a gear combination in which you think

you can make it home most effectively, and set the front derailleur over the chainring you have picked.

3. Wrap the chain over the chainring and the rear cog you have chosen, bypassing the rear derailleur entirely.

4. Remove any overlapping chain, making the chain as short as you can and still be able to connect the ends together.

5. Connect the chain with the chain tool as described in Chapter 4, Section IV-9.

6. Ride home.

III-13: BROKEN FRONT DERAILLEUR CABLE

Your chain will be on the inner chainring, and you will still be able to use all of your rear cogs. You have three options, depending on which chainring you want for your return ride:

Option 1. Leave it on the inner ring and ride home.

3.9 **bypassing damaged rear derailleur**

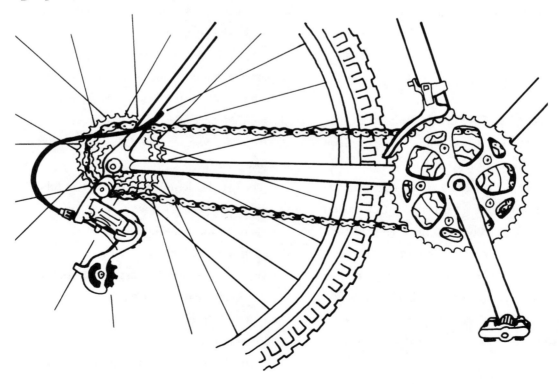

Option 2. Tighten the inner derailleur stop screw until the derailleur sits over the middle chainring (Fig. 3.10). Leave the chain on the middle ring and ride home.

Option 3. Bypass the front derailleur by removing the chain from the derailleur and putting it on the big chainring. You can do this either by opening the derailleur cage with a screwdriver or by disconnecting and reconnecting the chain with a chain tool (Chapter 4, Section IV-7, 9, 10, 11). Note: You have probably noticed by now that a chain tool is one of the handiest items you can take along. Like the American Express ads say: "Don't leave home without it."

III-14: BROKEN REAR DERAILLEUR CABLE

If your cable breaks, your chain will be on the smallest rear cog. You will still be able to use all three front chainrings. You have three options:

Option 1. Leave it on the small cog and ride home.

Option 2. Move the chain to a larger cog, push inward on the derailleur with your hand, and tighten the high-end adjustment screw on the rear derailleur (usually the upper one of the two screws) until it lines up with a larger cog (see Fig. 3.11). Move the chain to that cog and ride home. You may have to fine-tune the adjustment of the derailleur stop screw to get it to run quietly without skipping.

Option 3. If you do not have a screwdriver, you can push inward on the rear derailleur while turning the crank with the rear wheel off of the ground to shift to a larger cog. Jam a stick in between the derailleur cage plates to prevent it from moving back down to the small cog (Fig. 3.12).

emergency

3.10 tightening the inner front derailleur stop screw

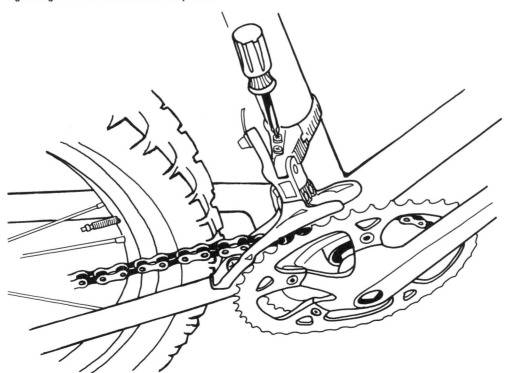

broken
rear
derailleur
cable

broken
seat rails
—
broken
seatpost
—
broken
handlebar

III-15: BROKEN BRAKE CABLE

Walk home, or ride slowly and carefully home if the trail is not dangerous.

III-16: FLAT SUSPENSION FORK

Not much you can do here. If you have a leaking air-sprung fork, you will just have to ride back with it bottoming out the whole way. Go slowly and keep your weight back.

III-17: BROKEN SEAT RAILS OR SEATPOST CLAMP

If you can't tape or tie the saddle back on, try wrapping your gloves or some clothing over the top of the seatpost to pad it. Otherwise, remove the seatpost and ride home without it.

III-18: BROKEN SEATPOST SHAFT

Splint it internally with a stick and ride very carefully. Failing that, remove the seatpost and ride home standing up.

III-19: BROKEN HANDLEBAR

It's probably best to walk home. You could splint it by jamming a stick inside and ride home very carefully, but the stick could easily break, leaving you with no way to control the bike. A sudden collision between your face and the ground would follow.

III-20: TRAIL SAFETY: AVOIDING GETTING LOST OR HURT, AND DEALING WITH IT IF YOU DO

Mountain biking in the back country can be dangerous. A rash of deaths and injuries in the mid-1990s underscores the need to prepare properly and to take personal responsibility for your own and others' safety when riding in deserted country. Two deaths near Moab, Utah, in the summer of 1995 highlight the risks inherent in the sport we love.

The two died in Moab while riding the Porcupine Rim trail, a favorite of visiting moun-

3.11 broken rear derailleur cable
— Option 2

tain bikers. The account of these two riders pinpoints a number of details that cost them their lives. The pair got lost on the descent off Porcupine Rim, missed the turn into Jackass Canyon, and then headed instead into Negro Bill Canyon — which divides the Porcupine Rim trail from Moab's most famous ride, the Slickrock Trail. It may come as a surprise that people could die and go undiscovered for 17 days so close to a main highway into town (which was right below them) and two heavily traveled trails. But apparently they hadn't told anyone of their plans to ride this trail, so no one in town noticed when they did not return.

Their parents, not hearing from them for a few days, called the sheriff, and a search was mounted.

Once lost, they abandoned their bikes and tried to walk down to the road, instead of riding back the way they had come. That road and the Colorado River are very close as the crow flies and are visible at a number of points ... but, due to the

numerous cliffs, are quite difficult to reach. They climbed, fell or slid down to a ledge from which they apparently were unable to climb either up or down, and there they perished from exposure.

They died on a ledge, in such a way that they were very difficult to spot from the air. They had placed no items to indicate their positions to airborne spotters. Had searchers found their bikes, they could have concentrated the search on a small area. Regrettably, their bikes and helmets were picked up by a pair of passing riders who did not leave word with the authorities.

Eventually, a helicopter searcher saw the bodies on the ledge, and a Forest Service ranger rappelled 160 feet down to them. He was able to then walk out unaided, indicating that perhaps the riders were so injured, exhausted, delirious or hypothermic that they had been unable to take the same route out.

Cliffs, steep hills and an array of other natural features can also pose a risk. In the fall of 1995,

trail safety

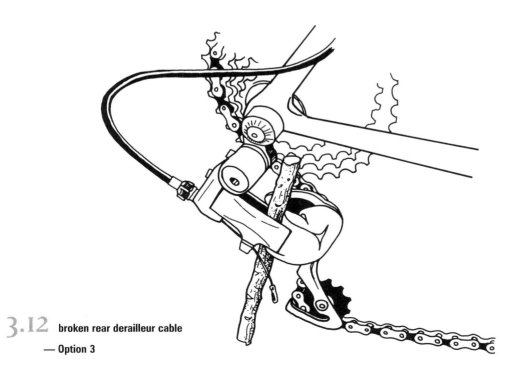

3.12 **broken rear derailleur cable**
— Option 3

another Moab rider barely managed to jump off his bike before it went hurtling over the edge of a cliff and dropped some 400 feet. Anyone who has ridden much in Moab can tell you that there are countless other places exposed enough to present a similar threat.

Even in seemingly safe areas, the risks can be high. Pro rider Paul Willerton came close to meeting his end on a relatively standard, cliff-less, but isolated, trail near Winter Park, Colorado. Unable to walk after crashing and breaking his leg, Willerton had to drag himself many miles using only his arms.

We all tend to think that nothing like this will ever happen to us. But things like this can happen, far too easily. This shouldn't discourage you from riding in the back country. It should encourage you to think and utilize the following 12 basic back-country survival skills — they could make the difference between life and death.

1. Always take plenty of water. You can survive a long time without food, but not without water.

2. Tell someone where you are going and when you expect to return. If you know of someone who is missing, call the police or sheriff.

3. If you find personal effects on the ground, assume it could indicate that someone is lost or in trouble. Report the find and mark the location.

4. If you get lost, backtrack. Even if going back is longer, it is better than getting stranded.

5. Don't go down something you can't get back up.

6. Bring matches, extra clothing and food, and perhaps a flashlight and an aluminized emergency blanket, in case you have to spend the night out or need to signal searchers.

7. If the area is new to you, go with someone who is familiar with it, or take a map and compass, and know how to use them.

8. Wear a helmet. It's hard to ride home with a cracked skull.

9. Bring basic first aid and bike tools, and know how to use them well enough to keep yourself and your bike going.

10. Walk your bike when it's appropriate. Falling off a cliff is a poor alternative to taking a few extra seconds or displaying less bravado. Try riding difficult sections to improve your bike handling, but if the exposure is great or a mistake leaves you injured a long way from help, find another place to practice those moves.

11. Don't ride beyond your limits if you are a long way out. Take a break. Get out of the hot sun. Avoid dehydration and bonk by drinking and eating enough.

12. Teach your friends all these things.

Keep in mind that your decisions not only affect you, but they could also affect your riding partners and countless others. Realize that endangering yourself can also endanger the person trying to rescue you. Search and rescue parties are usually made up of helpful people, who will gladly come and save you, but no one appreciates being put in harm's way unnecessarily.

In summary, make appropriate decisions when cycling the back country. Learn survival skills, and prepare well. Recognize that, just because you have a $4000 bike and are riding on popular trails, you are not immune to danger. When ignorance makes us oblivious to danger, it sadly becomes the danger itself.

chains

tools

chain lubricant
12-inch ruler
chain tool
lots of rags

OPTIONAL

solvent
 (citrus-based)
chain-cleaning tool
old water bottle
 or jar
caliper
pliers
solvent tank
Shimano link
 spacing tool
 (TL-CN24)
Rohloff chain-
 elongation indicator
Rohloff cog wear
 indicator
Lubrication (Level 1)

"A chain is only as strong as its weakest link" — *ANONYMOUS*

"A sausage is only as good as its last link" — *BLUTO*

A bike chain is a simple series of links connected by rivets. Rollers surround each rivet between the link plates and engage the teeth of the cogs and chainrings. It is an extremely efficient method of transmitting mechanical energy from your pedals to your rear wheel. In terms of weight, cost and efficiency, the bicycle chain has no equal ... and believe me, people have tried to improve on it.

To keep your bike running smoothly, you do have to pay at least some attention to your chain. It needs to be kept clean and well-lubricated in order to utilize your energy most efficiently, shift smoothly, and maximize chain life. Chains need to be replaced frequently to prolong the working life of other, more expensive, drive-train components. This is because, as a chain's internal parts wear, it gets longer, thus contacting gear teeth differently than intended.

IV-1: LUBRICATION

When lubricating the chain, use a lubricant intended for bicycle chains. If you want to get fancy about it, you can assess the type of conditions in which you ride and choose a lubricant intended for those conditions. Some lubricants are dry and pick up less dirt in dry conditions, some are sticky and therefore less prone to washing off in wet conditions.

1. Drip a small amount of lubricant across each roller (Fig. 4.1), periodically moving the chain to give easy access to the links you are working on. If you are in a hurry, you can turn the crank slowly while dripping lubricant onto the chain as

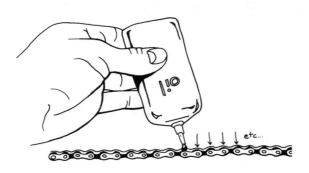

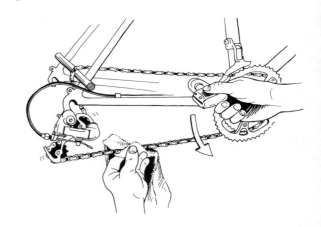

chain cleaning

it goes by. This is better than not lubricating the chain, but it will cause you to apply too much lubricant. That, in turn, will cause the chain to pick up dirt faster, and you will wear out your chain sooner.

2. Wipe the chain off lightly with a rag.

In wet conditions, expect to require more lubricant (after every ride, or even several times during a rainy ride). The lubricant for wet conditions needs to adhere well to the chain and not be easily washed off; this usually means a thick and sticky lubricant—even a grease. For dry conditions, less quantity of a dry lubricant that does not pick up dirt is preferable.

IV-2: CLEANING

Cleaning the chain can be accomplished in a number of ways.

Frequent wiping and lubrication

The simplest way to maintain a chain is to wipe it down frequently and then lubricate it. If this is done prior to every ride, you will never need to clean your chain with a solvent. The lubricant softens the old sludge buildup, which is driven out of the chain when you ride. The problem is that the lubricant also picks up new dirt and grime.

If new dirt and grime is wiped off before it is driven deep into the chain, and the chain is re-lubricated frequently, the chain will stay clean and supple. If you use one of the new chain waxes (wax mixed with solvent) and you apply it frequently, the drain will stay very clean as well as lubricated. Chain cleaning can be performed with the bike standing on the ground or in a bike stand.

1. With a rag in your hand, grasp the lower length of the chain (between the bottom of the chainring and the rear derailleur lower jockey wheel).

2. Turn the crank backward a number of revolutions, pulling the chain through the rag (Fig. 4.2). Periodically rotate the rag to present a cleaner section of it to the chain.

3. Lubricate each chain roller as above.

IV-3: CHAIN-CLEANING UNITS

Several companies make chain-cleaning units that scrub the chain with solvent while it is still on the bike. These types of chain cleaners are generally made of clear plastic and have two or three rotating brushes that scrub the chain as it moves through the solvent bath (Fig. 4.3). These units offer the advantage of letting you clean your chain without removing it from the bike.

4.3 using solvent-bath chain cleaner

Regularly removing your chain is a pain and it shortens chain life. Most chain cleaners come with a non-toxic, citrus-based solvent. For your safety and other environmental reasons, I strongly recommend that you purchase non-toxic citrus solvents for your chain cleaner, even if the unit already comes with a petroleum-based solvent. If you're cautious and you recycle used petroleum solvent, then go ahead and use it.

Citrus chain solvents often contain some lubricants as well, so they won't dry the chain out. The effective combination of lubricant and solvent is why diesel fuel used to have such a following as a chain cleaner. A really strong solvent without lubricant (acetone, for example) will displace the oil from inside the rollers. It will later evaporate, leaving a dry, squeaking chain, that is hard to rehabilitate. The same can happen with a citrus-based solvent without a lubricant included, especially if the chain is not allowed to dry long enough.

Procedure

1. Remove the top and pour in solvent up to the fill line.

2. Place the chain-cleaning unit up against the bottom of the chain, and reinstall the top so that the chain runs through it.

3. Turn the bike's crank backward (Fig. 4.3).

4. Lubricate as above (section IV-1).

IV-4: REMOVAL AND CLEANING

You can also clean the chain by removing it from the bicycle and cleaning it in a solvent. I recommend against it, because repeated disassembly weakens the chain, except in the case of a chain with a master link.

On a road bike, chain breakage is less of an issue, but mountain-bike chains are prone to breakage because of the conditions in which they are used. A chain that breaks while riding generally does it during shifting of the front derailleur while pedaling hard. This can pry a link plate open so that the head of a rivet pops out of it, tearing the chain apart. Chain disassembly and reassembly expands the size of the rivet hole where you put it together, allowing the rivet to pop out more easily. Shimano supplies special "subpins" for reassembly of their chains that are meant to prevent this. A hand-opened "master link" can avoid the chain weakening of pushing pins out. Master links are standard on Taya chains and will be on Sachs chains of 1998 and beyond; the aftermarket "Super Link" from Lickton Cycle can also be installed into any chain.

If you do disassemble the chain (see section IV-7 for instructions), you can clean it well, even without a solvent tank. Just drop your chain into an old jar or water bottle half filled with solvent. Using an old water bottle or jar allows you to clean the chain without touching or breathing the solvent — something to be avoided even with citrus solvents.

chains

removal

Procedure

1. Remove the chain from the bike (section IV-7 below).

2. Drop it in a water bottle or jar.

3. Pour in enough solvent to cover the chain.

4. Shake the bottle vigorously (low to the ground, in case the top pops off).

5. Hang the chain to air dry.

6. Reassemble it on the bike (see section IV-8-11 below).

7. Lubricate it as above (section IV-1).

Allow the solvent in the bottle to settle for a few days so you can decant the clear stuff and use it again. I'll say it throughout the book — it is important to use a citrus-based solvent. It is not only safer for the environment, it is gentler on your skin and less harmful to breathe. Wear rubber gloves when working with any solvent, and use a respirator meant for volatile organic compounds if you are not using a citrus-based solvent. There is no sense in fixing your bike so it goes faster if you end up becoming a slower, sickly bike rider.

IV-5: CHAIN REPLACEMENT

As the rollers, pins and plates wear out, your chain will begin to get longer. That, in turn, will hasten the wear and tear on the other parts of your drivetrain. An elongated chain will concentrate the load on each individual gear tooth, rather than distributing it over all of the teeth that the chain contacts. This will result in the gear teeth becoming hook-shaped and the tooth valleys becoming wider. If such wear has already occurred, a new chain will not solve the problem. A new chain will not mesh with deformed teeth, and it is likely to skip whenever you pedal hard. So, before all of that extra wear and tear takes place, get in the habit of replacing your chain on a regular basis.

How long it takes for the chain to "stretch" will vary, depending on chain type, maintenance, riding conditions, and strength and weight of the rider. Figure on replacing your chain every 500 to 1000 miles, especially if ridden in dirty conditions by a large rider. Lighter riders riding mostly on paved roads can extend replacement time to 2000 miles.

IV-6: CHECKING FOR CHAIN ELONGATION

The simplest method is to employ a chain-elongation indicator, such as the model made by Rohloff (Fig. 4.4). The indicator falls completely into the chain if the chain is worn out. If the chain is still in good shape, the indicator's tooth will not go all of the way in.

Another way is to measure it with an accurate ruler. Chains are measured on an inch standard, and there should be exactly an integral number of links in one foot.

1. Set one end of the ruler on a rivet edge, and measure to the rivet edge at the other end of the ruler.

2. The distance between these rivets should be 12 inches exactly. If it is 12 1/8 inches or greater, replace the chain; if it is 12 1/16 inches or more, it is a good idea to replace it (and a necessity to do so if you have any titanium or alloy cogs or an 11-tooth small cog). Chain manufacturer Sachs recommends replacement if elongation is 1 percent, or 1/2-inch in 100 links (50"). If the chain is off of the bike, you can hang it next to a new chain; if it is more than a half-link longer for the same number of links, replace it.

IV-7: CHAIN REMOVAL

The following procedure applies to all standard derailleur chains except those with a "master link". Master-link equipped chains include all

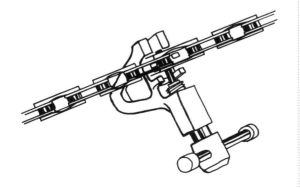

4.5 removing rivet

4.6 one complete chain link

Taya chains, chains with Lickton's "Super Link", and "Power Link"-equipped Sachs chains; all of these chains snap open by hand at the master link (see section IV-11), although they can also be opened at any other link with a chain tool as described below.

1. Place any link over the back teeth on a chain tool (Fig. 4.5).

2. Tighten the chain-tool handle clockwise to push the link rivet out. Unless you have a Shimano chain and a new "subpin" for it (in which case you push the rivet completely out), be careful to leave a millimeter or so of rivet protruding inward from the chain plate to hook the chain back together when reassembling.

IV-8: CHAIN INSTALLATION

1. Determine the chain length:

If you are putting on a new chain, determine how many links you'll need in one of two ways.

Method 1. Assuming your old chain was the correct length, compare the two and use the same number of links.

Method 2. If you have a standard long-cage mountain bike rear derailleur on your bike, wrap the chain around the big chainring and the biggest cog without going through either

removal and installation

4.7 determining chain length

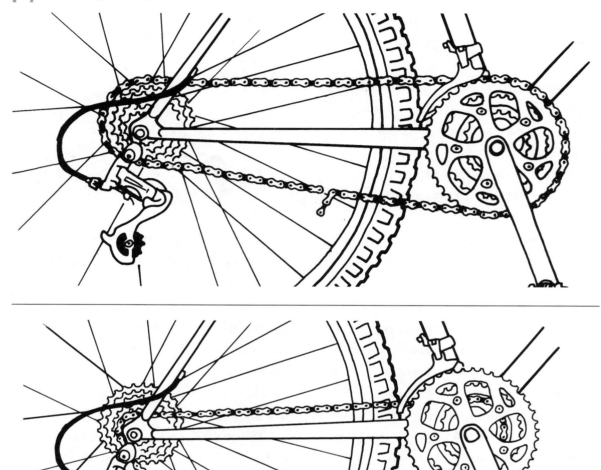

4.8 chain assembly

connecting chains

derailleur. Bring the two ends together until the ends overlap; one full link (Fig. 4.6) should be the amount of overlap (Fig. 4.7). Remove the remaining links, and save them in your spare tire bag so you have spares in case of chain breakage on the trail.

2. Route the chain properly:

Shift the derailleurs so that the chain will rest on the smallest cog in the rear and on the smallest chainring up front.

Starting with the rear derailleur pulley that is farthest from the derailleur body (this will be the bottom pulley once the chain is taut), guide the chain up through the rear derailleur, going around

4.9 replacing rivet

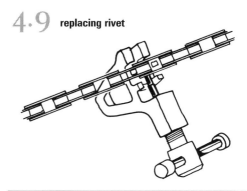

4.10 loosening a stiff link

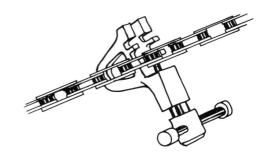

the two jockey pulleys. Make sure the chain passes inside of the prongs on the rear derailleur cage.

Guide the chain over the smallest rear cog.

Guide the chain through the front derailleur cage.

Wrap the chain around the smallest front chainring.

Bring the chain ends together so they meet.

3. Connect the chain:

Connecting a chain is much easier if the link rivet that was partially removed when the chain was taken apart is facing toward you. Positioning the link rivet this way allows you to use the chain tool (Fig. 4.8) in a much more comfortable manner (driving the rivet toward the bike, instead of back at you).

IV-9: CONNECTING A STANDARD CHAIN

1. Push the ends together, snapping the end link over the little stub of pin you left sticking out to the inside between the opposite end plates. You will need to flex the link open as you push the link in to get the pin to snap into the hole.

2. Push the rivet through with the chain tool (Fig. 4.9) until the same amount protrudes on either end.

3. Free the stiff link (Fig. 4.15), either by flexing it laterally with your fingers (Fig. 4.16), or, better, by using the chain tool's second set of teeth as below.

4. Put the link over the set of teeth on the tool closest to the screw handle (Fig. 4.10).

5. Push the pin a fraction of a turn to spread the plates apart.

IV-10: CONNECTING A SHIMANO CHAIN

1. Make sure you have a Shimano "subpin," which looks like a black rivet with a point on one end. It is twice as long as a standard rivet and has a breakage groove at the middle of its length. It comes with a new Shimano chain. If you are re-installing an old Shimano chain, get a new subpin at a bike shop. If you don't have a subpin and are going to connect it anyway, follow the procedure above in section IV-9, but be aware that the chain is now more likely to break than if it had been assembled with the proper subpin.

2. Remove any extra links, pushing the appropriate rivet completely out.

3. Line up the chain ends.

4. Push the subpin in with your fingers, pointed end first. It will go in about halfway.

5. With the chain tool, push the subpin through

4.11 snapping Shimano link

4.12 Taya chain master link

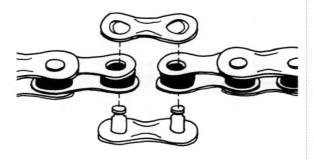

until there is only as much left protruding at the tail end as the other rivets in the chain.

6. Break off the leading half of the subpin with a pair of pliers (Fig. 4.11).

7. The chain should move freely. If not, flex it laterally with your thumbs at this rivet (Fig 4.16).

IV-11: CONNECTING AND DISCONNECTING A MASTER LINK

A. Taya chain connecting

1. Connect the two ends of the chain together with the master link that has two rivets sticking out of it (Fig. 4.12).

2. Snap the outer master link plate over the rivets and into their grooves. To facilitate hooking each keyhole-shaped hole over its corresponding rivet, flex the plate with the protruding rivets so that the ends of the rivets are closer together.

Disconnecting

1. Flex the master link so that the pins come closer together.

2. Pull the plate with the oval holes off of the rivets.

B. Lickton's Super Link and Sachs Power Link

These links are the same; Sachs licenses Lickton's

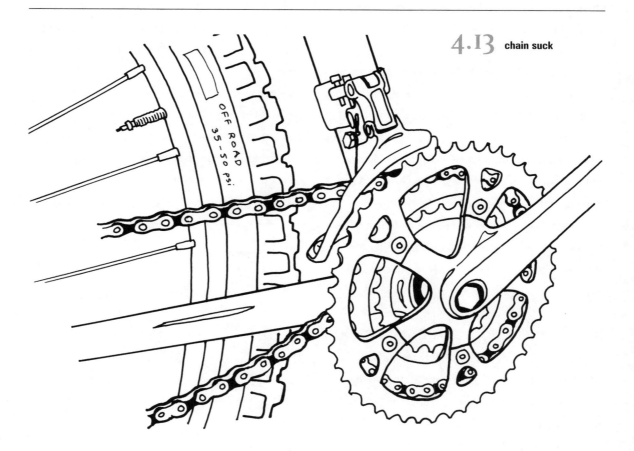

4.13 chain suck

design. The link is made up of two symmetrical links, each of which has a single pin sticking out of it. There is a round hole in the center of each plate that tapers into a slot on the end opposite the pin.

Connecting

1. Put the pin of each half of the link through the hole in each end of the chain; one pin will go down and one up.

2. Pull the links close together so that the each pin goes through the center hole in the opposite plate.

3. Pull the chain ends apart so that the groove at the top of each pin slides to the end of the slot in each plate.

Disconnecting

1. Push the chain ends toward each other so that the pins come to the center hole in each plate.

2. Pull the two halves of the master link apart.

TROUBLESHOOTING CHAIN PROBLEMS

IV-12: CHAIN SUCK

Chain suck occurs when the chain does not release from the bottom of a chainring and pulls up rather than running straight to the lower rear derailleur jockey wheel. It will come around and get "sucked" up by the chainring until it hits the chainstay (Fig. 4.13). Sometimes, the chain becomes wedged between the chainstay and the inner chainring.

A number of things can cause chain suck. To eliminate it, try the simplest methods first.

Reducing chain suck

1. Clean and lube the chain and see if it improves; a rusty chain will take longer to slide off of the chainring than will a clean, well-lubed chain.

2. Check for tight links by watching the chain move through the derailleur jockey wheels as you slowly turn the crank backwards. Loosen tight links by flexing them side to side with your thumbs.

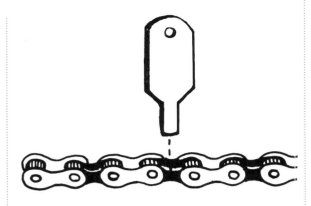

4.14 **checking link spacing with Shimano's TL-CN24 tool**

3. If chain suck persists, check that there are no bent or torn teeth on the chainring. Try straightening any broken or torn teeth you find with pliers. File off burrs.

4. If your chain still sucks, try another chain with wider spacing between link plates (if it is too narrow, it can pinch the chainring). You can use a caliper to compare link spacing of various chains or use Shimano's link-spacing tool (TL-CN24) that checks link-plate separation (Fig. 4.14).

5. Another approach is to replace the inner (and perhaps middle) chainring with a thin stainless steel (or shiny chromed) chainring. The thin, slick rings will release the chain more easily.

6. If the problem persists, a new chainring or an "anti-chain suck" device that attaches under the chainstays may help. Ask at your bike shop about what is available.

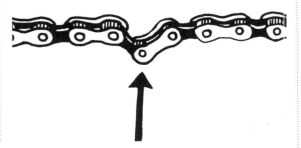

4.15 **stiff link**

IV-13: SQUEAKING CHAIN

Squeaking is caused by dry or rusted surfaces inside the chain rubbing on each other.

1. Wipe down and lubricate the chain.

2. If the squeak does not go away after a single ride with fresh lubricant, replace the chain. (If the initial remedy does not work, the chain is too dry inside and probably rusted as well. They seldom heal from this condition. Life is too short and bike riding is too joyful to put up with the sound of a squeaking chain.)

IV-14: SKIPPING CHAIN

There can be a number of causes for a chain to skip and jump as you pedal.

A. Stiff links

1. Turn the crank backward slowly to see if a stiff chain link (Fig. 4.15) exists; a stiff link will be visible because it will be unable to bend properly as it goes through the rear derailleur jockey wheels. It will deflect the jockey wheels when passing through.

2. Loosen stiff links by flexing them side to side between the index finger and thumb of both hands (Fig. 4.16) or by using the second set of teeth on a chain tool (Fig. 4.10). Set the stiff link over the teeth closest to the screw handle, and push the pin a fraction of a turn to spread the link.

3. Wipe down and lubricate the chain.

B. Rusted chain

A rusted chain will squeak. If you watch it move through the rear derailleur, it will look like many links are tight; they will not bend easily and will cause the jockey wheels to jump back and forth.

1. Lubricate the chain.

2. If this does not fix the problem after a few miles of riding, replace the chain.

C. Worn-out chain

If the chain is worn out, it will be elongated and will begin to skip because it does not mesh well with the cogs. A new chain will fix the problem, if it has not gone on long enough to ruin some cogs.

1. Check for chain elongation as described above in section IV-6.

TROUBLE— SHOOTING

2. If the chain is worn out, replace it.

3. If replacing the chain does not help, or makes matters worse, see the next section .

D. Worn cogs

If you just replaced the chain, and it is now skipping, at least one of the cogs is worn out. If this is the case, the chain will probably skip on the cogs you use most frequently and not on others.

1. Check each cog visually for wear. If its teeth are hook-shaped, the cog is shot and should be replaced. Rohloff makes a simple tool that checks for cog wear by putting tension on a length of chain wrapped around the cog. If chain links on the tool can be lifted off of the cog while under tension, the cog is worn out.

2. Replace the offending cogs or the entire cassette or freewheel. See cog installation in Chapter 6.

3. Replace the chain as well, if you have not just done so. An old chain will wear out your new cogs rapidly.

E. Misadjusted rear derailleur

If the rear derailleur is poorly adjusted or bent, it can cause the chain to skip, by lining the chain up between gears.

1. Check that the rear derailleur shifts equally well in both directions and that the chain can be pedaled backward without catching.

2. Adjust the rear derailleur by following the procedure described under the rear derailleur section in Chapter 5, section V-2.

F. Sticky shift cable

If the shift cable does not move freely enough to let the derailleur spring, push the chain under the cog, the chain will jump off under load. Frayed, rough, rusted, or worn cables or housings will cause the problem, as will overly thick cables or kinked or sharply bent housings.

Replacing the shift cables and housings (Chapter

5) should eliminate the problem.

G. Loose rear derailleur jockey wheel(s)

A loose jockey wheel on the rear derailleur can cause the chain to skip by letting it move too far laterally.

1. Check that the bolts holding the jockey wheel to the cage are tight and use the appropriately sized (usually 3mm) Allen wrench.

2. Tighten the jockey-wheel bolts if necessary. Hold the Allen wrench close to the bend so that you don't have enough leverage to over-tighten the bolts. If the jockey-wheel bolts loosen regularly, put Loctite on them.

H. Bent rear derailleur or derailleur hanger

If the derailleur or derailleur hanger is bent, adjustments won't work. You will probably know when it happened, either when you shifted your derailleur into your spokes, when you crashed onto the derailleur, or when you pedaled a stick or a tumbleweed through the derailleur.

1. Unless you have a derailleur hanger alignment tool and know how to use it (Chapter 14, Fig. 14.5), take the bike to a shop and have them check and correct the dropout hanger alignment. Some bikes, especially those made out of aluminum, have a replaceable (bolt on) right rear dropout and derailleur hanger, which you can purchase and bolt-on yourself.

2. If a straight derailleur hanger does not correct the misalignment, your rear derailleur is bent. This is generally cause for replacement of the entire derailleur (See Chapter 5). With some derailleurs, you can just replace the jockey-wheel cage, which is usually what is bent. If you know what you are doing and are careful, you can sometimes bend a bent derailleur cage back with your hands. It seldom works well, but it is worth a try if your only other alternative is to replace the entire rear

chains

TROUBLE—
SHOOTING

derailleur. Just make sure you don't bend the derailleur hanger in the process.

I. Worn derailleur pivots

If the derailleur pivots are worn, the derailleur will be loose and will move around under the cogs, causing the chain to skip. Replacing the derailleur is the solution.

J. Bent rear derailleur mounting bolt

If the mounting bolt is bent, the derailleur will not line up straight. To fix it, get a new bolt and install it following the "upper pivot overhaul" section (V-33) in Chapter 5. Observe how the spring-loaded assembly goes together during disassembly to ease reassembly.

the transmission
derailleurs, shifters, and cables

"Most Americans want to be somewhere else, but when they get there, they want to go home" — HENRY FORD

tools

3mm, 4mm, 5mm
    and 6mm Allen
wrenches
flat-blade and
    Phillips
screwdrivers
    (small and
    medium)
cable cutter
indexed housing
    cutter (Shimano)
pliers
grease
chain lubricant
rubbing alcohol

There is nothing like having your derailleurs working smoothly, predictably and quietly under all conditions. Knowing that you can shift whenever you need to inspires confidence when riding on difficult single-track sections. It really is a lot more pleasant to ride through beautiful terrain without the grinding and clunking noises of an out-of-whack derailleur.

Improperly adjusted rear derailleurs are a common problem even though derailleur adjustments are easy provided the equipment is clean and in good working order. A few simple adjustments to the limit screws and the cable tension and you are on your way. Once you see how easy it is, you will probably keep yours in adjustment all of the time.

V.A: THE REAR DERAILLEUR

The rear derailleur is one of the most complex parts on a bike (Fig. 5.1). It moves the chain from one rear cog to another, and it also takes up chain slack when the bike bounces or the front derailleur is shifted.

The rear derailleur bolts to a hanger on the rear dropout. Two jockey wheels (pulley wheels) hold the chain tight and help guide the chain as the derailleur shifts. Depending on the model, a rear derailleur has one or two springs that pull the jockey wheels tightly against the chain, creating a desirable amount of chain tension.

Except on Shimano's new reverse-action Rapid-Rise rear derailleurs, increasing the tension on the rear derailleur cable moves the derailleur inward toward the larger cogs. When the cable tension is released, a spring between the derailleur's two parallelogram plates pulls the chain back toward the smallest cogs. The Rapid-Rise derailleurs work in exactly the opposite fashion. The two limit screws on the rear derailleur prevent the derailleur from moving the chain too far to the inside (into the spokes) or to

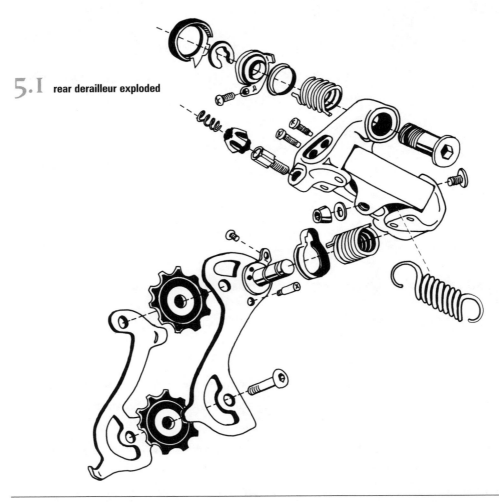

5.1 rear derailleur exploded

the outside (into the dropout). In addition to limit screws, most rear derailleurs have a cable-tensioning barrel adjuster located at the back of the derailleur, where the cable enters it (Fig. 5.3). This can be used to fine tune the shifting adjustment to land the chain precisely on each cog with each click of the shifter. Rear derailleurs also often have a "B" tension screw at the back of the derailleur rotating it around its mounting point to control the space between the bottom of the cogs and the upper jockey wheel.

V-1: REAR DERAILLEUR INSTALLATION

1. Apply a small amount of grease to the derailleur's mounting bolt and then thread the bolt into the large hole on the right rear dropout.

2. Pull the derailleur back so that the "B" adjusting screw or tab on the derailleur ends up behind the tab on the dropout (Fig. 5.2).

3. Tighten the mounting bolt until the derailleur fits snugly against the hanger.

4. Route the chain through the jockey wheels and connect it. (See Chapter 4, Sections IV-8 to IV-11)

5. Install the cables and housings (see Sections V-6 to V-13 below).

6. Pull the cable tight with a pair of pliers, and tighten the cable-fixing bolt.

7. Follow the adjustment procedure described below.

5.2 **right rear dropout**

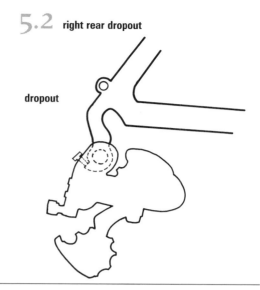

dropout

5.3 **limit screws and barrel adjuster**

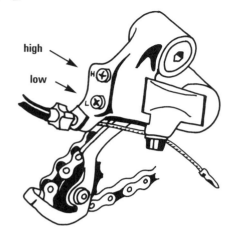

high

low

V-2: ADJUSTMENT OF REAR DERAILLEUR AND RIGHT-HAND SHIFTER

Perform all of the following derailleur adjustments with the bike in a bike stand or hung from the ceiling. That way, you can turn the crank and shift gears while you put the derailleur through its paces. After adjustment off of the ground, test the shifting while riding. Derailleurs often perform differently under load than in a bike stand.

Before starting, lubricate or replace the chain (Chapter 4) so that the whole drivetrain runs smoothly.

A. Limit screw adjustments

The first, and most important, rear derailleur adjustment is the limit screws. Properly set, these screws (Fig. 5.3) should make certain that you will not ruin your frame, wheel or derailleur by shifting into the spokes or by jamming the chain between the dropout and the smallest cog. It is never pleasant to see your expensive equipment turned into shredded metal. All it takes is a small screwdriver to turn these limit screws. Remember, it's lefty loosey, righty tighty for these screws.

B. High-gear-limit screw adjustment

This screw limits the outward movement of the rear derailleur. You tighten or loosen this screw until the derailleur shifts the chain to the smallest cog quickly but does not overshift.

How do you determine which limit screw works on the high gear? Often, it will be labeled with an "H," and it is usually the upper of the two screws (Fig. 5.3). If you're not certain, try both screws. Whichever screw, when tightened, moves the derailleur inward when the chain is on the smallest cog is the one you are looking for. On most derailleurs, you can also see which screw to adjust by looking in between the derailleur's parallelogram side plates. You will see one tab on the back end of each plate. Each is designed to hit a limit screw at one end of the movement. Shift into your highest gear, and notice which screw is touching one of the tabs; that is the high-gear-limit screw.

Procedure

1. Shift the chain to the large front chain ring.

2. While slowly turning the crank, shift the rear derailleur to the smallest rear cog (highest

high-
gear-limit
screw
adjustments

gear) (Fig. 5.4).

3. If there is hesitation in the chain's shifting movement, loosen the cable a little to see if it is stopping the derailleur from moving out far enough (this does not apply to Rapid-Rise rear derailleurs). Do this by turning the barrel adjuster on the derailleur or shift lever clockwise, or by loosening the cable-fixing bolt.

4. If the chain still won't drop smoothly and without hesitation to the smallest cog, loosen the high-gear-limit screw a quarter turn at a time, continuously repeating the shift, until the chain repeatedly drops quickly and easily.

5. If the derailleur throws the chain into the dropout, or it tries to go past the smallest cog, tighten the high-gear-limit screw a quarter turn and re-do the shift. Repeat until the derailleur shifts the chain quickly and easily into the highest gear without throwing the chain into the dropout.

C. Low-gear-limit screw adjustment

This screw stops the inward movement of the rear derailleur, preventing it from going into the spokes. This screw is usually labeled "L," and it is usually the bottom screw (Fig. 5.3). You can check which one it is by shifting to the largest cog, maintaining pressure on the shifter, and turning the screw to see if it changes the position of the derailleur.

1. Shift the chain to the inner chainring on the front. Shift the rear derailleur to the lowest gear (largest cog) (Fig. 5.5). Do it gently, in case the limit screw does not stop the derailleur from going into the spokes.

2. If the derailleur touches the spokes or shoves the chain over the largest cog, tighten the low-gear-limit screw until it does not.

3. If the derailleur cannot bring the chain onto the largest cog, loosen the screw a quarter turn.

low-gear-limit screw adjustment

5.4 high gear

Repeat this step until the chain shifts easily up to the cog, but does not touch the spokes.

D. Cable-tension adjustment:
Indexed rear shifters

With an indexed shifting system (one that "clicks" into each gear), it is the cable tension that determines whether the derailleur moves to the proper gear with each click.

1. With the chain on the large chainring in the front, shift the rear derailleur to the smallest cog.

5.5 **low gear**

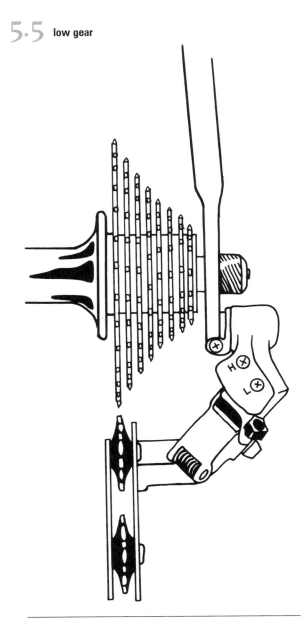

Keep clicking the shifter until you are sure it will not let any more cable out (or keep pushing the thumb lever with Rapid-Rise).

2. Shift back one click; this should move the chain smoothly to the second cog.

3. If the chain does not climb to the second cog, or if it does so slowly, increase the tension in the cable by turning either the derailleur cable barrel adjuster (Fig. 5.3) or the shifter barrel adjuster (Fig. 5.6) counterclockwise. Do the opposite with a Rapid-Rise derailleur. If you run out of barrel adjustment range, re-tighten both adjusters, loosen the cable-fixing bolt and pull some of the slack out of the cable. Tighten the fixing bolt and repeat the adjustment.

4. If the chain overshifts the second cog or comes close to overshifting, decrease the cable tension by turning one of the barrel adjusters clockwise (or increase the tension with a Rapid-Rise derailleur).

5. Keep adjusting the cable tension in small increments while shifting back and forth between the two smallest cogs until the chain moves easily in both directions.

6. Shift to the middle chainring in the front and onto one of the middle rear cogs. Shift the rear derailleur back and forth a few cogs, again checking for precise and quick movement of the chain from cog to cog. Fine-tune the shifting by making small adjustments to the cable-tensioning barrel adjuster.

7. Shift to the inner ring in the front and to the largest cog in the rear. Shift up and down one click in the rear, again checking for symmetry and precision of chain movement in either direction between the two largest cogs. Fine tune the barrel adjuster until you get it just right.

8. Go back through the gears. With the chain in the middle chainring in front, the rear derailleur should shift smoothly back and forth between any pair of cogs. With the chain on the big chainring, the rear derailleur should shift easily on all but perhaps the largest one or two cogs in the rear. With the chain on the inner chainring, the rear derailleur should shift easily on all but perhaps the two smallest cogs.

N O T E

If the shifter barrel adjuster does not hold its adjustment, your derailleur's performance will get

the transmission

cable-tension
adjustment
—
indexed
rear
shifters

5.6 shifter barrel adjuster

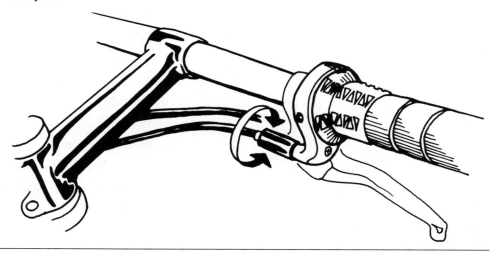

non-indexed
rear
shifters

steadily worse as you ride. This has been a problem with some XTR shifters, which, unlike most barrel adjusters, have no springs or notches to hold the adjuster in place. If you have this problem, there are a couple of things you can do, besides getting a new shifter. One is to put Finish Line "Ti-Prep" on the threads to create a bit more friction; I have found this to be a temporary fix only. Loctite or scoring the threads crosswise with a screwdriver blade may also help, although I have not tried either. One fool-proof solution, though a bit of a hassle, is to keep the shifter barrel adjuster turned all of the way in and make all cable tension adjustments with the barrel adjuster on the rear derailleur. This will not work with adjuster-free Rapid-Rise rear derailleurs, though.

E. Cable-tension adjustment: Non-Indexed rear shifters

If you do not have indexed shifting, adjustment is complete after you remove the slack in the cable. With proper cable tension, when the chain is on the smallest cog, the derailleur should move as soon as the shift lever does. If there is free play in the lever, tighten the cable by turning the cable barrel adjuster on the derailleur or shifter counterclockwise. If your rear derailleur and shifter don't have barrel adjusters, loosen

5.7 chain gap adjustment of SRAM derailleur

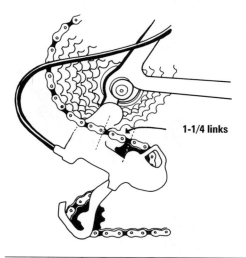

1-1/4 links

the cable clamp bolt, pull some slack out of the cable with pliers, and re-tighten the clamp bolt.

F. Final details of rear derailleur adjustment: "B-screw" adjustment

You can get a bit more precision by adjusting the small screw ("B-screw") that changes the derailleur's position against the derailleur hanger tab on the right rear dropout. Viewing from behind with the chain on the inner chainring and largest cog (Fig. 5.5), adjust the screw so that the upper jockey wheel is close to the cog, but not pinching the chain against the cog. Repeat

on the smallest cog (Fig. 5.4). You'll know that you've moved it in too closely when it starts making noise.

SRAM (a.k.a.: Grip Shift) suggests setting the B-screw on its ESP derailleurs with the chain on the middle chainring and largest cog. Viewing from the drive side, turn the screw so that the length of chain across the "chain gap" (from where the chain leaves the bottom of the cog to its first contact at the top of the upper jockey wheel) one- to one-and-a-quarter links (Fig. 5.7), where one link is a complete male-female link pair (Fig. 4.6).

Note on shifting trouble: If you cannot get the rear derailleur to shift well, or it makes noise in even mild cross gears no matter what you do, or it throws the chain off despite your best efforts, refer to the chain-line discussion under "Troubleshooting" at the end of this chapter.

V.B: THE FRONT DERAILLEUR

The front derailleur moves the chain over the chainrings. The working parts consist of a steel cage, a linkage and an arm attached to the shifter cable. The front derailleur is attached to the frame, usually by a clamp surrounding the seat tube (Fig. 5.8). Some Shimano models attach to the face of the bottom bracket. Shimano's top-of-the-line XTR front derailleur mounts both to the face of the bottom bracket and to a braze-on boss (or band clamp) on the seat tube (Fig. 5.9); Shimano also offers an XTR front derailleur with a standard seat-tube band clamp.

V-3: FRONT DERAILLEUR INSTALLATION: BAND TYPE

1. Clamp the front derailleur around the seat tube.

2. Adjust the height and rotation as described in section V-5A on the following page.

3. Tighten the clamp bolt (Fig. 5.8).

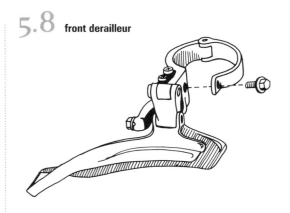

5.8 front derailleur

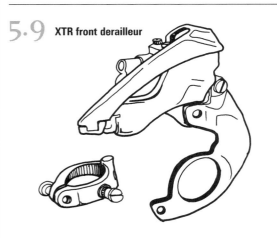

5.9 XTR front derailleur

V-4: FRONT DERAILLEUR INSTALLATION: BOTTOM-BRACKET-MOUNTING TYPE

1. Remove the bottom bracket (see Chapter 8, sections VIII-10 and VIII-11).

2. Slip the derailleur bracket over the right-hand bottom bracket cup, and start the cup into the bottom bracket shell a few threads.

3. With less expensive models, place the C-shaped derailleur stabilizer around the seat tube to fix the rotational adjustment. With the XTR bottom-bracket-mounted derailleur, loosely screw the mounting bolt into the special braze-on designed for it. (If the frame does not have the braze-on, a separate XTR seat-tube band clamp with a threaded hole in the side is used (Fig. 5.9). The band will need to be bent to fit an ovalized seat tube.)

V

the transmission

front
derailleur

5.IO-II proper cage alignment

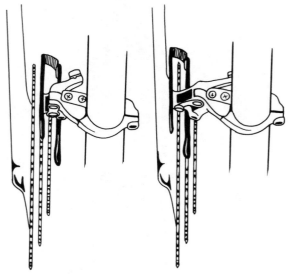

5.I2 proper clearance

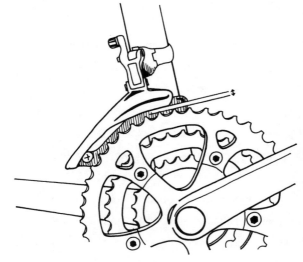

4. Tighten the right-hand bottom bracket cup against the bottom bracket face.

5. With the XTR bottom-bracket-mounted derailleur, tighten the mounting bolt into the braze-on (or band clamp hole).

6. Complete the bottom bracket installation (see Chapter 8, sections VIII-7, 8, 9).

N O T E

There are no (or limited) height and rotational adjustments on these derailleurs, and they must be used with the chainring size for which they were intended. They can be turned only slightly to line up better with the chain.

The XTR front derailleur has two mounting-bolt holes for either a 46- or 48-tooth chainring. The derailleur's rotational adjustment can be fine-tuned without the braze-on: the band clamp can be twisted around the seat tube a few degrees.

V-5: FRONT DERAILLEUR AND LEFT HAND SHIFTER ADJUSTMENT

A. Position adjustments

With a seat-tube-clamp front derailleur, the position is adjusted with a 5mm Allen (or 8mm box) wrench on the band clamp bolt. Bottom-bracket face-mounted front derailleurs have little or no vertical or rotational (twist about the seat tube) adjustments.

I. Position the height of the front derailleur so that the outer cage passes about 1mm to 2 mm (1/16 to 1/8 inch) above the highest point of the outer chainring (Fig. 5.12).

2. Position the outer plate of the derailleur cage parallel to the chainrings (or to the chain in the lowest and highest gears) when viewed from above. Check this by shifting to the big chainring and smallest cog and sighting from the top (Fig. 5.11). Many derailleurs (Sachs, most Shimano, Suntour) need the outer face of the cage exactly parallel to the chainring; check this by measuring the space between the cage and the inner side of the crankarm as it passes by. The cage of some derailleurs flares wider at the tail (Shimano XTR is one example). The outer tail of the derailleur cage

5.13 limit screws

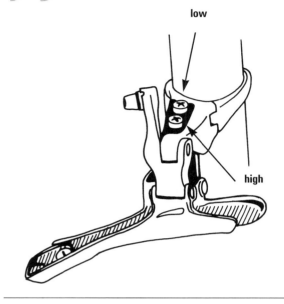

low

high

on these models needs to be out a bit from parallel to the plane of the frame in order to parallel the chain. Similarly, when on the inner chainring and largest cog, the inner cage plate should parallel the chain, making the tail a bit in from parallel with the plane of the frame (Fig. 5.10).

NOTE

Height and rotational adjustments of the seat-tube-clamp version of Shimano's differential-plate XTR front derailleur are set in the same manner as standard front derailleurs.

B. Limit-screw adjustments

The front derailleur has two limit screws that stop the derailleur from throwing the chain to the inside or outside of the chainrings. These are usually labeled "L" for low-gear (small chainring) and "H" for high gear (large chainring) (Fig. 5.13). On most derailleurs, the low gear screw is closer to the frame; however, Shimano XTR differential-plate derailleurs have the limit-screw positions reversed, but their adjustment is the same.

If in doubt, you can determine which limit screw

controls which function by the same trial-and-error method outlined above for the rear derailleur. Shift the chain to the inner ring, then tighten one of the limit screws. If turning that screw moves the front derailleur outward, then it is the low-gear-limit screw. If turning that screw does not move the front derailleur, then the other screw is the low-gear-limit screw.

C. Low-gear-limit screw adjustment

1. Shift back and forth between the middle and inner chainrings.

2. If the chain drops off of the little ring to the inside, tighten the low-gear-limit screw (clockwise) one quarter turn, and try shifting again.

3. If the chain does not drop easily onto the inner chainring when shifted, loosen the low-gear-limit screw one quarter turn and repeat the shift.

D. High-gear-limit screw adjustment

1. Shift the chain back and forth between the middle and outer chainring.

2. If the chain jumps over the big chainring, tighten the high-gear-limit screw one quarter turn and repeat the shift.

3. If the chain is sluggish going up to the big chainring or does not go up at all, loosen the high-gear-limit screw one quarter turn and try the shift again.

E. Cable-tension adjustment

1. With the chain on the inner chainring, remove any excess cable slack by turning the barrel adjuster on the shifter (Fig. 5.6, except on left shifter) counterclockwise (or loosen the cable-fixing bolt, pull the cable tight with pliers, and tighten the bolt).

2. Check that the cable is loose enough to allow the chain to shift smoothly and repeatedly from the middle to the inner chainring.

3. Check that the cable is tight enough so that

V

the transmission

front
derailleur
cable-tension
adjustment

the derailleur starts to move as soon as you move the shifter.

N O T E

This tension adjustment should work for indexed as well as friction shifters. With indexed front shifting, you may want to fine-tune the barrel adjuster to avoid noise from the chain dragging on the derailleur in some cross gears, or to get more precise shifting.

Another note: Some front derailleurs have a cam screw at the end of the spring to adjust spring tension. For quicker shifting to the smaller rings, increase the spring tension by turning the screw clockwise.

Note on shifting trouble: If you cannot get the front derailleur to shift well, or it rubs in cross gears no matter what you do, or it throws the chain off despite your best efforts, refer to the chain-line discussion under "Troubleshooting" at the end of this chapter.

V.C: THE SHIFT CABLES AND HOUSINGS

In order for your derailleurs to function properly, you need to have clean, smooth-running cables (also called "inner wires"). Because of all the muck and guck that you encounter on a mountain bike, you need to regularly replace those cables. As with replacing a chain, replacing cables is a maintenance operation, not a repair

operation. Do not wait until cables break to replace them. Replace any cables that have broken strands, kinks, or fraying between the shifter and the derailleur. You should also replace housings (also called "outer wires") if they are bent, mashed, just plain gritty or the color clashes with your bike (this is really important).

CABLE INSTALLATION/REPLACEMENT

V-6: PROCEDURE FOR BUYING CABLES

1. Buy new cables and housing with at least as much length as the ones you are replacing.

2. Make sure that the cables and housing are for indexed systems. These cables will stretch minimally, and the housings will not compress in length. Under its external plastic sheath, indexed housing is not made of steel coil like brake housings; it is made of parallel (coaxial) steel strands of thin wire. If you look at the end, you will see numerous wire ends sticking out surrounding a central Teflon tube (make sure it has this Teflon liner, too) (Fig. 5.14).

3. Buy two cable crimp caps (Fig. 5.14) to prevent fraying, and a tubular cable housing end (ferrule) for each end of every housing section. These ferrules will prevent kinking at the cable entry points, cable stops, shifters and derailleurs.

While you're at it, buying rubber cable donuts (Fig. 5.25) or sheathing for bare-cable runs is worthwhile to protect your frame.

4. It is a good idea to buy a bunch of cables, cable caps and ferrules (Fig. 5.14) to keep on hand in your work area. They're cheap, and you should be changing cables regularly without having to make a special trip to the bike shop every time you need a little cable-end cap.

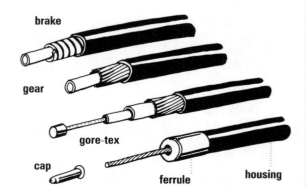

5.14 **cable types and housings**

brake

gear

gore-tex

cap

ferrule

housing

5.15-16 housing length

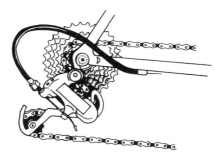

enough length at the rear derailleur so that the derailleur can swing forward (Fig. 5.16) and backward (Fig. 5.15) freely.

3. With a nail or toothpick, open each Teflon sleeve-end that has been smashed shut by the cutter.

4. Place a ferrule over each housing end (Fig. 5.14).

V-8: REPLACING CABLE IN THUMB SHIFTERS, RAPIDFIRE PLUS, RAPIDFIRE SL OR ORIGINAL RAPIDFIRE LEVERS

1. Shift both levers to the gear setting that lets the most cable out. This will be the highest gear position for the rear shift lever (small cog), and the lowest for the front (small ring).

2. Pull out the old cable and recycle it.

3. The recessed hole into which the cable head seats should be visible right up against the barrel adjuster. Thread the cable through the hole and out through the barrel adjuster (Figs. 5.17 and 5.18).

4. Guide the cable through each housing segment and cable stop. Slotted cable stops on the frame allow you to slip the cable and housing in and out from the side.

V-7: CUTTING THE HOUSING TO LENGTH

1. Use a special cutter like those from Park, Shimano or Wrench Force (see Chapter 1 tools). Standard wire cutters will not cut index-shift housing.

2. Cut the housing to the same lengths as your old ones. If you have no old housings to compare with, cut them so that the housing curves smoothly from cable stop to cable stop, and turning the handlebars does not pull or kink them. Allow for

V-9: XTR RAPIDFIRE CABLE-REPLACEMENT INSTRUCTION:

Shimano XTR shifters sold in 1996 and later have

5.17 thumb shifter

5.18 Rapidfire shifter

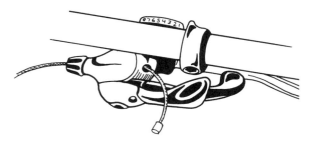

the transmission

cutting
cable housing
to length

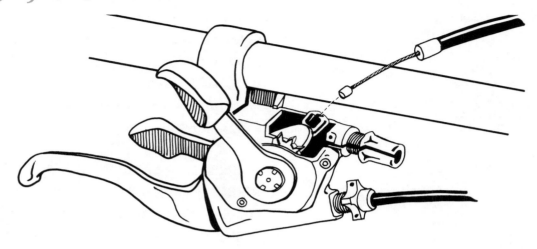

a plastic cover over the wire-end hook and also have a slotted barrel adjuster and shifter body.

1. Shift the smaller (upper and forward) finger-operated lever until the shifter lets out all of the cable.

2. Turn the shifter barrel-adjuster so the cable slit is lined up with the slot in the shifter body (Fig. 5.19); the slot is on the opposite side from the gear indicator.

3. Unscrew the Phillips-head screw on the plastic cover; it will not come completely out (where you could lose it), being retained in the cover by a plastic ring. Open the cover.

4. Pull the old cable down out of the slot, and pull the cable head out of the hook.

5. Slip the new cable head into the cable hook (Fig. 5.19), and pull the cable into the slot. Turn the barrel adjuster so the slots no longer line up.

6. Close the cover and tighten the screw (gently!).

7. Guide the cable through each housing segment and cable stop. Slotted cable stops allow you to slip the cable and housing in and out from the side.

NOTE

Replacing the thin cables connected to the XTR "Rapidfire Remote" bar-end-mounted shifters requires buying the thin double-headed cables and housings from Shimano. The small heads simply slip through the holes in both sets of shift levers (on the bar and on the bar end) from the back side. You install the little plastic cable head caps onto the metal cable heads to keep them from pulling back through. That's it!

V-10: REPLACING CABLE IN GRIP SHIFT

The Grip Shift lever must be disassembled to replace the cable.

1. Disconnect the derailleur cable.

2. Roll or slide the handlebar grip away from the Grip Shift to allow room for the shifter to slide apart.

3. With a Phillips screwdriver, remove the triangular plastic cover holding the two main sections together.

4. Pull the outer shifter section away from the main body to separate it from the inner housing. Watch for the spring to ensure that it does not fall out. It can be nudged back into place if it does (Figs. 5.20 and 5.21).

5. Pull the old cable out and recycle it.

6. Clean and dry the two parts if they are dirty; a rag and a cotton swab are usually sufficient. Finish Line offers a cleaning and grease kit

5.20 **Grip Shift right shifter**

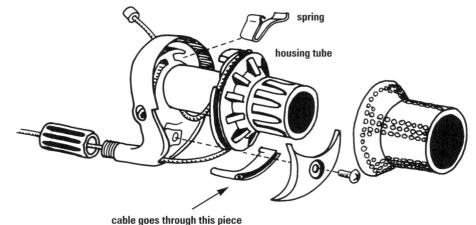

spring

housing tube

cable goes through this piece

5.21 **Grip Shift left shifter**

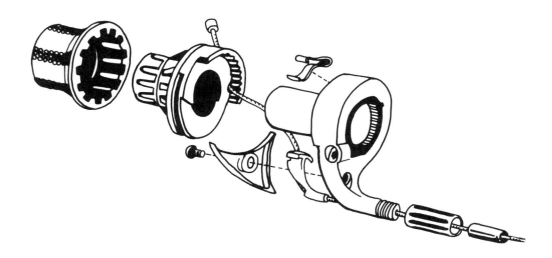

replacing
Grip Shift
cables

specifically designed for Grip Shift shifters. A really gummed-up shifter may require solvent and compressed air to clean and dry it.

7. Using a non-lithium grease, lubricate the inner housing tube and spring cavity, all cable grooves, and the indexing notches in the twister. Grip Shift recommends a silicone-based Teflon grease; SRAM and Finish Line sell such lubes.

8. Thread the cable through the hole, seating the cable end in its little pocket.

9. For the rear shifter, loop the cable once around the housing tube, and exit it through the barrel adjuster (Fig. 5.20). For the front shifter,

the cable routes directly into its guide (Fig. 5.21).

10. Make sure the spring is in its cavity in the housing; hold the spring in with a small amount of grease if need be.

11. Slide the outer (twister) body over the inner tube. Be sure that the shifter is in the position that lets the most cable out. (On models with numbers, line up the highest number with the indicator mark on rear shifters, lowest number on front shifters.)

12. Lift the cable loop into the groove in the twister (Fig. 5.20), and push straight inward on it as you pull tension on the cable exiting the

shifter. The twister should slide in until flush under the housing edge; you may have to jiggle it back and forth slightly while pushing in to get it properly seated.

13. Replace the cover and screw.

14. Check that the shifter clicks properly.

15. Slide the grip back into place.

16. Guide the cable through each housing segment and cable stop. Slotted cable stops allow you to slip the cable and housing in and out from the side.

attaching rear derailleur cables

V-11: ATTACH CABLE TO REAR DERAILLEUR

1. Put the chain on the smallest cog so the rear derailleur moves to the outside.

2. Run the cable through the barrel adjuster, and route it through each of the housing segments until you reach the cable-fixing bolt on the derailleur. Make sure that the rear shifter is on the highest setting; this ensures that the maximum amount of cable is available to the derailleur.

3. Pull the cable taut and into its groove under the cable-fixing bolt (Fig. 5.22).

5.22 attaching rear derailleur cable

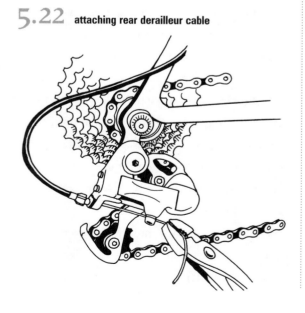

5.23 **pull cable tight before tightening with Allen wrench**

4. Tighten the bolt. On most derailleurs this takes a 5mm Allen wrench.

V-12: ATTACH CABLE TO FRONT DERAILLEUR

1. Operate the shifter to allow the most cable out (granny gear setting). Shift the chain to the inner ring so that the derailleur moves farthest to the inside.

2. Connect the cable to the cable-anchor groove under the bolt on the derailleur arm while pulling the cable taut with pliers (Fig. 5.23). Make sure you do not hook up a top-pull front derailleur from the bottom, or vice versa. Some older derailleur models require housing to run all of the way to a stop on the derailleur.

V-13: FINAL CABLE TOUCHES

A high quality cable assembly includes the cable-housing-end ferrules throughout, and crimped cable caps (Fig. 5.24); cables are clipped about 1cm to 2cm past the cable clamp-bolts. Also, little rubber cable donuts (Fig. 5.25) or pieces of thin cable sheathing are installed to keep the bare cables from scratching the frame's finish.

V-14: GORE-TEX CABLES

If you are using Gore-Tex cables, follow the instructions on the package, since these require very special treatment in order to work properly. The Gore Tex needs to be removed with a knife from the cable the last inch or so before the cable fixing bolt, as well as from all of the cable that is inside the shift lever or Grip Shift. A long

5.24 crimp cable ends

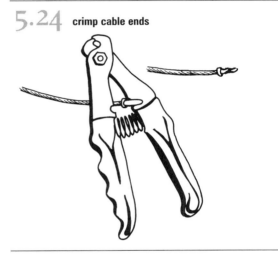

plastic tube covers the cable its entire length from shifter to derailleur (Fig. 5.14). A little rubber accordion seal (called a "Grub") at the fixing bolt covers the end of the cable-cover tube and keeps dirt and water out of it.

V-15: CABLE LUBRICATION

New cables and housings with Teflon liners do not need to be lubricated. Old cables can be lubricated with chain lubricant. Grease sometimes slows their movement, but some manufacturers recommend (and supply) their own molybdenum disulfide grease for cables.

1. Pull the housing segments out of their slotted cable stops; there is no reason to disconnect the cable.

2. Coat with lubricant the areas of the cable

5.25 little rubber donuts

that will be inside of the cable housing segments.

NOTE

If you do not have slotted cable stops, you might as well replace the cables and housings, since an old cable will have a frayed end and will be hard to put back through the housing after lubrication. Another reason to keep cables, housing ferrules and cable ends in stock.

V-16: EASY STEPS TO REDUCE CABLE FRICTION

Besides replacing your cables and housings with good quality cables and lined housings, there are other specific steps you can take to improve shifting efficiency.

1. The most important friction-reducing step is to route the cable so that it makes smooth bends, and so that turning the handlebars does not increase the tension on the shift cables.

2. Choose cables that offer particularly low friction. "Die-drawn" cables, which have been mechanically pulled through a small hole in a piece of hard steel called a die, move with lower friction than standard cables. Die-drawing flattens all of the outer strands and smooths the cable surface. Thinner cables and lined housings with a large inside diameter also reduce friction. Low-friction Gore-Tex cables are coated with Gore-Tex and are further sealed end-to-end with a plastic sheath (Fig. 5.14).

3. Shifting to smaller cogs can be quickened by

the transmission

reducing cable friction

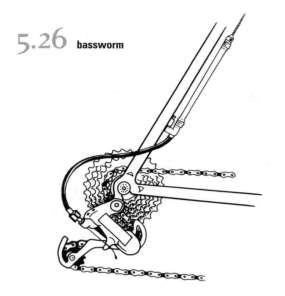

5.26 bassworm

increasing the size of the derailleur-return spring. You can buy an after-market stiffer spring designed specifically for your derailleur. You can also try Grip Shift's "Bassworm", a piece of surgical tubing that acts as a cable-return spring and keeps the cable clean where it enters the housing. It is hooked into the final cable stop and slipped over the cable just in front of the last segment of cable housing, pulled tight, and the set screw on its end is tightened down onto the cable (Fig. 5.26).

4. Hydraulic shifting, with a master cylinder at the shifter and a slave cylinder at the derailleur connected by fluid-filled hydraulic tubing, is available from Safe Systems. The system eliminates the cable, save for a stub at either end. The system is impervious to dirt and costs plenty.

shifter replacement

V.D: THE SHIFTERS

Twist shifters, thumb shifters and Rapidfire levers (Figs. 5.27, 5.28, and 5.29) all move the derailleurs, but they go about it in very different ways.

V-17: BAR END AND GRIP REPLACEMENT/INSTALLATION

Replacing shifters requires removing at least grips and bar ends, and often brake levers as well. Shifters are generally labeled right and left, but if you're in doubt, you can tell which is which because the right one has a lot more clicks. Obviously, this is not true with friction shifters.

1. Remove bar ends, usually with a 5mm Allen wrench.

2. Remove grips by peeling them back at either end, squirting water or rubbing alcohol underneath, and twisting back and forth while sliding them off. If you are planning on replacing them, you can cut the grips off.

3. Squirt water or rubbing alcohol inside when replacing grips.

V-18: REPLACING SHIFTERS WITH INTEGRATED BRAKE LEVERS

If you are replacing the entire brake lever/shift lever unit:

1. Remove the old brake lever and shifter.

2. Slide the new brake lever/shifter onto the bar, making sure that you put the right shifter on the right side and vice versa.

3. Slide the grip back into position.

4. Mount the bar end, if you have one.

5. Rotate the brake lever to the position you like.

6. Tighten the brake-lever-fixing bolt.

V-19: REPLACING THE SHIFTER UNIT ON INTEGRAL BRAKE/SHIFT LEVER (I.E., RAPIDFIRE)

1. After shifting to the high-gear position to release the maximum amount of cable, unbolt the old shift lever from the brake lever body.

2. Position the new shifter exactly like the old one.

3. Replace the bolt and tighten it.

4. Reinstall/replace cable and tighten it.

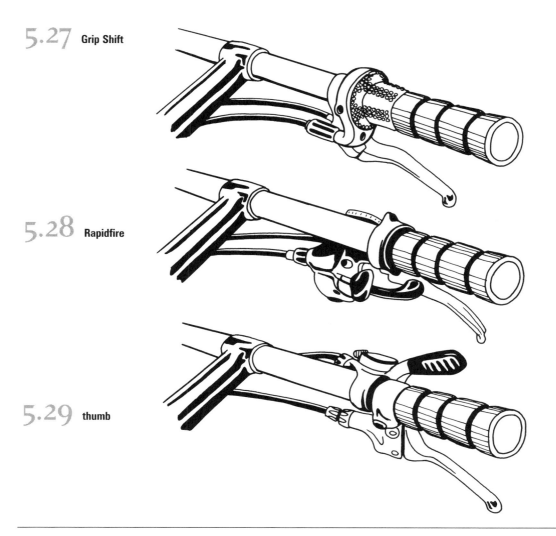

5.27 **Grip Shift**

5.28 **Rapidfire**

5.29 **thumb**

replacing
shifter units

NOTE

RapidFire Remote installation: Mount the lower lever to the end of the bar end with a 2mm hex key, as described in section V-9.

V-20: REPLACING GRIP SHIFT

1. Remove the old shifter. Replace the brake lever if you had to remove it to get the old shifter off.

2. Loosen and slide the brake lever inward to allow room for the Grip Shift.

3. Slide the appropriate (right or left) Grip Shift on with the cable-exit barrel pointing inward.

4. Slide on the plastic washer over the bar that separates the grip from the Grip Shift.

5. Replace the grip (and bar end).

6. Butt the Grip Shift up against the grip with the plastic washer separating them. Rotate the shifter until the cable-exit barrel is oriented so it will not interfere with the brake lever.

7. Tighten the Grip Shift to the handlebars with a 3mm Allen wrench.

8. Butt the brake lever up against the Grip Shift (or space it apart if you prefer), and rotate the brake lever to the position you like, and tighten it down.

9. Reinstall/replace cable and tighten it.

V-21: TOP-MOUNTED THUMB SHIFTERS

1. Remove the bar end, grip, brake

5.30 thumb shifter exploded

lever and old shifter.

2. Slide on the new shifter.

3. Slide on the brake lever, grip and bar end.

4. Tighten the bar end and brake lever in the position you want.

5. Tighten the shifter in the position that is comfortable for you that allows easy access to the cable-barrel adjuster and free cable travel.

6. Reinstall/replace cable and tighten it.

V.E: SHIFTER MAINTENANCE

V-22: GRIP SHIFT

Grip Shift (Fig. 5.27) requires periodic lubrication. The exploded diagrams in Figs. 5.20 and 5.21 and Section V-10 detail how to take a shifter apart, clean it and grease it. Use only non-lithium (preferably silicone-based Teflon) grease. As long as you have the shifter disassembled, you might as well replace the cable (Section V-10), since shifter disassembly is required for the task.

V-23: RAPIDFIRE SL AND RAPIDFIRE PLUS

Shimano Rapidfire SL and Rapidfire Plus

shifters (Fig. 5.28) are not designed to be disassembled by the consumer. Squirting a little chain lube inside every now and then is a good idea, though. If a Rapidfire Plus lever stops working, it requires purchasing a new shifter unit. The brake lever does not need to be replaced; just bolt the new shifter to it.

Sometimes the gear indicator unit stops working, and it can even jam the lever and stop it from reaching all of the gears. This was most common in the 1993 and 1994 models. The indicators can be removed from the shifter with a small screwdriver. The indicator's link arm needs to be stuck back into the hole from whence it came. Once the indicator jams, you can expect it to happen again; eventually, you will want to replace the lever or replace or dispense with the indicator.

V-24: ORIGINAL RAPIDFIRE

Shimano's first attempt at a two-lever mountain shifter did not work very well and if you are having trouble with yours, I recommend throwing it out and getting a new system. You know you have original Rapidfire if the thumb operates both the down- and up-shift levers. Newer Rapidfire SL and Plus levers (Fig. 5.28) require the thumb only for downshifting; the forefinger reaches around to perform the upshifts.

V-25: THUMB SHIFTERS

Indexed (click) thumb shifters (Fig. 5.30) are not to be disassembled further than removing them from their clamp. Periodic (semi-annual or so) lubrication with chain lube is recommended and is best accomplished from the back side once the shifter assembly is removed from its clamp.

Frictional (non-clicking) thumb shifters can be disassembled, cleaned, greased, and reassembled.

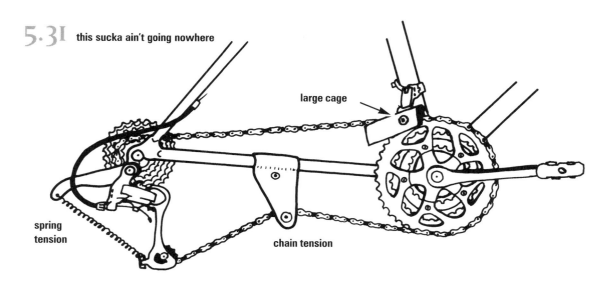

5.31 **this sucka ain't going nowhere**

large cage

spring tension

chain tension

Put the parts back the way you found them. You can avoid the hassle of disassembly by squirting chain lube in instead.

V-26: SPECIAL DOWNHILL-SPECIFIC DRIVETRAIN ADAPTATIONS

Tension arms, rollers, chain guards and giant front derailleur cages have become a part of downhill racing, due to the extraordinary demands it places on a chain drive system. These after-market products are outside of the scope of this book, but things like the chain tensioners and front derailleur cage extensions (Fig. 5.31) are fairly obvious in their function and quite easy to service.

Internal-planetary-gear hubs eliminate the derailleurs while adding weight and complexity; unless you are experienced at it avoid disassembling these puppies.

V-27: CONTINUOUSLY VARIABLE TRANSMISSIONS (CVTS)

Continuously Variable Transmissions regularly appear and disappear from the bike market. They are usually chain or belt driven and are intended to provide the rider with every possible gear

combination within the system's range. So far, none of them has proved viable in the market-place, so I haven't included any in this book.

V.F: DERAILLEUR MAINTENANCE

V-28: JOCKEY WHEEL MAINTENANCE

The jockey wheels on a derailleur will wear out over time. For best performance, standard jockey wheels should be overhauled every 200-500 miles. That should take care of the guck that the chain and the trail regularly deliver to them. The mounting bolts on jockey wheels also need to be checked regularly. If a loose jockey-wheel bolt falls off while you are riding, you will need to follow the procedure for a broken rear derailleur on the trail in Chapter 3.

Standard jockey wheels have a center bushing sleeve made of either steel or ceramic. Some expensive models have cartridge bearings. A washer with a curved rim facing inward is usually installed on both sides of a standard jockey wheel. Some jockey wheels also have rubber seals around the edges of these washers.

V-29: PROCEDURE FOR OVERHAULING STANDARD JOCKEY WHEELS

1. Remove the jockey wheels by undoing the bolts that hold them to the derailleur (Fig. 5.32). This usually takes a 3mm Allen wrench. Note which wheel goes on the top and bottom.

2. Wipe all parts clean with a rag. Solvent is usually not necessary but can be used.

3. If the teeth on the jockey wheels are broken or worn off, replace the wheels.

4. Smear grease over each bolt and sleeve and inside each jockey wheel.

5. Reassemble the jockey wheels on the derailleur. Make sure you replace the top jockey wheel on top and visa versa. Be sure to orient the cage plate properly (the larger part of the cage plate should be at the bottom jockey wheel).

V-30: CARTRIDGE BEARING JOCKEY WHEEL OVERHAUL

If the cartridge bearings in high-end jockey wheels (bottom, Fig. 5.32) do not turn freely, they can usually be overhauled.

1. With a single-edge razor blade, pry the plastic cover off one or, preferably, both sides of the bearing.

2. With a toothbrush and solvent, clean the bearings. Use citrus-based solvent, and wear gloves and glasses to protect skin and eyes.

3. Blow the solvent out with compressed air or your tire pump and allow the parts to dry.

4. Squeeze new grease into the bearings and replace the covers.

V-31: REAR DERAILLEUR OVERHAUL

Except for the jockey wheels and pivots, most rear derailleurs are not designed to be disassembled. If the pivot springs seem to be operating

5.32 **jockey wheel exploded**

effectively, all you need to do is overhaul the jockey wheels (see above), and clean and lubricate the parallelogram and spring as follows.

V-32: MINOR WIPE AND LUBE

1. Clean the derailleur as well as you can with a rag, including between the parallelogram plates.

2. Drip chain lube on both ends of every pivot pin

3. If you have the clothespin-type spring in the parallelogram (as opposed to the full coil spring running diagonally from one corner of the parallelogram to the other), put a dab of grease where the spring end slides along the underside of the outer parallelogram plate.

V-33: UPPER PIVOT OVERHAUL

1. Remove the rear derailleur; it usually takes a 5mm Allen wrench to unscrew it from the frame and to disconnect the cable.

2. With a screwdriver, pry the circlip (Fig. 5.33) off of the threaded end of the mounting bolt. Don't lose it; it will tend to fly when it comes off.

3. Pull the bolt and spring out of the derailleur.

4. Clean and dry the parts with or without the

use of solvent.

5. Grease liberally, and replace the parts.

6. Each end of the spring has a hole that it needs to go into. If there are several holes, and you don't know which one it was in before, try the middle one. (If the derailleur does not keep tension on the chain well enough, you can later try another hole that increases the spring tension.)

7. Push it all together, and replace the circlip with pliers.

V-34: LOWER PIVOT OVERHAUL

1. Locate and unscrew the tall cage-stop screw on the derailleur cage (Fig. 5.1); it is located near the upper jockey wheel. It is designed to maintain tension on the lower pivot spring and is what prevents the cage from springing all of the way around. Once the screw is removed, slowly guide the cage around until the spring tension is relieved.

2. Unscrew the lower pivot bolt using a 4mm, 5mm, or 6mm Allen wrench. Be sure to hold the jockey wheel cage to keep it from twisting.

3. Determine in which hole the spring end has been placed. Remove the spring.

4. Clean and dry the bolt and the spring with a rag. Solvent may be used if necessary.

5. Grease all parts liberally.

6. Replace the spring ends in their holes in either piece. Use the middle hole if you have a choice and aren't certain which it came out of.

7. Screw the bolt back into the jockey-wheel cage plate.

8. Twist the jockey wheel-cage plate counterclockwise to tension the spring, and replace the cage stop screw.

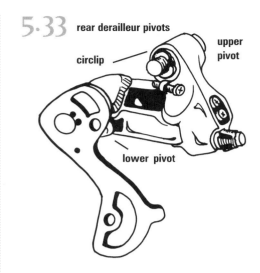

5.33 rear derailleur pivots

circlip

upper pivot

lower pivot

V-35: PARALLELOGRAM OVERHAUL

Very few derailleurs can be completely disassembled. Those that can have removable pins holding them together. The pins will have circlips on the ends that can be popped off with a screwdriver to remove the pins. If you have such a type, disassemble it in a box so the circlips do not fly away. With this type of derailleur, disassemble it carefully. Make note of where each part belongs so that you can get it back together again. Clean all parts, grease them, and reassemble.

V-36: REPLACING STOCK BOLTS WITH LIGHTWEIGHT VERSIONS

Lightweight aluminum and titanium derailleur bolts are available as replacement items for many derailleurs. Removing and replacing jockey wheel bolts is simple, as long as you keep all of the jockey wheel parts together and put the inner cage plate back on the way it was. Upper and lower pivot bolts are replaced following the instructions outlined earlier in this chapter for overhauling the pivots (Sections V-33 and V-34).

the transmission

V

Troubleshooting REAR derailleur and RIGHT—hand shifter problems

TROUBLESHOOTING REAR DERAILLEUR AND RIGHT—HAND SHIFTER PROBLEMS

Rear derailleur and right—hand shifter problems

Once you have made the adjustments outlined above, your drivetrain should be quiet and have all the gears lined up; the drivetrain should stay in gear, even if you turn the crank backwards. If you cannot fine-tune the adjustment so that each click with the right shifter results in a clean, quick shift, you need to check some of the following possibilities. For skipping- and jumping-chain problems, see also the "Troubleshooting" section at the end of Chapter 4.

V-37: SHIFTER COMPATIBILITY

Check to see if your shifter is compatible with your derailleur. This is especially important if either of them were not original equipment on your bike. Be certain, if the shifter is a different brand than your derailleur, that they are nonetheless designed to work together. The most common example of this is SRAM's Grip Shift, which is specifically designed to work with a Shimano rear derailleur. SRAM now manufactures it's own SRAM ESP derailleur, which works only with a longer-pull Grip Shift designed for it, incompatible with other derailleurs.

If your shifter and derailleur are incompatible, you will need to change one of them. Quality being equal, I suggest replacing the less costly item.

V-38: STICKY CABLES

Check your derailleur cables to be sure that they run smoothly through the housing. Sticky cable movement will cause sluggish shifting.

Lubricate the cable by smearing it with chain lube or a specific lubricant that came with your shifters (Section V-15).

If lubricating the cable does not help; replace the cable and housing (see Sections V-6 to V-14).

V-39: BENT REAR DERAILLEUR HANGER

A bent hanger will hold the derailleur crooked and bedevil shifting. Instructions for straightening the hanger are in Chapter 14, Section XIV-5.

V-40: BENT OR WORN-OUT REAR DERAILLEUR CAGE

A bent derailleur cage will line the jockey wheels up at angle. Mild bending can be straightened by hand, eyeballing the crank for reference.

V-41 LOOSE PIVOTS (WORN-OUT REAR DERAILLEUR)

A loose and floppy rear derailleur will not shift well. Replace it.

TROUBLESHOOTING FRONT DERAILLEUR AND LEFT—HAND SHIFTER PROBLEMS

V-42: CHAIN SUCK

For chain suck problems, see Troubleshooting at the end of Chapter 4 (Fig. 4.13).

V-43: CHAIN LINE

If, (1), your chain falls off to the inside no matter how much you adjust the low-gear-limit screw, cable tension, and derailleur position, or (2) you have chain rub, noise, or auto-shift problems in mild cross-gears that are not corrected with derailleur adjustments, you have chain-line problems.

Chain line is the relative alignment of the front chainrings with the rear cogs; it is the imaginary line connecting the center of the middle chainring with the middle of the cogset (Fig. 5.34). This line should in theory be straight and parallel with the vertical plane of the bicycle. Even owners of new bikes may find they have poor chain lines, due to mismatched cranks and bottom brackets.

Chain line is adjusted by moving or replacing the bottom bracket to move the cranks left or right. You can roughly check the chain line by placing a long straight edge against the middle chainring and back to the rear cogs; it should come out in the center of the rear cogs. Continue on for a more precise method, if you want to get your shifting as good as possible.

V-44: PRECISE CHAIN-LINE MEASUREMENT

You will need a caliper. The position of the middle chainring, as measured as the distance from the center of the seat tube to the center of the middle chainring, is often called the chain line, although this is only the front end point of the line.

1. Find the middle chainring position, or front end point of the chain line (**CLF** in Fig. 5.34).

a. Measure from the left side of the down tube to the outside of the large chainring (d1 in Fig. 5.34). (Do not measure from the seat tube, as it may be ovalized).

b. Measure the distance from the right side of the down tube to the inside of the inner chainring (**d2** in Fig. 5.34).

c. Add these two measurements, and divide the sum by two.

$$CLF = (d1 + d2)/2$$

2. Find the rear end point of the chain line (**CLR** in Fig. 5.34), which is the distance from the center of the plane of the bicycle to the center of the cogset.

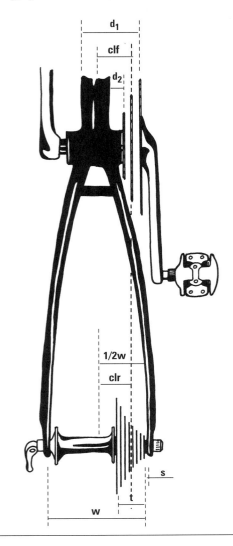

5.34 **measuring chain line**

a. Measure the thickness of the cog stack, end to end (**t** in Fig. 5.34).

b. Measure the space between the face of the smallest cog and the inside face of the dropout (**S** in Fig. 5.34).

c. Measure the length of the axle from dropout to dropout (**W** in Fig. 5.34); this dimension is also called "axle overlock dimension", referring to the distance from locknut face to locknut face on either end. Generally, on any mountain bike since 1989 or so, this will be 135mm.

d. Subtract one-half of the thickness of the cog

V

the transmission

TROUBLE—
SHOOTING
FRONT
DERAILLEURS
AND
SHIFTERS

stack and the distance from the inside face of the right rear dropout from one half of the rear axle length. **CLR = W/2 - t/2 - S**

3. If CLF = CLR, your chain line is perfect. This, however, almost never occurs on a mountain bike, due to considerations about chainstay clearance, prevention of chain rub on large chainrings in cross gears, and inward movement range of the front derailleur. Shimano specifies a "chain line" (meaning CLF, the front end point of the chain line) as 47.5mm for bikes with a 68mm-width bottom bracket shell, and 50mm for 73mm-width shells (both of these specified dimensions are plus-or-minus 1mm). CLF, the rear-end point of the chain line, on the other hand, usually comes out around 44.5mm. Shimano's specifications, then, are primarily intended to avoid chainring rub on chainstays, not on ideal shifting.

Your bike will shift best and run quietest if you get the chain line at around 45mm, but you may have some problems there, such as: (a) your inner and middle chainrings might rub the chainstays, (b) your front derailleur may bottom out on the seat tube before moving inward enough to shift to the inner chainring (this is particularly a problem with bikes with oversized seat tubes), and (c) when crossing to the smallest cog from the inner and even middle chainring, the chain may rub on the next larger ring (this is not a problem if you simply avoid those cross gears).

My general recommendation is to have the chainrings in toward the frame as far as you can without rubbing the frame or losing front derailleur shifting performance due to bottoming out on the seat tube.

4. To improve the chain line, move the chainrings, since there is little or nothing you can do with the rear cog position. The chainrings are moved by using a different bottom bracket, by exchanging your bottom bracket spindle for a longer one, or by moving the bottom bracket right or left (bottom bracket

**TROUBLE—
SHOOTING
FRONT
DERAILLEURS
AND
SHIFTERS**

5.35 **third eye chain catcher**

installation and overhauling is covered in chapter 8).

NOTE

Some new bikes have terrible chain lines that can only be corrected by buying a new bottom bracket. This usually has to do with a conceptually impaired bean-counting product manager selecting the parts. Product managers know that customers often pay more attention to the quality of the cranks on the bike and little attention to the quality of the bottom bracket — an unseen part. With a cheap bottom bracket the cranks will sit way too far out, and the chain line will stink. You will have to replace the longer bottom bracket with a shorter one if you want to shift decently. Good shops will replace the bottom bracket before selling it to you.

ANOTHER NOTE

The chain line can also be off if the frame is out of alignment (Chapter 14, Section XIV-6). If that's the case, it is probably something you cannot fix yourself.

5. If improving the chain line does not fix your problem, or if you don't want to mess with the chain line, buy and install a Third Eye Chain Watcher (Fig. 5.35). This is an inexpensive plastic gizmo that clamps around the seat tube next to the inner chainring. Clamp it on and adjust the position so that it nudges the chain back on when it tries to fall off to the inside.

the wheels

tires, rims, hubs and cogs

"I'm just sitting here watching the wheels go round and round.

I really love to watch them roll." — JOHN LENNON

Early bicycles may have existed without pedals and steering systems, but they always had wheels. After all, without wheels, it ain't a bike! With the exception of recent molded composites, wheels on mountain bikes are strung together with spokes. The hub is at the center, and its bearings allow the wheel to turn freely around an axle. The rim is supported and aligned by the tension on the spokes. On most bikes, the rim serves as both support for the tire and as a braking surface. On the rear wheel, a cassette freehub or freewheel allows the wheel to spin while coasting and engages when force is applied to the pedals (Fig. 6.1).

The tires provide grip and traction for propulsion and steering. The air pressure in the tire is your first line of suspension and is the primary suspension system on most mountain bikes. On virtually all mountain bikes, inner tubes keep the air inside the tires.

This chapter addresses how to: fix a flat or replace a tire or tube; true a wheel; fix a broken spoke or bent rim; overhaul hubs; change rear cogs; and lubricate cassettes and freewheels. Have at it.

VI.A TIRES

Replacing or repairing tires and inner tubes

VI-1: REMOVING THE TIRE

1. Remove the wheel (See Chapter 2, Section II-2 and II-11).

2. If your tire is not already flat, deflate it.

tools

spoke wrench
13mm, 14mm,
   15mm, 16mm
   cone wrenches
17mm open-end
   wrench (or an
   adjustable
   wrench)
screwdriver
5mm, 6mm and
   10mm Allen wrenches
grease
oil
chain whip
cassette lockring
remover
large adjustable
   wrench
freewheel remover,
   if your bike
   does not have
   a cassette
pump
tire levers
tube patch kit

OPTIONAL

truing stand
wheel-dishing tool
linseed oil
tweezers
cog-wear indicator

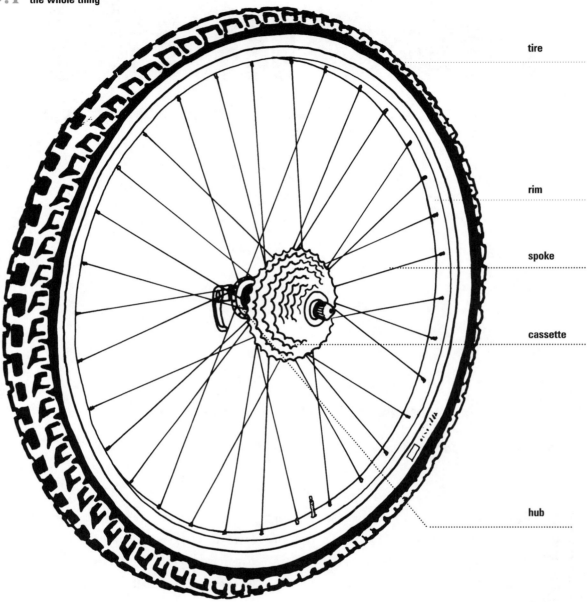

tire

rim

spoke

cassette

hub

tires

To deflate a Schrader valve (the kind of valve you would find on your car's tire), push down on the valve pin with something thin enough to fit in that won't break off, like a pen cap or a paper clip (Fig. 6.3).

Presta, or "French," valves are thinner and have a small threaded rod with a tiny nut on the end. To let air out, unscrew the little nut a few turns, and push down on the thin rod (Fig. 6.2). To seal, tighten the little nut down again (with your fingers only!); leave it tightened down for riding.

NOTE

If you have deep-section rims (i.e., Spinergy, Zipp or Hed), you will probably have "valve extenders"— thin threaded tubes that screw onto the valve stems. To deflate them, you need to insert a thin rod (a spoke is perfect) inside to release the air.

6.2 **presta valve**

6.3 **schrader valve**

letting air out

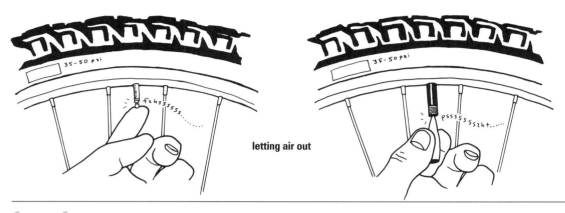

6.4-6.5 **removing tires with levers**

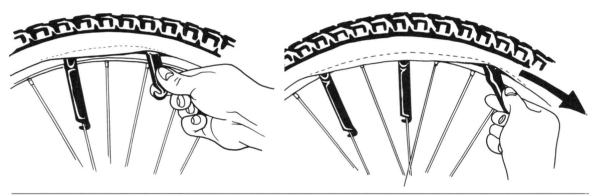

To install valve extenders so they seal properly and allow easy inflation, you need to unscrew the little nut on the Presta valve against the mashed threads at the top of the valve shaft (they are mashed to keep the nut from unscrewing completely off). Back the nut firmly into these mashed threads with a pair of pliers so it stays unscrewed and does not tighten back down against the valve stem and prevent air from going in when you pump it. You also should wrap a turn or two of Teflon pipe thread tape around the top threads on the valve stem before screwing on the valve extender to seal it; if you do not, air will leak out when pumping, and the pressure gauge on your pump will not give an accurate reading of the pressure in the tire. Tighten the valve extender onto the valve stem with a pair of pliers.

3. If you can push the tire bead off of the rim with your thumbs without using tire levers, by all means do it, since there is less chance of damaging either the tube or the tire.

4. If you can't get it off with your hands alone, insert a tire lever, scoop side up, between the rim sidewall and the tire until you catch the edge of the tire bead.

5. Push down on the lever until the tire bead is pulled out over the rim (see illustration above of tire removal with levers). If the lever has a hook on the other end, hook it onto the nearest spoke. Otherwise, keep holding it down.

6. Place the next lever a few inches away, and do the same thing with it (Fig. 6.4).

7. If needed, place a third lever a few inches farther on, pry it out, and continue sliding this lever

**tire
removal**

6.6 removing the inner tube

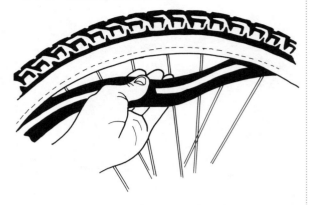

around the tire, pulling the bead out as you go (Fig. 6.5). Some people use their fingers under the bead to slide the tire off, but beware of cutting your fingers on sharp tire beads.

8. Once the bead is off on one side, pull the tube out (Fig. 6.6).

If you are patching or replacing the tube, you do not need to remove the other side of the tire from the rim. If you are replacing the tire, the other bead should come off easily with your fingers. If it does not, use the tire levers as outlined above.

VI-2: PATCHING AN INNER TUBE

1. If the leak location is not obvious, put some air in the tube to inflate it until it is two to three times larger than its deflated size. Be careful. You can explode it if you put too much air in, especially with latex or urethane tubes.

2. Listen/feel for air coming out, and mark the leak(s).

3. If you cannot find the leak by listening, submerge the tube under water. Look for air bubbling out (Fig. 6.7), and mark the spot(s).

Keep in mind that you can only patch small holes. If the hole is bigger than the eraser end of a pencil, a round patch is not likely to work. A slit of up to an inch or so can be repaired with a long oval patch.

VI-3: STANDARD PATCHES

1. Dry the tube thoroughly near the hole.

2. Rough up and clean the surface about a 1-inch radius around the hole with a small piece of sandpaper (usually supplied with the patch kit). Do not touch the sanded area, and don't rough up the tube with one of those little metal "cheese graters" that come with some patch kits. (They tend to do to your tube what they do to cheese.)

3. Use a patch kit designed for bicycle tires that have the thin, usually orange, gummy edges surrounding the black patches. Rema and Delta are common brands.

4. Apply patch cement in a thin, smooth layer all over an area centered on the hole (Fig. 6.8). Cover an area that is bigger than the size of the patch.

5. Let the glue dry until there are no more shiny, wet spots.

6. Remove the foil backing from the patch (but not the cellophane top cover).

7. Stick the patch over the hole, and push it down in place, making sure that all of the gummy edges are stuck down.

8. Remove the cellophane top covering, being careful not to peel off the edges of the patch (Fig. 6.9). Often, the cellophane top patch is scored. If you fold the patch, this cellophane will split at the scored cuts, allowing you to peel outward and avoid pulling

6.7 checking for puncture

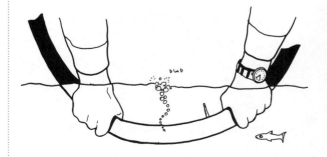

tubes

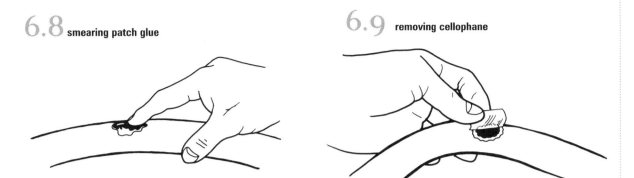

6.8 **smearing patch glue**

6.9 **removing cellophane**

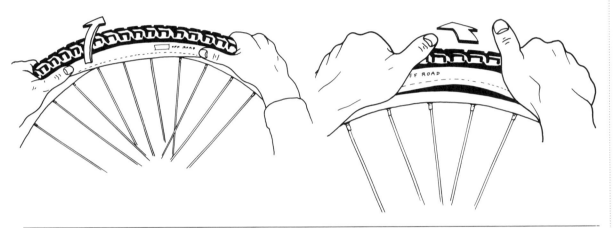

$6.10\text{-}11$ **installing tire by hand**

the newly-adhered patch away from the tube.

VI-4: GLUELESS PATCHES

There are a number of adhesive-backed patches on the market that do not require cement to stick them on. Most often, you simply need to clean the area around the hole with the little alcohol pad supplied with the patch. Let the alcohol dry, peel the backing, and stick on the patch. The advantage of glueless patches is that they are very fast to use, take little room in a seat bag, and you never open your patch kit to discover that your glue tube is dried up. On the downside, I have not found any that stick nearly as well as the standard type. With a standard patch installed, you can inflate the tube to look for more leaks without having to put the tube back in the tire. If you do that with a glueless patch,

it usually lifts the patch enough to start it leaking. You must install it in the tire and on the rim before putting air in it after patching.

VI-5: INSTALLING PATCHED OR NEW TUBE

Feel around the inside of the tire to see if there is still anything sticking through that can puncture the tube. This is best done by sliding a rag all the way around the inside of the tire. The rag will catch on anything sharp, and saves your fingers from being cut by whatever is stuck in the tire.

1. Replace any tire that has worn-out areas (inside or out) where the tread-casing fibers appear to be cut or frayed.

2. Examine the rim to be certain that the rim tape is in place and that there are no spokes or anything else sticking up that can puncture the tube. Replace

**patching
inner
tubes**

6.12 seating the tube

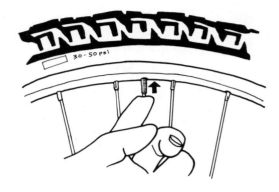

30-50 psi

the rim tape if necessary.

3. By hand, push one side bead of the tire onto the rim.

4. (Optional) Smear baby powder around the inside of the tire and on the outside of the tube, so the two do not adhere to each other. Don't inhale the stuff.

5. Put just enough air in the tube to give it shape. Close the valve, if Presta.

6. Push the valve through the valve hole in the rim.

7. Push the tube up inside the tire all of the way around.

8. Starting at the side opposite the valve stem, push the tire bead onto the rim with your thumbs. Be sure that the tube doesn't get pinched between the tire bead and the rim.

9. Work around the rim in both directions with your thumbs, pushing the tire onto the rim (Fig. 6.10). Finish from both sides at the valve (Fig. 6.11). You can usually install a mountain bike tire without tools. If you cannot, use tire levers, but make sure you don't catch any of the tube under the edge of the bead. Finish the same way, at the valve.

10. Re-seat the valve stem by pushing up on the valve after you have pushed the last bit of bead onto the rim (Fig. 6.12). You may have to manipulate the tire so that all the tube is tucked under the tire bead.

11. Go around the rim and inspect for any part of the tube that might be protruding out from under the edge of the tire bead. If you have a fold of the tube under the edge of the bead, it can blow the tire off the rim either when you inflate it or while you are riding. It will sound like a gun went off next to you and will leave you with an unpatchable tube.

12. Pump the tire up. Generally, 45-50 psi is a good amount. Much more, and the ride gets harsh. Much less, and you run the risk of a pinch flat or "snake bite."

VI-6: PATCHING TIRE CASING (SIDE WALL)

Unless it is an emergency, don't do it! If your casing is cut, get a new tire. Patching the tire casing is dangerous. No matter what you use as a patch, the tube will find a way to bulge out of the patched hole, and when it does your tire will go flat immediately. Imagine coming down a steep decent and suddenly your front tire goes complete flat — you get the picture. In emergency situations, you can put layers of non-stretchable material, such as a dollar bill, an empty energy bar wrapper (or two), even a short section of the exploded tube (double thickness is better) between the tube and tire (see Chapter 3, Section III-3B, Fig. 3.1).

VI-7: TIRE SEALANTS

Slime is primordial green goo filled with chopped fibers. When sloshing around in an inner tube, it flows to punctures and seals them. There are other tire sealants of different brands and colors as well; these instructions generally apply to them as well. Tire sealants can virtually eliminate flat tires other than sidewall cuts.

Only use Slime in a tube with a Schrader valve (Fig. 1.1, 6.3) without cuts in it and with the valve in good condition. You can put it in a tube with a slow leak; simply inject it as below, pump it up, and spin the wheel for about five minutes.

A. Slime installation into a tube that's already installed in a tire.

1. Shake Slime bottle.

2. Remove valve core using valve cap/core-remover packaged with the Slime.

3. Rotate the wheel so the valve stem is at the 4 o'clock position.

4. Cut off the bottle spout, and connect the bottle spout and valve stem with the supplied surgical tubing.

5. Squeeze the bottle slowly to inject the Slime.

6. Stop squeezing after injecting 4oz.; wait several minutes to clear the stem.

7. Remove the surgical tube.

8. Screw the valve core firmly back into the valve stem in a clockwise direction.

9. Inflate the tube.

If the tube has a leak, spin the wheel for five minutes to spread the Slime around in the tube.

NOTE

If you have Presta valves (Figs. 1.1 and 6.2), and you want to use tire sealant, you can purchase tubes with it already installed.

B. Maintaining tire-sealant-filled tubes

Pumping: Always have the stem at 4 o'clock and wait a minute for Slime to drain away; if you don't, Slime will leak out, eventually clogging the valve.

Sealing punctures:

1. If you find your tire flat, pump it up and ride it a bit to see if it seals.

2. If you get numerous punctures, you may need to pump repeatedly and ride before the tube seals up.

3. Pinch flats, caused by pinching the tube between the tire and rim, are hard to seal because the two "snake-bite" holes are on the side. Try laying the bike on the same side as the holes.

4. Imbedded nails and other foreign objects can

be removed; spin the wheel to seal the hole.

5. Punctures on the rim side of the tube will not seal, as the Slime is thrown to the outside.

6. Sidewall gashes need to be patched, and the tire needs to be replaced.

VI.B RIMS & SPOKES
VI-8: TRUING A WHEEL

level 2

For more information on truing wheels, see Chapter 12 on wheel building, section XII-4.

If your wheel has a wobble in it, you can fix it by adjusting the tension on the spokes. An extreme bend in the rim cannot be fixed by spoke truing alone, since the spoke tension on the two sides of the wheel will be so uneven that the wheel will rapidly fall apart.

1. Check that there are no broken spokes in the wheel, or any spokes that are so loose that they flop around. If there is a broken spoke, follow the replacement procedure in the following section, VI-9. If there is a single loose spoke, check to see that the rim is not dented or cracked in that area. I recommend replacing the rim if it is. If the rim looks okay, mark the loose spoke with a piece of tape, and tighten it up with the spoke wrench until it feels the same tension as adjacent spokes on the same side of the wheel (pluck the spoke and listen to the tone). Then follow the truing procedure below.

2. Grab the rim while the wheel is on the bike, and flex it side to side to check the hub bearing adjustment. If the bearings are loose, the wheel will clunk side to side. The hub will need to be tightened before you true the wheel, or the wheel will behave erratically. Follow the hub adjustment procedure, Section VI-12D, steps 28-31 in this chapter.

3. Put the wheel in a truing stand, if you have one. Otherwise, leave it on the bike. Suspend the bike in

6.13 tightening and loosening spokes

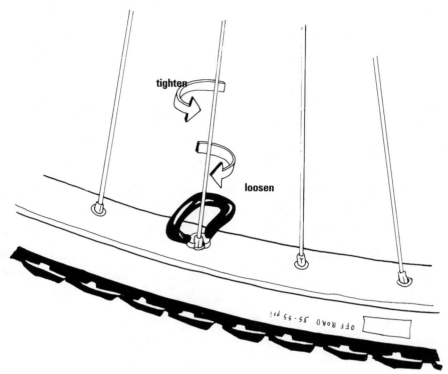

tighten

loosen

OFF ROAD 35-55 psi

truing a wheel

a bike stand or from the ceiling, or turn it upside down on the handlebars and saddle.

4. Adjust the truing stand feeler, or hold one of your brake pads so that it scrapes the rim at the biggest wobble.

5. Where the rim scrapes, tighten the spoke (or spokes) that come(s) to the rim from the opposite

side of the hub, and loosen the spoke(s) that come(s) from the same side of the hub as the rim scrapes (Figs. 12.16 and 12.17-or 6.14 and 6.15). This will pull the rim away from the feeler or brake pad.

When correcting a wheel that is laterally out of true (wobbles side-to-side), always tighten spokes in pairs: one spoke coming from one side of the wheel,

6.14-15 lateral truing

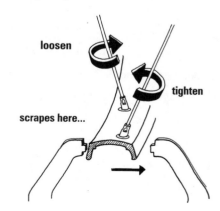

loosen

tighten

scrapes here...

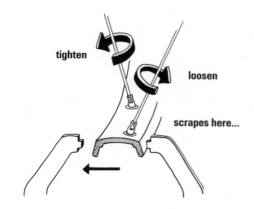

tighten

loosen

scrapes here...

hubs

6.16 **weaving a new spoke**

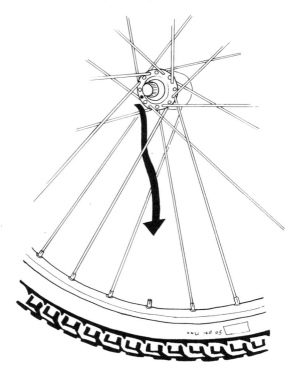

the other from the opposite side. Tightening spokes is like opening a jar upside down. With the jar right-side up, turning the lid to the left opens the jar, but this reverses when you turn the jar upside down (try it and see). Spoke nipples are just like the lid on that upside-down jar. In other words, when the nipples are at the bottom of the rim, counter-clockwise tightens, and clockwise loosens (Fig. 6.13). The opposite is true when the nipples to be turned are at the top. It may take you a few attempts before you catch on, but you will eventually get it. If you temporarily make the wheel worse, simply undo what you have done and start over.

It is best to tighten and loosen by small amounts (about a quarter-turn at a time), decreasing the amount you turn the spoke nipples as you move away from the spot where the rim scrapes the hardest. If the wobble gets worse, then you are turning the spokes the wrong direction.

6. As the rim moves more toward center, readjust the truing-stand feeler or the brake pad so that it again finds the most out-of-true spot on the wheel.

7. Check the wobble first on one side of the wheel and then the other, adjusting spokes accordingly, so that you don't end up pulling the whole wheel off center by chasing wobbles only on one side. As the wheel gets closer to true, you will need to decrease the amount you turn the spokes to avoid over-correcting.

8. Accept a certain amount of wobble, especially if truing in a bike, since the in-the-bike method of wheel truing is not very accurate and is not at all suited for making a wheel absolutely true. If you have access to a wheel-dishing tool, check to make sure that the wheel is centered (Chapter 12, section XII-5).

VI-9: REPLACING A BROKEN SPOKE

level 2

Go to the bike store and get a new spoke of the same length. Remember: the spokes on the front wheel are usually not the same length as the spokes on the rear. Also, the spokes on the drive side of the rear wheel are almost always shorter than those on the other side.

1. Make sure you are using the proper thickness and length spoke.

2. Thread the spoke through the spoke hole in the hub flange. If the broken spoke is on the drive side of the rear wheel, you will need to remove the cassette cogs or the freewheel to get at the hub flange (Sections VI-16 and VI-17).

3. Weave the new spoke in with the other spokes just as it was before (Fig. 6.16). It may take some bending to get it in place.

4. Thread it into the same nipple, if the nipple is in good shape. Otherwise, use a new nipple; you'll

6.17 front hub with cartridge bearing

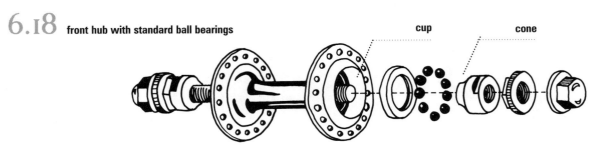

6.18 front hub with standard ball bearings   **cup**   **cone**

---

need to remove the tire, tube, and rim strip to
install it.

5. Mark the new spoke with a piece of tape, and
tighten it up about as snugly as the neighboring
spokes on that side of the wheel.

6. Follow the steps for truing a wheel as outlined
above, section VI-8.

VI.C HUBS

VI-10: OVERHAULING HUBS

Hubs should turn smoothly and
noiselessly. If they are regularly maintained, you can expect them to still be
running smoothly when you are ready
to give up on the rest of your bike.

There are two general types of hubs: the standard
"cup-and-cone" type, and the "sealed bearing" (or
"cartridge bearing") type. All hubs have a "hub shell"
that contains the axle and bearings and is connected to the rim with spokes, or in the case of disc
wheels, by sheets of composite material.

Standard "cup-and-cone" hubs have loose ball

bearings that roll along very smooth bearing surfaces called the "bearing races" or "cups," with an
axle going through the center of the hub. These hubs
also have conical-shaped nuts threaded onto the
axle called "cones" (Fig. 6.18). These cones press the
bearings gently inside the cups and guide the bearings as they travel along the bearing races. The cone
surface that comes in contact with the bearings has
been machined in high-quality hubs to minimize friction. The operation of the hub depends on the
smoothness and lubrication of the cones, ball bearings, and bearing races. Outside of the cones are
one or more spacers (or washers) followed by
threaded locknuts that tighten down against the
cones and spacers to keep the hub in proper adjustment. The rear hub will have more spacers on both
sides, especially on the drive side (Fig. 6.27).

The term "sealed-bearing" hub is a bit of a misnomer, since many cup-and-cone hubs offer better
protection against dirt and water than some sealed-
bearing hubs. The phrase "cartridge-bearing hub" is
more accurate, since the distinguishing feature of

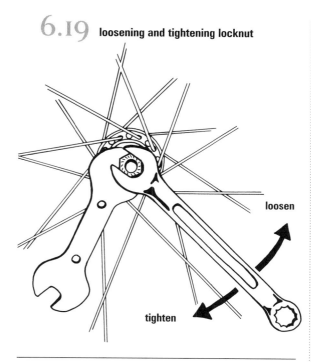

6.19 **loosening and tightening locknut**

loosen

tighten

these hubs is that the bearings, races and cones are all assembled as a complete unit at the bearing factory, and then plugged into a hub shell machined to accept the cartridge. Cartridge-bearing front hubs have two bearings, one on either end of the hub shell (Fig. 6.17). Rear hubs (Fig. 6.26) have at least that, and often come with additional bearing cartridges to stabilize the rear cassette (the part onto which the rear cogs are attached).

Cartridge-bearing hubs can have any number of axle assembly types. Some have a threaded axle with locknuts quite similar to a cup-and-cone hub. Much more common on mountain bikes are aluminum axles, often very thick with correspondingly large bearings. Their end caps usually snap on or are held on with set screws or circlips. The large diameter axles and bearings are meant to prevent independent movement of the legs of suspension forks or rear suspension assemblies.

VI-11: ALL HUBS

1. Remove the wheel from the bike (Chapter 2,

Sections II-2 and II-11).

2. Remove the quick-release skewer or the nuts and washers holding the wheel onto the bike.

VI-12: OVERHAUL STANDARD "CUP-AND-CONE" HUB, FRONT OR REAR

Take some time to evaluate the hub's condition before disassembling it. That will help you to isolate problems. Spin the hub while holding the axle, and turn the axle while holding the hub. Does it turn roughly? Is the axle bent or broken? Wobble the axle side to side. Is the bearing adjustment loose?

N O T E

Some hubs with large rubber seals covering the axle nuts (Shimano STX comes to mind) can squeal hideously, even though the inside workings of the hub are in good shape. The squeal can be caused by dust in the seal, or mis-seating of it against the hub face. The seal can be pulled off by squeezing and yanking it. Brush it off, put it back into its mating grooves on the hub, and it will probably be silent.

a. Disassembly:

1. Set the wheel flat on a table or workbench. Slip a cone wrench of the appropriate size (usually 13mm, 14mm or 15mm) onto the wrench flats on one of the cones. On a rear wheel, work on the non-cog side.

2. Put an appropriately sized wrench or adjustable wrench on the locknut on the same side.

3. While holding the cone with the cone wrench, loosen the locknut (Fig. 6.19). This may take considerable force, since these are often fastened together very tightly to maintain the hub's adjustment. Make sure that you are unscrewing the locknut counter-clockwise ("lefty loosey, righty tighty").

4. As soon as the locknut loosens, move the cone wrench from the cone on top to the cone on the opposite end of the axle, in order to hold the axle in place as you unscrew the lock nut. It will generally

6.20 removing dustcap

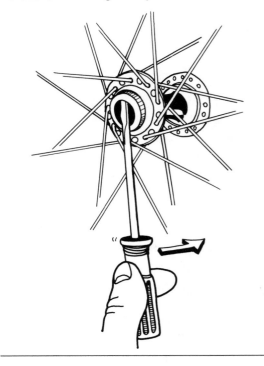

unscrew with your fingers; use a wrench on it if necessary to get past any damaged threads.

5. Slide any spacers off. If they will not slide off, the cone will push them off when you unscrew it. Please note that some spacers have a small tooth or "key" that corresponds to a notch on the axle.

6. Unscrew the cone off of the axle. Again, you may need to hold the opposite cone with a wrench and use a wrench on this cone. An easy way to keep track of the various nuts, spacers and cones is to lay them down on your work bench in the order they were removed, or you can slide a twist-tie through all the parts in the correct order of orientation. Either method serves as an easy guide when reassembling the hub.

7. Put your hand over the end of the hub from which you removed the nuts and spacers (to catch any bearings that might fall out), and flip the wheel over. Have a rag underneath the wheel to catch stray bearings.

8. Pull the axle up and out, being careful not to lose any bearings that might fall out of the hub or that might be stuck to the axle. Leave the cone, spacers and locknut all tightened together on the opposite end of the axle from the one you disassembled. If you are replacing a bent or broken axle, measure the amount of axle sticking out beyond the locknut. Put the cone, spacers and locknut on the new axle identically.

9. Remove all of the ball bearings from both sides of the hub. They may stick to a screwdriver with a coating of grease on the tip, or you can push them down through the center of the hub and out the other side with the screwdriver. Tweezers or a small magnet might also be useful for removing bearings. Put the bearings in a cup, a jar lid, or the like. Count the bearings, and make sure you have the same number from each side.

10. Gently pop off the seals that are pressed into either end of the hub shell with a screwdriver (Fig. 6.20). Be careful not to deform them; leave them in if you can't pop them out without damage. If they are not removed, it is tedious, but not impossible, to clean the dirty grease out of their concave inside with a rag and a thin screwdriver.

b. Cleaning:

11. Wipe the hub shell out with a rag. Remove all dirt and grease, from the bearing surfaces. Using a screwdriver, push a rag through the axle hole through the hub and spin it to clean out any grease or dirt. Wipe off the outer faces of the shell. Finish with a very clean rag on the bearing surfaces. They should shine and be completely free of dirt or grease. If you let your hub go too long between overhauls, the grease may have solidified and glazed over so completely that you will need a solvent to remove it. Use gloves and solvent. If you have a rear cassette hub, take this opportunity to lubricate the

hubs

cassette. (See "Lubricating cassettes and freewheels" later in this chapter.)

12. Wipe down the axle, nuts and cones with a rag. Clean the cones really well with a clean rag. Again, solvent may be required if the grease has solidified. Get any dirt out of the threads on the disassembled axle end, as the cone will then push this into the hub upon reassembly.

13. Wipe the grease and dirt off of the seals. A rag over the end of a screwdriver is sometimes useful to get inside. Again, glaze-hard grease may have to be removed with a solvent. Keep solvent out of the freehub body.

N O T E

Using new ball bearings when overhauling standard "cup-and-cone" hubs assures round, smooth bearings; however, do not avoid performing an overhaul just because you don't have any new ball bearings. Inspect the ball bearings carefully. If there is even the slightest hint of uneven wear or pitting on the balls, cups or cones, throw the bearings out and complete the overhaul with new bearings. Err on the side of caution.

14. Wipe the bearings off by rubbing all of them together between two rags. This may be sufficient to clean them completely, but small specks of dirt can still adhere to them, so I prefer to take the next step as well.

15. If you are overhauling low-quality hubs, skip to step 16.

Super clean and polish the bearings. I prefer to wash them in a plugged sink with an abrasive soap like Lava, rubbing them between my hands as if I were washing my palms. This really gets them shining, unless they are caked with glaze-hard grease. Make sure you have plugged the sink drain! This method has the added advantage of getting my hands super clean for the assembly step. It is silly to

contaminate your super-clean parts with dirty hands. If there is hardened glaze on the bearings, soak them in solvent. If that does not remove it, go buy new bearings at the bike shop. Take a few of the old bearings along so you are sure to buy the right size.

16. Dry all bearings and any other wet parts. Inspect the bearings and bearing surfaces carefully. If any of the bearings have pits or gouges in them, replace all of them. Same goes for the cones. A lack of sheen or a patina on balls and cones indicates wear and is cause for replacement. Most bike shops stock replacement cones. If the bearing races (or cups) in the hub shell are pitted, the only thing you can do is buy new hubs. Regular maintenance can prevent pitted hub bearing races.

c. Assembly and lubrication:

17. Press the seals or dust covers in on both ends of the hub shell.

18. Smear grease with your clean finger into the bearing race on one end of the hub shell. I like using light-colored or clear grease so that I can see if it gets dirty, but any bike grease will do. Grease not only lubricates the bearings, it also forms a barrier to dirt and water. Use enough grease to cover the

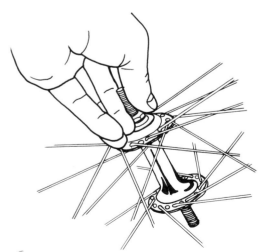

6.21 **holding axle to flip wheel over**

assembly and
lubrication
of cup-and-
cone hubs

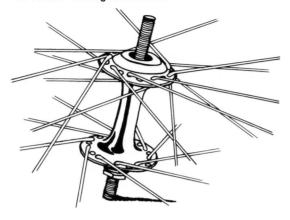

6.22 setting axle on floor

balls halfway. Too much grease will slow the hub by packing around the axle.

19. Stick half of the ball bearings into the grease, making sure you put in the same number of bearings that came out. Distribute them uniformly around in the bearing race.

20. Smear grease on the cone that is still attached to the axle, and slide the axle into the hub shell. Lift the wheel up a bit (30-degree angle), so you can push the axle in until the cone slides into position, and keeps all the bearings in place. It is important to replace the axle and cone assembly into the same side of the hub from which it was removed on rear hubs due to spacing for cogs.

21. Holding the axle pushed inward with one hand to secure the bearings, turn the wheel over (Fig. 6.21).

22. Smear grease into the bearing race that is now facing up. Lift the wheel and allow the axle to slide down just enough so that it is not sticking up past the bearing race. Make sure no bearings fall out of the bottom. If the race and bearings are properly greased and the axle remains in the hub shell, they are not likely to fall out.

23. While the top end of the axle is still below the bearing race, place the remaining bearings uniformly around in the grease. Make sure you have insert-

ed the correct number of bearings.

24. Slide the axle into place by setting the wheel down on the table, so that the wheel rests on the lower axle end, seating the cone up into the bearings (Fig. 6.22).

25. Using your fingers, screw the top cone down into place, seating it snugly onto the bearings. Covering the top cone with a film of grease is also a good idea.

26. In correct order, slide on the washer and any spacers. Watch for those washers with the little tooth or "key" that fits into the lengthwise groove in the axle.

27. Use your finger to screw on the locknut. Note that the two sides of the locknut are not the same. If you are unsure about which way the locknut goes back on, check the orientation of the locknut that is on the opposite end of the axle (this locknut was not removed during this overhaul and is assumed to be in the correct orientation). As a general rule, the rough surface of the locknut faces out so that it can get a better hold on the dropout.

6.23 tightening and loosening locknut

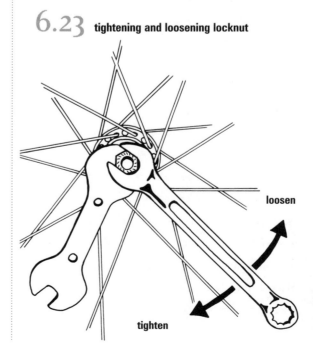

loosen

tighten

d. Hub adjustment:

28. Thread the cone onto the axle until it lightly contacts the bearings. The axle should turn smoothly without any roughness or grinding, and there should be a small amount of lateral play. Thread the locknut down until it is snug against the cone. The slight looseness will be taken out when the quick-release skewer is tightened down with the wheel in the frame. If the hub is a bolt-on type without a quick-release skewer, you don't want any play in it.

29. Place the cone wrench into the flats of the hub cone. Tighten the locknut with another wrench (Fig. 6.23). Tighten it about as tightly as you can against the cone and spacers, in order to hold the adjustment. Be aware that you can ruin the hub if you accidentally tighten the cone down against the bearings instead of against the locknut.

30. If the adjustment is off, loosen the locknut while holding the cone with the cone wrench. If the hub is too tight, unscrew the cone a bit. If the hub is too loose, screw the cone in a bit.

31. Repeat Steps 28-30 until the hub adjustment feels right. It should have a slight amount of end play so that the pressure of the quick-release skewer will compress it to perfect adjustment. Tighten the locknut firmly against the cone to hold the adjustment.

N O T E

You may find that tightening the locknut against the cone suddenly turns your "Mona Lisa" perfect hub adjustment into something slightly less beautiful. If it is too tight, back off both cones (with a cone wrench on either side of the hub, each on one cone) a fraction of a turn. If too loose, tighten both locknuts a bit. If still off, you might have to loosen one side and go back to step 29. It's rare that I get a hub adjustment perfectly "dialed-in" on the first try, so expect that you are going to have to tinker with the adjustment a bit before it's right.

32. Put the skewer back into the hub. Make sure that the conical springs have their narrow ends to the inside.

33. Install the wheel in the bike, tightening the skewer. Check that the wheel spins well without any side play at the rim. If it needs readjustment, go back to Step 31.

34. Congratulate yourself on a job well done! Hub overhaul is a delicate job, and it makes a difference in the longevity and performance of your bike.

VI-13: OVERHAUL CARTRIDGE-BEARING HUB

Cartridge-bearing hubs generally do not need much maintenance; however, if you ride through water above your hubs, you can expect water and dirt to get through any kind of seal. If the ball bearings inside the cartridges get wet, they should be overhauled or replaced.

There are many types of cartridge-bearing hubs, and it is outside the scope of this book to explain how to disassemble every one of them. Generally, there will be an end cap that can be removed by just pulling it off, by loosening a set screw on the cap, or by unscrewing the axle from either end with two 5mm Allen wrenches; the ends of the axle on either end will have a 5mm hex cut inside. Once the end cap is removed, you can often smack the end of the axle with a soft hammer or on a table, and it will push the opposite bearing out (Fig. 6.24). Pop the other bearing out the same way. The axle usually has a shoulder on either side, internal to the bearings, which can be used to force the bearings out. Simply tap the axle with a soft hammer and the shoulder should force the bearings out of the hub. Cartridge bearings are vulnerable to lateral stress; if you have to use a lot of force to pound them out, they will need to be replaced. Be careful when tap-

VI

hubs

overhauling
cartridge
bearing hubs

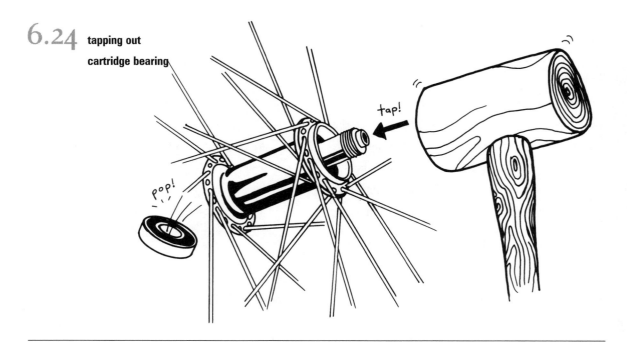

6.24 **tapping out cartridge bearing**

tap!

pop!

ping them back in; hold one of the old bearings against each new bearing, and hit the old bearing with the hammer.

Once the cartridge bearings are out, you can sometimes overhaul them (otherwise you'll need to buy new ones):

1. Gently pop the bearing covers off with a single-edge razor blade (Fig. 6.25).

2. Squirt citrus-based solvent into the bearing under pressure (wear rubber gloves and protective glasses) to wash out the grease, water and dirt. Scrub with a clean toothbrush.

3. Blow out the bearing with compressed air to dry

it out.

4. Pack it with grease and snap the bearing covers back on.

5. Reassemble the hub the opposite way it came apart. Sometimes a light tap on either end of the axle with a soft hammer will free the bearings from a side load (something akin to a pinched cartridge bearing) that will make the hub noticeably hard to turn.

NOTE

Reassembling the bearings of most new cartridge-bearing hubs is relatively easy: simply press the bearings with your hand, or use the shoulder on the axle as a punch to press the bearings into place. In most cases, even a soft hammer is not necessary; however, with older model cartridge-bearing hubs (Suntour, Sanshin, Specialized, and others), it isn't so easy. The tolerance between the hub cups and the outer surface of the bearing is so tight that these bearings must be pressed in or pounded in with a hammer. A direct blow from a hammer would ruin the bearing, so with these types of hubs, it is best to use either an old cartridge bearing or a similar-sized piece of metal to tap the bearings into the hub.

overhauling cartridge—bearing hubs

6.25 **removing bearing seal**

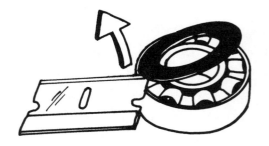

VI

cassettes n' cogs

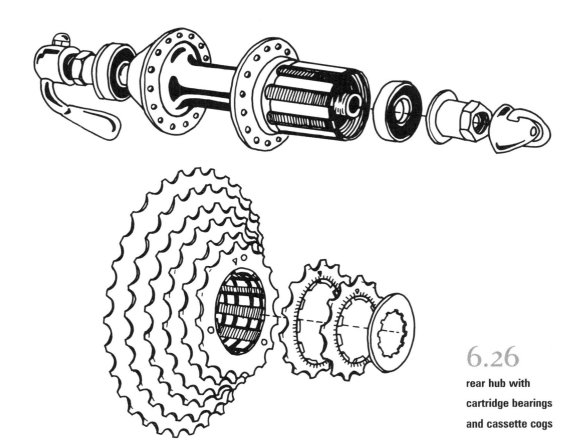

6.26

**rear hub with
cartridge bearings
and cassette cogs**

6.27

**rear hub with
standard ball
bearings
and freewheel**

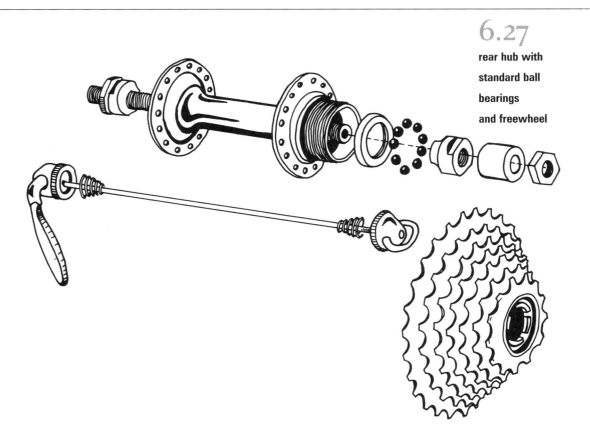

rear hub
diagrams

6.28 cleaning cogs

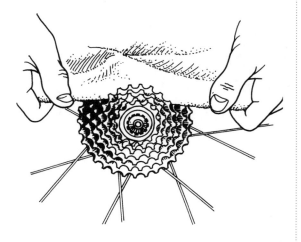

VI-14: GREASE GUARD HUBS

Wilderness Trail Bikes, Suntour and others make high-end hubs, some labeled Grease Guard, that have small grease ports on them that accept a small-tipped grease gun. The tip in this type of grease gun is about the size of the tip of a pencil. Injecting grease into these grease ports forces grease through the bearings from the inside out, squeezing the old grease, and whatever else is in area of the bearing surfaces, out of the outer end. Grease injection systems do not eliminate the need for overhauling your hubs. Grease injection merely extends the amount of time between overhauls; furthermore, these systems are only as good as you are about using them.

VI.D CASSETTES, FREEWHEELS AND COGS

Both freehub cassettes and freewheels are free-wheeling mechanisms, meaning that they allow the rear wheel to turn freely while the pedals are not turning.

A freehub cassette is an integral part of the rear hub. The cogs slide onto the cassette, engaging longitudinal splines on the cassette body.

A freewheel is a separate unit with the cogs

attached to it. The entire freewheel threads onto the drive side of the rear hub. Thread-on freewheels have fallen out of fashion relative to cassettes; they are more difficult to interchange cogs and do not support the drive side of the hub axle.

Most cassettes and freewheels rely on a series of pawls that engage when pressure is applied to the pedals, but allow the bike to freewheel when the rider is coasting.

Most cassettes can be lubricated without removing them from the hub. Changing gear combinations is accomplished by removing the cogs from the cassette body and putting on different ones.

Freewheels can be removed with a freewheel tool. Entire freewheels with different gear combinations can also be switched this way to adapt the bike to different terrain or for a special event.

6.29 using chain whip

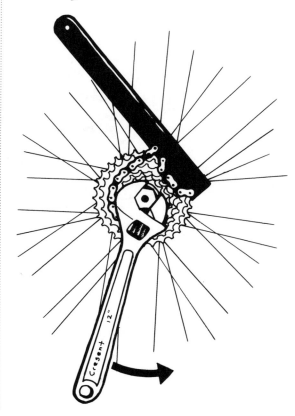

VI-15: CLEANING REAR COGS

The quickest, though perfunctory, way to clean the rear cogs is to slide a rag back and forth between each pair of cogs (Fig. 6.28). The other way is to remove them (See "Changing cassette cogs" below) and wipe them off with a rag or immerse them in solvent.

VI-16: CHANGING CASSETTE COGS

1. Get out a chain whip, a cassette lockring remover, a wrench (adjustable or open) to fit the remover, and the cog(s) you want to install. (Some very old cassettes have a threaded smallest cog instead of a lockring. These require two chain whips and no lockring remover.)

2. Remove the skewer.

3. Wrap the chain whip around a cog at least two up from the smallest cog, wrapped in the drive direction to hold the cassette in place.

4. Insert the splined lock-ring remover into the lockring. It is the metallic ring with a splined hole holding the smallest cog in place. Unscrew it in a counterclockwise direction while using the chain whip to keep the cassette from turning (Fig. 6.29). If the lockring is so tight that the tool pops out and damages it, put the skewer through the hub and tool without the springs and tighten it. Loosen the lock-ring a fraction of a turn, remove the skewer, and unscrew it the rest of the way.

5. Pull the cogs straight off. Some cassette cogsets are all single cogs separated by loose spacers, some cogsets are bolted together, and some are a combination of both.

6. Clean the cogs with a rag or a toothbrush and perhaps some solvent.

7. Inspect the cogs for wear. If the teeth are hook-shaped, they may be ripe for replacement. Rohloff also makes a cog wear indicator tool (Fig.1.5). If you

have access to one, use it following the accompanying instructions.

8. a. If you are replacing the entire cogset, just slide the new one on. Usually, one spline is wider than the others (Fig. 6.30).

b. If you are installing a nine-speed cassette, see the note under step 9.

c. If you are replacing some individual cogs within your cogset, be certain that they are of the same type and model. For example, not all 16-tooth Shimano cogs are alike. Most cogs have shifting ramps, differentially shaped teeth, and other asymmetries. They differ with model as well as with sizes of the adjacent cogs, so you need to buy one for the exact location and model. Install them in decreasing numerical sequence with the numbers facing out.

Bolt-together cogsets disassembled for cleaning can be put back together or not. There are two kinds of bolt-together cogsets: one with three long thin bolts holding the stack of cogs and spacers together (Fig. 6.26), and one with cogs bolted to an aluminum spider that has internal splines to fit on the cassette body. For the type with the three bolts, just unscrew the

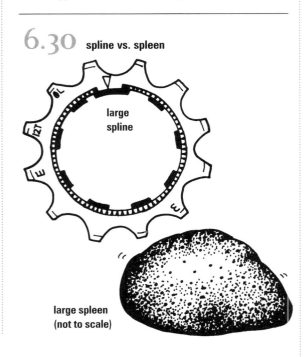

6.30 **spline vs. spleen**

large spline

large spleen
(not to scale)

bolts, take it apart, and put in the replacement cogs.

To save time and trouble with bolt-together cogsets in the future, you can put the cogs back on the cassette body individually and throw out the bolts.

9. Tighten the lockring back on with the lockring remover and wrench. (If you have the old type with the thread-on first cog, tighten that on with a chain whip instead.) Make sure that all of the cogs are seated and can't wobble side to side, which would indicate that the second cog is sitting against the ends of the splines. If they are loose, loosen the lockring, line up the second cog until it falls in place, and tighten the lockring again.

NOTE ON COMPATIBILITY

The above instructions for removing and replacing cogs apply for 8-, 7-, and 6-speed cogsets. The freehub body is different for each, so make sure you only use an 8-speed cogset on an 8-speed freehub body, etc.

NOTE ON 11-TOOTH COGS

Some 8-speed freehub bodies will not accept 11-tooth cogs (for instance, 1992-1994 XTR freehub bodies will not accept 11-28 or 11-30 cogsets). To accept the small 11-tooth cog, the splines of current freehub bodies stop about 2mm before the outer end of the freehub body. You can file the last 2mm of splines off of an old-style 8-speed freehub so it will accept an 11-tooth cog.

NOTE ON 9-SPEED CASSETTES

Ritchey's "2 X 9"system (front double, rear nine) features a 9-speed cassette that fits on an 8-speed freehub. The ninth cog is large (33 teeth or more) and is bowl-shaped. It takes advantage of some under-utilized space on the inboard end of the freehub body and spaces the teeth the same distance from the next cog as the spacing throughout the cassette.

Installing a Ritchey 9-speed cassette: Most freehubs from Shimano as well as other companies have a steel ring against the inboard end of the cassette body. Remove this ring (it pulls straight off), and put on the Ritchey ninth cog. XT and XTR freehubs have a thicker aluminum ring inboard; replace this thick ring with the thinner steel ring supplied with the Ritchey cog, and put on the ninth cog. Slide on the 8-speed cassette and tighten it down with the lockring as in step 9.

CAUTION ON 9-SPEED

To avoid the derailleur hitting the spokes when on the bowl-shaped cog, you must use an "OCR" ("Off-Center Rear") rim; Ritchey and Bontrager supply them. The spoke holes on these rims are offset to the non-drive side and angle the drive-side spokes further away from the cogs.

VI-17: CHANGING FREEWHEELS

If you have a freewheel (Fig. 6.27) and want to switch it with another one, follow this procedure. Replacing individual cogs on an existing freewheel is beyond the scope of this book, and is rarely done these days due to unavailability of spare parts.

1. Get out the appropriate freewheel remover for your freewheel, a big adjustable wrench to fit it, and the freewheel you are replacing it with.

2. Remove the quick-release skewer, and take the springs off of it.

3. Slide the skewer back in from the non-drive side, place the freewheel remover into the end of the freewheel so that the notches or splines engage, and thread the skewer nut back on, tightening it against the freewheel remover to keep it from popping out of its notches.

4. Put the big adjustable wrench onto the flats of the freewheel remover, and loosen it (counterclockwise). It may take considerable force to free it, and you may even need to put a large pipe on the end of the wrench for more leverage. Have the tire on the

ground for traction as you do it. Once the freewheel pops loose, be careful to not keep unscrewing it without loosening the skewer nut, as this could snap the skewer in two.

5. Loosen the skewer nut a bit, unscrew the freewheel a bit more, etc., until it spins off freely and there is no longer any danger of having the freewheel remover pop out of the notches it engages.

6. Remove the skewer and spin off the freewheel.

7. Grease the threads on the hub and the inside of the new freewheel.

8. Thread on the new freewheel by hand. Tighten it either with a chain whip, the freewheel remover and a wrench, or by putting it on the bike and pedaling.

9. Replace the skewer with the narrow ends of its conical springs facing inward.

VI-18: LUBRICATING CASSETTES AND FREEWHEELS

Lubricating cassettes and freewheels can usually be accomplished simply by dripping chain lube into them.

If yours is the kind of cassette with the teeth on the faces of the hub shell and cassette, just drip oil into the crease between the cassette and the hub shell as you turn the cassette counterclockwise.

a. If it is the standard kind of cassette:

1. Disassemble the hub axle assembly (see Section VI-12).

2. Wipe clean the inside of the drive-side bearing surface.

3. With the wheel laying flat and the cassette pointed up toward you, flow chain lube in between the bearing surface and the cassette body, as you spin the cassette counterclockwise. You will hear the clicking noise smooth out. Keep it flowing until old black oil flows out of the other end of the cassette.

You can inject lubricant under pressure into most cassettes with a Morningstar "Freehub Buddy" tool. The hub dust cover is removed, the Freehub Buddy is pressed in the bearing, and lube is inserted through a hole in the tool into the cassette body. Spray lube cans with thin plastic tubes, narrow-tip grease guns, oil cans, and other lubricant delivery systems work with the Freehub Buddy by means of various adaptors. This is about the only way to inject thick lubricants (like grease) for warm conditions into a freehub.

4. Wipe off the excess lube, and continue with the hub overhaul.

b. If it is a freewheel:

1. Wipe dirt off of the face of the fixed part of the freewheel surrounding the axle.

2. With the wheel lying flat, and the cogs facing up toward you, drip lubricant into the crease between the fixed and moving parts of the freewheel or cassette as you spin the cogs in a counterclockwise direction. You will hear the clicking noise inside get smoother as you get lubricant in there. Keep the flow of lubricant going until old, dirty oil flows out the back side around the hub flange.

3. Wipe off the excess oil.

Once you have the freehub or freewheel reassembled, go ride your bike!

Lubricating cassettes and freewheels

brakes

"Well, I predict that if you think about it long enough you will find yourself going round and round and round and round until you finally reach only one possible, rational, intelligent conclusion. The law of gravity and gravity itself did not exist before Isaac Newton. No other conclusion makes sense."

— ROBERT M. PIRSIG, from Zen and the Art of Motorcycle Maintenance

Oh, well. We came after Newton, so we need a good set of brakes.

TYPES OF BRAKES

In 1996, when we published the first edition of this book, mountain biking was still dominated by the trusty, old cable-actuated cantilever brake (Figs. 7.10 and 7.11), but in less than a year, brakes patterned after Shimano's V-brake had completely taken over the new-bike market. There's a good reason for that. V-brakes offer more flexibility than cantilevers; since they do not require a cable hanger, V-brakes can be used on rear suspension frames without added complexity, and parallel-push V-brake designs allow use of different rims without pad readjustment. Still, there are plenty of cantilever brakes out there. They work, they're light and simple, offer good mud clearance, and, above all, they stop your bike. V-brakes and cantilevers pivot on the same bosses attached to the frame and fork.

There are several other options when it comes to mountain-bike brakes, as well. For rear-suspension frames, linkage brakes that mount on the cantilever bosses offer the same advantage as V-brakes by operating without a cable stop. They rely on an articulated linkage that pulls both brake arms toward one another. The introduction of the V-brake has pretty much dried up the market for other linkage designs.

Some hydraulic brakes mount on the cantilever bosses and are also useful on rear-suspension bikes. On these brakes, the pads are driven straight toward the rim by hydraulic pressure.

Roller cams and U-brakes also mount on bosses attached to the frame and fork. You should know that the brazed-on bosses for these brakes are positioned higher than those used for standard

tools

2.5mm, 3mm, 4mm, 5mm, 6mm Allen wrenches
9mm and 10mm open end wrenches
small adjustable wrench
pliers
grease
screwdriver

cantilevers. Roller cams and U-brakes peaked in popularity in the late 1980s, but there are still a few around.

Unlike most other brakes that use the edge of the rim as a braking surface, disc brakes have hydraulically driven pads that pinch a hub-mounted disc — much like those on a motorcycle or a car. An advantage of disc brakes is that the rim (and hence the tire and tube) does not get hot on a long downhill, resulting in fewer flat tires. As these units have become lighter and simpler, their popularity has grown. One indication of that popularity is that major fork manufacturers, like Rock Shox, Manitou and Marzzochi, have collaborated with disc brake makers to develop a standard for mounting disc brakes on bikes.

VII-1: RELEASING BRAKES TO REMOVE A WHEEL

V-brakes (Fig. 7.12): Hold the pads against the rim and pull the cable noodle back and up to release it from the brake arm link.

Cantilevers (Fig. 7.23) and U-brakes (Fig. 7.41): Hold the pads against the rim and pull the head of the straddle cable out of the hook at the end of one brake arm (see Chapter 2, Fig. 2.1).

Magura hydraulic rim brakes (Fig. 7.33): If the brake has a stiffening arch over the wheel (Fig. 7.33), pull its left end off of the bolt head it slips over. If the brake has a quick-release lever on one side (Fig. 7.33, 7.34), open it and pull the brake bracket off of the brake boss. If there is no quick release, you will have to unscrew the mounting bolt on one side to pull off the brake bracket.

Other types: See the section on the particular brake.

VIIA: CABLES & HOUSINGS

Given that cables transfer braking force from the levers to the brakes, their proper installation and maintenance are critical to good brake performance. If there is excess friction in the cable system, the brakes will not work properly, no matter how well the brakes, calipers and levers are adjusted. Each cable should move freely and be replaced if there are any broken strands.

VII-2: CABLE TENSIONING

As brake pads wear and cables stretch, the cable needs to be shortened. The barrel adjuster on the brake lever (Fig. 7.1) offers adjustment to

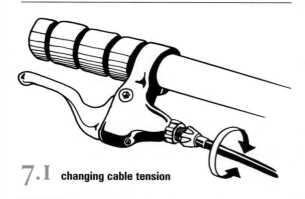

7.1 changing cable tension

mitigate these kind of changes. The cable should be tight enough that the lever cannot be pulled to the grip, yet loose enough that the brakes (assuming they are centered and the wheels are true) are not dragging on the rims.

VII-3: INCREASING CABLE TENSION

1. Back out the barrel adjuster (exploded in Fig. 7.2) by turning it counterclockwise (Fig. 7.1), after loosening the locknut.

2. Adjust the tension so that the brake lever does not hit the grip when the brake is applied. Lock in the tension by tightening the locknut down against the lever body while holding the

barrel adjuster. Note: Some levers, like Shimano's XTR, do not have a locknut on the barrel adjuster.

3. You may find that you need to tighten the cable more than by simply fiddling with the barrel adjuster. If you need to take up more slack than the barrel adjuster allows you to, tighten the cable at the brake. First, screw the barrel adjuster most of the way in. This leaves some adjustment in the system for brake setup and cable stretch over time. Loosen the bolt clamping the cable at the brake. Check the cable for wear. If there are any frayed strands, replace it. (See "Cable installation," section VII-6 this page.) Otherwise, pull the cable tight, and re-tighten the clamping bolt. Tension the cable as needed with the barrel adjuster.

VII-4: REDUCING CABLE TENSION

1. Back out the locknut on the barrel adjuster (Fig. 7.2) a few turns (counterclockwise).

2. Turn the barrel adjuster clockwise (Fig. 7.1) until your brake pads are properly spaced from the rim.

3. Tighten the locknut clockwise against the lever body to lock in the adjustment.

4. Double-check that the cable is tight enough so that the lever cannot be squeezed all the way to the grip.

VII-5: CABLE MAINTENANCE

1. If the cable is frayed or kinked or has any broken strands, replace it. (See "Cable installation," section VII-6 this page.)

2. If the cable is not sliding well, lubricate it. If you have it, use molybdenum disulfide grease; otherwise, try a chain lubricant. Standard lithium-based greases can gum up on cables and eventually restrict movement.

3. To lubricate, open the brake (via the cable quick release as when you remove a wheel; see section VII-1).

4. Pull each section of cable housing out of each slotted cable stop. If your bike does not have slotted cable stops, you will have to pull out the entire cable.

5. Slide the housing up the cable, rub lubricant with your fingers on the cable section that was inside the housing, and slide the housing back into place.

6. If the cable still sticks, replace it.

VII-6: CABLE INSTALLATION

1. Remove the old cable, making sure not to lose any parts of the cable clamps or straddle-cable holders.

N O T E

When installing a new cable, it is a good idea to replace the housings as well, even if you don't think they need to be. Daily riding in particularly dirty conditions means that cables and housings may have to be replaced every couple of months. As with chains and derailleur cables, brake cable replacement is a maintenance operation, not a repair operation; don't wait until a cable breaks or seizes up to replace it.

2. Purchase good-quality cables and lined housings.

Cables: Try using die-drawn cables; they have been pulled through a constricting die and will pull with less friction, because the exterior strands have been flattened.

N O T E

Some cables even come coated in Teflon or Gore-Tex. Gore-Tex RideOn cables and housings, when properly installed, can reduce friction significantly and stay that way, by virtue of being completely sealed. The Gore-Tex must be peeled off of the cable the last couple of inches on either end—where it enters the brake lever and clamps to the brake; if this is not done, the Gore-Tex coating can get completely wadded up and prevent cable movement. A thin plas-

7.2 cable installation at brake lever

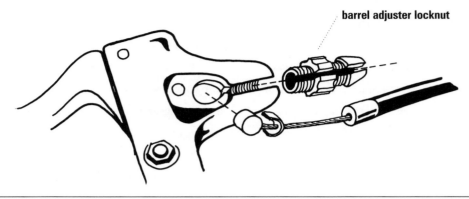

barrel adjuster locknut

tic tube sheaths the cable end to end, including through the housing sections to seal out crud. A rubber accordion-like seal (called the "Grub") covers the end of the plastic tube at each brake and prevents the access of dirt at its one possible entry point.

Housing: Most brake-cable housing is spiral-wrapped to prevent splitting under braking pressure (see Chapter 5, Fig. 5.14). Teflon-lined housing reduces friction and is a must on a mountain bike.

3. Cut the housing sections long enough to reach the brakes, and route them so that they do not make any sharp bends. If you are replacing existing housing, look at the bends before removing it. If the bends are smooth and do not bind when the wheel is turned, cut the new housings to the same lengths. If not, cut each new segment longer than you think necessary and keep trimming it back until it gives the smoothest path possible for the cable, without the cable tension being affected by steering. Use a cutter specifically designed for cutting housings, or a sharp side-cutter.

4. After cutting, make sure the end faces are flat. If not, flatten them with a file or a clipper.

5. If the end of the Teflon liner is mashed shut after cutting, open it up with a sharp object like a nail or a toothpick.

6. Slip a ferrule over each housing end for sup-

port (see Chapter 5, Fig. 5.14).

7. Decide which hand you want to control which brake (the standard is the right hand controlling the rear brake).

8. Tighten the adjusting barrel to within one turn of being screwed all of the way in. Rotate the barrel adjuster and locknut so that their slots line up with those on the lever and lever body (Fig. 7.2).

9. Insert the round head of the cable into the lever's cable hook (Figs. 7.2, 7.9, and 7.11).

10. Pull the cable down into the lined-up slots on the barrel and nut. Once the cable is in place, turn the barrel so that the slots are offset to prevent the cable from slipping back out. If you have an old lever that is not slotted, you will have to feed the entire length of the cable through the hole in the lever body.

11. For the front brake, skip to step 12.

Hopefully, you have slotted cable stops on your frame. They make cable installation a lot easier. Assuming that you do, slide the rear brake cable through the housing sections and then route the cable and housing from the brake lever to the brake, snapping the housing and cable into each slotted stop from the side. If you don't have slotted stops, you will have to feed the cable through the hole in each cable stop.

brakes

With new cables and lined housing, it is usually best not to use a lubricant on the cable. It can gum up inside the housing and attract dirt. Some manufacturers, however, supply lubricants specifically for this purpose with their cables and housings.

For the rear brake, skip to step 13.

12. With a suspension fork and a cantilever brake, terminate the front brake housing at the stop on the brake arch (Fig. 7.5); the housing stops at the "noodle" guide tube on a V-brake (Fig. 7.12). For cantilevers without suspension, you may have a cable stop that is integral to the stem or one attached to the headset (Fig. 7.4). I recommend bypassing any integral cable stop on the stem or stem through-hole, as these require readjustment of the front brake with any change in stem height.

Instead, use a collar that slips around the stem above the headset (Fig. 7.3), or one that slips into the headset stack between locknuts (Fig. 7.4).

13. Attach the cable to the brake. (See section on your type of brake.) Pull it taut and tighten the cable-clamping bolt (Fig. 7.6, for cantilevers). Pull the lever as hard as you can and hold it for 60 seconds to stretch the new cable.

14. Adjust cable tension with the lever barrel adjuster (as in sections VII-2, 3, and 4).

15. Cut off cable ends about $2\frac{1}{2}$" past the cable-fixing bolts. Crimp end caps on all exposed cable ends to prevent fraying (Fig. 5.24 in Chapter 5), and bend the extra to the side.

Once the cable has been properly installed, the lever should snap back quickly when released. If it

7.3-5 **examples of cable hangers**

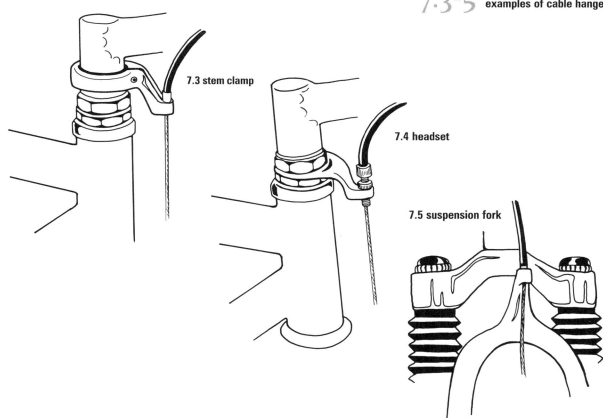

7.3 stem clamp

7.4 headset

7.5 suspension fork

straddle
cables

7.6 tightening cantilever brake cable

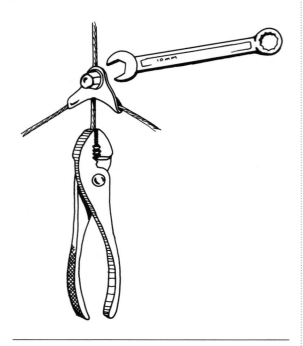

does not, re-check the cables and housings for free movement and sharp bends. Release the cable quick release, and check the levers for free movement. With the cable still loose, check that the brake pads do not drag on the tire as they return to the neutral position; make sure the brake arms rotate freely on their pivot bosses, and check that the brake arm return springs pull the pads away from the rims. Reconnect the cable quick release and follow the adjustment instructions for your particular type of brake.

VIIB: BRAKE LEVERS

The levers must operate smoothly and be set up so that you can easily reach them while riding.

VII-7: LEVER LUBRICATION/SERVICE

1. Lubricate all pivot points in the lever with grease or oil if sticky.

2. Check return spring function for levers that have them.

3. Make sure that the lever or lever body is not bent in a way that hinders movement.

4. Check for stress cracks, and, if you find any, replace the lever.

VII-8: LEVER REMOVAL, INSTALLATION, AND POSITIONING

Levers mount on the bar inboard of the grip and bar end. They are also mounted inboard of twist shifters and outboard of thumb shifters (Figs. 7.7 and 7.8). Some manufacturers offer integrated systems that include both lever and shifter in a single unit (Fig. 7.11).

1. If installed, remove the bar end by loosening the mounting bolt and sliding it off.

2. Remove the handlebar grip by lifting the edges on both ends, squirting water or rubbing alcohol underneath, and twisting it until it becomes free and slides off.

3. If installed, remove the twist shifter by loosening the mounting bolt and sliding it off.

4. Loosen the brake lever's mounting bolt with an Allen wrench and slide the lever off.

5. Slide the new lever on, and replace the other parts in the order in which they were installed. Slide the grips on using rubbing alcohol (it dries quickly) as a lubricant; water works, too, but the grips will twist for a few rides.

6. Make certain the levers do not extend beyond the ends of the bars. Rotate them and slide them inward to your preference.

7. Tighten all mounting bolts on levers, shifters, and bar ends.

VII-9: REACH AND LEVERAGE ADJUSTMENTS

Some levers have a reach adjustment set screw; usually it's on the lever body just under the barrel adjuster (Figs. 7.9 and 7.10). If you have

brake
levers

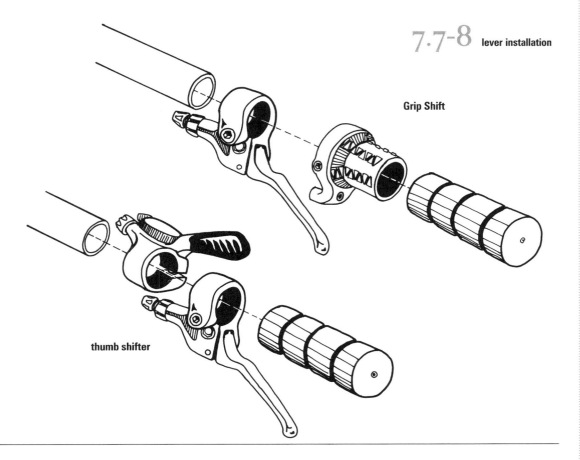

7.7-8 **lever installation**

Grip Shift

thumb shifter

small hands, you may want to tighten the reach set screws so the levers are closer to the bars when released.

Some brakes also have a leverage adjustment (Figs. 7.9 and 7.11), which moves the cable end in or out relative to the lever pivot. To adjust the leverage, some levers have a threaded shaft on the cable hook (like Avid and XTR—see Fig. 7.11); some have removable inserts; some have adjustable settings of a set screw (Fig. 7.9); others yet use a rotating notched eccentric disc. The closer the cable passes by the pivot, the higher the leverage, but the less cable the lever pulls, and vice versa.

Safety note: The levers for V-brakes have intentionally low leverage (with high cable pull), due to the high leverage of the long brake arms. If you use a lever from a cantilever brake with a

V-brake, you can end up on your nose. Always start with V-brake levers adjusted to lowest leverage (cable passing furthest from the lever pivot), and increase from there if you wish.

VIIC: BRAKE CALIPERS
VIIC1: V-BRAKES

V-brakes have tall, cantilever-like arms, a horizontal cable-hook link on top of one arm, and a cable clamp on the top of the other. A curved aluminum guide pipe, or "noodle", hooks into the horizontal link and takes the cable from the end of the housing and out through the link and directs it toward the cable clamp on the opposite arm (Figs. 7.12 and 7.13). V-brakes usually, although not always, have long, thin brake pads with threaded posts. Some V-brakes, like Shimano XT and XTR (Fig. 7.12) and Avid Arch Supreme have

brake
calipers

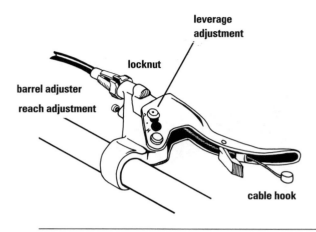

leverage
adjustment

locknut

barrel adjuster
reach adjustment

cable hook

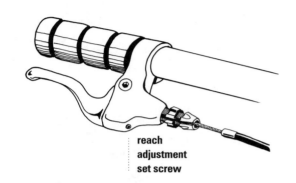

reach
adjustment
set screw

"parallel-push" linkages which move the brake pads horizontally rather than in an arc around the brake boss like a cantilever. Simple V-brake designs mount the pad directly to the arm so that it moves in a cantilever-like arc (Fig. 7.13).

V-brakes are extremely powerful and can be very grabby if used with a cantilever brake lever; it is important that you use the levers that were designed for use with the brake.

VII-10: V-BRAKE LEVER INSTALLATION

V-brake lever installation to the bars is the same as any others (Section VII-8, Figs. 7.7 and 7.8), with the exception of Avids, which have a C-shaped band holding them on, rather than a complete through-bored clamp. This design allows the levers to be pulled straight off of the bars without removing the grips, bar ends, etc.

VII-11: LEVERAGE ADJUSTMENT

Some levers have allow a certain amount of adjustment to vary the distance between the lever pivot and the head of the cable. To start with, set it at the position that offers the weakest leverage, where the head of the cable is farthest from the

pivot. Only increase the leverage if you become very confident in using the brakes. On Shimano XTR and Avid, a threaded adjuster performs the adjustment (Fig. 7.11); on Shimano XT, leverage is adjusted by installing or removing a series of inserts; on Shimano DX and M600, leverage is adjusted by loosening a small bolt on the upper face of the lever arm with a 3mm Allen key, sliding the leverage adjuster up and down, and re-tightening the bolt (Fig. 7.9). M600 and DX levers have a hook with a cover to hold the cable end far out at the end of the lever (Fig. 7.9); the cable passes over a grooved trough above the pivot whose

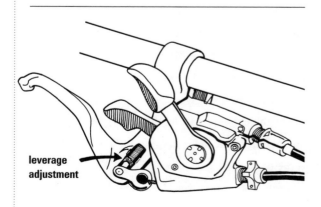

leverage
adjustment

7.11 **integrated shift/brake levers**

height setting determines the leverage.

VII-12: V-BRAKE INSTALLATION AND ADJUSTMENT

a. Brake mounting

1. Grease the cantilever boss on your frame or fork.

2. With Shimano and Dia-Compe V-brakes, slide each brake arm on, inserting the spring pin into the center hole of the boss. Tighten the brake bolt with washer into the boss.

With Avid Arch Supreme brakes, slide two supplied washers onto each brake boss to prevent binding of the brake pivot cartridge bearings. Slide the brake on and tighten the bolt. Bolt each end of the pivot arch, using the supplied bolts and washers, to the hole in the arm adjacent to each brake pad.

B. Pad adjustment

These instructions apply to threaded pad posts. For V-brakes with unthreaded pad posts (Dia-Compe 747), it is best to follow the pad adjustment procedure for cantilever brakes, Section VII-18, coupled with the pad offset in step 4 below. Dia-Compe 747s do not hold the adjustment of their pads well, no matter how much you tighten the eye-bolt nut on the unthreaded pad posts. You may be able to increase the friction between the eye-bolt washers and the curved brake arm by sanding the contacting surfaces on the arms and washers. The brakes will not look as nice, but they may at least work.

3. Roughly adjust each pad by loosening the pad nut, pushing the arm toward the rim, and tightening the pad nut with the pad flat against the rim.

4. Determine the proper amount of pad offset from the brake arms: While holding the pads against the rim, measure the space between the end of the link to the inside edge of the opposite brake arm (Fig. 7.14); this length should be at least

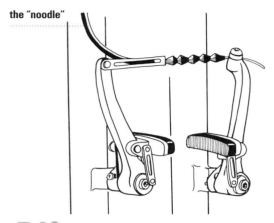

the "noodle"

7.12 **Shimano V-brake**

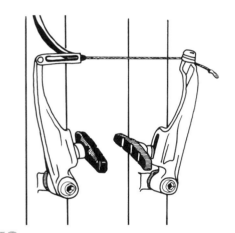

7.13 **simple V-brake**

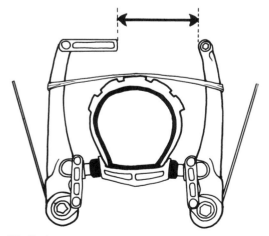

7.14 **finalizing pad to rim adjustment**

V-brake installation and adjustment

7.15 pad replacement on V-brakes

7.16 V-brake pad holder assembly

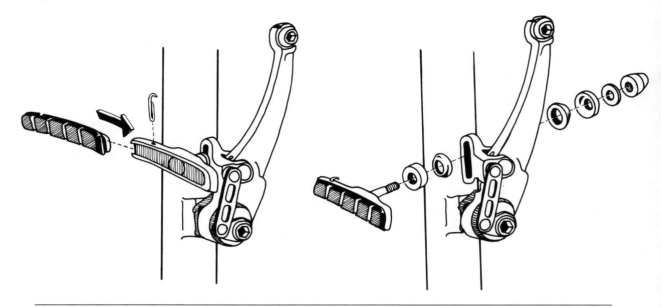

39 mm. If it is less than 39mm, the end of the noodle can hit the opposite arm when the brake is applied, particularly as the pads wear. Obviously, this would prevent the brakes from grabbing the rims, which is not what you have in mind when you apply the brakes; this becomes more of an issue the narrower the rim is.

Threaded-post pads are offset from the brake arms by concave washers of various thicknesses nesting over convex washers on either side of the mounting tab (Fig. 7.16). The pad offset, which is adjusted by the spacer stack, should be set so that the top of each brake arm is a little outside of vertical relative to the brake mounting bolt when the brake is applied (i.e., the arms are approximately parallel). On Shimano V-brakes, as they come out of the box, the concave washer on the pad side is 6mm thick, and 3mm thick on the nut side; Avid offers more options, using a 1mm flat washer and 3mm and 5mm concave washers, which can be stacked in combinations. Interchange the washers from side to side to set the offset.

5. Finalize the pad-to-rim adjustment: On brakes

with vertical return springs, like Shimano and Avid, flip the springs off of their retention pins and connect the tops of the arms together with a rubber band to lightly hold the pads against the rim (Fig. 7.14). Otherwise, hold the pad against the rim or put a rubber band around the brake lever after you have connected the cable.

6. Loosen the pad fixing nut, and then tighten the pad fixing nut with the pad held flat against the rim. Toe-in is not necessary or recommended. The pad's top edge should be about 1mm below the edge of the rim.

7. Re-hook the return springs to the retention pins.

N O T E

On Shimano XT, XTR and Avid Arch Supremes, the V-brake linkage keeps the pad moving horizontally as it contacts and leaves the rim surface; when interchanging wheels, as long as the rims have parallel braking surfaces, there is no need to adjust the pads; the only necessary adjustment is to the cable length.

C. . Threading the cable to the brake through the curved alloy guide pipe (the "noodle").

For the rear brake, pick the one of the two noo-

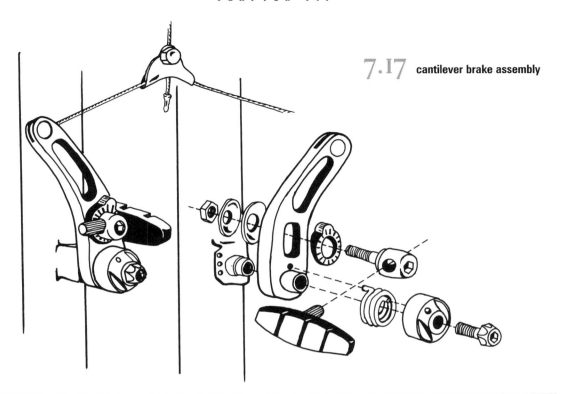

7.17 **cantilever brake assembly**

brakes

dles whose angle fits your frame the best for a smooth cable path. Hook the head of the noodle into the notch in the horizontal link.

7. Slip the rubber accordion boot onto the cable, big end first, and over the tip of the noodle (Fig. 7.12). An O-ring ("cable donut") on the cable butted up against the narrow end of the boot is a good idea to prevent the boot from falling off of the noodle and keep the cable cleaner. If you are using Gore-Tex RideOn cables, you can dispense with the boot and use Gore's little "Grub" seal instead. The Grub seals the end of the Gore plastic sheath, which should be cut to terminate halfway between the guide pipe tip and the cable fixing bolt.

8. Connect the cable to the fixing bolt on the opposite arm.

9. Set the cable length so that there is 1mm to 1.5 mm of space between each pad and the rim. Tighten the cable fixing bolt with the lever barrel adjuster screwed out one turn. Make sure the wheel is centered in the frame or fork.

D. Brake centering/ spring tension adjustment

10. a. Some V-brakes (Shimano) use a vertical

return spring adjusted by a screw at the mounting pivot on each arm (Fig. 7.12); turn the screw clockwise to move the arm farther from the rim, and vice versa. A quick way to increase spring tension or center the brakes on the trail is to bend the vertical springs outward (after pulling them off the retention pins on the back of the arms) without fooling with the screws.

b. Dia-Compe 747s use a spring adjuster cam rotated by a 5mm Allen key; turn it toward the imprinted "H" or "L" for more or less spring tension.

c. Avid Arch Supremes have an innovative (and very quick) way to set spring balance. While lightly squeezing the lever so the pads touch the rim, loosen and re-tighten the plastic knob at the top of the arch. The W-shaped spring passes through the knob and hooks on the arms; it automatically finds its balance point when the knob is loosened.

d. If your V-brake springs do not adjust with any of the above three methods, look at spring tension adjustment for cantilever brakes, Section VII-20, since any of the spring configurations used in cantilevers could be built into a V-brake.

brake
centering/
spring
tension
adjustment

NOTE

If a brake arm does not turn freely on the boss, the boss may be damaged. Bulged or mushroomed bosses can be filed and sanded smaller; bent or broken ones must be replaced (hopefully they are the bolt-on type; otherwise new ones must be welded on).

ANOTHER NOTE

Parallel-push V-brakes, like high-end Shimano and Avid, often do not hold their pad centering adjustment, especially when new. You may frequently find that one pad is very close to or rubbing the rim after a ride in which they started centered. This is because, especially as the pivots break in, any bit of grit in any of the numerous pivots will change the return friction on one side relative to the other side. Brake adjustment is an exercise in symmetry; it can be easily thrown off.

11. Squeeze the brake lever hard a number of times to stretch the cable and make sure it does not slip at the anchor bolt.

VII-13: V-BRAKE PAD REPLACEMENT

Pad replacement on high-end V-brakes with removable pad inserts:

1. With a pair of pliers, remove the cotter pin from the top of the pad holder

2. Slide the old pad out out of its groove in the pad holder (Fig. 7.15).

3. Slide in the new pad, paying attention to the "R" and "L" markings for right and left and the "Forward" direction arrow, if present. Right and left must be heeded, as the backs of these pads only have a slot for the cotter pin on one end. Avid pads have two cotter pin slots and can be oriented either way.

4. Replace the cotter pin, and check that the pad is secure in the holder.

NOTE

Avid pads are not interchangeable with Shimano XT and XTR, whose pad holders have a curved groove; Avid pad holders have a straight groove, even though the pad itself is curved. The pads are flexible enough that they can be jammed into each other's holders in a pinch, but the outer curvature of the pad will not match that of the rim.

VII-14: PAD REPLACEMENT ON V-BRAKES WITH ONE-PIECE PAD AND THREADED POST:

1. Note how the washers are stacked on the pad post (Fig. 7.16).

2. Unscrew the shoe fixing nut and remove the old pad from the arm.

3. Replacing the concave and convex washers as they were, bolt the new pad to the arm. The convex washers are placed on either side of the brake arm with flat sides facing in (Fig. 7.16). The concave washers are placed adjacent to the convex washers so that the concave and convex surfaces meet and allow angular adjustability of the pad.

4. Follow pad adjustment procedure, Section VII-12B.

VII-15: PAD REPLACEMENT ON V-BRAKES WITH UNTHREADED PAD POSTS:

Follow pad replacement and adjustment procedures for cantilever brakes, Sections VII-17 and VII-18.

VIIC2: CANTILEVER BRAKES
VII-16: INSTALLATION

1. Grease the brake bosses. Avoid getting grease inside the brake boss or on the bolt threads; they are treated with thread-lock goop to prevent them from vibrating loose.

2. Follow the installation directions that came

7.18   cylindrical clamp brake

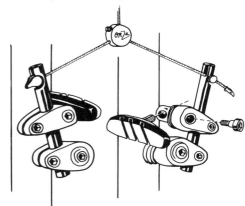

7.19   threaded post brake

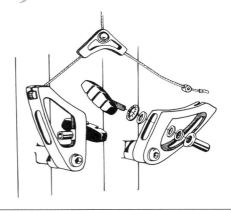

with your brakes, if you have them. If not, follow the general installation instructions below.

3. Make sure you install the brakes with all of the parts in the order in which they were packaged together. In particular, the springs will often be of different colors not interchangeable from left to right.

4. If the brake has a separate inner sleeve bushing to fit over the cantilever boss, install that first. Slip the brake and return spring over it.

5. Determine what sort of return system your brakes use. If the brake arms have no spring-tension adjustment, or a set screw on the side of one of the arms for adjusting spring tension, go to Step

6. Such brakes utilize the hole in the cantilever boss to anchor the bottom end of the spring. If the brake arms have a large nut surrounding the mounting bolt for adjusting spring tension, skip to Step 8. These brakes do not use the hole in the cantilever boss as a spring anchor.

6. Slip the brake onto the boss, inserting the lower end of the spring into the hole in the cantilever boss (if the boss has three holes, try the center hole first; use a higher hole to make the brake snappier, a necessity with lower-quality or old brakes). You also want to make sure that the top end of the spring is inserted into its hole in the brake arm as well.

7. Install and tighten the mounting bolt into the cantilever boss. Skip the next three steps.

8. Slip the brake (with any included bushings) onto the cantilever boss.

9. Install the spring so that one end inserts into the hole in the brake arm and the other inserts into the hole in the adjusting nut.

10. Install and tighten the mounting bolt while holding the adjusting nut with the appropriate open-end wrench (usually 15mm), so that the pad is touching the rim. This facilitates pad adjustment later.

VII-17: PAD REPLACEMENT AND INSTALLATION

1. Remove the old pad, if applicable.

2. Install the new pad. Most cantilevers rely on an eye bolt with an enlarged head and a hole through it to accept the pad post. Some cantilevers (Avid, for example) have a slotted clamp with a hole for the pad post. A few cantis use a threaded pad post that passes through a slot in the brake arm.

3. If your brake spring can be adjusted so that it

7.20 **distance of pad to fixing bolt (a) and angle against rim (c)**

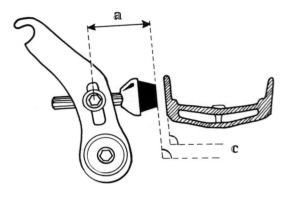

holds the pad against the rim, set it up that way now. It will make the pad adjustments much easier. If not, you will have to push each arm toward the rim as you adjust the pad (Figs. 7.25 and 7.26).

cantilever brake pad adjustment

VII-18: PAD ADJUSTMENT

There are five separate adjustments (a. through e. in Figs. 7.20, 7.21, 7.22) that must be made for each pad. These adjustments are quite easy with some brakes and a real pain in the rear with others.

a. offset distance of the pad from the brake arm (extension of the pad post) (Fig. 7.20a.);

b. vertical pad height (Fig. 7.21b.);

7.21 **up and down (b) and twist (d)**

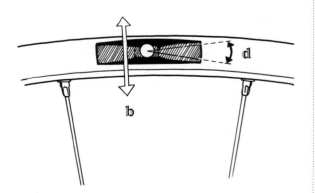

c. pad swing in the vertical plane for mating with the rim's sidewall angle (Fig. 7.20c.);

d. pad twist to align the heel and toe of the pad with the rim's curvature (Fig. 7.21d.);

e. pad swing in the horizontal plane to set toe-in (Fig. 7.22e.).

Cantilevers that feature a cylindrical brake arm are by far the easiest to adjust (Fig. 7.18). Pad adjustment is simple because the pad is held to the cylinder with a clamp that offers almost full range of motion. Avid, OnZa, Gravity Research Pipe Dreams, and Dia Compe VC900 all rely on this type of system. All other cantilevers employ a single pad eye-bolt to hold all five adjustments. It requires a bit of manual dexterity to hold all five adjustments simultaneously while tightening the bolt.

With all types of cantilevers:

1. Loosen the pad clamping bolt, lubricate the pad-fixing threads, and set the pad offset, (a., Fig. 7.20), by sliding the post in or out of the clamping hole. The farther the pad is extended away from the brake arm, the greater the angle of the brake arm will be from the plane of the wheel. A benefit of this is that leverage is increased (see straddle cable angle in Figs. 7.25 and 7.26). Drawbacks are: the brake feels less firm, since less lever pull force is required; and heel clearance of rear brake arms is reduced, particularly for small frames. A good way to start off is with the post clamped in the center of its length.

NOTE

With threaded-post pads, pad offset is set by placing spacers between the brake arm and the pad; lube the pad threads.

2. Roughly adjust the vertical pad height, (b., Fig. 7.21), by sliding the pad-clamping mechanism up and down in the brake arm slot. With cylindrical-clamp brakes, loosen the bolt clamping the pad

brakes

7.22 **brake pad toe-in (e)**

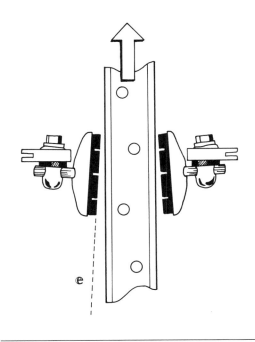

e

holder to the brake arm, and snug the bolt back up, once the rough adjustment is reached. With all other types, leave the pad bolt just loose enough so that you can move the pad easily, and continue.

3. Adjust pad swing in the vertical plane, (c., Fig. 7.20), so that the face of the pad meets the rim flat with its top edge 1mm to 2mm below the top of the rim. Fine tune this adjustment by simultaneously sliding the pad up or down.

4. Adjust the pad twist, (d., Fig. 7.21), so that the top edge of the pad is parallel to the top of the rim. Modern pads are quite long and require precision with this adjustment. With cylindrical-clamp brakes, the pad-securing bolt may now be tightened.

5. Finally, adjust the pad toe-in (e., Fig. 7.22). The pad should either be adjusted flat to the rim, or toed in so that, when the forward end of the pad touches the rim, the rear end of it is 1mm to 2mm away from the rim.

If the pad is toed out, the heel of it will catch

and tend to chatter, making an obnoxious squealing noise. If the brake arms are not stiff, or they fit loosely on the cantilever boss, the same thing will happen when flat; toe-in is a must and will have to be adjusted frequently as the pads wear to keep them quiet.

On cylindrical-arm brakes with two fixing bolts (Fig. 7.18), toe-in is adjusted by again loosening the bolt that holds the vertical height adjustment of the pad. Since you have already tightened the other bolt that holds the pad in place, you simply loosen this second bolt and swing the pad horizontally until you arrive at your preferred toe-in or flatness setting. Tighten the bolt again, and you are done with pad adjustment.

With any brake using a single bolt to hold the pad as well as control its rotation, you now have a tricky task of holding all of the adjustments you have made and simultaneously tightening the nut. Most eye-bolt systems are tightened with a 10mm wrench on the nut on the back of the brake while the front is held with a 5mm Allen wrench. Help from someone else to either hold or tighten is useful here. Probably the trickiest brake to adjust has a big toothed or notched washer between the head of the eye bolt and a flat brake arm (Fig. 7.17). The washer is thinner on one edge than the other, so rotating it (by means of the tooth or notch) toes the pad in or out. With this type, you must hold all of the pad adjustments as you turn this washer, and then keep it and the pad in place as you tighten the nut. It's not an easy job, and the adjustment changes as you tighten the bolt.

The other common type has a convex or concave shape to the slotted brake arm, and cupped washers separate the eye bolt head and nut from the brake arm (Shimano, most Dia Compe, Ritchey (Fig. 7.23), Paul, etc.). The concave/convex surfaces

**cantilever
brake
pad
adjustment**

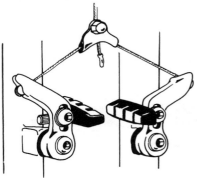

7.23 **standard cantilever brake**

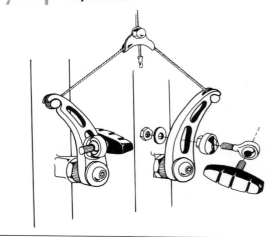

7.24 **ball joint brake**

allow the pad to swivel , and tightening the bolt secures everything. Again, you may not get it on the first try. Threaded posts also employ such washers.

N O T E

Some of these curved-face brakes do not hold their toe-in adjustment well; you may need to sand the brake arm faces and washers to create more friction between them.

Brakes with a cylindrical arm and a clamp secured only by the pad eye bolt (WTB, SRP, etc.) are adjusted functionally the same as the curved-face ones with cupped washers.

Campagnolo used a rare, but simple method to adjust using a ball-joint at each pad eye bolt (Campagnolo, see Fig. 7.24).

disc brakes

VII-19: STRADDLE CABLE ADJUSTMENT

The straddle cable should be set so that it pulls on the brake arms in such a way as to provide optimal braking. This is not always the adjustment that produces the highest leverage, since sometimes brake feel (i.e., modulation of braking) is improved when leverage is reduced. In general, I recommend setting it for high leverage and reducing it from there to improve modulation

With any lever arm, the mechanical advantage is highest when the force is applied at right angles to the lever arm. For general purposes, set the straddle cable so that it pulls as close to 90 degrees to the brake arm as you can (Fig. 7.25). An esoteric and more precise argument is that, once the pad hits the rim, the actual lever arm is the line from the face of the pad to the cable attachment point on top of the arm (since the pad, not the brake boss, now becomes the fulcrum); if you set the straddle cable at 90 degrees from this line, the leverage is maximized (Fig. 7.26).

With low-profile brake arms, a 90-degree straddle-cable angle results in a short straddle cable set very low and close to the tire. Make sure that you allow at least an inch of clearance over the tire to prevent mud or a bulge in the tire from engaging the brake.

The straddle cable usually has a metal blob on one end, and the other end is clamped to one brake arm by an anchor bolt (Fig. 7.27). The blob fits into the slotted brake arm and acts as a quick release for the brake.

With Shimano cantilevers built since 1988, the brake cable connects directly to the cable clamp on one brake arm, and a link wire hooks to the other arm. On post-1993, Shimano cantilevers, the cable passes through a link-wire holder holding not only a link wire but also a fixed length of

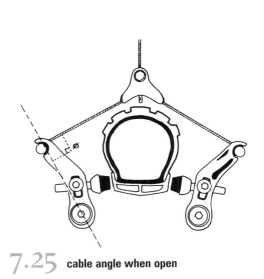

7.25 cable angle when open

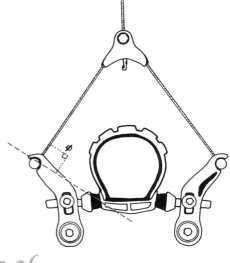

7.26 cable angle when closed

cable housing (Fig. 7.29). The brake cable passes directly through the link-wire holder and housing segment to the cable clamp on the brake arm. The mechanic has no choice of straddle cable settings; it is predetermined.

Between 1988 and 1993, Shimano brakes did not have the housing segment on the link wire holder; the holder was instead clamped to the brake cable, and its position was set by a plastic gauge. If you have this type and no gauge, simply set the

cable length from link wire holder to brake arm the same on both sides.

Some brakes do not have a cable clamp on either brake arm; both arms are slotted to accept the blob on the end of a straddle cable or link wire. In this case, a small cylindrical clamp forms a second blob on the end of the straddle cable (Fig. 7.28), or a link wire holder that holds two link wires is used.

With any straddle cable, after setting its length,

hydraulic and linkage brakes

7.27-29 straddle cables

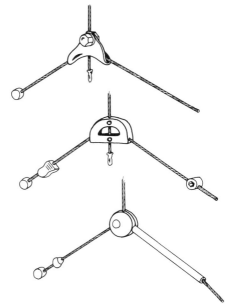

7.30 offset straddle hanger

for rear suspension

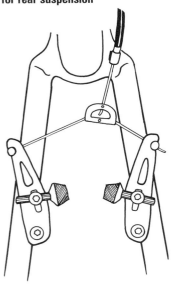

the straddle cable holder position is set by loosening the bolt or set screws that hold it onto the end of the brake cable and sliding it up on the brake cable. Tighten it in place (Fig. 7.6). It is set properly when the brake engages quickly, and the lever cannot be pulled closer than a finger's width from the bar. Some cable slack can be taken up with the barrel adjuster on the brake lever.

The lateral position of the straddle-cable holder can be changed with set screws as well. The holder should generally be centered on the straddle cable, but, sometimes, the brake cable pulls asymmetrically as it comes around the seat tube. In these cases, the straddle-cable holder may need to be offset for the brakes to work (Fig. 7.30).

VII-20: SPRING TENSION ADJUSTMENT

The spring tension adjustment centers the brake pads about the rim and also determines the return spring force. There is only one adjustment to make on brakes with a single set screw on the side of one brake arm. Turn the screw until the brakes are centered and the pads hit the rim simultaneously when applied (Fig. 7.31). Higher spring tensions can be achieved by moving the spring to a higher hole in the brake boss.

Some brakes rely on large tensioning nuts surrounding the mounting bolt and do not utilize the holes in the brake bosses as anchors (Fig. 7.17). On these, the tensioning nuts may be turned on both arms to get the combination of return force and centering you prefer. You must loosen the mounting bolt while holding the tensioning nut with a wrench. Turn the nut to the desired tension, and, while holding it in place with the wrench, tighten the mounting bolt again (Fig. 7.32).

On really old brakes without a tension adjustment, centering is accomplished by removing the

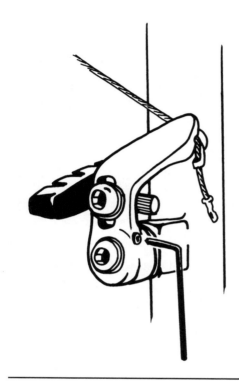

7.31 **adjusting return spring tension with a set screw**

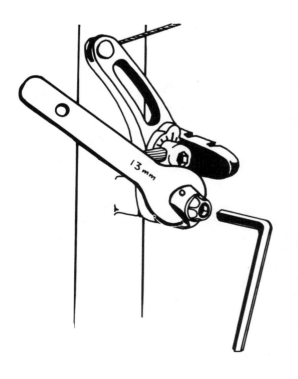

7.32 **adjusting return spring tension**

spring
tension
adjustment

brake arm and moving the spring to another hole on the boss. It is a rough adjustment at best, and some bosses do not have more than a single hole. When this adjustment fails, you can twist the arm on the boss to tighten or loosen the spring a bit. That, of course, is an even rougher adjustment.

<u>N O T E</u>

If the brake arms do not rotate easily (or at all) on the brake post, there is too much friction. Remove the brake and check that the post is not bent or split, in which case a new one needs to be screwed in or welded on. If not bent, the post is probably too fat to slide freely inside the brake arm, either due to paint on it or bulging or mushrooming of the post due to over-tightening of the brake mounting bolt. In this case, if it's the replaceable type, screw a new post into the frame or fork. Otherwise, file and sand the circumference of the post to reduce its diameter. File and sand uniformly, only a little at a time; avoid making it too small.

VII-2I: CANTILEVER LUBRICATION/ SERVICE

The only lubrication necessary on cantilever brakes is on the cables, levers, and brake arms. This should be performed whenever braking feels sticky. Lever and cable lubrication is covered in Section VII-5. Cantilevers can be lubricated by removing them, cleaning and greasing the pivots, and replacing them.

VIIC3: HYDRAULIC RIM BRAKES

This refers to brakes that are fully hydraulic and are mounted on the cantilever bosses. The most common type is Magura (Fig. 7.33), and these instructions, while possibly applicable to others, focus on Maguras. I cover it in detail, because the

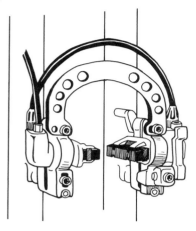

7.33 **Magura hydraulic brake**

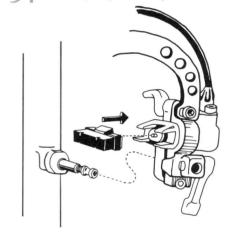

7.34 **installing Magura brake pad**

Magura owner's manual is an inscrutable translation from German.

The advantages of the Magura brake, in addition to its great stopping power, are that it is practically maintenance free and simple to adjust. The system is completely sealed from dirt, and there are no cables and housings to wear. Pads are replaced simply by pulling them out by hand and pushing new ones in. A screw on the lever adjusts pad-to-rim spacing as easily as turning a barrel adjuster on a cable-actuating lever.

A hydraulic brake works like a car brake in that pressure on brake fluid inside hydraulic tubes trans-

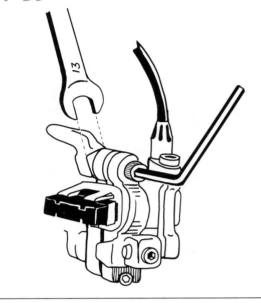

7.35 installing and/or adjusting elbow

mits the braking force from the lever to the wheel.

NOTE

The "master cylinder" is the hydraulic cylinder inside the lever, and each "slave cylinder" (or "wheel cylinder") is the cylinder driving each brake pad (one cylinder for each pad).

VII-22: MOUNTING MAGURA BRAKE LEVERS:

Hydraulic levers are installed onto the bars with a 4mm or 5mm Allen wrench, as with cable-actuating levers.

VII-23: INSTALLATION AND ADJUSTMENT OF MAGURA BRAKE CALIPERS ONTO CANTILEVER BRAKE BOSSES:

1. Snap a C-shaped plastic ring around each slave cylinder.

2. Assemble the adaptor brackets around the plastic ring on each slave cylinder with the supplied 4mm bolts, installing the L-shaped elbow behind the top bracket hole (Fig. 7.35). Right and left brake cylinders

are normally determined by having the crossover tube connecting the cylinders toward the bike (Fig. 7.33) i.e. the tube from the lever and the bleed hole are to the outside).

NOTE

The adaptor brackets (Fig. 7.33) are asymmetrical and can be reversed from left to right to move the slave cylinder closer to the rim or vice versa. Normal mounting is with the bracket imprinted with "Magura" on the right when facing the brake.

3. Slide a D-shaped washer onto the boss with the flat side of the washer up. A thick washer with a set screw must be used with some suspension forks to clear the fork brace.

4. Bolt the adaptor bracket to the cantilever boss with a bolt and washer. If mounting a bracket with the quick-release feature, first screw the mounting bolt with the spool-shaped head a few turns into the brake boss. Slide the quick-release unit over the mounting slot on the adaptor bracket (Fig. 7.34). Push the bracket onto the brake boss so the mounting bolt head comes through the hole in the quick-release unit. Flip the quick-release lever up to its closed position. Tighten the mounting bolt with a 5mm Allen key. You can now remove this side of the brake by merely flipping the quick-release lever down and pulling the bracket straight off. To install, push the bracket onto the boss so the bolt head sticks out through the hole in the quick-release unit, and flip the lever up.

5. Set the pad position: Sliding the adaptor bracket up and down adjusts the height of the brake cylinder. Loosening the mounting bolt and the two bolts holding the bracket together allows the cylinder to be slid in or out and rotated. Using these adjustments in tandem, set the pad-to-rim contact so that the pad hits the rim flat, about 2mm below its upper edge. See to it that the pad holders

do not drag on the tire. When retracted, the pads should sit 2mm to 3mm away from the rim.

6. Once the brake is set to the proper position, the elbows need to be positioned (Fig. 7.35) to support the brake and simplify repositioning after removal. Loosen the bolt above the pad cylinder. With a 13mm open-end wrench, rotate the elbow until it contacts the inner side of the seatstay or fork leg, and tighten the bolt (Fig. 7.35). Aftermarket elbows are available to fit certain suspension forks better.

7. If you have the "Brake Booster" arch (Fig. 7.33), loosely bolt it onto the right bracket adaptor through its right-side, oval mounting hole. Swing the arch over the wheel and slide it laterally until the booster's bottom left hole lines up with and slips over the bolt head on the left bracket. Tighten the top bolt on the right bracket to fix the booster in place. When releasing the brake, pull the left side of the booster off of the bolt head, and leave it attached to the right cylinder when pulling it off.

8. To fine-tune pad-to-rim spacing, especially as the pads wear, tighten the adjustment screw on the lever. Some systems take a 2mm Allen key; the screw is under the lever. Newer systems have a finger-operated knob on the front of the lever.

VII-24: MAGURA HOSE ROUTING

The hoses cannot go through cable stops, so you secure them to the frame by means of plastic draw ties or with little plastic or aluminum clips that snap over the tube and press or bolt into the frame's cable guides. Make sure there are no kinks in the hoses and that they do not stick out from the bike enough to hit your legs or hook on obstacles. Damaging hoses is to be avoided, as braking goes away if they are punctured.

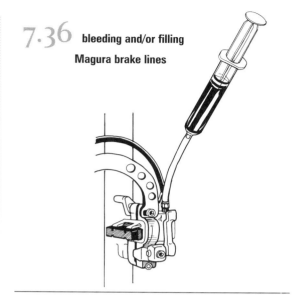

7.36 bleeding and/or filling Magura brake lines

Unless your frame is very small or very large, you may be able to get away with simply attaching the brakes to the frame as they come out of the box, already filled and bled, saving yourself the time and effort of bleeding the brakes. Skip to "Cutting brake lines" if you are adjusting the hose length.

VII-25: MAGURA PAD REPLACEMENT

Pad replacement is very simple.

1. Once the wheel is off, grab the pad and pull it straight out (Fig. 7.34).

2. Push the new pad in, paying attention to the rotation-indicator arrow on it. That's it!

VII-26: BLEEDING MAGURAS

Sponginess of brakes indicates the need for bleeding air from the lines. Bleeding is not a maintenance operation that needs to be done regularly; the fluid stays clean, and air does not get in unless the system is opened or gets damaged.

The air bubbles will rise toward the highest point in the system, so they should be up in the lever after any ride, meaning that it will not take much new fluid to drive them out.

1. Back up the 2mm micro-adjustment screw

bleeding
Magura
hydraulic
brakes

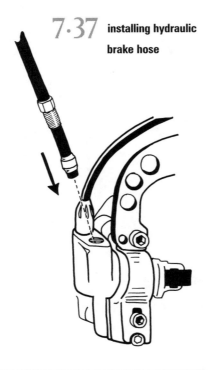

7.37 installing hydraulic brake hose

under the lever and the 2mm reach-adjustment screw on top of the lever, or on newer models, back up the single knob on the front the lever.

2. Keeping the bleed bolt at the lever closed, remove the bleed bolt (Fig. 7.33) on the right brake slave cylinder.

IMPORTANT

Never squeeze the lever while the system is open; fluid will squirt out.

3. The Magura syringe has a tube with a barbed fitting on the end (Fig. 7.36). Fill the syringe with Magura brake fluid or low-viscosity mineral oil (never with automotive brake fluid), invert it, and push out any air with the plunger. Screw the fitting into the bleed hole on the wheel cylinder (Fig. 7.36). (In a pinch, a squirt bottle of fluid can be used instead of the syringe, but it is easy to allow air in this way. You will need another person to hold the bottle tip tightly into the bleed hole and squeeze the bottle while you open and close the lever bleed bolt.)

4. Tip the bike or rotate the lever on the bar so the lever bleed bolt is at its highest point, and remove the bolt from the lever.

5. Push fluid into the brake wheel cylinder with the syringe (Fig. 7.36). Let it push fluid out of the lever.

NOTE

A cleaner way to do this is to screw in a piece of tubing with a barbed fitting into the lever bleed hole. Have the tube drain into a bottle of fluid.

6. While the fluid is still flowing, re-install the bleed bolt at the lever and tighten it. Make sure the bolt and washer are free of grit.

7. Remove the syringe or bottle from the wheel cylinder, leaving a dome of fluid bulging from the hole. Put the bolt back in, and tighten it; again, the bolt and washer must be free of grit.

If the bubbles have all been driven out, the brake will no longer feel spongy. Repeat until it is right. You may need to bleed it again after riding; the bubbles will have collected at the lever.

8. Adjust the pad spacing and lever reach as you wish with the two 2mm bolts or the single knob on the lever.

VII-27: CUTTING MAGURA HYDRAULIC BRAKE TUBES

1. Pull the plastic cover off of the crossover tube sleeve nut and slide it up the tube to get it out of the way. Unscrew the main tube sleeve nut with an 8mm wrench and pull the tube out (Fig. 7.37).

IMPORTANT

Again, never squeeze the brake lever while the system is open.

2. Cut the hose to length with a sharp blade, making sure it is a perpendicular cut. For every end you cut, you must have a brass "olive" fitting from Magura (Fig. 7.37); get them in advance.

3. Slide the 8mm sleeve nut up the tube.

7.38 **disc brake**

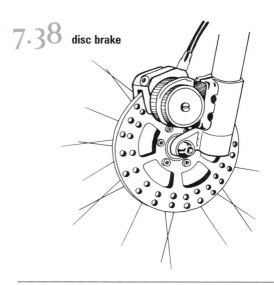

4. Slide the brass olive on, with the step-cut end toward the sleeve nut.

5. Stick the hose into the brake cylinder hole (Fig. 7.37), and screw in the sleeve nut by hand. Tighten the nut with an 8mm wrench. Push the plastic cover back onto the crossover tube sleeve nut.

6. If shortening the tubing, bleeding may not be necessary unless the brakes feel spongy. If installing new tubing, make the connection at the brake lever the same way. Fill and bleed the line following the "Bleeding" instructions.

VIIC4: DISC BRAKES
VII-28: ADJUSTMENT

Disc brakes have two pads that grab a disc (Fig. 7.38); most cars and motorcycles have brakes like this. They need need to be adjusted so that the disc turns parallel to the pads without rubbing them (or rubbing lightly, in the case of floating systems). They also need to be adjusted to stop quickly, well before the lever pulls to the grip. It is beyond the scope of this book to go into great detail about each individual type. Instead, you should refer to the instruction manual on the particular brake.

In general, cable-activated disc brakes can be

adjusted by tensioning the cable the same way as you would on a cantilever brake. On such brakes, only the caliper is hydraulic. The rest operates on the same principle as a cantilever brake.

The pads can usually be moved closer to the disc by turning a bolt that reduces the fluid volume in the caliper.

On fully hydraulic systems, volume in the entire system can often be adjusted at either the lever or at the caliper. If the brakes feel spongy, bleeding the air out of the system may be necessary. Unless your brakes have specific bleeding instructions, have the factory or a shop certified by the manufacturer perform this service.

To perform anything other than what is outlined in theses admittedly general statements, refer to the instruction manual included with your braking system.

VIIC5: LINKAGE BRAKES

There are so many vastly different linkage brakes (Fig. 7.39) besides V-brakes on the market that it would not be possible to include them all in detail here. Linkage brakes are often quite similar to cantilevers or V-brakes and are adjusted, centered and mounted in much the same way.

If in doubt, refer to specific instructions from

7.39 **linkage brake**

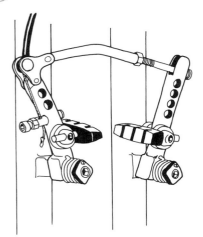

7.40 u-brake

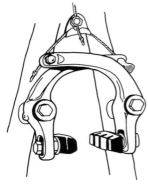

the manufacturer.

VIIC6: U-BRAKES
VII-29: U-BRAKE INSTALLATION

U-brakes (Fig. 7.40) mount on the same bosses that roller-cams do. They cannot be mounted on cantilever bosses, which would be too low.

1. Grease the pivots
2. Slide the arms onto the pivots
3. Screw in the mounting bolts.
4. Attach the straddle cable yoke to the brake cable
5. Attach the straddle cable to the cable clamp on one arm.
6. An easy way to set the position of the straddle cable yoke on a chainstay-mounted U-brake is to squeeze the lever to the grip after slipping the yoke up against the bottom bracket cable guide. Then tighten it in place. This is the highest it could be set on the cable and allows the longest possible straddle cable.

VII-30: U-BRAKE ADJUSTMENT

1. Set the rear straddle cable yoke position on the brake cable as outlined above. On a front brake, set it about 2 inches above the brake.
2. Tighten the straddle cable while pulling it

tight with a pair of pliers and squeezing the pads against the rim with your hand. Make sure you have tightened the anchor bolts enough that the cables do not slip.

3. Check that you cannot pull the lever closer than a finger's width from the grip. Tension the cable as needed with the straddle cable yoke or the lever barrel adjuster.

4. Set the spring tension by releasing the straddle cable, loosening the mounting bolt and swinging the pad away from the rim; then tighten the mounting bolt. Center the brake by setting the spring tension on one arm first, followed by the other arm in the same fashion. If your brake has a small Allen set screw on the side of one arm, use it to make fine spring-tension adjustments.

VII-31: U-BRAKE PAD REPLACEMENT AND POSITIONING

U-brakes rely on brake pads with threaded posts. Install them with the original spacers in their original orientation. The pads should hit the center of the braking surface and should have a small amount of toe-in. There is no adjustment for spacing from the brake arm. Hold the pad in place with your hand while tightening the nut with a wrench. As the pads wear, they tend to slide up on the rim and hit the tire, so check this adjustment frequently. You should also regularly clear hardened mud from inside of the brake arms; it can build up here on U-brakes and abrade the tire sidewalls.

VIIC7: ROLLER-CAM BRAKES
VII-32: ROLLER-CAM REMOVAL AND INSTALLATION

Roller-cam brakes (Fig. 7.41) mount on U-brake

brakes

7.41 roller-cam brake

bosses attached to the fork and either the chainstays or the seatstays. These are mounted further from the hub than cantilever bosses, and, like U-brakes, they will not work on standard cantilever bosses.

Roller-cams are removed by first pulling the cam plate out from between the rollers on the ends of the arms. Remove the mounting bolt and pull the arms off of the bosses.

Installation is performed in reverse. Grease the bosses and the inside of the pivots as well as the edges of the cam plate and the mounting bolts.

VII-33: ROLLER-CAM ADJUSTMENT

1. Check that the pulleys spin freely, and loosen them with a 5mm Allen wrench on the front and an open-end wrench on the back. The pulleys should rest on the narrow portion of the cam, which gives the greatest mechanical advantage when the brakes are applied. You change pad spacing by changing the location of the cam on the cable.

2. Use a 17mm wrench on the nut surrounding the mounting bolt to center the brake or to adjust spring tension. Loosen the mounting bolt, make small adjustments to the 17mm nut, and tighten the mounting bolt down again.

3. Once the adjustments are set, tighten the cam onto the cable so it will not slip.

VII-34: ROLLER-CAM PAD POSITIONING AND REPLACEMENT

The pad eye bolt is held on the front with a 5mm Allen wrench. The bolt in the back is adjusted using a 10mm open wrench. The pads should be toed in slightly. As the pads wear, they tend to slide up the rim and rub the tire, so check this adjustment periodically.

VII-35: BRAKE TROUBLESHOOTING

The first thing to check with any brake is that it stops the bike!

1. While the bike is stationary, pull each lever and see that it firmly engages the brake while the lever still is at least a finger's width away from the handlebar grip. If not, skip to "Cable tensioning" in Section VII-2 to VII-4 (or to "Hydraulic rim brakes," Section VII-26 if that is what you have).

2. Move at 10 mph or so, and apply each brake one at a time. By itself, the rear brake should be able to lock up the rear wheel and skid the tire, and the front brake alone should come on hard enough that it will cause the bike to pitch forward. Careful. Don't overdo it.

If you can't stop the bike quickly, you must make some adjustments and, perhaps, do a little cleaning. A brake works by forcing the brake pads into contact with the rim (or disc) to create friction. Anything that reduces the ability of these surfaces to generate friction against each other compromises braking. With this in mind, it should be obvious that these surfaces need to be clean and dry, that they should line up well with each other, and that

TROUBLE-
SHOOTING

the mechanism to pull them into contact should move freely and pull at an angle that offers high mechanical advantage.

That said, you can probably generate the following brake inspection list to perform frequently:

1. Cable length: Check that the cable is short enough to pull the pads against the rims without the levers contacting the grips, and long enough to allow the wheels to turn without dragging on the pads when centered between them. See "Cable tensioning" in Section VII-2 to VII-4 below to adjust.

2. Clean rims: Check for and remove any grease or glaze buildup on rims and pads. Grease can be removed with rags or solvent, and lightly buffing surfaces with sandpaper will remove glaze. Solvent residues on pads and rims cause brake squeal. You can remove such residues with soap and water.

TROUBLE-
SHOOTING

3. Pad wear: Check that the pads are not excessively worn (Fig. 7.42); if they have grooves, make sure these are not worn off). Make sure the pads contact the rims effectively (Figs. 7.20 to 7.22). Dig out any rocks or pieces of aluminum that are embedded in the pads to prevent rim damage (Fig. 7.43). Beware of lip formation on the top edge of the pad over the rim edge as the lower part of the pad wears away; this lip can prevent the pad from releasing from the rim. Replace or adjust pads as needed, and adjust the brake (see section under your brake) to get the desired response.

4. Cable wear: Check the cables for fraying, wear, and free movement, and check that the angle the cable meets each cantilever brake arm is close to 90 degrees (pulling at right angles generates the most leverage). If replacing, see "Cable installation," Section VII-6. Recognize that cables, housings, and pads are maintenance items; replace them frequently with good-quality ones. Even new, poor quality pads can require more than twice as much distance to stop as good ones!

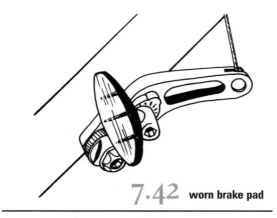

7.42 **worn brake pad**

5. Centered brakes: Check that the brakes are centered (the pads are spaced equally from either side of the rim) and that they apply and return easily. Readjust as needed (see adjustment section for your brake).

6. Toe-in: If the brakes squeal, and the rims and pads are clean (2. and 3., above), toe the pads in so that the forward corner of each pad touches the rim while the trailing corner is a millimeter or so away from it (Fig. 7.22c.); see pad adjustment under your brake type. The flimsier the brake arms, or the looser they are on the brake bosses, the more toe-in that is required.

7. Brake boss flex: If the seatstays or the fork legs are too flexible, applying the brakes will bow them outward and decrease braking pressure. This can be counteracted by attaching a horseshoe-shaped "brake booster" connecting the brake mounting bolts and bridging over the tire. These boosters are available for V-brakes, cantilevers, hydraulic rim brakes (see Fig. 7.33), U-brakes, roller cams and other linkage brakes.

7.43 **cleaning dirt from brake pad**

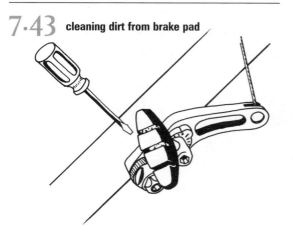

cranks and bottom brackets

"If you don't have time to do it right the first time,

you must have time to do it over again." — ANONYMOUS

The crank and bottom bracket is the power center for you and your bike. It is through this system that your energy is converted into forward movement of the bike. The crankset consists of the crankarms, bottom bracket, chainrings, chainring bolts and crank bolt (Fig. 8.1).

Any problem in the crankset can result in a large drop in available propulsion. The forces applied here are so large that expensive damage can easily occur if parts are not set up correctly. All parts need to be secured very tightly to oppose these large forces and prevent ruining expensive parts by using them when loose.

VIIIA: CRANKARMS AND CHAINRINGS

VIII-1 CRANK REMOVAL AND INSTALLATION

Depending on the crankset, you will either need a socket wrench or a large Allen wrench to remove the crank bolt, and a crank puller (Figs. 1.2 and 1.3) to take off the crankarms.

Most current crank bolts take either an 8mm Allen wrench or a 14mm socket wrench. Older systems may take a 15mm socket or a 7mm Allen, and you may still run across a few of those old French TA cranks with 16mm bolts.

A. Removal

1. Older cranksets have a dust cap covering the crank bolt. If it's there, remove it with either a 5mm Allen wrench, a two-pin dust cap tool, or a screwdriver.

2. Remove the crank bolt, using the appropriate wrench (Fig. 8.2). Make sure you bring the washer out with the bolt (Fig. 8.1), if there is one (if you leave it in, you will not be able to pull the crank off).

NOTE

Some cranks, like Shimano XTR (Fig. 8.8), are self-pulling (i.e., require no crank puller). The crank bolt

tools

5mm and 8mm Allen wrenches
pliers
file
crank puller
crank bolt wrenches (Allen or socket)
chainring nut tool
Shimano splined bottom-bracket cup tool
3/8-inch drive socket screwdriver
adjustable pin tool
lockring spanner
pin spanner

O P T I O N A L
shop-style fixed-cup installation tool

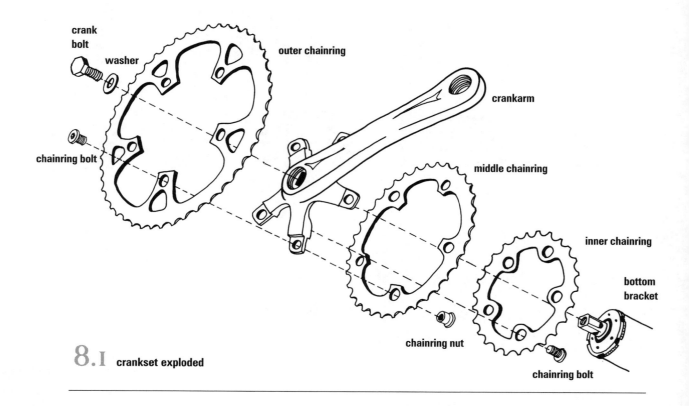

crank bolt

washer

outer chainring

chainring bolt

crankarm

middle chainring

inner chainring

bottom bracket

chainring nut

chainring bolt

8.1 **crankset exploded**

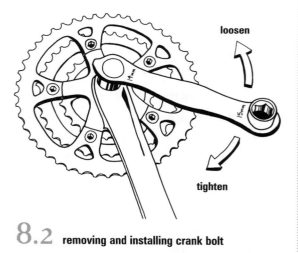

loosen

tighten

8.2 **removing and installing crank bolt**

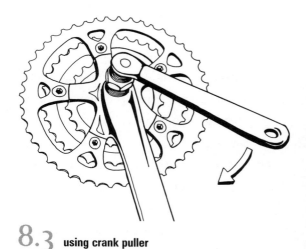

8.3 **using crank puller**

has a lip held down by a ring threaded into the crank; as the bolt is unscrewed, its lip pushes on the ring and pushes the crank off. Sometimes it doesn't work and the ring unscrews. In this case, you need to hold the ring with an adjustable pin tool while you unscrew the bolt with an 8mm Allen key.

3. Holding the crank puller (Fig. 1.3) in your hand,

unscrew its center push bolt so that the inner and outer threaded ends of the tool are flush.

4. Thread the crank puller into the hole in the crankarm. Be sure that you thread it in (by hand) as far as it can go; otherwise, you will not engage enough crank threads when you tighten the push bolt, and you will damage the threads. Future crank removal

depends on those threads being in good condition.

5. Tighten the push bolt clockwise (Fig. 8.3), either with the socket wrench or the included handle, until the crankarm pulls off of the spindle. Unscrew the puller from the crankarm.

B. Installation

1. Slide the crankarm onto the bottom bracket spindle. Clean off all grease from both parts. Grease allows the soft aluminum crank to slide too far onto the steel spindle and could deform the square hole in the crank.

2. Install the crank bolt. Apply grease to the threads, and tighten (Fig. 8.2). Here is where a torque wrench comes in handy; tighten it to about 35 to 45 foot-pounds. If you're not using a torque wrench, make sure the bolt is quite snug, but don't muscle it into submission, unless you are very small, in which case you may even need a cheater bar.

3. Replace the dust cover, if your crank has one.

4. Removing and reinstalling the right crank arm could affect shifting, so check the front derailleur adjustment. (See Chapter 5, Section V-5.)

5. You're done. Go ride your bike.

VIII-2 CHAINRINGS

You should get into the habit of checking your chainrings regularly. They do wear out and need to be replaced. It's hard to say how often, so include chainrings as part of your regular maintenance checklist. Check your chainrings for wear, when you replace your chain.

The chainring teeth should be checked periodically for wear; the chainring bolts should be checked periodically for tightness; the chainrings themselves should be checked for trueness by watching them as they spin past the front derailleur.

8.4 **chainring shifting ramps**

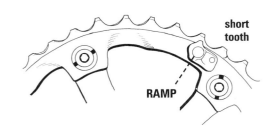

short
tooth

RAMP

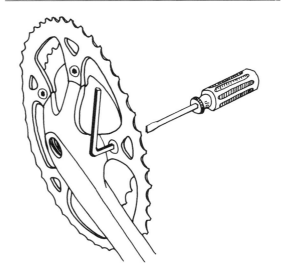

8.5 **removing and installing chainring bolts**

1. Wipe the chainring down and inspect each tooth. The teeth should be straight and uniform in size and shape. Caution: Don't be deceived by the seemingly erratic tooth shapes designed to facilitate shifting; check if they repeat regularly. Shifting ramps on the inner side (Fig. 8.4), meant to speed chain movement between the rings, often look like cracks.

If the teeth are hook-shaped, the chainring needs to be replaced. The chain should be replaced as well (see Chapter 4, Section IV-5), since this tooth shape effectively changes the spacing between teeth and accelerates wear on the chain. Note: Another wear evaluation method

crankarm
removal
and
installation
—
chainrings

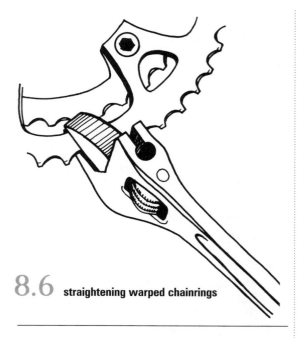

8.6 **straightening warped chainrings**

is to lift the chain from the top of the chainring; the greater the wear of either part, the further the chain separates. If it lifts more than one tooth, at least the chain, and perhaps the chainring, needs to be replaced.

2. Remove minor gouges in the chainrings with a file.

3. If an individual tooth is bent, try carefully bending it back with a pair of pliers or a crescent wrench. It will likely break off; take the message and buy a new chainring.

4. While turning the crank slowly, watch where the chain exits the bottom of the chainring. See if any of the teeth are reluctant to let go of the chain. That can cause chain suck. Locate any offending teeth and see if you can correct the problem. If the teeth are really chewed up or cannot be improved with pliers and a file, the chainring should be replaced.

VIII-3 CHAINRING BOLTS

Check that the bolts are tight by turning them clockwise with a 5mm Allen wrench (Fig. 8.5). If,

as you try to tighten the bolt, the nut on the back side turns, hold it with a two-pronged chainring-bolt tool designed especially for this purpose, or a screwdriver (Fig. 8.5).

VIII-4 WARPED CHAINRINGS

Looking down from above, turn the crank slowly and see whether the chainrings wobble back and forth relative to the plane of the front derailleur.

If they do, make sure there is no play in the bottom bracket. If there is play, adjust your bottom bracket (step 15, Section VIII-8). It is normal to have a small amount of chainring wobble and flex when you pedal hard, but excessive wobbling will compromise shifting. Small, localized bends can be straightened with a crescent wrench (Fig. 8.6). If it's really bent, replace it.

VIII-5 BENT CRANKARM SPIDERS

If you installed a new chainring and are still seeing serious back-and-forth wobble, chances are high that the spider arms on your crank are bent. If the crank is new, this is a warranty item, so take it to your bike shop.

VIII-6 CHAINRING REPLACEMENT

A. Replacing either of the two largest chainrings (Fig. 8.7) is easy.

8.7 **outer and middle chainrings**

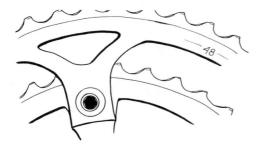

8.8 removing and installing post-1996 Shimano XTR chainrings

chainring
replacement

1. Simply unscrew the five 5mm Allen bolts holding them on the chainring (Fig. 8.5). You may need to hold the nut on the backside with either the specially made tool I mentioned before or a thin screwdriver.

2. Install the new rings, lubricate the bolts, and tighten them (Fig. 8.5).

NOTE

Any time you change the outer chainring size, you must reposition the front derailleur for proper chainring clearance, as described in Chapter 5, Section V-5.

B. To replace the inner chainring:

1. Pull off the crankarm (Section VIII-1, Figs. 8.2 and 8.3).

2. Remove the 5mm Allen bolts holding the chainring on. They are threaded directly into the crankarm (Fig. 8.1).

3. Install the new ring, and lube and tighten the bolts.

NOTE

Some chainring spiders do not have separate chainrings.

At the high end, 1996 and later Shimano XTR cranks rely on a thread-on cassette system that allows you to spin off all three chainrings from the crankarm as a single unit (Fig. 8.8). After removing a circlip (by prying it off with a screwdriver), a special lockring tool loosens the chainring-cassette-securing lockring; a female-threaded tool that goes on the crank bolt holds the lockring tool in place (Fig. 8.8). Once the cassette is off, you can interchange chainrings within the set or simply pop on a whole new set.

Economical cranks often have chainrings riveted to the crank or riveted to each other and bolted to the crank as a unit. In either case, you have no choice of chainring sizes, if, for instance, you want a lower gear on that $1000 full-suspension bike some penny-pinching product manager

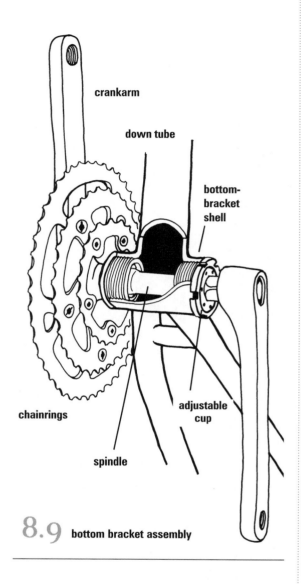

crankarm

down tube

bottom-
bracket
shell

chainrings

adjustable
cup

spindle

8.9 bottom bracket assembly

equipped with such a crank. If the chainrings are damaged, you must either replace the entire crank or the chainring set with an identical one.

4. Replace the crankarm (Section VIII-1, Fig. 8.2). Now ride your bike.

VIIIB: BOTTOM BRACKETS

Most bottom brackets thread into the frame's bottom bracket shell (Fig. 8.9). Simple enough, but it's important to remember that not all of these threads are the same.

Almost all mountain bikes use English standard threads. That translates into a 1.370-inch diameter and a thread pitch of 24 threads per inch. These numbers are usually engraved on the bottom bracket cups. If you are replacing a bottom bracket, make sure that the new cups have the same threads. It is important to remember that the threads on the drive side of an English standard bottom bracket are left-hand threads. In other words, the right-hand cup is tightened by turning counterclockwise (Fig. 8.16). Meanwhile, the threads on the left cup are right-hand threads and are, therefore, tightened clockwise.

English-threaded mountain-bike bottom brackets come in two bearing spacing widths for two different bottom-bracket shell widths. The standard bottom bracket shell width is 68mm, and most bottom brackets will have stamped or printed on them something like: "68-114", which means 68mm shell width and 114mm spindle length. The other, less common bottom bracket shell width is 73mm, and the bottom bracket would have a demarcation like: "73-118".

Other threads you may run across are Italian (with a 36mm diameter), French and Swiss (both of these come in 35mm diameter, but use different thread directions). These thread patterns are very rare on mountain bikes.

The most common type of bottom bracket in the 1990s is the Shimano-style cartridge bottom bracket with splined cups (Fig. 8.10). The most common bottom bracket in the 1980s and before was the "cup-and-cone" style with loose ball bearings (Fig. 8.11). Another recent bottom bracket type has a sealed cartridge bearing on either end secured by an adjustable cup and lockring at either end (Fig. 8.12). Shimano's latest high-end bottom brackets have a large spindle with splined, rather than

8.10-14 **types of bottom brackets**

8.10 Shimano cartridge

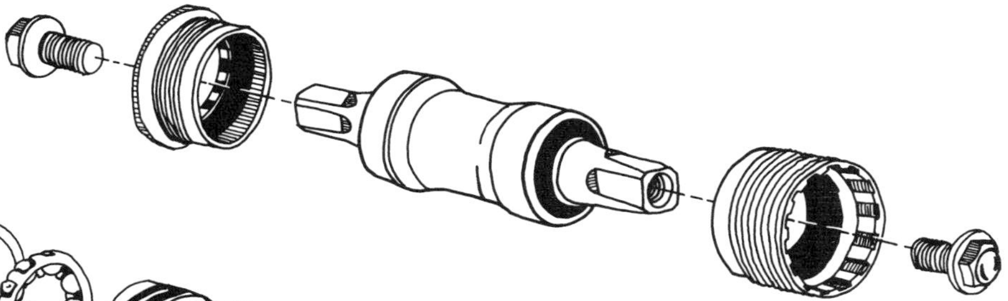

8.11 standard bearing

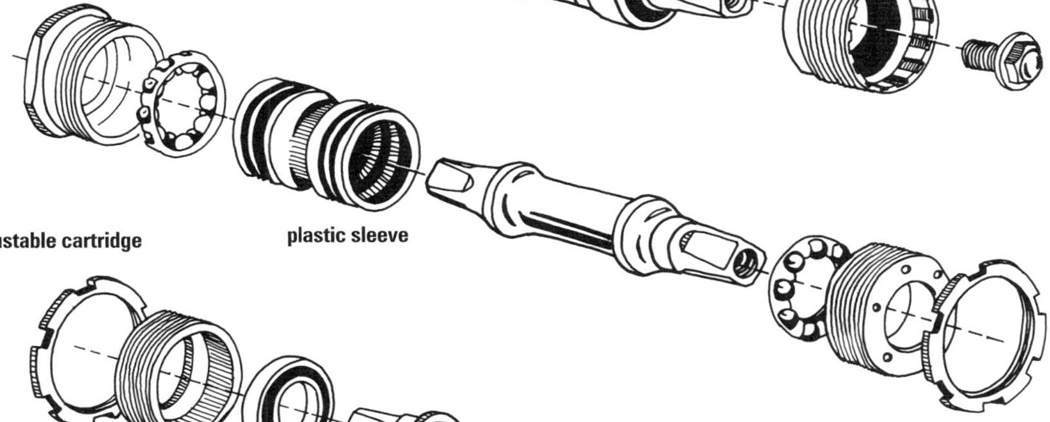

plastic sleeve

8.12 adjustable cartridge

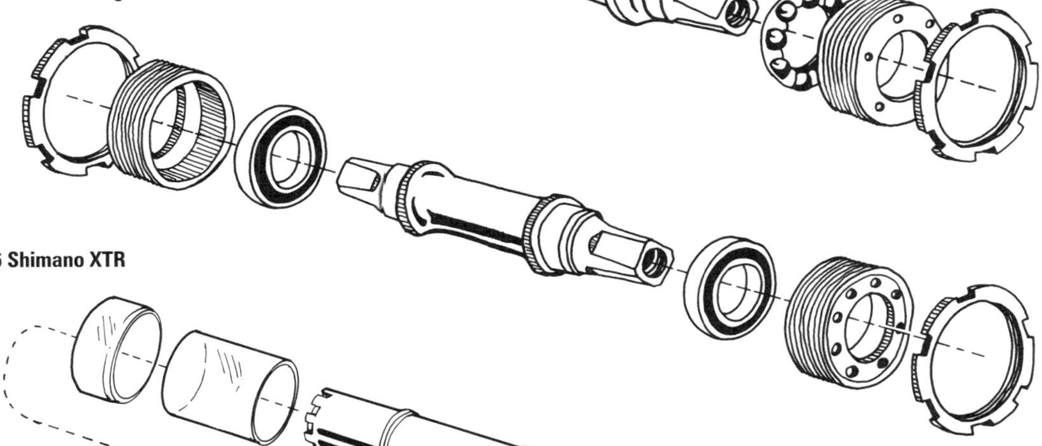

8.13 1996 Shimano XTR

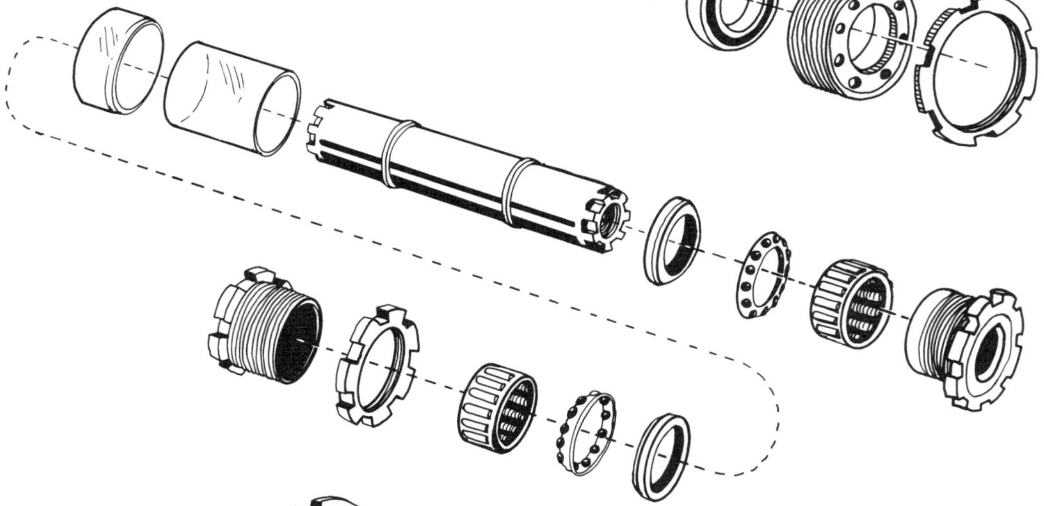

8.14 Mavic cartridge

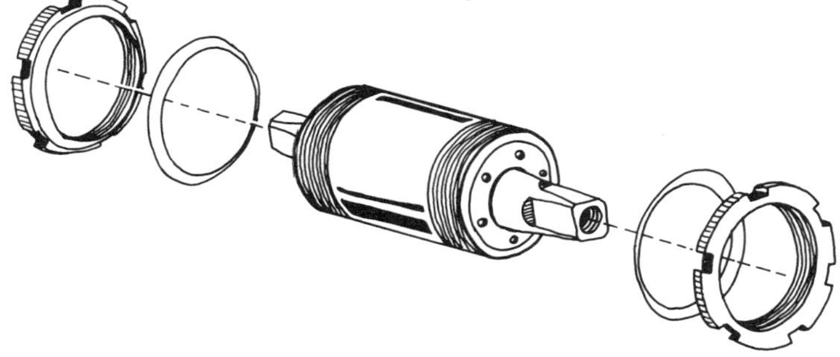

cranks and
bottom brackets

bottom
brackets

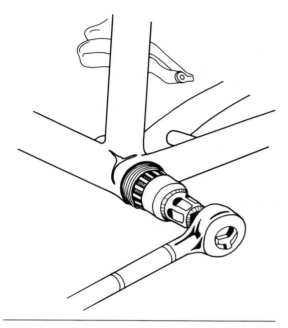

8.15 tightening and loosening Shimano-style cartridge bottom bracket with socket wrench and splined bottom-braket tool.

square, ends, and four sets of bearings: two sets of tiny balls, and two sets of needle bearings (Fig. 8.13).

Some bottom brackets do not thread into the bottom bracket shell. One type utilizes cartridge bearings held into an unthreaded bottom bracket shell by snaprings in machined grooves. Another type is the Mavic-style cartridge, threaded on each end (Fig. 8.14); it slips into the bottom-bracket shell and is held in place by lockrings threaded onto the cartridge.

VIIIC: BOTTOM-BRACKET INSTALLATION

level 2 The most important item in bottom-bracket installation is to put the right bottom bracket in. If a bike has the wrong length bottom bracket spindle, the chainrings will not line up well with the rear cogs (i.e., the center ring should be in line with

the center of the cogset; this is called chain line). Some bikes come from the factory with the wrong length bottom bracket. No amount of fiddling with the derailleurs will get such a bike to shift properly. Get a bottom bracket specifically recommended for your crankset, and with the proper thread and bottom-bracket shell width for your frame. Before installing a new bottom bracket of a different brand and model than your crank, see Fig. 5.34, and read the chain line section (V.H) at the end of chapter 5.

VIII-7 INSTALLATION OF SHIMANO CARTRIDGE-SEALED BOTTOM BRACKETS (AND CLONES)

As of this writing, most mountain-bike bottom brackets are Shimano-style sealed cartridge units (Fig. 8.10) that are installed with a splined tool (Fig. 1.3 and Fig. 8.15).

1. Slide the cartridge into the bottom-bracket shell, paying particular attention to the right and left markings on the cartridge. The cup with the

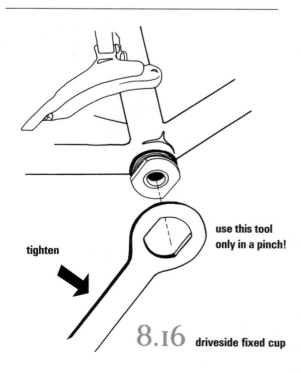

tighten

use this tool only in a pinch!

8.16 driveside fixed cup

bottom—bracket installation

138

raised lip and left-hand thread is the drive-side cup (the left-hand cup in Fig. 8.10).

2. Using the splined cup tool with either an open-end wrench or a 3/8-inch drive socket wrench on it, tighten the right (drive-side) cup until the lip seats against the face of the bottom bracket shell (as in Fig. 8.15, except on the drive side); recommended torque is in Appendix E.

NOTE

Since almost all mountain bikes have English threads, this cup should tighten counterclockwise.

3. Insert the non-drive side cup, and, with the same tool, turn it clockwise until it fits tightly against the cartridge (Fig. 8.15). (See Appendix E for recommended torque.) There is no adjustment of the bearings to be done; you can now put on the crank.

VIII-8 INSTALLATION OF CUP-AND-CONE BOTTOM BRACKETS

Cup-and-cone (or "loose-ball") bottom brackets (Fig. 8.11) use ball bearings that ride between cone-shaped bearing surfaces on the spindle and cup-shaped races in the threaded cups. One cup, called the fixed cup (the left-hand cup in Fig. 8.11), has a lip on it and fits on the drive side of the bike. The other, called the adjustable cup (the right-hand cup in Fig. 8.10), has a lockring that threads onto the cup and against the face of the bottom bracket shell. The individual ball bearings are usually held together by a retaining cage, which varies in shape depending on bottom bracket. Some folks prefer to do without the retainer; it works fine either way.

In order for loose-ball bottom brackets to turn smoothly, it is important that the bearing surfaces of the cups are parallel. Since the cups thread into the bottom bracket shell, the threads on both sides of the shell must be lined up with each other, and the end faces of the shell must be par-

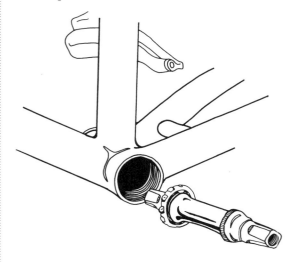

8.17 placing axle in shell

allel. If you have any doubts about your frame and are installing an expensive bottom bracket, it is a good idea to have the bottom bracket shell tapped (threaded) and faced (ends cut parallel) by a qualified shop possessing the proper tools.

1. Unless you have a shop fixed-cup tool, have a shop install the fixed cup for you. The shop tool assures the cup goes in straight and very tightly. The tool pictured in Fig. 8.16 can be used in a pinch, but it can let the cup go in crooked and will slip off before you get it really tight. The fixed cup must be very tight (see Appendix E for torque) so it does not vibrate loose. Remember that English-threaded fixed cups are tightened counterclockwise.

2. Wipe the inside surface of the both cups with a clean rag, and put a thin layer of clean grease on the bearing surfaces. Put enough so that the balls will be half-covered; any more is wasted and attracts dirt.

3. Wipe the axle with a clean rag.

4. Figure out which end of your bottom bracket spindle (or axle) is the drive side. The drive side may be marked with an "R," or you can simply tell by choosing the side with the longer end (when

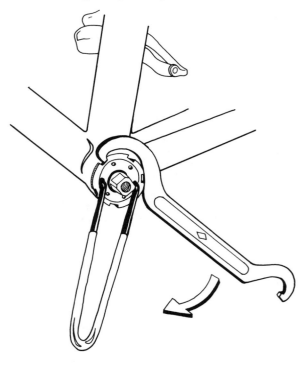

8.18 tightening lockring

measured from the bearing surface). If there is writing on the spindle, it will usually by right-side up for a rider on the bike. If there is no marking and no length difference, the spindle orientation is irrelevant.

5. Slide one set of bearings onto the drive-side end of the axle (Fig. 8.17). If you're using a retainer cage, make sure you put it on right. The balls, rather than the retainer cage, should rest against the axle bearing surfaces. Since there are two types of retainers with opposite designs, you need to be careful to avoid binding, as well as smashing of the retainers. If you're still confused, there is one easy test: If it's right it'll turn smoothly; if it's wrong it won't.

If you have loose ball bearings with no retainer cage, stick them into the greased cup. Most rely on nine balls; you can confirm that you are using the correct number by inserting and removing the axle

and checking to make sure that they are evenly distributed in the grease with no extra gap for more balls.

6. Slide the axle into the bottom bracket so it pushes the bearings into the fixed cup (Fig. 8.17). You can use your pinkie to stabilize the end of the axle as you slide it in.

7. Insert the protective plastic sleeve (shown in Fig. 8.11) into the shell against the inside edge of the fixed cup. The sleeve keeps dirt and rust from falling from the frame tubes into the bearings, so, if you don't have one, get one.

8. Now turn your attention to the other cup. Place the bearing set into the greased adjustable cup. If you are using a bearing retainer, make sure it is properly oriented.

9. Without the lockring, thread the adjustable cup (clockwise) by hand into the shell over the axle, assuring that it is going in straight. Screw the cup in as far as you can be hand, ideally all the way until the bearings seat between the axle and cup.

10. Locate the appropriate tool for tightening the adjustable cup. Most cups have two holes that accept the pins of an adjustable cup wrench called a "pin spanner" (Fig. 1.3). The other common type of adjustable cup has two flats for a wrench; on this type, you may use an adjustable wrench.

11. Carefully tighten the adjustable cup against the bearings, taking great care not to overtighten. Turn the axle periodically with your fingers to ensure that it moves freely. If it binds up, you have gone too far; back it off a bit. The danger of overtightening is that the bearings can force dents into the bearing surfaces of the cups, and the bottom-bracket axle will never turn smoothly again.

12. Screw the lockring onto the adjustable cup, and select the proper tool for your lockring. Lockrings come in different shapes, and so do

lockring spanners; make sure yours mate properly with each other.

13. Tighten the lockring against the face of the bottom-bracket shell with the lockring spanner, while holding the adjustable cup in place with a pin spanner (Fig. 8.18). If you turn the bicycle upside down, you can pull down harder on the wrenches.

14. As you snug the lockring up against the bottom-bracket shell, check the bottom-bracket spindle periodically, since the lockring pulls the cup out of the shell minutely and loosens the adjustment. The spindle should turn smoothly without free play in the bearings. I recommend installing and tightening the drive-side crankarm onto the drive end of the spindle (Fig. 8.2) at this time so you can push the crank from side to side to check for free play.

15. Adjust the cup so that the axle play is just barely eliminated. While holding the cup in place, tighten the lockring as tightly as you can (Fig. 8.18) so the bottom bracket does not come out of adjustment while riding (recommended torque is in Appendix E; tightening it as tightly as you can is about right). You may have to repeat this step a time or two until you get the adjustment just right.

VIII-9 INSTALLATION OF OTHER TYPES OF BOTTOM BRACKETS

The two bottom-bracket types mentioned earlier in this chapter probably represent about 95 percent of the mountain bikes in circulation. There are, however, a few variations worth mentioning.

A. Cartridge-bearing bottom brackets with adjustable cups (Fig. 8.12) are reasonably easy to install. These come with a pair of adjustable cups for both ends. With this type, you simply install the drive-side cup and lockring, slide the cartridge

bearing in (if it is not pressed into the cup), slip the spindle in, and then install the other bearing, cup and lockring. Tighten each lockring while holding the adjustable cup in place with a pin spanner (Fig. 8.18). Adjust for free play as in Section VIII-8, steps 11-15.

The advantage of having two adjustable cups is that you can center the cartridge by moving it side-to-side in the bottom-bracket shell. If the chainrings end up too close or too far away from the frame (see "chain line" discussion and Fig. 5.34 in the Troubleshooting section at the end of Chapter 5, Section V.H), you can move one cup in and one out to shift the position of the entire cartridge.

Sometimes cartridge-bearing bottom brackets bind up a bit during adjustment and installation. A light tap on each end of the axle usually frees them.

B. An unthreaded bottom-bracket shell with snap-ring grooves uses a type of bottom bracket without cups (not pictured); snaprings retain the bearings. This type was popular at the beginning of the 1980s and has virtually disappeared on new bikes. With a cupless bottom bracket, seat the cartridge bearings against the stops on either end of the spindle. Install one snap-ring with snap-ring pliers into the groove in one end of the shell. Push the entire assembly of axle and two bearings in from the other side of the bottom-bracket shell. Install the other snap-ring, and you're done.

C. Mavic cartridge bottom brackets (Fig. 8.14) require either end of the bottom-bracket shell to be chamfered at an angle to seat the angled lockrings. You need to go to a shop equipped with the Mavic tool for this. Once this is done, you simply slip the cartridge into the shell, slide on one of the angled plastic rings from either end (pictured in Fig. 8.14), and screw on a lockring, angled side inward, from either side. Holding the cartridge

other
bottom-
bracket
installation

with a pin spanner, tighten the lockring on either side (Fig. 8.18). The beauty of Mavic bottom brackets is that they work independently of the bottom-bracket-shell threads, so they can be installed in shells with ruined or non-standard threads. Mavic stopped producing them in 1995, so they are hard to find.

VIIID: OVERHAULING THE BOTTOM BRACKET

level 2

A bottom-bracket overhaul consists of cleaning or replacing the bearings, cleaning the axle and bearing surfaces, and re-greasing them. With any type, both crankarms must be removed.

VIII-10 OVERHAULING SHIMANO CARTRIDGE-SEALED BOTTOM BRACKETS

Standard sealed Shimano-style cartridge bottom brackets (Fig. 8.10) are sealed units and cannot be overhauled. They must be replaced when they stop performing properly. Remove them by unscrewing the cups with the splined cup tool (Fig. 8.15). Remove the cranks as in Section VIII-1, and install a new bottom bracket as directed in Section VIII-7, above.

VIII-11 OVERHAULING CUP-AND-CONE BOTTOM BRACKETS

Cup-and-cone bottom brackets (Fig. 8.11) can be overhauled entirely from the non-drive side, after you have removed the crankarms as described in Section VIII-1.

1. Remove the lockring with the lockring spanner (as in Fig. 8.18, with the lockring spanner and the rotation direction reversed).

2. Remove the adjustable cup with the tool that fits yours (usually a pin spanner (Fig. 1.3), installed into the cup as in Fig. 8.18).

3. Leave the fixed cup in place, and check that it is tightened hard into the frame by putting a fixed cup wrench on it and turning it counterclockwise (Fig. 8.16).

4. Clean the cups and spindle with a rag. There should be no need for a solvent unless the parts are really glazed.

5. Clean the bearings, without removing them from their retainer cages, with a citrus-based solvent. A simple way to do it is to shake the bearings about in a plastic bottle with solvent in it. A toothbrush may be required, and a solvent tank is certainly handy if you have access to one. If your bearings are not shiny and in perfect shape, go ahead and replace them. Balls with dull luster and/or rough spots or rust on them should be replaced.

6. Wash the bearings in soap and water to remove the solvent and any remaining grit. Towel them off thoroughly, and then let them dry completely. An air compressor is handy here.

7. Follow the installation procedure described in Section VIII-8.

8. Install the crankarms as in Section VIII-1, (Fig.8.2.)

VIII-12 OVERHAULING OTHER TYPES OF BOTTOM BRACKETS

If any cartridge-bearing bottom bracket becomes difficult to turn, the bearings must be replaced. If they are pressed into cups, then you may also have to buy new cups. Be doubly sure to get the correct size.

1. Reverse the installation procedure outlined above in Section VIII-9 to remove your bottom bracket.

2. Replace the bearings.

3. Reinstall your bottom bracket (Section VIII-9) and crankarms (Section VIII-1).

4. You're done. Go ride your bike.

TROUBLESHOOTING-CRANK AND BOTTOM-BRACKET NOISE

VIII-13 CREAKING NOISES

Those mysterious creaking noises can be enough to drive you nuts. Just as you think you have your bike tuned to perfection, a little noise comes along to ruin your ride, and these annoying little creaks, pops and groans can be a bear to locate. Pedaling-induced noises can originate from almost anything connected to your crankset, like movement of the cleats on your shoes or of the crankarms on the bottom-bracket spindle, loose chainrings, or poorly adjusted bearings. Of course, they could also originate from seemingly unrelated components like your seat, seatpost, frame, wheels, or handlebars.

Before spending hours overhauling your drivetrain, spend some time trying to isolate the source of the noise. Try different pedals and shoes and wheels. Pedal out of the saddle, and pedal without flexing the handlebars. If the source of the creak turns out to be the saddle, seatpost, wheels, or handlebars, turn to the appropriate chapter for directions on how to correct the problem.

If the creaking is in the crank area

1. Check to make sure that the chainring bolts are tight, and tighten them if they are not (Fig. 8.5).

2. If that does not solve the problem, make certain that the crankarm bolts are tight (Fig. 8.2). If they are not, the resulting movement between the crankarm and the bottom-bracket spindle is a likely source of noise. If your crank is of a different brand than your bottom bracket, check with the manufacturers or your local shop to make sure that they are recommended for use together. Incompatible cranks and spindles will never prop-

erly join and are a potential problem area.

3. The bottom bracket itself can creak due to improper adjustment, lack of grease, cracked bearings, worn parts, or loose cups. All of these things require adjustment or overhaul procedures, outlined in Section VIII.C of this chapter.

4. Now for the bad news. If creaking persists, the problem could be rooted in your frame. Creaks can originate from cracks in and around the bottom-bracket shell, so be sure to check for that. The threads in your bottom bracket shell could also be worn to the point that they allow the cups to move slightly. Neither of these is a good sign, unless, of course, you were hoping for an excuse to buy a new frame.

VIII-14 CLUNKING NOISES

1. Crankarm play: Grab the crankarm and push on it side-to-side.

a. If there is play, tighten the crank arm bolt (Fig. 8.2; torque spec is in Appendix E).

b. If there is still crankarm play and you have a cup-and-cone bottom bracket (Fig. 8.11) or a cartridge-bearing bottom bracket with a lockring on either side (Fig. 8.12), adjust the bottom bracket spindle end play (see steps 11-15 in Section VIII-8).

c. If bottom-bracket adjustment does not eliminate crankarm play, or you have a non-adjustable cartridge bottom bracket (Fig. 8.10), the bottom bracket is loose in the frame threads. With a cup-and-cone bottom bracket, you can go back to Section VIII-8, and start over, making sure that the fixed cup is very tight. A cheater bar (extension tube) may need to be used on the fixed-cup wrench to tighten it to high enough torque. Adjustable-cup lockrings need to be equally tight (Fig. 8.18), once the spindle end play is adjusted properly.

d. The lockrings and fixed-cup flanges must be flush with the bottom bracket shell all of the way around; if they are not, the bottom bracket must be removed, and the bottom-bracket shell must be faced (cut parallel) by a shop equipped with a facing cutter.

e. If the crankarm play persists, or the bottom-bracket fixed cup or lockring will not tighten up completely, the bottom-bracket cups are stripped or undersized, or the frame's bottom-bracket-shell threads are stripped or oversized. Either way, it's an expensive fix, especially the frame replacement option! Get a second opinion if you reach this point. If you can find a Mavic bottom bracket (Fig. 8.14), you can still use the frame.

2. Pedal end play: Grab each pedal and wobble them to check for play. See "Overhauling pedals," Section IX.B in Chapter 9 if they are loose.

VIII-15 HARD-TO-TURN CRANKS

If the cranks are hard to turn, you really ought to overhaul your bottom bracket (see Section VIII.C, above) — unless you want to continue intensifying your workout or boosting the egos of your cycling companions. The bottom bracket may be shot and needs to be replaced.

VIII-16 INNER CHAINRING DRAGS ON CHAINSTAY

Your bottom bracket spindle is too short, the square hole in your crankarm is deformed so that the crank slides on too far, or you have switched to a larger inner chainring. A misaligned frame, with either bent chainstays or a twisted bottom-bracket shell, can cause chainring rub as well. With an adjustable cartridge-bearing bottom bracket with a lockring on either end, it is possible that the entire bottom bracket is offset to the left.

If the bottom-bracket spindle is too short, you need a new one of the correct length.

If the square hole in the crank is badly deformed, you need a new crankarm. Otherwise it will continue to loosen up and cause problems.

If the chainring is too large, get a smaller one.

A badly misaligned frame needs to be replaced.

If the bottom bracket is offset, loosen the lockrings, screw the left cup in further, back the right cup out some, adjust out the end play, and tighten the lockrings back down (Fig. 8.18).

N O T E

See Section V.H at the end of Chapter 5 (Fig. 5.34) on chain line to establish proper crank-to-frame spacing.

pedals

"For everything, turn, turn, turn..." — *THE BYRDS*

To best serve its purpose, a bicycle pedal needs only to be firmly attached to the crankarm, and provide a stable platform for the shoe. A simple enough task. But you'd be amazed at the different approaches that have been taken to achieve this goal. For this book, however, we only focus on the two basic types of mountain-bike pedals. The standard cage-type pedal with a toeclip and strap (Fig. 9.2), is the simplest and cheapest. The "clip-in" (Fig. 9.1), pedal has spring-loaded shoe retention like a ski binding, and is probably the most common version used on mid- to high-end mountain bikes. Clip-in pedals are sometimes called "clipless", since they have no toeclip.

Cage-type pedals are fairly common on lower-end bikes. They are relatively unintimidating for the novice rider, and the frame (or "cage") that surrounds the pedal provides a large, stable platform (Fig. 9.2). Without a toeclip, the top and bottom of the pedal are the same and you can use just about any type of shoe. If you mount a toeclip without a strap, it can keep your foot from sliding forward and still allow easy release in almost any direction. When you add a toe strap and cleats, the combination works well to keep your foot on the pedal while riding even the roughest of single track. When tightened, the strap allows you to pull up on the upward part of the pedal stroke — giving you more power and a more fluid pedal stroke. Of course, as you add clips and straps, the pedal becomes harder to enter and exit, and boots or shoes with aggressive tread designs become increasingly difficult to use.

Clip-in models (Fig. 9.1) offer all of the advantages of a good clip-and-strap combination, yet allow easy entry and exit from the pedal. These

tools

15mm pedal wrench
small and large
  adjustable
  wrenches
3mm, 4mm, 5mm,
  and 6mm
  Allen wrenches
screwdriver
pliers
knife
grease
oil (chain lubricant)

FOR OVERHAULING PEDALS:

7mm, 8mm, 9mm,
10mm, 17mm or
18mm open end
  wrenches
Shimano splined
pedal tool
  - or - Look splined
  pedal tool - or-
  snapring pliers
  for Time
13mm cone
  wrench
8mm socket
  wrench

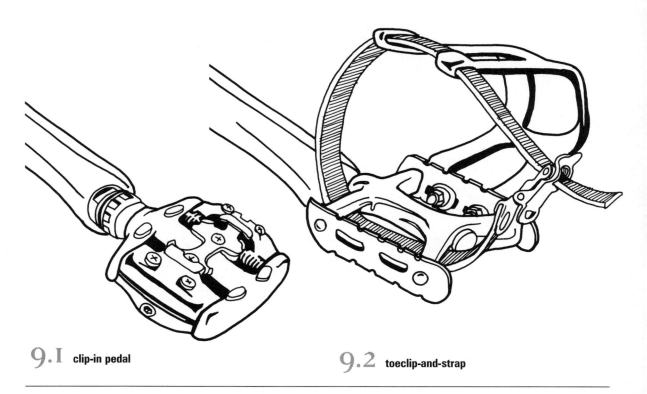

9.1 **clip-in pedal**

9.2 **toeclip-and-strap**

pedals are more expensive and require special shoes and accurate mounting of the cleats. Your choice of shoes is limited to stiff-sole models that accept cleats for your particular pedal. Once you have them dialed in, you will find that clip-in pedals waste less energy through flex and slippage and allow you to transfer more power directly to the pedals. This greater efficiency explains their almost universal acceptance among cross-country mountain-bike racers. Most clip-in mountain pedals are "SPD" style; SPD stands for Shimano Pedaling Dynamics, as Shimano was the originator of the first successful clip-in mountain pedal in the mid-1980s. "SPD-compatibility", shared by virtually all current clip-in mountain pedals, indicates that the cleat mounts with two side-by-side 5mm x 0.8mm-thread screws, spaced 14mm apart, screwing into a movable threaded cleat-mounting plate on a shoe with two longitudinal grooves in

the sole (Fig. 9.6). It does not mean that one company's cleat will necessarily work with the pedal of another company.

NOTE

Some pedal cleats do work with other brands of pedals. Appendix F is a cleat compatibility chart that shows how well those cleats work with particular pedals.

This chapter explains how to remove and replace pedals, how to mount the cleats and adjust the release tension with clip-in pedals, how to troubleshoot pedal problems, and how to overhaul and replace spindles on almost all mountain-bike pedals. Incidentally, in this chapter I use the terms "axle" and "spindle" interchangeably.

IX-1: PEDAL REMOVAL AND INSTALLATION

Note that the right pedal axle is right-hand

threaded and the left is left-hand (reverse) thread-ed. Both unscrew from the crank in the pedaling direction.

A. Removal:

1. Slide the 15mm pedal wrench onto the wrench flats of the pedal axle (Fig. 9.3). Or, if the pedal axle is designed to accept it, you can use a 6mm Allen wrench from the back side of the crank arm (Fig. 9.4). This is particularly handy on the trail, since you probably won't be carrying a 15mm wrench anyway. But, if you are at home and the pedal is on really tight, it'll probably be easier to use the standard pedal wrench. Some pedals, like the Time A.T.A.C. (Fig. 9.14) and Time TMT, have no wrench flats and can only be removed with a 6mm Allen wrench (Fig. 9.4).

2. Unscrew the pedal in the appropriate direc-tion. The right, or drive-side, pedal unscrews coun-terclockwise when viewed from that side. The left-side pedal is reverse threaded, so it unscrews in a clockwise direction when viewed from the left side of the bike. Once loosened, either pedal can be unscrewed quickly by turning the crank forward with the wrench engaged on the pedal spindle.

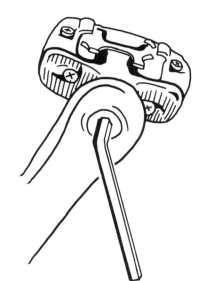

9.4 **removing pedal with a 6mm Allen wrench**

B. Installation:

1. Use a rag to wipe the threads clean on the pedal axle and inside the crankarm.

2. Grease the pedal threads.

3. Start screwing the pedal in with your fingers, clockwise for the right pedal, counterclockwise for the left.

4. Tighten the pedal with the 15mm pedal wrench (Fig. 9.3) or a 6mm Allen wrench (Fig. 9.4). This can be done quickly by turning the cranks backward with the wrench engaged on the pedal spindle.

IXA: SETTING UP CLIP-IN PEDALS

Setting up clip-in pedals involves installation and adjustment of the cleats on the shoes, and adjusting the pedal-release tension.

IX-2: INSTALLING AND ADJUSTING PEDAL CLEATS ON THE SHOES.

The cleat is important because its position determines the fore-aft, lateral (side-to-side) and

9.3 **removing pedal with 15mm wrench**

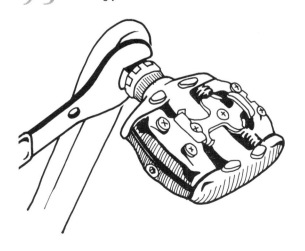

removing and installing clip-in pedals

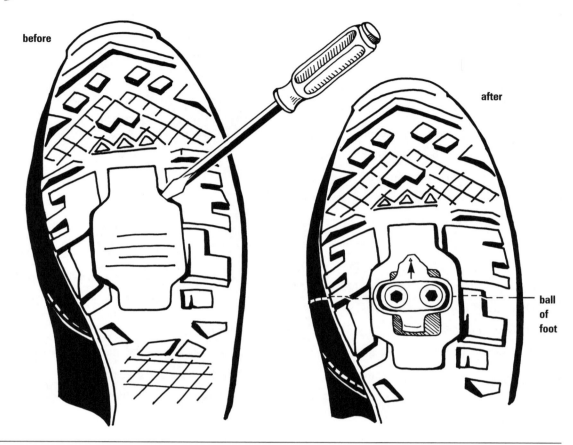

before

after

ball
of
foot

rotational position of your foot. If your pedals aren't properly oriented, it could eventually cause hip, knee or ankle problems.

1. If your shoe has a pre-cut piece of rubber covering the cleat-mounting area, remove it. Cut around the cover's outline with a knife, pry an edge up with a screwdriver (Fig. 9.5), and yank it off with some pliers. Warming it up with a hair dryer beforehand softens the glue.

2. Put the shoe on, and mark the position of the ball of your foot (the big bump behind your big toe) on the outside of the shoe. This will help you position the cleat so the ball of your foot will be over the pedal spindle. Take the shoe off, and continue drawing the line straight across the bottom of the shoe (Fig. 9.6).

3. If there are threaded holes in your shoe sole to accept the cleat screws, skip to step 4. If you do not have threaded shoe holes, you must install the backing plate and threaded cleat plate that came with your pedals. Remove the shoe's sock liner, put the rectangular backing plate inside the shoe over the two holes, and put the threaded plate on top of it.

4. Lube the cleat screw threads, and screw the cleat that came with your pedals to your shoe; this usually requires a 4mm Allen wrench. Make sure you orient the cleat in the appropriate direction. Some cleats have an arrow indicating forward (Fig. 9.6); if yours do not, the instructions accompanying your pedals probably specify which direction the cleat should point.

5. Position the cleat in the middle of its lateral- and rotational-adjustment range, and line up the mounting screws over the mark you made in Step 2 (Fig. 9.6).

setting up
clip-in
pedals
—
adjusting
release
tension
on clip-in
pedals

NOTE

Cleats for Time A.T.A.C. pedals (Fig. 9.14)have no lateral or rotational adjustment; just set the screws at your mark and tighten the cleat down, making sure the arrow on the cleat points forward. Put the cleat with the imprinted stars onto the right shoe for more float range; put it on the left shoe for less float. You may now tighten the screws, skip the remaining steps and go riding! (Incidentally, the older model Time TMT pedal, of which few were sold, also is set up the same way—with only fore-aft cleat adjustment, but the only shoe you could use with it was Time's mountain shoe of the time. The newer A.T.A.C. works with any SPD-compatible shoe.)

6. Snug the screws down enough that the cleat won't move when clipped in or out of the pedals, but don't tighten them down fully yet. Follow the same steps with your other shoe.

7. In order to set the lateral position, put the shoes on, sit on the bike, and clip into the pedals. Ride around a bit. Notice the position of your feet. Pedaling is more efficient the closer the feet are to the plane of the bike, but you don't want them in so far that they bump your cranks. Take the shoes off and adjust the cleats laterally, if necessary, to move the feet side to side. Get back on the bike and clip in again.

8. In order to set the rotational position, ride around some more. Notice if your feet feel twisted and uncomfortable. You may feel pressure on either side of your heel from the shoe. If necessary, remove your shoes and rotate the cleat slightly. Some pedals offer free-float, allowing the foot to rotate freely for a few degrees before releasing. Precise rotational cleat adjustment is less important if the pedal is free-floating.

NOTE

On Speedplay Frogs (Fig. 9.16), angle the cleat

slightly toward the outside of the shoe, and tighten the mounting screws just enough that the cleat can still turn. Clip into the pedal and rotate the heel inward until it just touches the crankarm. Tighten the cleat in this position (Frogs have no inward release; this sets the inward stop).

9. Once your cleat position feels right, trace the cleats with a pen so that you can tell if the cleat stays put. While holding the cleat in place, tighten the bolts down firmly. Hold the Allen wrench close to the bend so that you do not exert too much leverage and strip the bolts.

10. If the cleat holes are open to the inside of the shoe, place a waterproof sticker over the opening inside, and replace the sock liner.

11. When riding, bring the 4mm Allen wrench along, since you may want to fine-tune this adjustment over the course of a few rides.

IX-3: ADJUSTING RELEASE-TENSION ON CLIP-IN PEDALS

If you find the factory release-adjustment set-

9.7 **release tension adjustment**

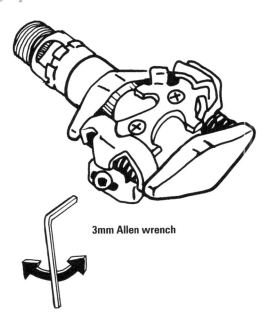

3mm Allen wrench

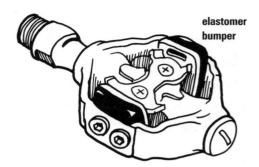

9.8 onZa clip-in pedal

ting to be too loose or too restrictive, you can adjust the release tension on most clip-in pedals; exceptions are Time and Speedplay. The adjusting screws are usually located at the front and rear of the pedal (Fig. 9.7). The screws affect the tension of the nearest set of clips. The adjusters are usually operated with a small (usually 3mm) Allen wrench. OnZa (Fig. 9.8) and Look SL3 (Fig. 9.15) pedals are adjusted differently; see Section IX-4 below.

1. Locate the tension-adjustment screws. They are usually on either fore and aft end of the pedal; you can see the screw in Figs.9.7 and 9.9-9.13.

2. To loosen the tension-adjustment, turn the screw counterclockwise, and to tighten it, turn it clockwise (Fig. 9.7). It's the classic "lefty loosey, righty tighty" approach. There usually are click stops in the rotation of the screw. Tighten or loosen one click at a time (one-quarter to one-half turn), and go riding to test the adjustment. Many types include an indicator that moves with the screw to show relative adjustment. Make certain that you do not back the screw out so far that it comes out of the spring plate.

NOTE

With Ritchey, Scott, Girvin, Topo, Wellgo and other

dual-rear-clip/dual-rear-spring pedals, you will decrease the amount of free-float in the pedal as you increase the release tension.

IX-4: ADJUSTING TENSION OF OTHER TYPES OF PEDALS

A. Medium-old Look mountain pedals have a single 5mm bolt that adjusts both sides. It has a large window like a ski binding with a pointer to show the relative adjustment. The even older, one-sided Look models have a small slotted screw in the center to adjust the tension. Current Look SL3 pedals (Fig. 9.15) have a 3mm adjustment screw with spring tension indicator on either side that is reached through a hole in the top of the rear clip.

B. OnZa clip-in pedals (Fig. 9.8) rely on elastomer bumpers to provide release tension. You adjust OnZas by changing the elastomer. Bumpers of varying hardness are included with the pedals. OnZa's black bumpers are the hardest, and the clear ones are the softest. There are several grades in between. The harder the bumper, the greater the release tension. To replace bumpers, unscrew the two Allen bolts that retain each bumper (Fig. 9.21). Pull the old bumper out, put in the new one. While you are at it, make sure that the Phillips screws that hold in the cleat guides are tight, since they have a tendency to loosen up and fall out.

C. Time pedals (Fig. 9.14) have no tension adjustment; they offer high retention and lots of float; yet they require low entry and release force — hence no adjustment.

D. Speedplay Frogs (Fig. 9.16) have no tension adjustment either; ease of exit can be adjusted by rotating the cleat on the shoe sole to reduce the release angle.

IXB: OVERHAULING PEDALS

Just like a hub or bottom bracket, pedal bearings and bushings need to be cleaned and re-greased regularly. Most pedals have a lip seal around the axle where it enters the pedal. Pedals without one get dirty inside very quickly.

1. Remove the pedal from the bike (Figs. 9.3 and 9.4) for overhauling.

There is a wide variation in mountain-bike pedal designs. This book is not big enough to go into great detail about the inner workings of every single model. Speaking in general terms, pedal guts fall into two broad categories: ones that have cartridge bearings and/or bushings (Figs. 9.13-9.16, and 9.21), and those that have loose ball bearings (Figs. 9.11, 9.10, and 9.18). Many pedals are closed on the outboard end and have a nut surrounding the axle on the inboard end (Figs. 9.9-9.16). The axle assembly installs into the pedal as a unit and is accessed by this inboard nut. The axle assemblies on older pedal designs — and some newer models — are accessed from the outboard end by removing a dust cap (Figs. 9.18 and 9.21).

2. Before you start, figure out how the pedal is put together so you will know how to take it apart; the following paragraphs and the illustrations on subsequent pages should help. In a few cases, what the pedal guts are like may not be clear until you have completed step 1 in the overhaul process.

Shimano pedals usually have two sets of loose bearings and a bushing, which come out as a complete axle assembly (Figs. 9.11 and 9.12). You will see the tiny ball bearings at the small end of the axle (Fig. 9.17).

Most Taiwan-made clip-in pedals use an inboard bushing and an outboard cartridge bearing (Figs.

9.13 and 9.21); Codas also have an additional needle bearing between the two other bearings. Brands include Wellgo, VP, Ritchey, Scott, Coda, Girvin, Topo, Nashbar, OnZa, Exus and Norco. Some of these are accessed from the crank side; others are accessed via an outboard dustcap. Speedplay pedals also have cartridge bearings and bushings; they differ in that they are opened like a clamshell.

All Look and Time mountain pedals have an inboard cartridge bearing and an outboard needle bearing (Figs. 9.14 and 9.15). The axle assembly is accessed from the crank side.

Some pedals — even clip-in models (older Tioga comes to mind) — have no bearings at all. Instead, they just use bushings inside a plastic axle sleeve.

IX-5: OVERHAULING PEDALS CLOSED ON THE OUTBOARD SIDE

This includes Shimano, Time, Look, Coda, Scott, Tioga, Exus and some VP and Wellgo models.

1. With the tool designed for your pedal (Figs. 1.2 and 1.3), remove the axle assembly by unscrewing the nut surrounding the axle where it enters the inboard side of the pedal (Fig. 9.9 and 9.10). See note below regarding thread direction.

Shimano, Look and Exus pedals take a plastic splined tool. Use a large adjustable wrench to turn the tool (Fig. 9.9). Most other pedals take a 17mm or 18mm open-end wrench (Fig. 9.10).

NOTE

The threads inside the pedal body are reversed from the crankarm threads on the axle; the internal threads on the drive-side pedal are left-hand threaded, and vice versa. That means the right axle assembly unscrews clockwise, and the left axle assembly unscrews counterclockwise. It's confusing, but unlike the crankarm threads, pedal axles are threaded so

pedals

overhauling
clip-in
and
standard
pedals

that pedaling forward tightens the assembly in. The nut is often plastic and can crack if you turn it the wrong way, so be careful. Hold the pedal body with your hand or a vise while you unscrew the assembly. The fine threads take many turns to unscrew.

Time and Look pedals: All Look and Time mountain pedals have a large inboard cartridge bearing and an outboard needle bearing cartridge. Look and Time bearings tend to stay very clean and seldom require overhaul.

There are three versions of Look clip-in mountain pedals. The oldest models, marketed under the Look and Campagnolo names, clip in only on one side and resemble Look road pedals in design and function. The newer Look models resemble most double-sided mountain clip-in pedals and take a large steel cleat. Axle assemblies in the older models are accessed with an 18mm open-end wrench, while the newer Looks (Fig. 9.15) require a special splined tool purchased separately.

Time A.T.A.C. and TMT pedal axles are removed via a snapring on the crank side (Fig. 9.14). Popping the snapring out requires inward-squeezing snapring pliers.

With Time or Look, skip to step 3.

Speedplay Frogs have a cartridge bearing and a needle bearing which can be re-greased without opening the pedal. Remove the Phillips screw from the outboard end of the pedal body and squirt grease in with a fine-tip bicycle grease gun until it squirts out the axle end. If you decide to open a Frog (reminds you of junior-high biology, doesn't it?), the pedal comes apart like a clamshell by unscrewing the single bolt on each side with a 2.5mm Allen wrench (Fig. 9.16). Before you put it back together, put a thin bead of automotive gasket sealer all of the way around the edge of one pedal half to seal out water.

2. Once you have removed the pedal body, take a look at the axle/bearing/bushing assembly. You will notice either one or two nuts on the thin end of the axle. These nuts serve to hold the bearings and/or bushings in place. Remove the nuts.

If the axle has just a single nut on the end (Figs. 9.13 and 9.16), simply hold the axle's large end with the 15mm pedal wrench and unscrew the little nut with a 9mm wrench (or whatever fits it). The nut will be very tight, since it has no locknut.

If the axle has two nuts on the end, they are tightened against each other. To remove them, hold the inner nut with a wrench while you unscrew the outer nut with another (Fig. 9.17).

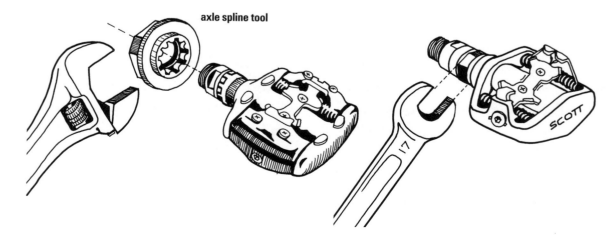

9.9 removing axle from Shimano clip-in pedal

axle spline tool

9.10 removing axle from Scott pedal

9.11-16 types of clip-in pedals

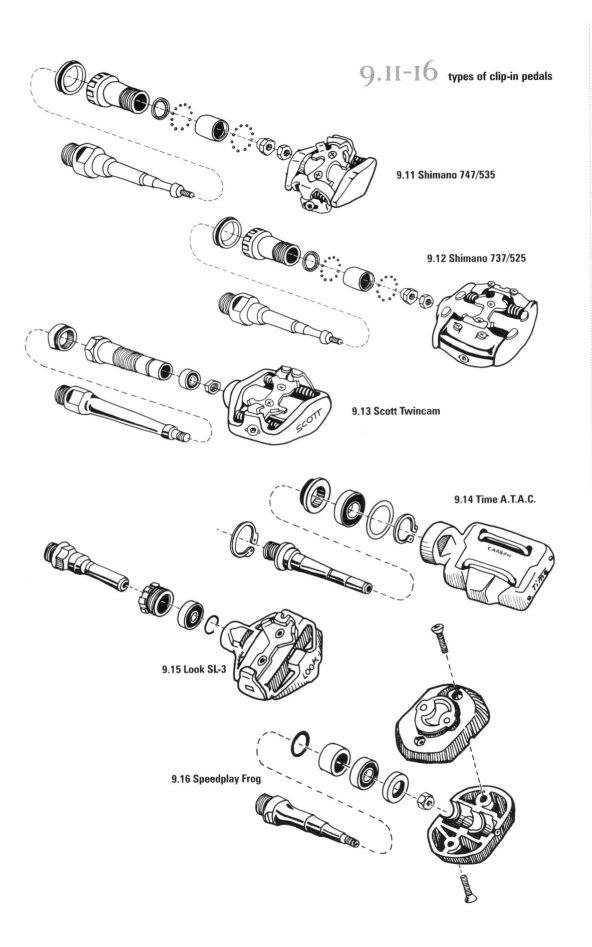

9.11 Shimano 747/535

9.12 Shimano 737/525

9.13 Scott Twincam

9.14 Time A.T.A.C.

9.15 Look SL-3

9.16 Speedplay Frog

pedals

overhauling
clip-in
and
standard
pedals

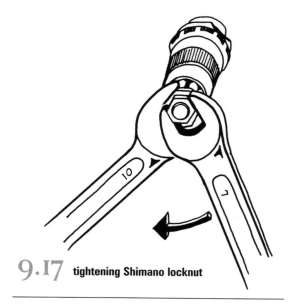

9.17 tightening Shimano locknut

Shimano and older Tioga pedals use two nuts in this fashion; on Shimanos, the inner nut acts as a bearing cone—be careful not to lose the tiny ball bearings as you unscrew the cone!

3. Clean all of the parts.

If it is a loose-bearing pedal, use a rag to clean the ball bearings, the cone, the inner ring that the bearings ride on at the end of the plastic sleeve (it looks like a washer), the bearing surfaces on either end of the little steel cylinder, the axle, and the inside of the plastic axle sleeve (Fig. 9.11 and 9.12). To get the bearings really clean, wash them in the sink in soap and water with the sink drain plugged; the motion is the same as washing your hands, and results in both the bearings and your hands being clean for a sterile reassembly. Blot dry.

If, on a pedal with a cartridge bearing (Figs. 9.13-9.16), the bearing is dirty or worn out, replace it. These usually have steel bearing covers that cannot be pried off without damaging them, nor can the covers be replaced

Needle bearings (Time, Look and Coda) can be cleaned with solvent and a thin toothbrush slipped inside the bearing cylinder.

On a bushing-only pedal, like older Tioga, just wipe down the axle and the inside of the bushings.

4. Lightly grease everything and reassemble it as it was, a simple process with bushings, cartridge bearings, and needle bearings— not so simple with loose bearings!

With a loose-bearing pedal, you have some exacting work to place the bearings on their races and screw the cone on while they stay in place. On a Shimano (Figs. 9.11 and 9.12), grease the bushing inside the plastic axle sleeve, and slide the axle into the sleeve. Slide the steel ring, on which the inner set of bearings rides, down onto the axle and against the end of the sleeve. Make sure that the concave bearing surface faces out, away from the sleeve. Coat the ring with grease, and stick half of the bearings onto the outer surface of the ring. Slip the steel cylinder onto the axle so that one end rides on the bearings. Make sure that all of the bearings are seated properly and none are stuck inside of the sleeve.

To prevent the bearings from piling up on each other and ending up inside the sleeve instead of on the races, grease the cone and start it on the axle a few threads. Place the remaining half of the bearings on the flanks of the cone. Being careful not to dislodge the bearings, screw the cone in until the bearings come close to the end of the cylinder but do not touch it. While holding the plastic sleeve, push the axle inward until the bearings seat against the end of the cylinder. Make sure that the first set of bearings is still in place. Screw the cone in. Tighten it with your fingers only, and loosely screw on the locknut.

5. Adjust the axle assembly. (Time and Look skip this step).

Pedals with a small cartridge bearing and a single nut on the end of the axle, like Exus, Coda, VP, Wellgo, Topo, Girvin, Speedplay and Scott, simply require that you tighten the nut against the cartridge bearing while holding the other end of the axle with the 15mm pedal wrench. This secures the inner ring of the cartridge bearing against the shoulder on the axle, and proper adjustment is assured.

On pedals with two nuts on the end of the axle, hold the cone or inner nut with a wrench and tighten the outer locknut down against it (Fig. 9.17). Check the adjustment for freedom of rotation, and be sure there is no play. Readjust as necessary by tightening or loosening the cone or inner nut and re-tightening the locknut.

6. Replace the axle assembly in the pedal body.

Smear grease on the inside of the pedal hole; this will ease insertion and act as a barrier to dirt and water. Screw the sleeve back in place with the same wrench you used to remove it (Figs. 9.9 and 9.10). Remember: Pay attention to proper thread direction (see note in Step 1)! Tighten carefully; it is easy to overtighten and crack the plastic nut.

7. Put the pedals back on your bike, and go ride.

IX-6: OVERHAULING LOOSE-BEARING PEDALS WITH A DUST CAP ON THE OUTBOARD END

NOTE

Many non-clip-in pedals are not worth the effort of overhaul, and all economical pedals are not accessible to overhaul. Assess the value of your pedals and your time before continuing.

1. Remove the dust cap with the appropriate tool. This could be a pair of pliers, a screwdriver, a coin, an Allen wrench or a splined tool made especially for your pedals (Fig. 9.18); it's pretty easy to figure out which one is needed to remove the cap.

2. As if you were overhauling a hub, hold the cone on the outboard end of the axle with a cone wrench, and unscrew the locknut.

3. Holding the pedal over a rag to catch the bearings, unscrew the cone. Keep the bearings from the two ends separate in case they differ in size or in number. Count them so you can put the right numbers back in when you reassemble the pedal. The guts should look like Fig. 9.18.

4. With a rag, clean the bearings, cones and bearing races. Clean the inside of the pedal body by pushing the rag through with a screwdriver. If there is a dust cover on the inboard end of the pedal body, you can clean that in place or after popping it out with a screwdriver.

5. If you want to get the bearings really clean, wash them in a plugged sink with soap and water. The motion is the same as washing your hands, and results in both the bearings and your hands being clean for a sterile reassembly. Blot dry.

6. If you removed it, press the inboard dust

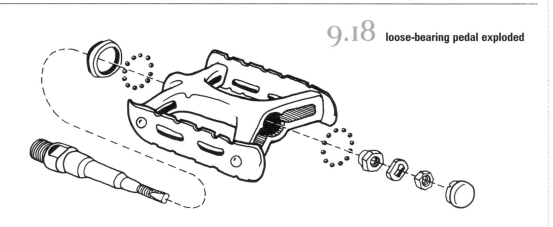

9.18 **loose-bearing pedal exploded**

9.19 dropping in bearings

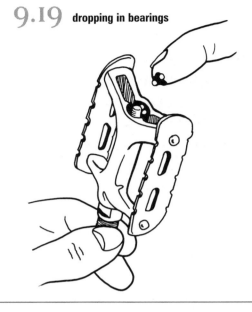

cover back into the pedal body. Smear a thin layer of grease in the inboard bearing cup and replace the bearings. Once all of the bearings are in place, there will be a gap equal to about half the size of one bearing.

7. Drop the axle in and turn the pedal over so that the outboard end is up. Smear grease in that end, and replace the bearings.

8. Screw the cone in until it almost contacts the bearings, then push the axle straight in to bring the cone and bearings together; this prevents the bearings from piling up and getting spit out as the cone turns down against them. Without turning the axle (which would knock the inboard bearings about), screw the cone in until it is finger-tight.

9. Slide on the washer and screw on the lock nut. While holding the cone with a cone wrench, tighten the lock nut (similar to Fig. 9.17, but you will be holding the cone with a 13mm or so cone wrench, not a 10mm standard open-end wrench).

10. Check that the pedal spins smoothly without play. Readjust as necessary by tightening or loosening the cone and re-tightening the locknut.

11. Replace the dust cap.

12. Put the pedals back on and go riding!

IX-7: OVERHAULING CARTRIDGE BEARING PEDALS WITH OUTBOARD DUSTCAP

Ritchey, OnZa (Fig. 9.8), some Wellgo, some VP, Nashbar and Norco, among others, have an axle end nut accessed from the outboard end by removing the dustcap. Inside is a brass bushing on the crank side and a sealed cartridge bearing on the outboard end.

1. Take off the dustcap; some take a 5mm or 6mm Allen wrench; others take a coin or a screwdriver.

2. Hold the crank end of the axle with a 15mm pedal wrench, and unscrew the nut on the outboard end with an 8mm socket wrench. The guts should look similar to Fig. 9.21

3. Push the axle out the inboard end, freeing the outboard cartridge bearing.

4. Clean and regrease the axle and the inside of the pedal body hole. Replace the cartridge bearing if necessary. On Ritcheys, the brass bushings inside the pedal body are also replaceable.

5. Push the axle back into the pedal body, slip the cartridge bearing onto the outboard end of the axle, and thread on the end nut.

9.20 removing locknut on onZa-type pedal

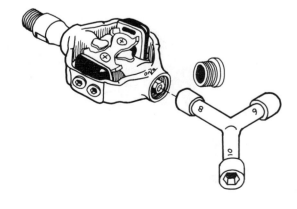

9.21 onZa clip-in pedal exploded

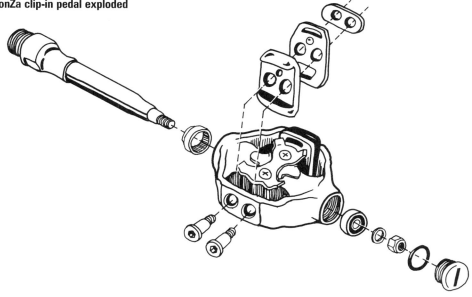

6. While holding the crank end of the axle with a 15mm pedal wrench, tighten the little nut down against the cartridge bearing.

NOTE

Ritcheys will still have side play at this point; the dustcap is an integral part of the assembly. Once it is tightened down, the play goes away.

7. Replace the dustcap.

8. Put the pedals back on your bike (Fig. 9.3), and you're done. Go ride.

IX-8: LIGHTEN YOUR BIKE WITH AN AFTERMARKET TITANIUM SPINDLE

Many manufacturers offer aftermarket titanium axles for high-end pedals. Some manufacturers offer only a titanium axle that is installed into the same sleeve, bushings and bearings as the one it replaces. Other manufacturers sell a complete assembly, including the sleeve, bushings and bearings.

If you are going to install a lightweight aftermarket axle or axle assembly into your pedals, make sure that you purchase one intended for your pedal brand and model. If all you are doing is replacing the axle, go ahead and follow the overhaul procedures outlined earlier in this chapter (Section IX-5 and IX-7). If you bought the entire assembly, just take out your old assembly. Again (I obviously feel the need to say this often), pay attention to the direction of the threads (see note in Section IX-5, Step 1). Using the procedures in Section IX-5 or IX-7, install the new assembly.

Reinstall your pedals (Fig. 9.3 or 9.4). You'll be amazed how much lighter your bike feels.... Or is that your wallet?

TROUBLESHOOTING PEDAL PROBLEMS

IX-9: CREAKING NOISE WHILE PEDALING

a. The shoe cleats are loose, or they are worn and need to be replaced (see Section IX-2).

b. Pedal bearings need cleaning and lubrication (see Section IX.B and IX-5 to IX-7).

c. The noise is originating from somewhere other than the pedals (see Chapter 8 Troubleshooting section).

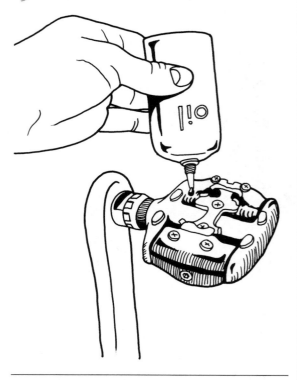

9.22 lubing release mechanism

IX-10: Release or entry with clip-in pedals is too easy or too hard

a. Release tension needs to be adjusted (see "Adjusting pedal release tension" in this chapter).

b. Pedal-release mechanism needs to be cleaned and lubricated. Clean off mud and dirt, and drip a dry chain lubricant on the springs and spring contacts (Fig. 9.22).

c. The cleats themselves need to be cleaned and lubricated. Clean off dirt and mud and put a dry chain lubricant or a dry grease like pure Teflon on the contact ends of the cleats.

d. The cleats are worn out: replace them (Section IX-2).

e. The knobs on the shoe sole that contact the pedal might be so tall that they prevent the cleat from engaging. Locate where the pedal edges contact the sole, and trim some of the rubber with a knife.

f. The clips on the pedal are bent down. Straighten

them if you can, or replace them. If you can't repair or replace the clips, you may have to replace the entire pedal.

g. If it is hard to clip into your pedals, check the metal cleat guide plate at the center of the pedal. It is held on with two Phillips screws, and they may be loose or have fallen out.

IX-11: YOU EXPERIENCE KNEE AND JOINT PAIN WHILE PEDALING

a. Cleat misalignment often causes pain on the sides of the knees, (see Section IX-2).

b. You need more rotational float. Consider a pedal that offers more float; those offering the most are the Time A.T.A.C. and Speedplay Frog.

c. If your foot naturally rolls inward (pronates), and your shoe and cleat are not allowing it to do so, then there is likely to be an increase in the tension on the iliotibial (I-T) band, the tendon connecting the hip and calf. This will eventually cause pain on the outside of the knee. You need to see a specialist, because you will probably need orthotics to correct the problem.

d. Fatigue and improper seat height can also contribute to joint pain. Pain in the front of the knee right behind the kneecap can indicate that your saddle is too low. Pain in the back of the leg behind the knee suggests that your saddle is too high.

CAUTION

If any of these problems result in chronic pain, consult a specialist.

saddles and seatposts

"Your view of the world pretty much depends on where you're sitting." — C. P. ELLKEY

tools

4mm, 5mm, 6mm
Allen wrenches
open-end wrenches
of various sizes
adjustable wrench
grease

After a few hours on the bike, I can pretty much guarantee that you will be most aware of one component on your bike: the saddle. It is the part of your bike with which you are most ... uh ... intimately connected. Nothing can ruin a good ride faster than a poorly positioned or bad saddle.

The seatpost connects it to the frame. Some have shock absorbing systems that cushion the ride. Some bikes, like the Softride, employ a flexible beam attached to the front of the frame instead of a seatpost.

X-1: SADDLES

Most bike saddles are simply made up of a flexible plastic shell, some padding, a cover and a pair of rails (Fig. 10-1). There are countless variations on (and a few notable exceptions to) this theme: Some have extra thick or high-tech padding; some have rails made of titanium, chromoly or even carbon fiber; others have synthetic covers, covers made from Kevlar, or covers made from the finest full-grain leather money can buy. You can expect to spend anywhere from $20 to $200 for a decent saddle, and price may not be the best indicator of what makes a saddle really good — namely comfort.

You have a lot of choices when you decide to pick a saddle. My best advice is to ignore weight, fashion and looks, and choose a saddle that is comfortable. I could go on for pages about hi-zoot gel padding, scientifically designed shells that flex in just the right places at just the right moment, and all sorts of factors that engineers consider when designing a saddle. None of it would count for squat if, after reading it, you ran out and bought a saddle that turned out to be a giant pain in the rear. People are different and saddles are different. Try as many as you can before buying one.

Determine which saddle shape and design is the most comfortable for your body and then — and only then — start looking at things like titanium rails, fancy covers and all of the other things that improve a saddle. I know a lot of people who

IO.I modern lightweight saddle

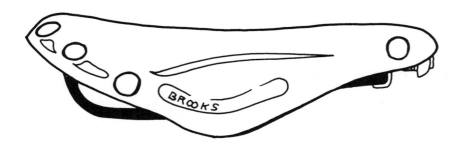

IO.2 Brooks leather saddle

need 300- or 400-gram saddles with tons of thick padding to feel comfortable on even a short ride. I know others who can ride for hours on a skinny little 200-gram Selle Italia Flite. It's a matter of preference and anatomy. Any decent bike shop worth its weight in titanium should let you try a saddle for a while before locking you into a sale.

Brooks and Idéale saddles have no plastic shell, foam padding or cover. They are simply constructed from a single piece of thick leather attached to a steel frame with large brass rivets (Fig. 10-2). This was the most commom saddle up until the 1980s. Brooks still makes them and even offers them with titanium rails these days. This sort of saddle requires a long break-in period and frequent applications of a leather-softening compound that comes with the saddle or from a shoe store. Like a lot of old bike parts, you either love 'em or hate 'em. If you're not familiar with them by now, go out and buy a modern saddle (Fig. 10-1).

A saddle with a plastic shell and foam padding requires little maintenance, except to keep it clean; check periodically that the rails are not bent or cracked (a good sign that you need to replace your saddle).

X-2: SADDLE POSITION

Even if you have found the perfect saddle, it can still feel like some medieval torture device if it isn't properly positioned. Saddle placement is the most important part of finding a comfortable riding position. Not only does saddle position affect how you feel on the bike, but with the saddle in the right place you suddenly become a much better rider. There are three basic elements to saddle position: tilt, fore-and-aft and saddle height (Fig. 10-3).

See Appendix C, Section C-3 for a detailed explanation of setting saddle and handlebar position. Following are some short guidelines.

Proper saddle height (Fig. 10-3) is key to transferring good power to the pedals. The ideal road-bike saddle height places your leg in a 90- to 95-

percent extension when you're riding; however, you may find that this position to be too high for riding single track. Make sure your seatpost is inserted past the limit line, however. Again, consult Appendix C.

In order to improve your balance and center of gravity when descending, you can bring the saddle height down— how far depends on you and the kind of riding you do. Pro downhillers prefer very low saddle heights when compared to pro cross-country riders.

The most common cause of numb crotch and butt fatigue is an improperly tilted saddle (Fig. 10-3). The general rule of thumb is that you should keep the saddle level when you first install it. After a while, some people find that they prefer a slight upward or downward tilt to their saddles. I strongly recommend against making that tilt much more than a quarter-inch. Too much upward tilt and you place too much of your body weight on the nose of the saddle. Too much downward tilt will cause you to scoot down the saddle as you ride. That puts unnecessary pressure on your back, shoulders and neck.

Fore-and aft-position (Fig. 10-3) determines where your butt sits on the saddle, the position of your knees relative to the pedals, and how much of your weight is transferred to your hands. Regardless of manufacturer, all saddles are designed to have your butt centered over the widest part. If this is not where you sit, reposition the saddle. You want to position the saddle so that you have a comfortable amount of bend in your arms, without feeling too cramped or stretched out. If you find that your neck and shoulders feel tighter than usual and your hands are going numb, then redistribute your weight by moving the saddle back. Fore-and-aft saddle position also affects

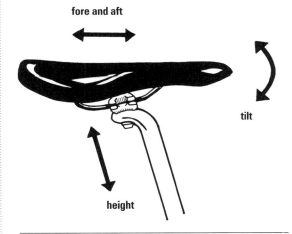

IO.3 saddle adjustments

fore and aft

tilt

height

how your legs are positioned relative to the pedals. Ideally, your fore-aft position should be such that your knee pushes straight down on the forward pedal when your crankarms are in a perfectly horizontal position.

Butt pain is intimately connected to handlebar position, as are other aches and pains. The shorter the upper-body reach and higher the handlebars, the more weight will go on the butt. On the other hand, the longer the reach and lower the bars, the more the pelvis rotates forward and moves the saddle pressure point from the sit bones to the soft tissue of the perineum and genital area. As a general rule, a novice rider will want a shorter reach and higher bars, and perhaps a correspondingly wider saddle, than an experienced rider. Once again, consult Appendix C.

X-3: SEATPOST MAINTENANCE

A standard seatpost requires little maintenance other than removing it from the frame every few months. When you do that, wipe it down, regrease it and the inside of the frame's seat tube, and then reinstall it. This keeps it clean and moving freely for the purposes of adjustability; it also should

saddle
position
—
seatpost
maintenance

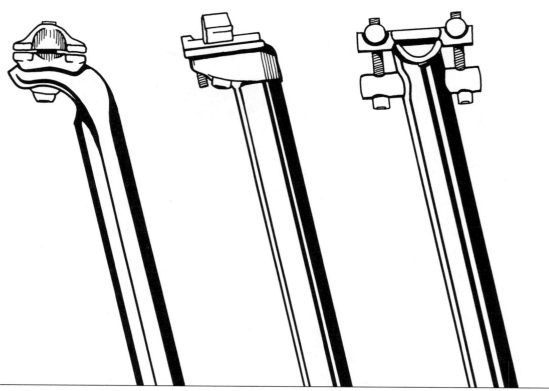

IO.4 single-bolt seatpost

IO.5 single-bolt seatpost with small adjusting bolt

IO.6 two-bolt seatpost

prevent the seatpost from getting stuck in the frame (a very nasty and potentially serious problem). I have outlined the procedures for installing a new seatpost and for removing a stuck seatpost later in this chapter.

Suspension seatposts require periodic tune-ups. I have outlined the steps further on in this chapter.

Regularly check any seatpost for cracks or bends so that you can replace it before it breaks with you on it.

X-4: INSTALLING A SADDLE

Most seatposts have either one (Fig. 10-4) or two bolts (Figs. 10-5 and 10-6) for clamping the saddle. The single-bolt systems have either a vertical bolt (Fig. 10-4) or a horizontal crosswise bolt. Remember those heavy posts on your first cheap bike? Those steel seatposts had the single horizontal bolt which pulled together a number of

knurled washers with ears to hold the saddle rails. Fortunately, most of us don't have these weak seatpost clamps that cannot hold up to adult use anymore, eschewing them for posts with one or two vertical bolts holding aluminum clamshell clamp pieces together. The two-bolt posts can rely on one of two systems. In one, the two bolts work together by pulling the saddle into the clamp (Fig. 10-6). On others, like the American Classic post, a smaller second bolt works to offset the force of the main bolt (Fig. 10-5). No matter what type you have, it is reasonably easy to figure out how to remove, install and adjust the saddle.

X-5: SADDLE INSTALLATION ON SEATPOST WITH A SINGLE VERTICAL CLAMP BOLT

Systems with a single vertical bolt (Fig. 10-4) usually have a two-piece clamp that fastens onto the

seatposts

10.7 saddle installation on single-bolt seatpost

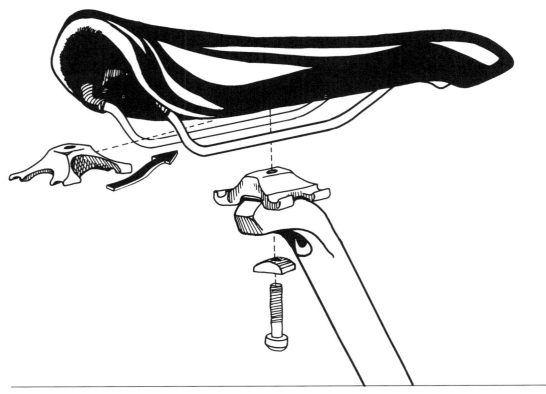

saddle rails. On most single-bolt models, saddle tilt is controlled by moving the clamp and saddle across a curved platform. Before you tighten the clamp bolt, make sure there is not a second, much smaller bolt (or "set screw") that adjusts seat tilt. If it does, skip to the next section (X-6).

1. Loosen the bolt until there are only a couple of threads still holding onto the upper clamp.

2. Turn the top half of the clamp 90 degrees and slide in the saddle rails. Do it from the back where the space between the rails is wider. You might need to remove it completely from the bolt if the clamp is too large. If you do disassemble the clamp, pay attention to the orientation of the parts so you can put it back together the same way.

3. Set the seat rails into the grooves in the lower part of the clamp, and set the top clamp piece on top of the rails (Fig. 10-7). Slide the saddle to the desired fore-aft position.

4. Tighten the bolt and check the seat tilt. Readjust if necessary.

X-6: SADDLE INSTALLATION ON SEATPOST WITH LARGE CLAMP BOLT AND SMALL SET SCREW

This type of post is illustrated in Fig. 10-5.

1. Loosen the large bolt until the top part of the clamp can either be removed or moved out of the way so that you can slide the saddle rails into place.

2. Set the saddle rails between the top and bottom sets of grooves in the seat clamp. Slide the saddle to the desired fore-aft position. Tighten the large bolt.

3. To change saddle tilt, loosen the large clamp bolt, adjust the saddle angle as needed by turning the set screw, and re-tighten the clamp bolt. Repeat until the desired adjustment is reached.

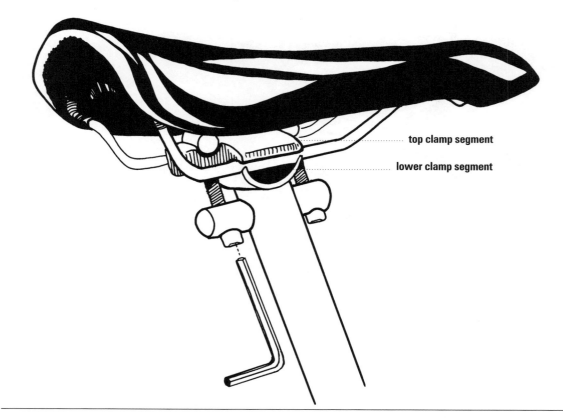

IO.8 saddle installation on two-bolt seatpost

top clamp segment

lower clamp segment

NOTE

On these types of seatposts, the set screw may be either vertical or horizontal. On those with a vertical set screw (Fig. 10-5), the screw is usually adjacent to the clamp bolt. A horizontal set screw is usually placed at the top front of the seatpost, pushing back on the clamp. With a horizontal set screw, push down on the back of the saddle with the clamp bolt loose to make sure the clamp and set screw are in contact.

X-7: INSTALLING SADDLE ON SEATPOST WITH TWO EQUAL-SIZED CLAMP BOLTS

This type of post is illustrated in Fig. 10-6.

1. Loosen one or both of the bolts and open the clamp enough that the saddle rails slide into their grooves between the two sides of the clamp.

2. Slide the saddle to the desired fore-aft posi-

tion. Tighten down one or both of the clamp bolts completely.

3. Loosen one clamp bolt and tighten the other to change the tilt of the saddle (Fig. 10-8). Repeat as necessary. Complete by tightening both bolts.

X-8: SEATPOST INSTALLATION INTO THE FRAME

1. Check for irregularities, burrs and other problems inside the seat tube, visually and with your finger; if there are some, you may need to sand or otherwise clean up inside the seat tube. It may be necessary for a bike shop to ream the seat tube if a seat post of the correct size will not fit.

2. Grease the seatpost and the inside of the seat tube. Grease the seat lug binder bolt. If you are using a sleeve or shim to adapt an undersized seatpost to fit your frame, grease it inside and out,

and insert it.

3. Insert the seatpost (Fig. 10-9), and tighten the seat binder bolt. Some binder bolts are tightened with a wrench (usually a 5mm Allen), and some have a quick-release lever. To tighten a quick release, flip the lever open so that it is directly in line with the body of the bolt — in other words, about halfway open. Finger-tighten the nut on the other end, and then close the lever (Fig. 10-10). It should be fairly snug, about tight enough to leave an impression in the heel of your hand for a few seconds. Open the lever, reposition the end nut, and close the lever again as necessary to get the right closing force.

4. After the saddle is attached, adjust the seat height to your desired position. It is a good idea to mark this height on the post with an indelible marker or a piece of tape. This way, if you remove it, you can just slide it right back into the proper place.

X-9: SUSPENSION SEATPOSTS

Shock-absorbing seatposts come equipped with some sort of spring —either a steel coil, an elastic polymer ("elastomer"), or an air cushion. The vertically moving elastomer spring type (Fig. 10-11) is probably the most common, and air shocks are the rarest. Some seatposts have linkages and swing the saddle on an arc, rather than up and down. There are a number of different suspension-seatpost designs out there and it is difficult — if not impossible — to write instructions that apply to all of them without being so general that those instructions become useless. Fortunately, most shock-absorbing seatposts are an aftermarket item and come with extensive instructions. I strongly recommend following the same regular maintenance schedule you would use for a standard seatpost, in addition to maintenance of the suspension components.

10.9 seatpost installation into the frame

10.10 closing quick-release seatpost binder

X-10: INSTALLING A SOFTRIDE SUSPENSION BEAM ONTO FRAME

level 2

The frame must be built to accept the beam, or you must purchase a retrofit kit from Softride to install it on a standard frame.

X

saddles and seatposts

suspension seatposts

IO.II suspension seatpost

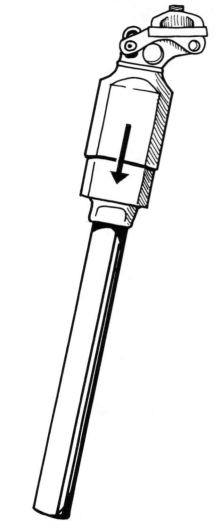

1. Attach the beam to the front frame-mounting bracket with a steel pin. The underside of the beam's nose has a small steel eyelet that fits between two tabs on the bracket, which is located on the top of the frame's top tube (Fig. 10-12). With a soft hammer, tap the included pin through the bracket, through the eye on the bottom of the beam, and out through the hole in the other side of the bracket.

2. Attach the beam to the rear frame-mounting bracket, located a few inches behind the front eyelet. The rear mount on the beam consists of two curved tabs, separated by the width of the frame's mounting bracket, that extend down. Long, curved slots in each tab (Fig. 10-12) are used to adjust the saddle height. Pass the bolt through one of the rectangular washers (with its knurled side pointing inward) and into the slot of one tab. Then pass it through the round end cap of the cylindrical frame mount, the frame mount itself and out through the second end cap, the other oval tab hole and the other rectangular washer. Screw on the nut after lining up the offset end cap holes so they fit into the mounting bracket with the bolt in place.

3. Swing the beam up to the desired height, with the fixing bolt loose. For starters, set it about an inch higher than what your normal seat height would be, to offset the beam's flex. If you reach the end of the adjustment in the bracket tab slots and the seat is still not as high as you need it to be, rotate the rear frame-mount end caps. The caps' offset holes offer two height positions for this very reason.

4. Tighten the fixing bolt. Readjust saddle height as needed.

X-II: REMOVING A STUCK SEATPOST

level 3 This is a Level 3 job because of the risk involved. This may be a job best done by a shop, because if you make a mistake you run the risk of destroying your frame. If you're not 100-percent confident in your abilities, go to someone who is — or at least to someone who will be responsible if they screw it up.

1. Remove the seat binder bolt. Sounds easy enough.

2. Squirt penetrating oil around the seatpost, and let it sit overnight. To get the most penetration, remove the bottom bracket (Chapter 8), turn

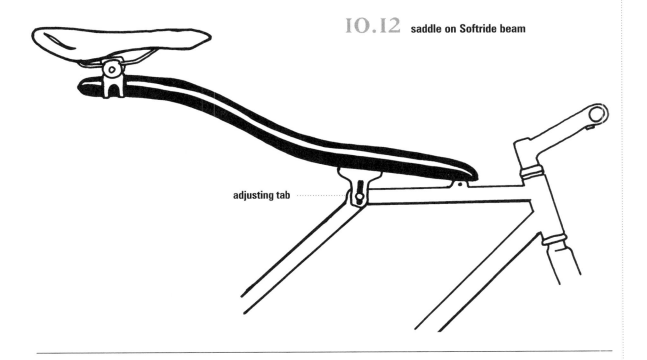

10.12 saddle on Softride beam

adjusting tab

the bike upside down, squirt the penetrating oil in from the bottom of the seat tube, and let it sit overnight.

3. The next day, stand over the bike and twist the saddle.

4. If Step 3 does not free the seatpost, you will need to move into the difficult and risky part of this procedure.

You will now sacrifice the seatpost. Remove the saddle and all of the clamps from the top of the seatpost. With the bike upside down, clamp the top of the seatpost into a large bench vise that is bolted to a very secure workbench. Congratulations, you have just ruined your seatpost. Don't ever ride it again.

Grab the frame at both ends, and begin to carefully apply a twisting pressure. Be aware that you can easily apply enough force to bend or crack your frame, so be careful. If the seatpost finally releases, it often makes such a large "pop" that you will think that you have broken many things!

5. If step 4 does not work, you need to go to a

machine shop and get the post reamed out of the seat tube.

If you *still* insist on getting it out yourself, you should really sit down and think about it for a while. Will the guy at the machine shop really charge you so much money that is now worth the risk of completely trashing your frame?

Have you thought about it for a while? And still you insist on doing this yourself? Okay, but don't say I didn't warn you.

Take a hacksaw and cut your seatpost off a little more than an inch above the seatlug on your frame. (Now you really have destroyed your seatpost, so, I don't have to warn about riding it again.) Remove the blade from the saw and wrap a piece of tape around one end. Hold on to the taped end and slip the other end into the center of the post. Carefully (no, make that very carefully) make two outward cuts about 60 degrees apart. Your goal is to remove a pie-shaped wedge from the hunk of seatpost stuck in your frame. Be careful, this is where many people cut too far and go right through the seatpost into the frame. Of course, you wouldn't do that, now would you? Once you've made the cut, pry or pull this piece out with a large screwdriver or a pair of pliers. Be careful here, too. A lot of over-enthusiastic home mechanics have damaged their frames by prying too hard here. But you wouldn't do that, would you?

Once the wedge is out, work the remaining piece out by curling in the edges with the pliers to free more and more of it from the seatpost walls. It should eventually work its way out.

Now, once your seatpost is out of the frame, remember to go back and re-read that part of this chapter outlining the regular maintenance procedures required for a seatpost. In other words, take out and apply grease every once in a while. You don't want to have to do this again, do you?

X-12: TROUBLESHOOTING PROBLEMS IN THE SEAT AND SEATPOST

1. Loose saddle.

Check the bolts. They are probably loose. Tighten the bolts and set the desired saddle tilt, after setting fore-aft saddle position (Section X-2). Check for any damage to the clamping mechanism, and replace the post if necessary. If you need help, look up the instructions that apply to your seatpost.

2. Stuck seatpost.

It can be a serious problem. Follow the instructions in Section X-11 carefully or you might damage your frame.

3. Saddle squeaks with each pedal stroke.

Put up with it or get a new saddle.

4. Creaking noises from the seatpost.

A seatpost can creak from moving back and forth against the sides of the seat tube while you ride. A dry seatpost can creak, so first try greasing it.

Some frames use a collar to adapt the seat tube to a certain seatpost diameter. Remember that the internal diameter of the seat tube is larger below the collar. I have seen bikes that creaked because the bottom of the seatpost rubbed against the sides of the seat tube below the extension of the collar. You can solve that problem by shortening the seatpost a bit with a hacksaw. If you do saw off the seatpost, make sure that you still have at least 3 inches of seatpost inserted in the frame for security.

If the creaking originates from the seatpost head where the saddle is clamped, you should check the clamp bolts. Lubricate the bolt threads and you will be able to tighten them a bit more.

Shock-absorbing seatposts can squeak as they move up and down. Try greasing the sides of the inner shaft. Grease the elastomers inside, too.

5. Seatpost slips down.

Tighten the frame binder bolt. If the seat-binder lug is pinched closed, and you still can't get it tight enough, you may be using a seatpost with an incorrect diameter, or the seat tube on your bike is oversized or has been stretched. Double check the seat-tube diameter with a pair of calipers. Your local shop may have one.

Try putting a larger seatpost in the frame, and replace yours if you find one that fits better. If the next size up is too big, you may need to "shim" your existing post. Cut a 1-inch x 3-inch piece of aluminum from a pop can. Pull the seatpost out, grease it and the pop-can shim, and insert both back into your frame. Bend the top lip of the shim over to prevent it from disappearing inside the frame. You may need to experiment with various shim dimensions until you find a piece that will go in with the seatpost and will also prevent slippage. Go ahead, they're cheap.

handlebars, stems and headsets

tools

metric Allen
   wrenches
headset wrenches
   sized for your
   particular
   headset
grease
rubbing alcohol
scissors, tin snips,
   or knife
mallet
hacksaw
round file
flat file
bike stand

OPTIONAL

bench vise
headset cup
   remover
star nut
   installation tool
headset fork
   crown race
   slide hammer
Shimano
   or Chris King
   tool to protect
   fork crown race
   when setting
   headset press
Chris King headset
   press inserts to
   protect bearings
   during
   installation
torque wrench

"If you don't change direction, you're liable to end up where you're headed." — ANONYMOUS

n a bike, you maintain or change your direction by applying force to your handlebars. If everything works properly, variations in that pressure will result in your front wheel changing direction. Pretty basic, right? Right, but there is a somewhat complicated series of parts between the handlebars and the wheel that makes that simple process possible. The parts of the steering system are illustrated in Fig. 11.1. In this chapter, we'll cover most of that system by going over handlebars, stems and headsets. This chapter is designed to start at the outside of the handlebars and move toward the middle.

XIA: BAR ENDS

XI-1: INSTALLATION OF BAR ENDS

1. Slide the shifters, brake levers and grips inward to make room at the end of the bar for the bar end. See "Grip removal," Section XI-3, for instructions on moving the grip, and Chapters 5 and 7 about shifters and brake levers.

2. Loosen the bolt on the bar-end clamp; it usually accepts a 5mm Allen wrench. Slide the bar end onto the bar (Fig. 11.2).

3. Tighten the clamp bolt enough that it just holds the bar ends in place. Rotate the bar ends to the position you like.

4. Tighten the clamp bolt. Make sure it is snug.

NOTES

The ends of some super-light handlebars can be damaged by bar ends. These bars come equipped with small cylindrical aluminum inserts that support the bar under the bar end. Similarly, some composite bars have an aluminum reinforcement at the end to support them under the bar end. These bars cannot be shortened, since the bar ends will not have the support they need.

• *Bar ends are meant to provide a powerful hand*

11.1 steering assembly (shown without brake levers for clarity)

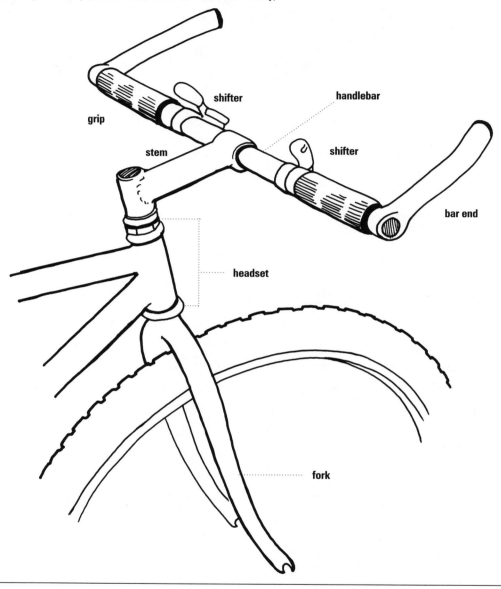

grip

shifter

handlebar

stem

shifter

bar end

headset

fork

bar ends

position while climbing, as well as an alternative stretched-out position while riding on smooth roads. They are not meant to be positioned vertically to provide a higher hand position. If you want your hands higher, get a taller, more vertical stem and perhaps bars that have a double bend to elevate the ends. This way you still have easy access to the brake levers.

· Some bar ends have features to provide adjustment in more planes than just rotationally about the bars.

Some (Profile) use a ball joint that fits over the end of the bar with one bolt for all adjustments and fixing to the bars. Other types (Syntace) use a second bolt that allows the bar end to twist about its axis.

XI-12 REMOVE BAR ENDS

1. Loosen bolt on bar-end clamp; it usually accepts a 5mm Allen wrench.
2. Pull the bar end off (Fig. 11.2).

II.2 **grip and bar-end assembly exploded**

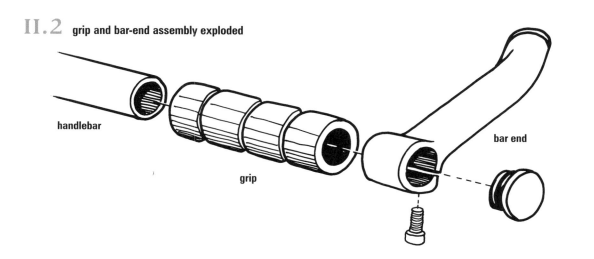

handlebar

grip

bar end

XIB: GRIPS

XI-3: GRIP REMOVAL

1. Remove bar ends and bar-end plugs (Fig. 11.2, Section XI-2).

2. Roll back an edge of the grip on itself.

3. Squirt water or, better yet, rubbing alcohol on the bar and the exposed grip underside (Fig. 11.3). Flip the rolled-up edge back down, and repeat Steps 2 & 3 on the other end of the grip.

4. Starting at the ends, twist the grip back and forth as you pull outward on it (Fig. 11.4). The wet sections will slip easily, and the dry middle section will get moving as the ends twist.

Pro trick: A syringe can be used to pierce the grip and inject rubbing alcohol under the center of the grip; it will slide off in seconds.

XI-4: GRIP INSTALLATION

1. Squirt rubbing alcohol or water inside the grip. Rubbing alcohol lubricates well and dries quickly (immediately, with a blast of compressed air!); water dries slowly, so the grip slips for a few days; hair spray, which is sometimes used for this, sucks to breathe and sets up permanently, thwarting subsequent removal and repositioning.

2. Twist the grip onto the bar.

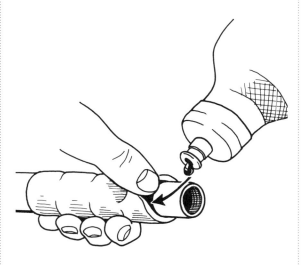

II.3 **using water to remove grip**

II.4 **grip removal**

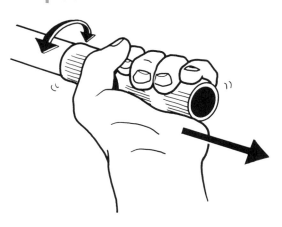

11.5 trimming grip to accommodate bar end

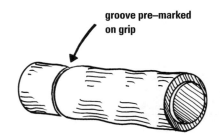

groove pre–marked
on grip

N O T E S

Some grips have a closed end. If you are going to use bar ends, you will need to cut off the closed end; you may also want to shorten the grip for your hand size or to adapt to a twist shifter. Some of these grips have a marked groove where they are meant to be cut with a pair of scissors (Fig. 11.5). Otherwise, you can cut them off anywhere you wish with scissors, tin snips, or a knife. If you have a thin, lightweight handlebar you can easily cut off the end of the grip by hitting the end of the grip with a mallet or hammer after it is installed on the bar; the bar will cut a nice hole in the grip end like a cookie cutter.

· Grips used alongside Grip Shift and other twist shifters are shorter than standard grips, since part of the hand is sitting on the twist grip. Grips specifically designed for Grip Shift shifters are readily available in bike shops. If you can't find them, just cut yours down to the proper length.

XIC: HANDLEBARS
XI-5: HANDLEBAR REMOVAL

1. Remove the bar ends and grips (Fig. 11.2), at least from one side. It is easier to remove grips when the bar is clamped into the stem than when it is sitting on a workbench, so, if you are moving the parts to another bar, remove them while the bar is still on the bike. For instructions for removing bar ends and grips, see Sections XI-2 and XI-3.

2. Remove brake levers and shifters. (Turn to Chapter 7 for information on brake levers and Chapter 5 for shifters.)

3. Loosen the bolt on the stem clamp surrounding the bar. This usually takes a 5mm Allen wrench.

4. Pull the bar out.

XI-6: HANDLEBAR INSTALLATION

1. Remove the stem-clamp bolt, grease its threads, and replace it. Grease the inside of the stem clamp, and grease the clamping area in the center of the bar.

2. Twist the bar to the position you find most comfortable. With a standard, single-bend bar, I prefer rotating the bar to the point that the ends point up and back, but it's all a matter of preference.

XI-7: HANDLEBAR MAINTENANCE AND REPLACEMENT SCHEDULE

A bike cannot be controlled without handlebars, so you never want one to break on you. Do not look at your bars as a permanent accessory on your bike. All aluminum bars will eventually fail. If titanium, steel or carbon-fiber bars are repeatedly stressed above a certain level, they will eventually fail as well. What that level is depends on the particular bar. The trick is not to be riding them when they fail.

Keep your bars clean. Regularly inspect the bars for cracks, crash-induced bends, corrosion and stressed areas. If you find any sign of wear or cracking, replace the bars. Never straighten a bent handlebar. Replace it! If you crash hard on your bike, consider replacing your bars even if they look fine. If you have had a crash and see no

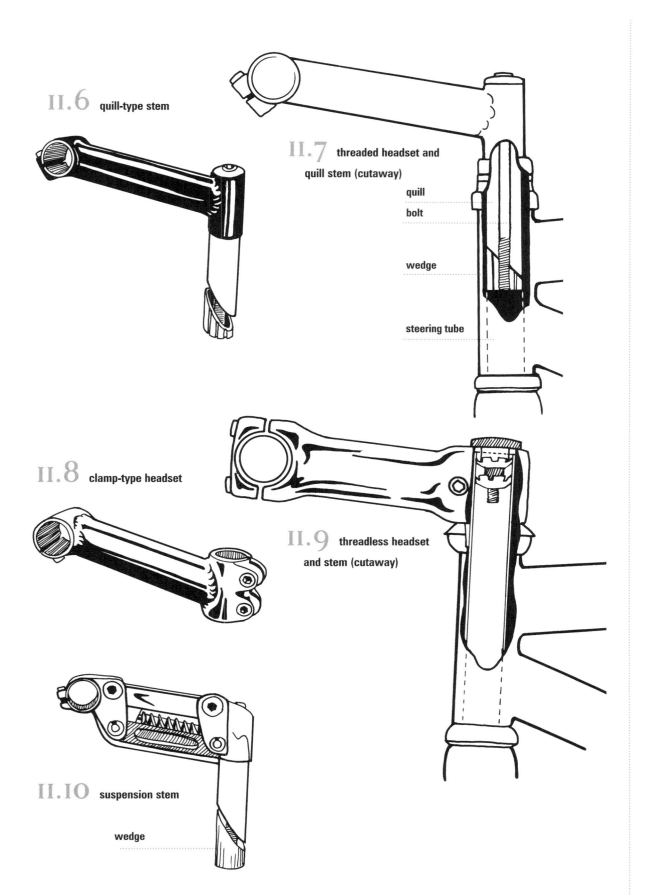

handlebars, stems and headsets

II.6 quill-type stem

II.7 threaded headset and quill stem (cutaway)

quill

bolt

wedge

steering tube

II.8 clamp-type headset

II.9 threadless headset and stem (cutaway)

stems

II.10 suspension stem

wedge

problems with the bars, remove the bar ends and check whether the bar is bent at the edges of the bar end. A carbon-fiber bar can be broken internally and the damage may not be visible from the outside. If your bars have taken an extremely hard hit, its a good idea to replace them rather than gamble on their integrity.

The Italian stem and bar manufacturer, 3T, recommends replacing stems and bars every four years. As with a stem, if you rarely ride the bike, this is overkill. If you ride hard and ride often, every four years may not be frequent enough. Do what is appropriate for you, and be aware of the risks.

XID: STEMS

The stem connects to the fork-steering tube and clamps around the handlebar. Stems come in one of two basic types: for (1) threaded or (2) unthreaded fork-steering tubes. Some stems have shock-absorbing mechanisms with pivots and springs to provide suspension.

Stems for threaded steering tubes (Fig. 11.6) have

II.II   threadless headset cup held in place by stem

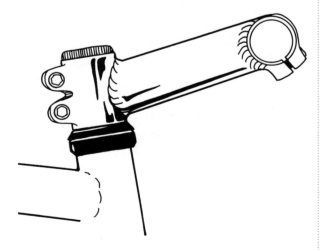

been the most common historically. They have a vertical "quill" that extends down into the steering tube of the fork, and binds to the inside of the steering tube by means of a wedge-shaped plug pulled up by a long bolt that runs through the quill (Fig. 11.7).

Stems for unthreaded fork-steering tubes (Fig. 11.8) have a clamping collar in place of the quill. Since the steering tube has no threads, the top headset cup slides on and off. In this case, the stem plays a dual role. It clamps around the steering tube to connect the handlebars to the fork, and it also keeps the headset in proper adjustment by preventing the top headset cup from sliding up the steering tube (Figs. 11.9 and 11.11).

Suspension stems are made for both threadless and threaded steering tubes. Some, like Softride (Fig. 11.10), use a parallelogram system with four pivots to prevent the handlebar from twisting as it moves up and down. Others, like Girvin, have a single pivot around which the bar swings in an arc. Both incorporate some sort of a spring for suspension, usually a steel coil or an elastic polymer ("elastomer"). Some suspension stems also come with a hydraulic damper to control the speed of movement.

XI-8: REMOVE STANDARD QUILL-TYPE STEM FROM THREADED FORK

1. Unscrew the stem-fixing bolt on the top of the stem. It should take three turns or so. Most stem bolts take a 6mm Allen wrench.

2. Tap the top of the bolt down with a mallet or hammer (Fig. 11.12) to disengage the wedge from the bottom of the quill. If the head of the bolt is recessed down in the stem so that a hammer cannot get at it, leave the Allen wrench in the bolt and tap the top of the Allen wrench until the wedge is free.

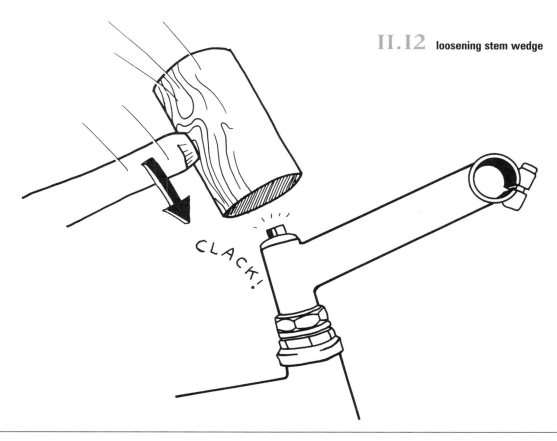

11.12 **loosening stem wedge**

CLACK!

handlebars, stems and headsets

3. Pull the stem out of the steering tube. If the stem will not budge, see Section XI-14A in this chapter.

XI-9: INSTALL AND ADJUST HEIGHT OF STANDARD STEM IN THREADED FORK

1. Grease the stem quill, the bolt threads, the outside of the wedge or conical plug, and the inside of the steering tube.

2. Thread the bolt through the stem and into the wedge or plug until it pulls it into place, but not so far as to prevent the stem from inserting into the steering tube.

3. Slip the stem quill into the steering tube (Fig. 11.7) to the depth you want. Make sure the stem is inserted beyond its height-limit line. Tighten the bolt until the stem is snug but can still be turned.

4. Set the stem to the desired height, line it up with the front wheel, and tighten the bolt. It needs to be tight, but don't overdo it. You can over-tighten the stem bolt to the point that you bulge out the steerer tube on your fork, so be careful.

XI-10: REMOVE CLAMP-TYPE STEM FROM THREADLESS STEERING TUBE

1. Loosen the horizontal bolts clamping the stem around the steering tube. Again, this should take about two or three turns.

2. With a 5mm Allen wrench, unscrew and remove the adjusting bolt in the top cap covering the top of the stem clamp and steering tube (Fig. 11.13). The fork can now fall out, so hold the fork as you unscrew the bolt.

3. With the bike standing on the floor, or while holding the fork to keep it from falling out, pull the cap and the stem off of the steering tube.

installation and adjustment of stem height on threadless steering tube

Leave the bike standing until you replace the stem, or slide the fork out of the frame, keeping track of all headset parts.

4. If the stem will not budge, see Section XI-14B in this chapter.

XI-11: INSTALL AND ADJUST HEIGHT OF STEM ON THREADLESS STEERING TUBE

level 2 Installing and adjusting the height of a stem on a threadless fork is much more complicated than installing and adjusting the height of a standard stem in a threaded fork. Here, the stem is an integral part of the headset (Fig. 11.9), so any change to the stem position alters the headset adjustment. That's why this step is listed with a Level 2 designation.

1. Stand the bike up on its wheels, so the fork does not fall out. Grease the top end of the steering tube. Loosen the stem clamp bolts, and grease their threads. Slide the stem onto the steering tube.

2. Set the stem height to the desired level. If you want to place the stem in a position higher than directly on top of the headset, you must put some spacers between the bottom of the stem clamp and the top piece of the headset. No matter what, there must be contact (either directly or through spacers) between the headset and the stem. Otherwise, the headset will be loose.

NOTE

Some manufacturers produce a pinch-binding headset-adjustment-holding ring with which you can raise or lower your stem without affecting the adjustment of your headset. You slide the ring onto the steering tube on top of the headset and below the stem. Once the headset position is set, you tighten the pinch bolt on the ring. After that is in place, you can raise the stem without throwing the headset out of adjustment.

11.13 loosening and tightening bolt on threadless-style headset

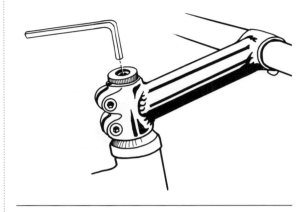

11.14 measuring distance between stem clamp and top of steering tube

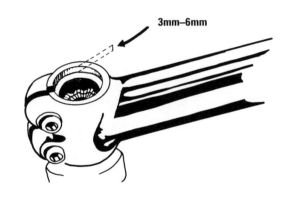

3mm–6mm

3. Check the steering tube length: In order to adjust the threadless headset, the top of the stem clamp (or spacers placed above it) should overlap the top of the steering tube by 3mm to 6mm (1/8"-1/4") (Fig. 11.14). If it does, skip ahead to step 4.

a. Steering tube too short: If the top of the stem clamp overlaps the top of the steering tube by more than 6mm (1/4"), the steering tube is too short to set the stem height where you have it. If you have spacers below the stem, remove some until the top edge of the stem clamp overlaps the top of the steering tube by 3mm to 6mm. If you cannot or do not want to lower the stem any fur-

handlebars, stems and headsets

ther, you either need a longer steering tube or a stem with a shorter clamp. Stems for threadless steering tubes with clamps of differing lengths are available. It's a lot cheaper and easier than replacing the steering tube or fork.

On most suspension forks, you can simply replace the steering tube and crown assembly and bolt your existing fork legs into it. With all but a few rigid (non-suspension) fork, you can't replace the steering tube without having it done by a frame builder. At this point, it's safer and probably cheaper to replace the fork.

b. Steering tube too long: If the top of the steering tube is less than 3mm (1/8") below the top edge of the stem clamp (or if it sticks up above the top of the stem clamp) you have a choice. If you want the option to raise the stem for a higher handlebar position, stack some headset spacers on top of the stem clamp until the spacers overlap the top edge of the steering tube by at least 3mm.

If, on the other hand, you are sure you will never want the stem any higher, then go ahead and cut off the excess tube. First, mark the steering tube along the top edge of the stem clamp and remove the fork from the bike. Make another mark on the steering tube 3mm below the first mark. Place the steering tube in a padded vise or bike-stand clamp. Using the lower mark as a guide, cut the excess steering tube off with a hacksaw or tube cutter.

There is a star-shaped nut that is inserted inside the steering tube (Fig. 11.9). The bolt through the top cap screws into it to adjust the headset bearings. If the star nut is already inside of the steering tube, and it looks like the saw is going to hit it, thread the adjusting bolt into the star nut and tap on the bolt with a hammer. That should move the star nut down.

Make your cut straight. Mark it straight by wrap-

ping a piece of paper around the steering tube and tracing along the top edge. If you are not sure your cut will be straight, start it a little higher and file it down flat to the marked line. If you really want to be safe, use a tool specifically designed to help you make a straight cut; Park Tool's "threadless saw guide" will do the trick. Remember that you can always shorten the steering tube a little more, but you cannot make it longer! So, apply the old adage of "measure twice, cut once." Use a round file on the inside of the tube and a flat file on the outside to file off any metal burrs left by the hacksaw or cutter.

When you have completed cutting and deburring, put the fork back in, replacing all headset parts the way they were originally installed (Fig. 11.18). Return to Step 1 above.

4. Check that the edges of the star-shaped nut are at least 12mm below the top edge of the steering tube. The nut must be far enough down that the bottom of the headset top cap does not hit it once the adjusting bolt is tightened. If the nut is not in deeply enough, you will need to drive it deeper into the steering tube after removing the stem. This is best done with the star nut installation tool (Fig. 1.4). The tool threads into the nut, and you hit it with a hammer until it stops; the star nut will now be set 15mm deep in the steering tube. If you do not have this tool, go to a bike shop and have the nut set for you. If you insist on doing it yourself, follow the steps to push the star nut in deeper outlined below. Just remember that it is easy to mangle the star nut if you do not tap it in straight.

a. Put the adjusting bolt through the top cap, and thread it six turns into the star nut.

b. Set the star nut over the end of the steering tube, and tap the top of the bolt with a mallet. Use the top cap as guide to keep it going in straight.

changing
steering
tube length

177

c. Tap the bolt in until the star nut is 15mm below the top of the steering tube.

NOTE

If the wall thickness of the steering tube is greater than standard, the stock headset star nut will not fit in, and it will just bend when you try to install it. Even pros sometimes ruin star nuts. Not a big problem, since replacements can be purchased separately. If yours goes in crooked, take a long punch or rod, set it on the star nut, and drive it all of the way out of the bottom of the steering tube. Dispose of the star nut, and get another.

If the internal diameter (I.D.) of the steering tube is undersized — (standard I.D. is 22.2mm (7/8″) on a one-inch steering tube, 25.4mm (1″) on a 11/8-inch steering tube, and 28.6mm (1-1/8″) on a 11/4-inch steering tube) — you cannot use the stock star nut from the headset for that size; get one of the correct size (the fork manufacturer often supplies, or at least stocks, them). In a pinch, you can make the stock star nut fit by bending each pair of opposite leaves of the star nut toward each other with a pair of channel-lock pliers to reduce the nut's width. Now you can insert the nut; be aware that it may not grip as well as a proper-sized one.

5. Install the headset top cap on the top of the stem clamp (or spacers you set above it). Grease the threads of the top-cap adjusting bolt, and thread it into the star nut inside the steering tube (Fig. 11.13).

6. Adjust the headset. The steps are outlined in Section XI-17.

XI-12: STEM MAINTENANCE AND REPLACEMENT SCHEDULE

A bike cannot be controlled if the stem breaks, so make sure yours doesn't break. Since aluminum has no fatigue limit, all aluminum parts will eventually fail. Steel and titanium parts repeatedly stressed more than about one-half of their tensile strength will eventually fail as well. Stems and handlebars are not permanent accessories on your bike. Replace them before they fail on you.

Clean your stem regularly. Whenever you clean it, look for corrosion, cracks, bends and stressed areas. If you find any, replace the stem immediately. If you crash hard on your bike, especially hard enough to bend the bars, replace your stem. It makes sense to err on the side of caution.

Italian stem maker 3T recommends replacing stems and bars every four years. As with a set of handlebars, if you rarely ride the bike, this is overkill. If you ride hard and ride often every four years may not be frequent enough. Do what is appropriate for you, and be aware of the risks.

XI-13: SETTING STEM AND BAR POSITIONS

Complete treatment of this subject is Appendix C, Section C-3. Here are some brief suggestions.

I recommend setting your handlebar twist so that the bends in the bars are pointed up and back. I also recommend setting your bar ends so that they are horizontal or tipped up between 5 and 15 degrees from horizontal.

Setting handlebar height and reach is very personal. Much depends on your physique, your flexibility, your frame, your riding style, and a few other preferences. This subject is covered in depth in the appendix on page 256. Since I do not know anything about you personally, I will leave you with a few simple guidelines:

· If you climb a lot, you will want your bars lower and further forward to keep weight on the front wheel on steep uphills.

· If you descend technical trails a lot, you will want your bars higher and with less forward reach.

• If you ride a lot on pavement, a low, stretched-out position is better aerodynamically. A low position means that the handlebar grips are about 7cm to 12cm lower than your saddle. A stretched-out position would place your elbow at least two inches in front of your knee at the top of the pedal stroke.

XI-14: REMOVING STUCK STEM

level 3   A stem can get stuck into (or onto) the steering tube due to poor maintenance. By periodically re-greasing the stem and steering tube, you will keep them sliding freely, and the grease will form a barrier to sweat and water getting in between the two. If your stem is really stuck, be careful; you can ruin your fork as well as your stem and headset trying to get it out. In fact, you're better off having a shop work on it, unless you really know what you are doing and are willing to accept the risk of destroying a

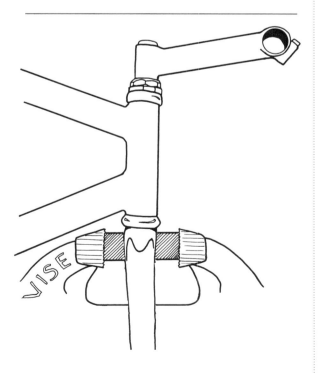

11.15 **clamping fork crown in vise**

lot of expensive parts.

A. Removing a stuck stem from a threaded fork

1. Unscrew the stem bolt on top of the stem three turns or more. Smack the bolt (or the Allen wrench in the bolt) with a mallet or hammer (Fig. 11.12) to completely disengage the wedge.

2. Grasping the front wheel between your knees, make one last attempt to free the stem by twisting back and forth on the bars. Don't use all of your strength, because you can ruin a fork and front wheel this way.

3. If your stem didn't budge, squirt penetrating oil around the stem where it enters the headset. Let the bike sit for several hours and add more penetrating oil every hour or so.

4. Turn the bike over, and squirt penetrating oil into the bottom of the fork steering tube so that it runs down around the stem quill. Let the bike sit for several hours and add more penetrating oil every hour or so.

5. Now that it is totally soaked in penetrating oil, try Step 2 again. If the stem does not come this time, you have to go to your workbench and use that heavy-duty vise. It's solidly mounted, isn't it? Good, because you'll need it to be.

6. Remove the front wheel (Chapter 2) and the front brake (Chapter 7). Put pieces of wood on both sides of the vise. Clamp the fork crown into the vise (Fig. 11.15). To fit it in the vise, you will at least have to remove the brakes. With a suspension fork remove the inner fork legs from the crown by loosening the crown bolts and yanking the legs out.

7. Grab both ends of the handlebar and twist back and forth. If this doesn't work, you may have to saw off the stem just above the headset and have the bottom of the stem reamed out of the steering tube by a machine shop. I told you that

handlebars, stems and headsets

removing a stuck stem

11.16 stick coin in crack to spread stem clamp

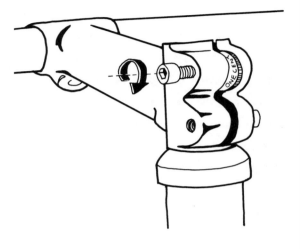

you should have gone to a bike shop.

B. Removing a stuck stem from a threadless fork

1. Remove the top cap (Fig. 11.13) and the bolts clamping the stem to the steering tube.

2. Spread the stem clamp by inserting a coin into the slot between each bolt end and the opposing unthreaded half of the binder lug (Fig. 11.16). Tighten each bolt against each coin so that it spreads the clamp slot open wider. The stem should come right off of the steering tube now.

N O T E

If your stem is the type that comes with a single bolt in the side of the stem shaft ahead of the steering tube (Fig. 11.9), loosen the bolt a few turns and tap it in with a hammer to free the wedge. It might still take some penetrating oil to free this type of stem from around the steering tube.

3. If it still will not come free, you may have to use a vise, following instructions 6 and 7 in the last section on freeing a quill-type stem. Failing that, your last resort is to saw through the steering tube at the base of the stem clamp and replace the stem, fork (or at least the steering tube) and headset.

XIE: HEADSETS

There are two basic types of headsets: threaded (Fig. 11.17) and unthreaded (Fig. 11.18). The different standard mountain-bike headset sizes are 1-, 1 1/8- and 1 1/4-inch.

The top bearing cup on a threaded headset has wrench flats, a toothed washer stacked on top of it, and a locknut that covers the top of the steering tube. That locknut tightens against the washer and top cup (Fig. 11.17). A brake cable hanger (Fig. 7.4, Chapter 7) and extra spacers may be included under the locknut.

Prior to the 1990s, practically all headsets and steering tubes were threaded. Dia-Compe's AheadSet pioneered the threadless headset, which is lighter because it eliminates the stem quill, bolt and wedge. The connection between the handlebars and the stem is more rigid than with an expanding stem wedge. Of course, fork manufacturers prefer threadless headsets, because they do not have to thread their forks and/or offer various lengths of fork steerers; steerer diameter is now the only variable.

On an unthreaded headset, the top cup and a conical compression ring slide onto the steering tube (Fig. 11.18). The stem clamps around the top of the steering tube and above the compression ring. A nut with two layers of spring-steel teeth sticking out from it (called a "Star Fangled Nut" by Dia-Compe) fits into the steering tube and grabs the inner walls (Fig. 11.9). A top cap sits atop the stem clamp and pushes it down by means of a long bolt threaded into the star nut to adjust the headset (Fig. 11.13). The stem clamped around the steering tube holds the headset in adjustment (Fig. 11.11).

Most headsets, threaded or threadless, use loose ball bearings held in some type of steel or plastic retainer (or "cage") (Figs. 11.17 and 11.18), so that

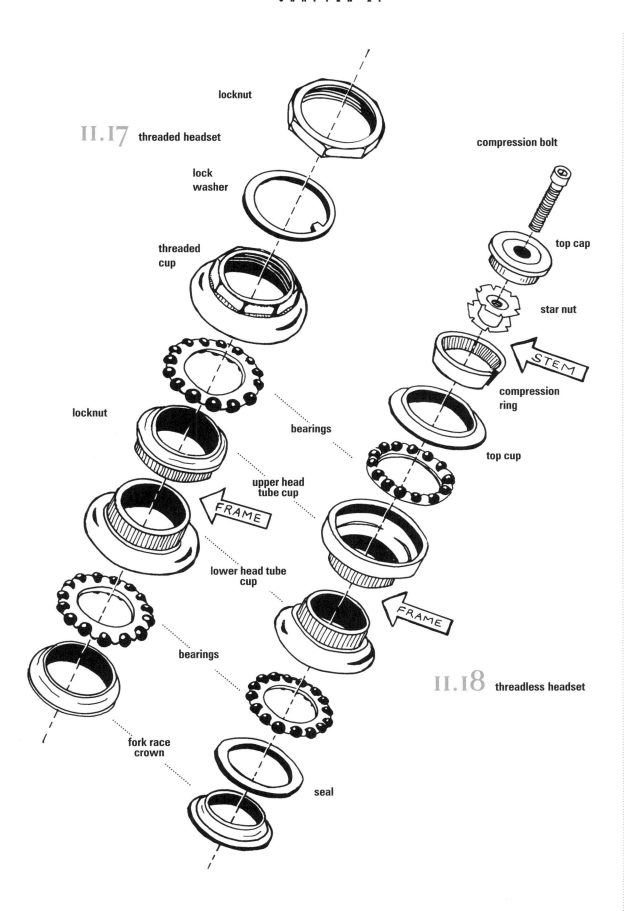

locknut

11.17 threaded headset

lock washer

threaded cup

locknut

bearings

upper head tube cup

lower head tube cup

FRAME

bearings

fork race crown

seal

compression bolt

top cap

star nut

compression ring

top cup

STEM

FRAME

11.18 threadless headset

handlebars, stems and headsets

headsets

II.19 needle bearings

you are not chasing dozens of separate balls around when you work on the bike. A variation on this (Stronglight) has needle bearings held in conical plastic retainers (Fig. II.19) riding on conical steel bearing surfaces.

Cartridge-bearing headsets usually employ "angular contact" bearings, since normal cartridge bearings cannot take the side forces encountered by a headset. Each bearing is a separate, sealed, internally greased unit.

XI-15: CHECK HEADSET ADJUSTMENT

If your headset is too loose, it will rattle or clunk while you ride. You might even notice some "play" in the fork as you apply the front brake. If your headset is too tight, the fork will be difficult to turn or feel gritty.

1. Check for headset looseness by holding the front brake and rocking the bike forward and back. Try it with the front wheel pointed straight ahead and then with the wheel turned at 90 degrees to the bike. Feel for back-and-forth movement (or "play") at the lower head cup with your other hand. If there is play, you need to adjust your headset because it is too loose.

N O T E

This task is more complicated with a suspension fork, and even with many brake types. There is always some side-to-side play in any suspension

fork, as well as in many brakes; this makes it hard to isolate whether the play you feel is from the headset, the fork, or the brakes. You have to feel each part as you rock the bike, and you may have to do some trial-and-error headset adjustment.

If the headset is loose, skip to the appropriate adjustment section, XI-16 or XI-17.

2. Check for headset tightness after picking up the front wheel, by holding the top tube, and turning the handlebars back and forth. Feel for any binding or stiffness of movement. Also, check for the chunk-chunk-chunk movement to fixed positions characterizing a pitted headset (if you feel this, you need a new headset; skip to Section XI-20). Lean the bike to one side and then the other; the front wheel should turn as the bike is leaned (be aware that cable housings can resist the turning of the front wheel). Lift the bike by the saddle so it is tipped down at an angle with both wheels off of the ground. Turn the handlebar one way and let go of it. See if it returns to center quickly and smoothly on its own. If the headset does not turn easily on any of the above steps, it is too tight, and you should skip to the appropriate adjustment section, XI-16 or XI-17.

3. If yours is a threaded headset, try to turn either the top nut or the threaded cup by hand. They should be so tight against each other that they can only be loosened with wrenches. If you can hand tighten or loosen either part by hand, you need to adjust your headset; go to section XI-16.

XI-16: ADJUSTING A THREADED HEADSET

level 2 The secret to good adjustment is simultaneously controlling the steering tube, the adjustable cup and the locknut as you tighten the latter two together.

Perform the adjustment with the stem installed. Not only does it give you something to hold onto that keeps the fork from turning during the installation, but there are slight differences in adjustment when the stem is in place as opposed to when it is not. Tightening the stem bolt can sometimes bulge the walls of the steering tube very slightly (Fig. 11.7), but just enough for it to shorten the steering tube and throw your original headset adjustment off.

1. Follow the steps outlined in Section XI-15, and determine whether the headset is too loose or too tight.

2. Put a pair of headset wrenches that fit your headset on the headset's top nut (which I will also call the "locknut") and top bearing cup (or "threaded cup" or "adjustable cup"). Headset nuts come in a wide variety of sizes, so make sure you have purchased the proper size wrench. Place the wrenches so that the top one is slightly offset to left of the bottom wrench. That way you can squeeze them together to free the nut (Fig. 11.20).

People with small hands or weak grip will need to grab each wrench out at the end to get enough leverage.

3. Hold the lower wrench in place and turn the top wrench counterclockwise about a quarter-turn to loosen the locknut. It may take considerable force to break it loose, since it needs to be installed very tightly to keep the headset from loosening up.

4. If the headset was too loose, turn the lower (or threaded) cup clockwise about one-16th of a turn while holding the stem with your other hand. Be very careful when tightening the cup; over-tightening it can ruin the headset by pressing the bearings into the bearing surfaces and make little

indentations. The headset then stops at the indentations rather than turns smoothly, a condition known as a "pitted" headset.

If the headset was too tight, loosen the threaded cup counterclockwise one-16th turn while holding the stem with your other hand. Loosen it until the bearings turn freely, but be sure not to loosen it to the point that you allow any play to develop.

5. Holding the stem, tighten the locknut clockwise with a single wrench. Make sure that the threaded cup does not turn while you tighten the locknut. If it does turn, you either are missing the toothed lock washer separating the cup and locknut (Fig. 11.17), or the washer you have is missing its tooth. In this case, remove the locknut and replace the toothed washer. Put it on the steering tube so that the tooth engages the longitudinal groove in the steering tube. Tighten the locknut on again.

You can adjust a headset without a toothed washer by working both wrenches simultaneously, but it is trickier and the headset often comes loose while riding.

II.20 **loosening headset locknut**

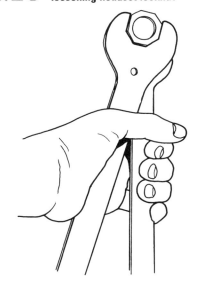

adjusting
threaded
headset

11.21 **tightening headset locknut**

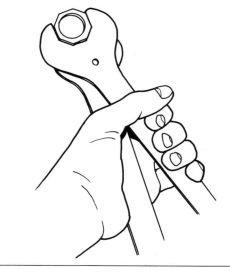

6. Check the headset adjustment again. Repeat Steps 4 and 5 until properly adjusted.

7. Once properly adjusted, place one wrench on the locknut and the other on the threaded cup. Tighten the locknut (clockwise) firmly against the washer(s) and threaded cup to hold the headset adjustment in place (Fig. 11.21).

8. Check the headset adjustment again. If it is off, follow Steps 2-7 again. If it is adjusted properly, make sure the stem is aligned with the front wheel, and go ride your bike.

N O T E S

If you constantly get what you believe to be the proper adjustment, and then find it to be too loose after you tighten the locknut and threaded cup against each other, your steering tube may be too long, causing the locknut to bottom out. Remove the stem and examine the inside of the steering tube. If the top end of the steering tube butts up against the top lip of the locknut, the steering tube is too long. Remove the locknut and add another spacer.

If you don't want to add another spacer, file off one or two millimeters of the steering tube. Be sure to deburr it inside and out, and avoid leaving filings in the bearings or steering tube threads. Replace the locknut and return to Step 5.

· Wheels Manufacturing makes a headset locknut called the "Growler." It replaces your locknut and will not come loose, even on bumpy terrain. It threads on just like a normal locknut and is adjusted the same way. The only difference between a Growler and a standard locknut is that the Growler is split down one side and has a pinch bolt bridging the split. Once your headset is adjusted, you tighten the pinch bolt to keep it in adjustment.

XI-17: ADJUSTING A THREADLESS HEADSET

Adjusting a threadless headset is much easier than adjusting a threaded one. It's a Level 1 procedure and usually takes only a 5mm Allen wrench.

1. Check the headset adjustment. Determine whether the headset is too tight or too loose.

2. Loosen the bolt(s) that clamp the stem to the steering tube.

3. If the headset is too tight, loosen the 5mm Allen bolt on the top cap about one-16th of a turn (Fig. 11.22).

If the headset is too loose, tighten the 5mm Allen bolt on the top cap about one-16th of a turn (Fig. 11.22). Be careful not to over-tighten it and pit the headset. If you're using a torque wrench, Dia-Compe recommends a tightening torque on this bolt of 22 inch-pounds.

Adjustment problems

a. If the cap does not move down and push the stem down, make sure the stem is not stuck to the steering tube. If it is, go to Section XI-14B earlier in this chapter.

b. Another hindrance comes in if the conical compression ring (Fig. 11.18) is stuck to the steering

adjusting
threaded
headset
—
adjusting
threadless
headset

tube, preventing adjustment via the top cap bolt. With the stem off, tap the steering tube down with a mallet, and then push the fork back up to free the compression ring. Grease the ring and the steerer, and reassemble.

c. If neither the stem nor the compression ring are stuck, yet the cap still does not push the stem down, the steering tube may be so long that it is hitting the lip of the top cap and preventing the cap from pushing the stem down. The steering tube's top should be 3mm to 6mm below the top edge of the stem. If the steering tube is too long, add a spacer, or cut or file some off the top.

d. Another thing that can thwart adjustment is if the star nut is not installed deeply enough, so the cap bottoms out on the star nut. The highest point of the star nut should be 12mm to 15mm below the top of the steering tube. Tap it deeper with a star-nut-installation tool, or put the bolt through the top cap, thread it five turns into the star nut, and gently tap it in with a soft hammer, using the top cap to keep it going in straight.

Once you have fixed the cause of the adjustment problem, return to step 1 above.

4. Tighten the stem clamp bolts. If using a torque wrench, Dia-Compe recommends a tightening torque of 130 inch-pounds. On two-bolt stems,

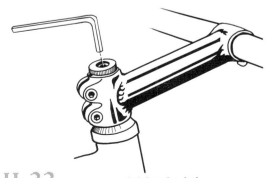

11.22 **loosening and tightening bolt on threadless-style headset**

11.23 **Chris King-style pressed sealed bearings**

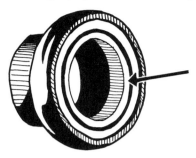

be sure to tighten them alternately, not putting the entire load on one and then going on to tighten the second.

5. Re-check the headset adjustment. Repeat Steps 2-4 if necessary. If it is adjusted properly, make sure the stem is aligned straight with the front wheel. Once the headset is adjusted properly, go find something else to do, because you are done.

XI-18: OVERHAUL THREADED HEADSET

Like any other bike part with bearings, headsets need periodic overhauls. If you use your bike regularly, you should probably overhaul your loose-bearing headset once a year. Headsets with sealed cartridge bearings usually never need to be overhauled; if a bearing fails, you either replace the bearing or, if it has press-in bearings (like Chris King and Dia-Compe's "S" series, Fig. 11.23), you replace the entire cup. If you have a Shimano cartridge-bearing headset, continue with these instructions. If you are replacing a Chris King or Dia-Compe "S" headset cup, move on to the instructions for headset removal.

A bike stand is highly recommended when overhauling a headset.

1. Disconnect the front brake cable (Chapter 7), and remove the stem by loosening the stem bolt three turns, tapping the bolt down with a hammer

handlebars, stems and headsets

overhauling threaded headset

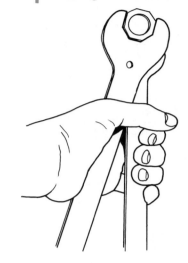

11.24 **loosening headset locknut**

to free the wedge (Fig. 11.12), and pulling it out.

2. Either turn your bike upside down or be prepared to catch your fork as you remove the upper portion of the headset. To remove the top headset cup, unscrew the locknut and threaded cup with headset wrenches. Place one on the locknut and one on the threaded cup. Loosen the locknut by turning it counterclockwise (Fig. 11.24). Unscrew the locknut and the cup from the steering tube. The headset washer or washers will slide off of the steering tube as you unscrew the threaded cup.

3. Pull the fork out of the frame.

4. Remove any seals that surround the edges of the cups. Make a point of remembering the position and orientation of each.

5. Remove the bearings from the cups. Be careful not to lose any. Separate top and bottom sets if they are of different sizes.

6. Clean or replace the bearings.

a. With standard ball-bearing or needle-bearing headsets, put the bearings in a jar or old water bottle along with some citrus-based solvent. Shake. If the bearings from the top and bottom are of different sizes, keep them in separate contain-

ers to avoid confusion.

b. With sealed-cartridge bearings, check to see if they turn smoothly. If they do not, buy new ones. Either way, skip to Step 8.

7. Blot the bearings dry with a clean rag. Plug the sink, and wash the bearings in soap and water in your hands, just as if you were washing your palms by rubbing them together. This helps keep your hands clean for the assembly steps as well. Rinse bearings thoroughly and blot them dry. Let them air dry completely.

8. Wipe all of the bearing surfaces with clean rags. Wipe the steering tube clean, especially the threads, and wipe the inside of the head tube clean with a rag stuck to the end of a screwdriver.

9. Inspect all bearing surfaces for wear and pitting. If you see pits (separate indentations made by bearings in the bearing surfaces), you need to replace the headset. If that's the case, skip to Section XI-20.

10. Apply grease to all bearing surfaces. A thin film will do, especially if you are using sealed cartridge bearings.

11. Turn the bike upside down in the bike stand. Place a set of bearings in the top cup and a set in the cup on the lower end of the head tube. Make sure you have the bearing retainer right side up so that only the bearings contact the bearing surfaces. If you have installed the retainer upside down, it will come in contact with one of the bearing surfaces, and the headset does not turn well. This is a bad thing, since assembling and riding it that way will turn the retainer into jagged chunks of broken metal. To be safe, double and triple check the retainer placement by turning each cup pair in your hand before proceeding. Most headsets have the bearings set up symmetrically top and bottom (Fig. 11.17). This way, the top

11.25 setting fork in head tube to seat bearings

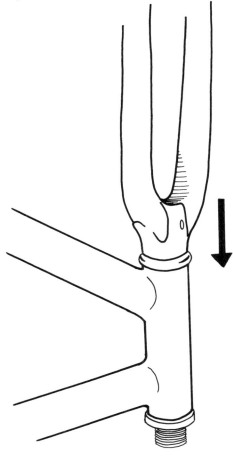

piece of each pair is a cup, and the bottom piece is a cone and the bearing retainer rides the same way in both sets. Some headsets, however, place both cups facing outward from the head tube (Fig. 11.18), so the bearing retainers are asymmetrical on either end of the head tube. Also, watch for asymmetry in ball size; Ritchey headsets have smaller balls on top than in the bottom.

NOTES

Stronglight or similar needle-bearing headsets come with two pairs of separate conical steel rings. These are the bearing surfaces that sit on either side of the needle bearings (Fig. 11.19). On each set of conical rings, you will find that one is smaller than the other. Place the smaller one on the lower sur-

face of each pair: the fork crown race and the cup on top of the head tube.

· If you have loose ball bearings with no bearing retainer, stick the balls into the grease in the cups one at a time, making sure that you replace the same number you started with in each cup.

12. Re-install any seals that you removed from the headset parts.

13. Drop the fork-steering tube into the head tube so that the lower headset bearing set seats properly (Fig. 11.25).

14. Screw on the top cup, with the bearings in it, onto the steering tube. Keeping the bike upside down at this point not only keeps the fork in place, it also prevents grit from falling into the bearings as you thread on the cup.

15. Slide on the toothed washer. Align the tooth in the groove going down the length of the steering tube threads (Fig. 11.17). If you have one, install the brake-cable hanger (Fig. 7.4) the same way. Screw on the locknut with your hand.

16. Turn the bike over. Grease the stem quill and insert it into the steering tube (Fig. 11.7). Make certain that it is in deeper than the imprinted limit line. Line the stem up with the front wheel, and tighten the stem bolt.

17. Adjust the headset as outlined in Section XI-16.

XI-19: OVERHAUL THREADLESS HEADSET

level 2

Either place the bike upside down in the work stand or be ready to catch the fork when you remove the stem.

1. Disconnect the front brake (Chapter 7), and unscrew the top cap bolt (Fig. 11.22) and the stem clamp bolts. Remove the top cap and the stem.

2. Remove the top headset cup by sliding the top

handlebars, stems and headsets

overhauling
threadless
headset

cup, conical compression ring, and any other spacers above it, off of the steering tube (Fig. 11.18). It may take a tap with a mallet on the end of the steering tube, followed by pushing the fork back up, to free the compression ring.

3. Pull the fork out of the frame.

4. Remove any seals that surround the edges of the cups. Remember the position and orientation of each.

5. Remove the bearings from the cups. Be careful not to lose any. Separate top and bottom sets if they are of different sizes.

6. Clean or replace the bearings:

a. With standard ball-bearing or needle-bearing headsets, put the bearings in a jar or old water bottle along with some citrus-based solvent. Shake. If the bearings from the top and bottom are of different sizes, keep them in separate containers to avoid confusion.

b. With sealed-cartridge bearings, check to see if they turn smoothly. If they do not, buy new ones. Skip to Step 8.

7. Blot the bearings dry with a clean rag. Plug the sink, and wash the bearings in soap and water in your hands, just as if you were washing your palms by rubbing them together. Your hands will get clean for the assembly steps as well. Rinse bearings thoroughly and blot them dry. Air dry completely.

8. Wipe all of the bearing surfaces with clean rags. Wipe the steering tube clean, especially the threads, and wipe the inside of the head tube clean with a rag on the end of a screwdriver.

9. Inspect all bearing surfaces for wear and pitting. If you see pits (separate indentations made by bearings in the bearing surfaces), you need to replace the headset. If so, skip to section XI-20 "Remove headset" on the next page.

10. Apply grease to all bearing surfaces. If you are using sealed-cartridge bearings, apply grease conservatively.

11. Turn the bike upside down in the bike stand. Place a set of bearings into the top cup and a set into the cup on the lower end of the head tube. Make sure you have the bearing retainer right side up so that only the bearings contact the bearing surfaces. If you have installed the retainer upside down, it will come in contact with one of the bearing surfaces, and the headset does not turn well. This is a bad thing, since assembling and riding it that way will turn the retainer into jagged chunks of broken metal. To be safe, double and triple check the retainer placement by turning each cup pair in your hand before proceeding. Most headsets have the bearings set up symmetrically top and bottom (Fig. 11.17). This way, the top piece of each pair is a cup and the bottom piece is a cone, and the bearing retainer rides the same way in both sets. Some headsets, however, place both cups (and hence the bearing retainers) facing outward from the head tube (Fig. 11.18).

NOTE

If you have loose ball bearings with no bearing retainer, stick the balls into the grease in the cups one at a time, making sure that you replace the same number you started with in each cup.

12. Re-install any seals that you removed from the headset parts.

13. Drop the fork-steering tube into the head tube so that the lower headset bearing set seats properly (Fig. 11.25).

14. Slide the top cup, with the bearings in it, onto the steering tube. Keep the bike upside down at this point; it not only keeps the fork in place, it also prevents grit from falling into the bearings as you put the cup on.

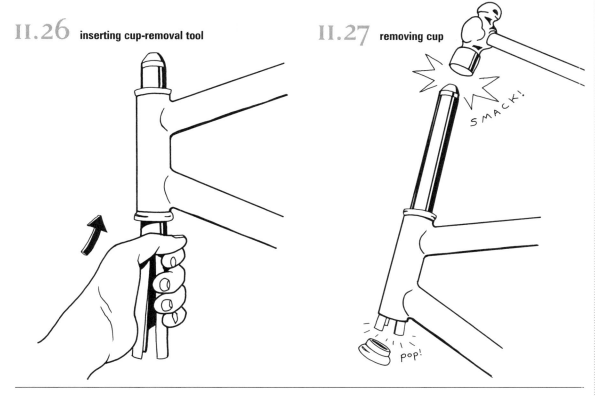

II.26 **inserting cup-removal tool**

II.27 **removing cup**

SMACK!

POP!

15. Grease the compression ring and slide it onto the (greased) steering tube, so the narrower end slides into the conical space in the top of the top cup (Fig. II.18). Slide on any spacers you had under the stem. Slide the stem on, and tighten one stem clamp bolt to hold it in place.

16. Turn the bike over. Check that the stem clamp extends 3mm to 6mm above the top of the steering tube. If it does, install the top cap on the top of the stem clamp and steering tube, and screw the bolt into the star nut set inside the steering tube.

If the steering tube is too long, remove the stem. Add a spacer or file the steering shorter until the stem clamp overlaps it by 3mm to 6mm. If the steering tube is too short, remove spacers from below the stem, if there are any. If there are no spacers to remove, try a new stem with a shorter clamp.

17. Adjust the headset (Section XI-17). Go ride your bike.

XI-20: REMOVE HEADSET

level 3

1. Open the headset and remove the fork and bearings by following Steps 1-5 either section XI-18 or XI-19, depending on headset type.

2. Slide the solid end of the headset-cup remover through one end of the head tube (Fig. II.26). As you pull the headset-cup remover through the head tube, the splayed-out tangs on the opposite end of the tool pull through the cup and spread out.

3. Strike the solid end of the cup remover with a hammer, and drive the cup out (Fig. II.27).

4. Remove the other cup by placing the cup remover into the opposite end of the head tube and repeating Steps 2 and 3 on the opposite end of the end tube.

5. a. If you have a suspension fork (or a rigid fork with a clamp-together crown), you will find a notch on the front and back of the fork crown under the fork crown race. Turn the fork upside

removing headset

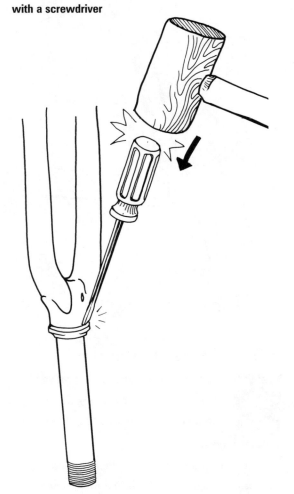

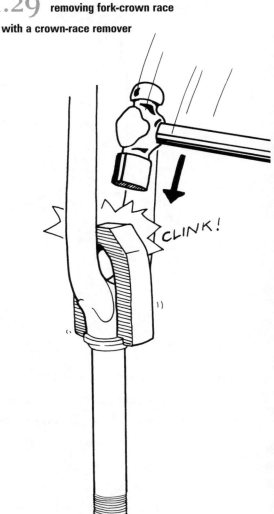

CLINK!

removing
headset

down so that the top of the steering tube is sitting on the workbench. Place the blade of a large screwdriver into the notch on one side of the crown so it butts against the bottom of the headset fork crown race. Tap the handle of the screwdriver with a hammer to drive the crown race up the steering tube a bit (Fig. II.28). Move the screwdriver to the groove on the other side, and tap it again to move that side of the crown race up a bit. Continue in this way, alternately tapping either side of the crown race up the steering tube, bit by bit, until it gets past the enlarged section of the steering tube and slides off.

b. If you have a rigid fork, you can use a screwdriver to tap the crown race off as outlined above (Fig. II.28). You can also do it more elegantly with a crown race remover or an appropriately sized bench vise. Stand the fork upside down on the top of the steering tube. Place the U-shaped crown race remover so it straddles the underside of the fork crown, and its ledges engage the front and back edges of the crown race. Smack the top of the crown race remover with a hammer to knock the race off (Fig. II.29).

To do it with a bench vise, flip the brakes out of the way and slide the fork in, straddling the center

XI

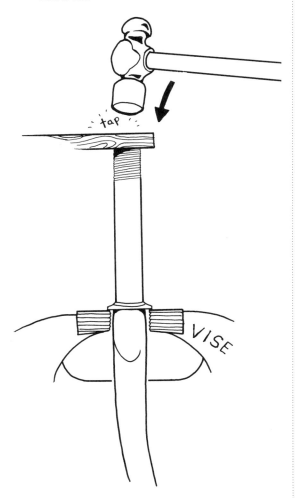

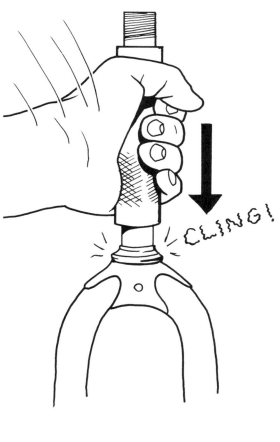

CLING!

handlebars, stems and headsets

shaft of the vise. Tighten the vise so its faces lightly contact the front and back of the fork crown with the lower side of the crown race sitting on top of them. Put a block of wood on the top of the steering tube to pad it. Strike the block with a hammer to drive the fork down and knock the crown race off of it (Fig. 11.30).

XI-21: INSTALL HEADSET

When you get a new headset, you can install it yourself if you have the necessary tools. Otherwise, get a shop to do it.

1. Frame and fork preparation: If this is a new frame (or one that has "eaten" headsets in the past), make sure that the head tube has been reamed and faced. If not, you will need a bike shop equipped with the proper tools to do it for you. Reaming makes the head tube ends round inside and of the correct diameter for the headset cups to press in. Facing makes both ends of the head tube parallel so the bearings can turn smoothly and uniformly.

The base of the steering tube also needs to be turned down to the correct diameter for the crown race. The crown race seat on top of the fork crown must be faced in a way that places the

installing
headset

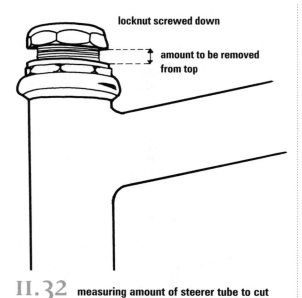

II.32 measuring amount of steerer tube to cut

locknut screwed down

amount to be removed from top

crown race parallel to the head tube cups. This is generally only a concern with rigid forks; suspension forks are usually shipped with the tube properly machined to accept the fork crown race.

The fork steerer (threaded or threadless) must also be cut to the proper length. **Remember, you can always go back and cut more off. You can't go back and add any, so be careful!** You can wait until the headset and stem (in the case of a threadless headset) are installed. Or you can figure out the length first. Measure the excess length as in Fig. 11.32, remove the top nut and cut that much off the top.

To calculate steerer length with a threaded headset, you need to know its stack height (the stack height is often listed in the headset owner's manual, or a bike shop can look it up in their Barnetts's Manual). Measure the length of the head tube and add the headset stack-height to this length. If you are adding extra spacers or a brake cable hanger between the headset nuts, add their thickness in as well. This figure represents the length that the fork-steering tube must be. If the

steering tube is already more than 3mm to 5mm shorter than this, you need to find another headset with a shorter stack height (or, if you have included spacers, remove a few). If the steering tube is longer than this sum, saw it down to length and then file off the burrs the hacksaw left on the inside and outside edges of the steering tube end.

You can pretty much follow the same steps if you are using a threadless headset. Add the headset stack-height to the length of the steering tube and the stem clamp, and subtract 3mm from the total. This is the length the steering tube should be from fork crown to top. I recommend not cutting until the headset is assembled and the stem is installed so you can see if you want some spacers under the stem to raise your bars higher.

If you do not know the headset stack-height, you're afraid you'll cut the steering tube too short, or you want to see how it goes together before you cut it down, continue with the installation and assembly. When you are ready, cut it to 3mm to 6mm below the top edge of the stem.

2. Put a thin layer of grease on the ends of the head-tube cups that will be pressed into the head tube, inside the hole in the fork-crown race, inside the ends of the head tube itself, and on the base of the steering tube.

3. Slide the fork-crown race down on the fork steering tube until it hits the enlarged section at the bottom. Slide the crown-race-slide punch up and down the steering tube, pounding the crown race down until it sits flat on top of its seat on the fork crown (Fig. 11.31). Some crown-race punches are longer and closed on the top and are meant to be hit with a hammer rather than be slid up and down by hand.

Hold the fork up against the light to see if there are any gaps between the crown race and the crown.

XI

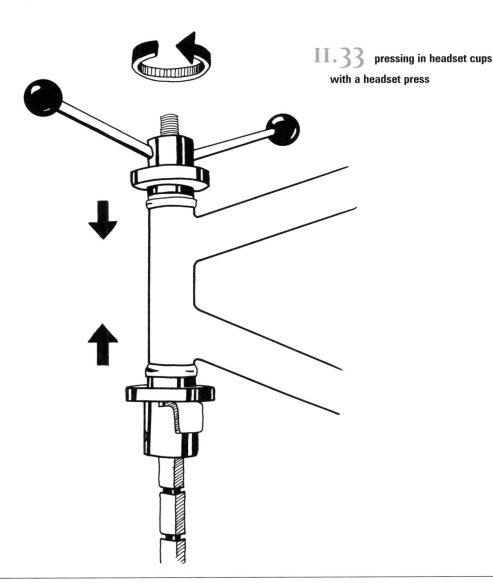

II.33 pressing in headset cups
with a headset press

handlebars, stems
and headsets

installing
headset

NOTE

Extra-thin crown races can be easily bent or broken by the crown-race punch. Chris King and Shimano both make support tools that sit over the race and distribute the impact from the punch.

4. Place the headset cups into the ends of the head tube. Slide the headset-press shaft through the head tube. Press the button on the detachable end of the tool and slide it onto the shaft until it bumps into one of the cups. Find the nearest notch on the shaft and release the button (Fig. II.33). Some headset presses use a system of spacers and cones on both ends of the cups. Follow the instruc-

tions to set yours up properly. Whatever you do, be certain that the parts that contact the cups are not touching the bearing races.

NOTE

Dia-Compe "S" and Chris King headsets have bearings that are pressed into the cups and cannot be removed (Fig. II.23). If you use a headset press that pushes on the center of the cups, you will ruin the bearings. You need a press that pushes the outer portion of the cup and does not touch the bearings. Chris King makes tool inserts for this that fit most headset presses, and Park has a headset press with large flat ends that also works.

5. Hold the lower end of the cup press shaft with a wrench. That will keep the tool from turning as you press in the cups. Tighten the press by turning the handle on the top clockwise (Fig. 11.33). Keep tightening down on the tool until the cups are fully pressed into the ends of the head tube. Examine them carefully to make sure there are no gaps between the cups and the ends of the head tube.

6. Liberally apply grease to all bearing surfaces. If you are using sealed-cartridge bearings, a thin film will do.

7. Install and adjust the headset, following Sections 11-18 and 11-16 for a threaded headset, and Sections 11-19 and 11-17 for a threadless one.

XI-22: TROUBLESHOOTING STEM, BAR AND HEADSET PROBLEMS

1. Bars slip.

Tighten the pinch bolt on the stem that holds the bars. If the clamp closes on itself without holding the bar securely, check that the bar is not deformed and the stem clamp is not cracked or stretched; replace any questionable parts. You can slide a shim made out of a beer can between the stem and bar to hold it better, but replacing parts is a safer option; there is always a reason why parts that are meant to fit together no longer do!

2. Bars make creaking noise while riding.

Loosen stem clamp, grease area of bar that fits in stem, slide bar back in place, and tighten stem bolt.

3. Bar end slips.

Tighten bar-end clamp bolt.

4. Stem is not pointed straight ahead.

Loosen bolt (or bolts) securing stem to fork steering tube, align stem with front wheel, and tighten stem bolt (or bolts) again. (With a threaded headset, the bolt you are interested in is a single vertical bolt on top of the stem; loosen it about two turns, and tap the top of the bolt with a hammer to disengage the wedge on the other end from the bottom of the stem (Fig. 11-12). With a threadless headset, there are one, two, or three horizontal bolts pinching the stem around the steering tube that need to be loosened to turn the stem on the steerer. Do not loosen the bolt on the top of the stem cap (Fig. 11.22); you'll have to readjust your headset if you do.

5. Fork and headset rattle or clunk when riding.

The headset is too loose. Adjust headset (Section XI-16 or XI-17).

6. Stem/bar/fork assembly does not turn smoothly but instead stops in certain fixed positions.

Headset is pitted and needs to be replaced. See Sections XI-20 and XI-21.

7. Stem/bar/fork assembly does not turn freely.

Headset is too tight. The front wheel should swing easily from side to side when leaning the bike or lifting the front end. Adjust the headset (Section XI-16 or 17, depending on type).

8. Stem is stuck in fork steering tube.

See Section XI-14.

wheel building

"A child of five could understand this.

Fetch me a child of five." — GROUCHO MARX

tools

**spoke wrench
truing stand
wheel dishing tool
13mm,14mm, 15mm
    cone wrenches
17mm open end
wrench (or
    an adjustable
    wrench)
spoke prep
    (follow
    application
    instructions
    on container)**

**OPTIONAL
linseed oil**

Congratulations. You have arrived at the task most often used to gauge the talents of a bike mechanic. Next to building a frame or fork, building a good set of wheels is the most critical and most creative of a bike mechanic's tasks. Despite the air of mystery surrounding the art of wheel building, the construction of a good set of bicycle wheels is really a pretty straightforward task.

Clearly, wheels are the central component of a bike. For any bike to perform well, its wheels must be well-made and properly tensioned. Once you learn how, it is quite rewarding to turn a pile of small parts into a set of strong and light wheels upon which you can bash around with confidence. You will be amazed at what they can withstand, and you will no longer go through life thinking that building wheels is just something the "experts" do. With practice, you can build wheels at your house that are just as good as any custom-

made set, and far superior to those built by machine.

This is not meant to be an exhaustive description of how to build all types of wheel-spoking patterns; there are entire books written on that. (If you are interested in a more comprehensive treatment of the subject of wheel building, I recommend reading "The Barnett's Manual," by John Barnett or "The Bicycle Wheel," by Jobst Brandt.) You can build great wheels following this method in the classic "three-cross" spoking pattern in which each spoke crosses over three other spokes (Fig. 12.1). So, let's get started.

XII-1: PARTS

1. Get together the parts you need: a rim, a hub (make sure that the hub you are using has the same number of holes as the rim does), properly sized spokes and nipples to match. I suggest getting the spokes from your local bike shop. This way, a mechanic can help make sure you are get-

12.1 the complete wheel

rim ....

valve hole ....

spoke ....

nipple ....

hub ....

12.2 spoke and nipple

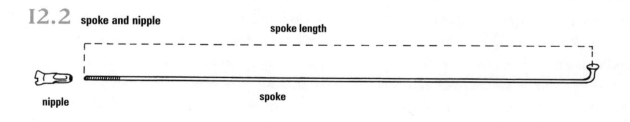

spoke length

nipple

spoke

ting the right spoke lengths (Fig. 12.2) and can counsel you on what gauges (thicknesses) of spoke to buy, as well as what rim makes sense for your weight and kind of riding you plan on doing. Remember: you must specify that you will be using a "three-cross" spoking pattern.

N O T E

If you are just replacing a rim on an old wheel, do not use the old spokes. You won't save all that much money re-using the old spokes, and the rounded-out nipples and weakened spokes will soon make you wish you had gone ahead and spent the extra money on a new set.

XII-2: LACING THE WHEEL

For the sake of brevity and clarity, I do not mention using spoke prep compound with every instruction to thread a nipple onto a spoke. While not necessary, I think that the wheel is improved if spoke prep is used, as it encourages the nipples to thread on more smoothly, takes up some of the slop between the spoke and nipple threads, and its thread-locking ability discourages the nipples from vibrating loose.

The spoke prep is applied to the spoke threads before putting each nipple on. You do not want too much, as it will be hard to adjust the nipples months and years down the off-road; you just want the spoke prep in the dips of the threads. You can get the right amount if you dip the threads of a pair of spokes into the spoke prep and then take two more dry spokes, and roll the threads of all four spokes together with your fingers.

NOTE

If you are building a rear wheel with an OCR (Off-Center Rear) rim drilled off center (Ritchey and Bontrager both have OCR models), make sure as you are lacing that you orient the rim so that the spoke holes are offset to the left (non-drive) side (see Fig. 12.3). The rim is meant to reduce wheel dish, so offsetting the nipples to the left reduces the otherwise very steep angle at which drive-side spokes normally hit the rim. The balanced left-to-right spoke tension should increase the lifetime of the wheel, and the lower spoke angle moves the drive-side spokes away from the rear derailleur. When using the chain on the dished titanium ninth (largest) cog of Ritchey's "2 x 9" drivetrain, the derailleur does not snag the spokes.

1. Divide your spokes into four separate groups, two sets for each side of each hub flange. Remember: if you are building a rear wheel, you should be working with two different spoke

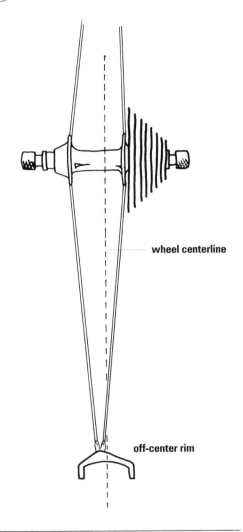

12.3 **"OCR" (off-center rear) rim laced correctly**

wheel centerline

off-center rim

lengths, since spokes on the right-hand side, or drive side, are almost always shorter.

2. Hold the rim on your lap with the valve hole away from you. Notice that the holes alternate being offset upward or downward from the rim centerline. With an OCR rim (Fig. 12.3), have the spoke holes offset downward, toward your lap.

3. Hold the hub in the center of the rim, with the right side of the hub pointing up. On a rear hub, the right side is the drive side. Front hubs are symmetrical; pick a side to be the right side. In the illustrations, the right side has the nut end of the

lacing
the
wheel
—
first set
of spokes

12.4 first half of right-side spokes placed in hub

12.5 first spoke – right side up

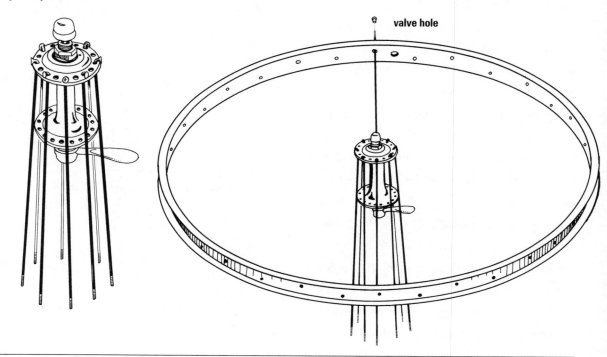

valve hole

12.6 first set of spokes laced

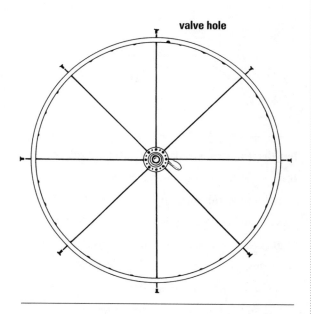

valve hole

quick release.

A. First set of spokes

4. Drop a spoke down into every other hole in the top (right side) hub flange, so that the spoke

heads are facing up (Fig. 12.4). Make sure if it's a rear wheel that you put the shorter spokes on the right side. Half of the holes you are looking at are normally countersunk deeper into the hub flange to seat the spoke head, so use those holes.

5. Put a spoke into the first hole to the left of the valve hole and screw the nipple on three turns (Fig. 12.5). Notice that this hole is offset upward (on an OCR rim, this means that the hole is offset upward from the centerline of the spoke holes, not the centerline of the rim). If the first hole to the left of the valve hole isn't offset upward, you have a mis-drilled rim, and you must offset all instructions one hole.

6. Working counterclockwise, put the next spoke on the hub into the hole in the rim four holes away from the first spoke, and screw a nipple on three turns. There should be three open rim holes between these spokes, and the hole you put the second spoke into should also be offset upward.

12.8 **lacing second set**

next spoke
of the
second set

valve hole

first spoke
of the first set

first spoke
of the second set

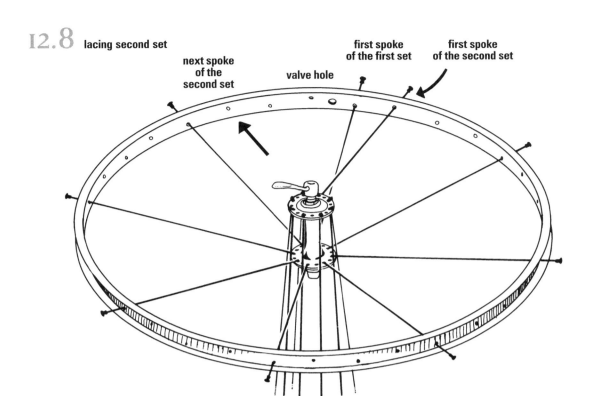

XII

wheel building

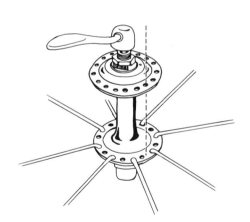

12.7 **spoke-hole offset**

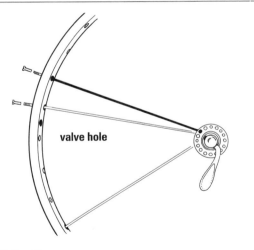

valve hole

12.9 **diverging parallel spokes**

**lacing the
wheel
—
second set
of spokes**

7. Continue counterclockwise around the wheel in the same manner. You should now have used half of the rim holes that are offset upward, and there should be three open holes between each spoke (Fig. 12.6).

8. Flip the wheel over.

B. Second set of spokes

9. Sight across the hub from one flange to the

other. Notice that the holes in one flange do not line up with the holes in the other; each hole lines up in between two holes on the opposite flange (Fig. 12.7).

10. Drop a spoke down through the hole in the top flange that is immediately to the right of the first spoke you installed (the spoke that is just to the right of the valve hole).

12.10 second set of spokes laced

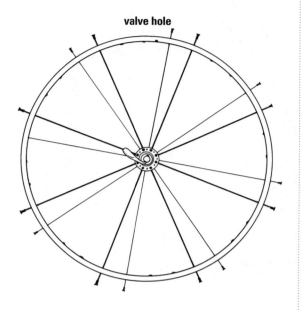

valve hole

12.11 placing third set of spokes in hub

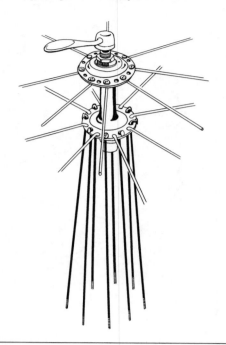

11. Put this new spoke into the second hole to the right of the valve hole, next to the first spoke you installed (Figs. 12.8 and 12.9). This hole will be offset upward from the rim centerline.

12. Thread the nipple on three turns.

13. Double check to make sure that the spoke you just installed starts at a hole in the hub's top (left side) flange that is one-half-a-hole space to the right of the hole in the lower flange where the first spoke you installed started. These two spokes should be diverging but still nearly parallel (Fig. 12.9).

14. Drop a spoke down through the hole in the top (left side) flange two holes away in either direction, and continue around until every other hole has a spoke hanging down through it (Fig. 12.8).

15. Working counterclockwise, take the next spoke and put it in the rim hole that is three holes to the left of the valve hole. This hole should be offset upward and four holes to the left of the spoke you just installed. Thread the nipple on three turns.

16. Follow this pattern counter-clockwise around the wheel (Fig. 12.10). You should have now used half of the rim holes that are offset upwards, as well as half of the total rim holes. The second set of spokes should all be in upwardly offset holes, one hole to the right of each spoke of the first set.

C. Third set of spokes

17. Drop spokes through the remaining holes on the right side of the hub, from the inside out (Fig. 12.11). Remember: if it's a rear wheel, these spokes should be shorter than the spokes used on the left side.

18. Flip the wheel over, grabbing the spokes you've just dropped through to keep them from falling out.

19. Fan the spokes out, so they cannot fall back down through the hub holes.

20. Grab the hub and rotate it counterclockwise as far as you can (Fig. 12.12).

21. Pick any spoke on the top (right hand) flange that is already laced to the rim. Now find the spoke five hub holes away in a clockwise direction.

12.13 lacing third set of spokes

first spoke of the third set

valve hole

first spoke of the first set

next spoke of the third set

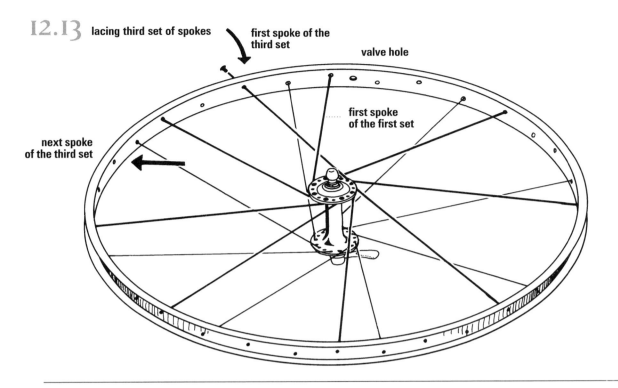

22. Take this new spoke, cross it under the spoke you counted from (the one five holes away), and stick it into the rim hole two holes counterclockwise from that spoke (Fig. 12.13). Thread a nipple on three turns.

23. Continue around the wheel, doing the same thing (Fig. 12.14). You may find that some of the

spokes don't quite reach far enough. If that's the case, push down on each one about an inch from the spoke elbow to help them reach.

24. Make sure that every spoke coming out of the upper side of the top flange (the spokes that come out toward you with their spoke heads hidden from view) crosses over two spokes and

12.12 rotating hub counterclockwise

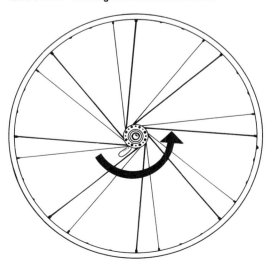

12.14 third set laced

valve hole

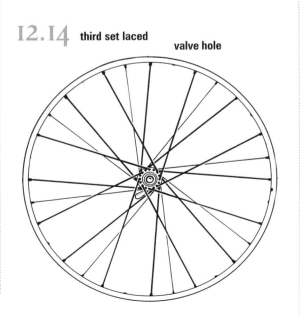

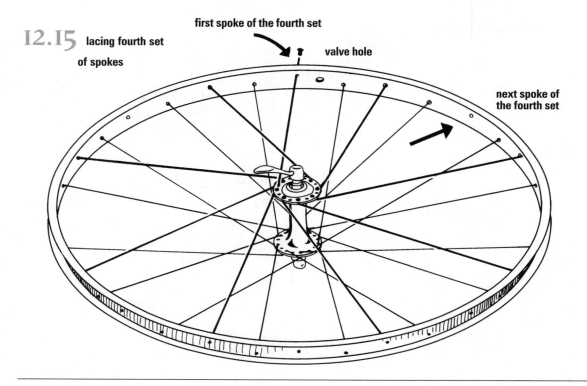

12.15 lacing fourth set of spokes

first spoke of the fourth set

valve hole

next spoke of the fourth set

under a third. All three of these "crossing" spokes come from the underside of the same flange, and have their spoke heads facing toward you. These "crossing" spokes begin 1, 3 and 5 hub holes counterclockwise from the spoke that you just inserted into the rim (Fig. 12.14). This is called a "three cross" pattern because every spoke crosses three others on its way to the rim (over, over, under). Every upwardly offset hole should now be occupied on the rim.

D. Fourth (and final) set of spokes

25. Drop spokes down through the remaining hub holes in the bottom flange from the inside out (like Fig. 12.11, but with the other side of the hub up).

26. Flip the wheel over, grabbing the spokes to keep them from falling back down through the holes.

27. Fan the spokes out.

28. Count in a counterclockwise direction to the spoke that is five hub holes from any spoke on the top (left) flange that is already laced to the rim.

29. Take that spoke, cross it over two spokes and under the spoke you counted from. Stick the spoke into the rim hole two holes clockwise from the spoke it crosses under (Fig. 12.15). Thread a nipple on three turns.

30. Continue around the wheel, doing the same thing (Fig. 12.1). You may find that some of the spokes don't quite reach far enough. If that's the case, push down on each one about an inch from the spoke elbow to help them reach.

31. Make sure that every spoke coming out from the upper side of the top flange (the spokes that come out toward you with their spoke heads hidden from view) crosses over two spokes and under a third (Fig. 12.1). All three of these "crossing" spokes come from the underside of the same flange, and have their spoke heads facing toward you. The "crossing" spokes begin 1, 3 and 5 hub holes clockwise from each spoke emerging from the top of upper (left) hub flange (Fig. 12.1). This is called a "three-cross" pattern because every spoke crosses three others on its way to the rim (over,

12.16 converging parallel spokes

valve hole

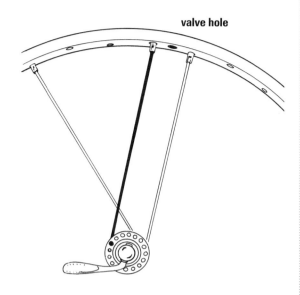

over, under). Every hole should now be occupied on the rim. The valve hole should be between "converging parallel" spokes (Fig. 12.16) to make room for the pump head when inflating the tire.

XII-3: TENSIONING THE WHEEL

1. Put the wheel in the truing stand.

2. Tighten each nipple with a spoke wrench until only three threads are visible beyond the bottom of the nipple (see Figs. 12.17-12.20 for rotation direction). Leaving three threads showing assumes that you are using standard-length nipples and not the long nipples that are rarely seen any more on high-quality wheels. With long nipples, tighten each until the spoke end is four threads from popping out of the top of the nipple toward the tube.

3. Press the spokes coming outward from the outer side of the hub flanges down with your thumb at the elbow to straighten out their line to the rim. Spokes coming out of the inner side of the flange do not need this.

4. Go around the wheel, tightening each nipple a half-turn. Do this uniformly, so that the wheel is not thrown out of true.

5. Check to see if the spokes are tight enough to give a tone when plucked. Squeeze pairs of spokes together and compare with a good wheel with spokes of the same gauge; your wheel should have considerably less tension at this point.

6. Repeat Steps 4 and 5 until the spokes all make a tone and are under less tension than an existing, good wheel.

XII-4: TRUING THE WHEEL

A. Lateral true

The side-to-side trueness is the most obvious wheel parameter when you spin it.

1. Make sure the hub axle has no end play. If it does, adjust the hub (see "Hub adjustment," Section VI-12D in Chapter 6) to eliminate the end play.

2. (Optional) Put a drop of linseed oil around each nipple on the tire side where it seats in the rim to lubricate the contact area between it and the inside of the rim hole.

3. Set the truing-stand feelers so that one of them scrapes the side of the rim at the worst lateral wobble (Figs. 12.17 and 12.18).

4. Ending a few spokes on either side of where the rim scrapes, tighten the spokes coming from the opposite side of the hub and loosen the spokes coming from the same side of the hub (Figs. 12.17 and 12.18). Start with a quarter-turn on nipples at the center of the scraping area and decrease the amount you turn each nipple as you move away in either direction. This pulls the rim away from the feeler. If it does the opposite, you are turning the nipples in the wrong direction. Remember: you normally turn something to the

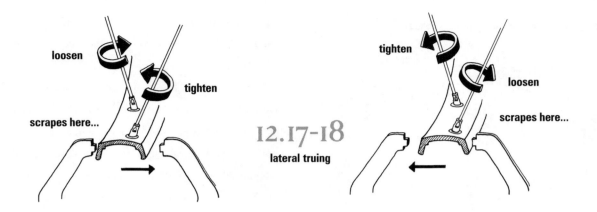

12.17-18

lateral truing

right to tighten and to the left to loosen, but tightening and loosening spoke nipples at the bottom of the wheel is the opposite of what you would normally do (Figs. 12.17-12.20). This is because the nipple head is underneath your spoke wrench. Try opening a jar that is upside down and you will immediately understand the principle involved.

5. Work around the wheel in this way, bringing in the feelers as the wheel gets truer.

B. Radial true

While not as obvious as side-to-side trueness, out-of-roundness is more important to the longevity of the wheel, since "uniformity of tension is the key to durability" — Portia Masterson of Self Propulsion in Golden, CO.

6. Set the truing-stand feelers so that they now contact the circumference of the rim, rather than the sides.

7. Bring the feelers in until they scrape against the highest spot on the rim (Fig. 12.19).

8. Tighten the spokes a quarter-turn where the rim scrapes. This will pull the rim inward. Decrease the amount of each turn (to an eighth-turn and less) as you move away from the center of the scraping area.

9. Work around the wheel this way, bringing the feelers in as the wheel becomes rounder. Loosen the spokes at a dip in the rim (Fig. 12.20).

If the spokes are too tight at this point, they will be hard to turn, and will creak and groan as you

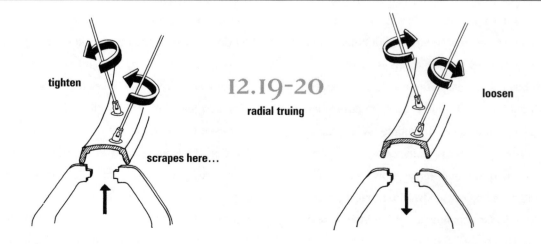

12.19-20

radial truing

turn them. When the spokes become hard to turn (i.e. the nipples feel on the verge of rounding off), loosen all of the spokes in the wheel a quarter-turn before continuing. Compare tension with a good wheel with the same gauge spokes; tension should still be lower in the wheel you are building.

XII-5: DISHING THE WHEEL

1. Place the dishing tool across the right side of the wheel, bisecting the center (Fig. 12.21).

2. Tighten or loosen the dishing gauge screw until the gauge contacts the outer face of the axle end nut (Fig. 12.21).

3. Flip the wheel over.

4. Place the dishing tool across the other side of the wheel.

5. Check the gap of the dishing gauge with this axle end-nut face (Fig. 12.22). Any gap between the dishing gauge and the axle end-nut face indicates the amount the rim is offset from the centerline of the wheel. If there is no gap, but an overlap instead, reset the dishing gauge on this side (the previously overlapped side). Then flip it over and check the other side (i.e., repeat Steps 3, 4 and 5 on the opposite side).

6. Put the wheel back in the truing stand.

7. Pull the rim toward the center (reducing the gap between the dishing tool and the axle-end face) by tightening the spokes on the opposite side of the wheel from the axle end that had the gap between it and the dishing gauge. Tighten a half-turn each. If the spokes start getting really tight (they creak a lot when the nipples start rounding off, and the spokes feel much tighter than the spokes in a comparable wheel), then loosen the spokes on the opposite side of the wheel.

8. Recheck the wheel with the dishing gauge by repeating Steps 1-5.

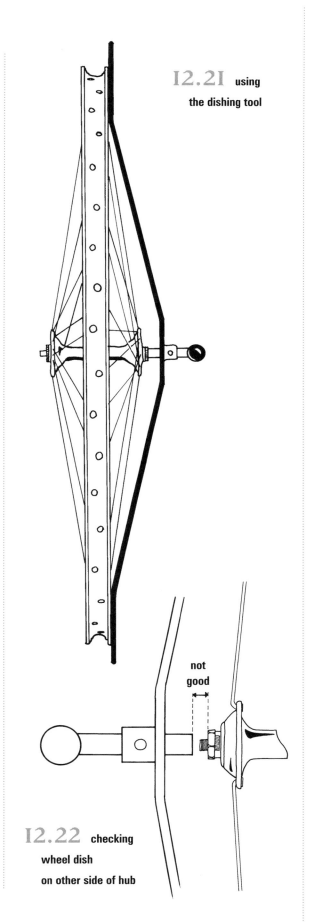

I2.2I using the dishing tool

not good

I2.22 checking wheel dish on other side of hub

XII

wheel building

dishing the wheel

9. If the wheel is still off dish (there is still a gap between the dishing gauge and the end nut when you flip it over), repeat Steps 6-8 until the dish is correct (the gap is zero).

10. Pre-stress the spokes by squeezing each pair of spokes together with your hands (Fig. 12.23). They will make a "ping" noise as they unwind. If pre-stressing throws the wheel way out of true, the spokes are probably too tight. Loosen them all an eighth-turn. Some loss of wheel "trueness" is normal. If the loss is minor, you may overlook it

11. Repeat "Truing the wheel" steps, followed by the "Dishing the wheel" steps, pre-stressing the spokes frequently as you go. Keep bringing in the accuracy this way.

12. Bring up the tension to that of a comparable wheel by making small tightening adjustments to every nipple, adjusting dish and true after each time around, until the wheel is as you want it.

13. If the rim is oily, wipe it down with a citrus-based biodegradable solvent.

14. Congratulate yourself on building your wheel, and show it off to your friends.

XII-6: COMMENTS

Your wheel has some features that you won't find on machine-built wheels. Most significantly, on your rear wheel, the "pulling spokes are to the outside." In plain speak, this means that you have a spoking pattern that resists the twisting force on the hub produced by pedaling forces on the chain. Half of the spokes are called "pulling" or "dynamic" spokes, and the other half are called "static" spokes. The pulling spokes are the ones directed in such a way that a clockwise twist on the hub increases the tension in them. If you look at the wheel from the drive side, you will see what I am talking about. On the other hand, the static spokes

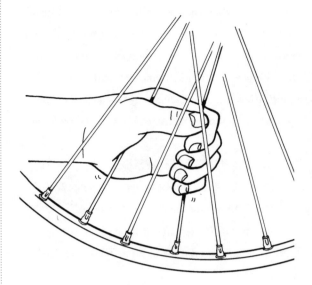

12.23 relieving tension

do not oppose a clockwise twist on the hub. In fact, their tension decreases when you stomp on the pedals. By placing all of the pulling spokes so that they come from the inside of the hub flanges out (i.e. the spoke heads are on the inward side of the flanges), we have attached the spokes doing the most work the farthest outward on the hub, increasing their angle to the rim, and hence their ability to oppose forces acting on the rim.

If you choose the appropriate parts for your weight and riding style, and have the proper spoke tension, then you should have a strong wheel that will last you a long time. Congratulations!

XIII

forks

"If you come to a fork in the road, take it." — YOGI BERRA

tools

- metric Allen wrenches
- metric open-end wrenches
- adjustable wrench
- needle-nose pliers
- safety glasses
- soft hammer
- long screwdriver
- non-lithium grease
- citrus degreaser

OPTIONAL

- torque wrench
- ruler or calipers
- a pair of dropout alignment tools
- solid bench vise
- snap-ring pliers
- air pump for fork
- metric socket wrenches
- bike stand
- medium thread lock compound (like Loctite 242)
- titanium bolt anti-seize compound

The fork serves a number of purposes. Most obviously, it connects the front wheel to the handlebars. Of course, the fork allows the bike to be steered, and supports the front brake. Forks also offset the front hub some distance forward of the steering axis. This offset distance (called the "fork rake"), combined with the steering axis (the "head angle") and the wheel size, determine how your bike is going to handle and steer.

All forks — suspended (Fig. 13.2) or rigid (Fig. 13.1) — provide at least a minimum amount of suspension by allowing the front wheel to move up and down. The simple facts that the steering axis angles the fork forward from vertical and that the front hub is offset further forward still, make it possible for the fork to flex along its length and absorb vertical shocks. Suspension forks add a much greater range of vertical wheel travel.

Virtually any mountain-bike fork is made up of a simple combination of components: the steering tube, the fork crown, the fork legs (sometimes called "blades"), the brake bosses (usually cantilever/V-brake posts, but there are also disc brake- and roller-cam/U-brake-mounts), and the fork ends (also called "dropouts" or "fork tips"). Figs. 13.1 & 13.2 illustrate these parts on both rigid and suspension forks. Mountain bike forks are manufactured from steel, aluminum, titanium, carbon fiber and countless mixes of these materials.

These days, a large percentage of mountain bikes come equipped with suspension forks (Fig. 13.2). Their most distinguishing feature is, of

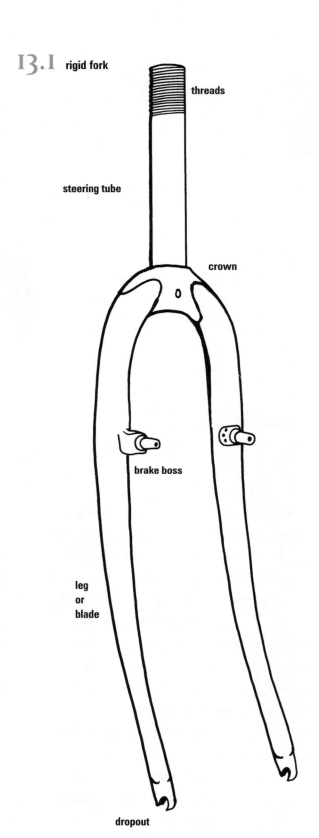

13.1 **rigid fork**

threads

steering tube

crown

the fork

brake boss

leg
or
blade

dropout

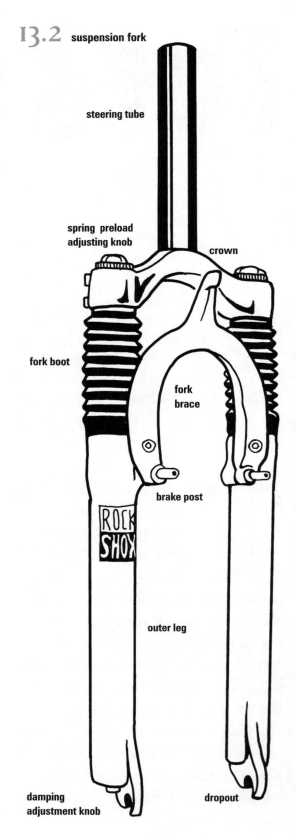

13.2 **suspension fork**

steering tube

spring preload
adjusting knob

crown

fork boot

fork
brace

brake post

ROCK
SHOX

outer leg

damping
adjustment knob

dropout

course, the spring inside. That spring can be made up of elastic polymer bumpers (elastomers), compressed air, steel or titanium coils, or a combination. A lot of suspension forks also include a damping system to control how fast the spring compresses and rebounds. It acts much like a shock absorber on a car or a door (you know-the thing that keeps your screen door from slamming).

Hydraulic damping systems are the most common, relying on the controlled movement of oil from one chamber to another. That flow is usually regulated by a system of holes that act to slow the rate of flow. Some dampers operate on a similar principle with compressed air instead of oil.

The most commonly used suspension fork design uses "telescoping" fork legs that consist of two sections: inner legs attached to the fork crown and steering tube, and outer legs attached to the front hub that slide up and down over the inner legs (Fig. 13.3). While this describes the vast majority of suspension forks, there are a number of variations that vie for a small piece of the fork market. Cannondale's "Head Shock" design incorporates rigid fork legs attached to a single shock unit inside the head tube. "Upside down" telescoping forks have thin lower legs sliding up and down inside fatter upper legs. There are also lots of "linkage" suspension forks on the market that use a system of pivots and movable arms attached to a spring.

XIII-1: FORK INSPECTION

For the most part, forks are pretty durable, but they do break sometimes. A fork failure can ruin your day, since the means of control of the bike is eliminated. Such loss of control usually involves the rapid transfer of your body directly

13.3 **how suspension fork works**

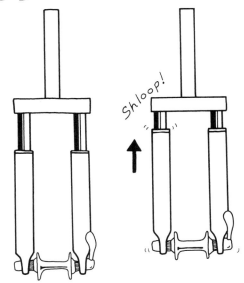

Shloop!

onto the ground resulting in substantial pain.

Ever since I first opened a frame shop, people have regularly brought me an amazing collection of forks that broke, sometimes with catastrophic consequences. Some had steering tubes broken either at the fork crown or in the threads. Others had fork crowns that broke or separated (releasing a fork leg or two), fork crown bolts that broke or fell out, fork legs that folded, cantilever posts that snapped, fork braces (supporting the brake cable) that broke off, and front dropouts that broke off. I have also seen results of air in air-sprung forks suddenly rushing out, bottoming out the fork, and of pivots on linkage forks breaking or falling apart. You can go a long way toward preventing problems like these by regularly inspecting your fork.

With that in mind, get into the habit of checking your fork regularly for any warning signs of impending failure — bends, cracks and stressed paint. If you have crashed your bike, give your fork a very thorough inspection. If you find any indication that your fork has been damaged,

XIII

forks

fork
inspection

replace it. A new fork is cheaper than emergency room charges, brain surgery, or an electric wheelchair.

When you inspect a fork, remove the front wheel, clean the mud off, and look under the crown and between the fork legs. Carefully examine all of the outside areas. Look for any areas where the paint or finish looks cracked or stretched. Look for bent parts, from little ripples in fork legs to skewed cantilever posts and bent dropouts (Fig. 13.4).

Put your wheel back in, and watch to see if the fork legs twist when you tighten the hub into the dropouts. Check to make sure that a true wheel centers under the fork crown. If it doesn't, turn the wheel around and put it back in the fork. That way you can confirm whether the misalignment is in your fork or your wheel. If the wheel lines up off to one side when it is in one way and off the same amount to the other side when it is in the other way, the wheel is off, and the fork is straight. If the wheel is skewed off to the same side in the fork no matter which direction you place the wheel, the fork is misaligned.

I recommend overhauling your headset annually (Chapter 11, Sections XI-18 and XI-19), and, when you do, carefully examine the steering tube for any signs of stress or damage. Check for bent, cracked or stretched areas, stripped threads (Fig. 13.4), bulging where the stem expands inside (threaded steerer) or crimping where the stem clamps around the top (threadless steerer).

Hold the stem up next to the steering tube to make sure that, when your stem is inserted to the depth you have been using it, the bottom of the stem is always over an inch below the bottom of the steering tube threads. If you expand your stem in the threaded region, you are asking for trouble; the threads cut the steering tube wall thickness down by about 50 percent, and each thread offers a sharp breakage plane along which the tube can cleave.

On telescoping suspension forks

Check that any clamp bolts are tight (ideally, you would do this with a torque wrench to check that they are tightened to the torque recommended by the fork manufacturer). If you have titanium clamp bolts on your fork crown and you do lots of fast and rough downhill riding, consider replacing them annually; the heads of titanium fork crown bolts have been known to snap off. Check for oil leaks, either from around the top of the outer leg or around the bolt at the bottom of the outer leg. Check for torn, cracked or missing seals around the top of the outer leg.

On linkage forks, there are a lot of bolts, pins and pivots that need to be checked regularly. Make sure that all bolts are tight and all pins have their circlips or other retaining devices in place so they do not fall out. Check for cracks and bends around the pivot points.

If you have any doubts about anything on your fork, take it to the expert at your bike shop. When it comes to forks, err on the side of caution. Replace them before they need it.

XIII-2: FORK DAMAGE

If your inspection has uncovered some damage that does not automatically require fork replacement, here are some guidelines to go by and means of repair.

A. Dents

Not all fork dents threaten the integrity of the fork. On a rigid fork, a small dent usually poses little risk. A large dent (Fig. 13.4), of course, does. On a suspension fork, almost any dent can

13.4 one messed-up fork

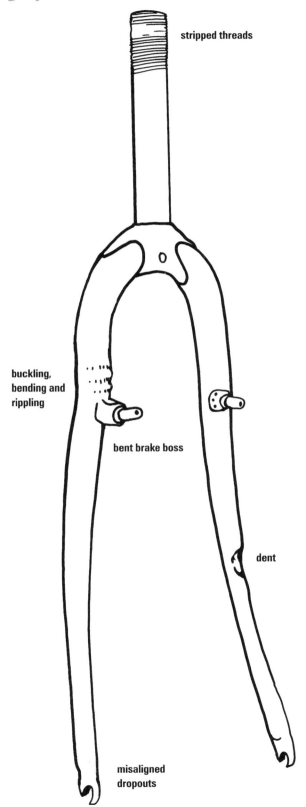

stripped threads

buckling,
bending and
rippling

bent brake boss

dent

misaligned
dropouts

adversely affect the fork's operation, even if it does not pose a breakage threat. Most suspension fork parts are replaceable. If, for example, an inner leg gets dented, you can get a new one and install it without replacing — or even removing — the fork.

B. Fork misalignment

Within limits, a rigid steel fork can be realigned if it is slightly off-center. (See Section XIII-5 in this chapter.) Suspension forks and aluminum, carbon-fiber, and titanium forks cannot be re-aligned. Don't try it!

C. Stripped steering tube threads

If the threads on the steering tube are damaged (Fig. 13.4) so that the headset slips when you try to tighten it, you need to replace it. The steering tube and fork crown assembly can usually be replaced on a suspension fork. You don't usually have that option when it comes to rigid forks, so you have to replace the whole thing.

D. Obvious bend, ripple or crease in fork legs

Replace the fork if ripples and bends are close to or as obvious as in Fig. 13.4. The poor handling and potential breakage pose too great a threat to your safety to be worth saving a few bucks.

E. Bent or stripped cantilever bosses

On most suspension forks, as well as some rigid forks, the cantilever studs can be unscrewed with an 8mm open-end wrench and replaced. It is a good idea to use a thread-locking compound like Loctite 242 on the threads of the new mount.

With few exceptions, bent or stripped cantilever bosses on a rigid fork (Fig. 13.4) usually mean that you have to buy a new fork. If you have a framebuilder in your area, he or she may be able to weld or braze a new one on a steel fork. You will also need to repaint the fork.

fork damage

XIII-3: MAINTAINING RIGID FORKS

Beyond touching up the paint on steel forks and performing regular inspections, the only maintenance procedure to do with a rigid fork is to check the alignment if your bike is handling badly. You can perform minor realignment on a steel fork if you find that it is off center; note that it is risky enough to qualify as a Level 3 job. Do not try to realign titanium, carbon-fiber or aluminum forks. (You've probably noticed that I am repeating myself here.)

XIII-4: CHECK FORK ALIGNMENT

You will need a ruler, a true front wheel and dropout alignment tools (Fig. 1.5). If you have an aluminum, titanium, carbon-fiber, or suspension fork, this procedure is diagnostic only, because you should not try to realign any of these forks. (Again, you might have noticed by now that I am repeating myself.) Checking the alignment may help explain bike-handling problems.

If you find the alignment to be off more than a couple of millimeters in any direction with any fork other than an unsuspended steel model, you need a new fork. If your fork is new, misalignment should be a warranty item.

If your steel fork is more than 8mm off in any direction, you ought to get a new fork. If the dropouts of a steel fork are slightly bent, you can realign them. You can also take a moderately bent (between 2mm and 8mm off) steel fork to a framebuilder or a bike shop for realignment. Make sure that whomever you take it to is properly equipped with a fork jig or alignment table and is well versed in the art of "cold setting" (a fancy term for bending) steel forks.

1. Remove the fork from the bike. (Chapter 11,

Sections XI-18 and XI-19)

2. With the front wheel out, measure the spacing between the faces of the dropouts (Fig. 13.5). Adult and high-quality children's' bikes should have a spacing of 100mm between the inner surfaces of the dropouts. (Some low-end kids' bikes have narrower spacing — about 90mm or so. If that's the type of bike you are working with, don't bother checking alignment; it isn't worth the trouble.) Remember that you are measuring the distance between the flat surfaces that meet the hub-axle faces, not between wheel-retaining bumps. Dropout spacing up to 102mm and down to 99mm is acceptable. Beyond that in either direction means a trip to the bike shop for a new fork. If you have a steel fork, you can go to a bike shop or framebuilder for realignment.

3. Clamp the steering tube of the fork in a bike stand or a padded vise. Install the dropout-alignment tools (Fig. 13.6). The tools are made so that they can be used on either the fork and the rear triangle of the bike, so they have two axle diameters and spacers for use in the wider rear dropouts. Move all of the spacers to the outside of the dropouts so that only the cups of the tools are placed inside of the dropouts. Install the tool so that the shaft is seated up against the top of the dropout slot. Tighten the handles down.

4. Ideally, the ends of the cups on the dropout aligning tools should be parallel and lined up with each other (Fig. 13.7). The cups of Campagnolo dropout-alignment tools are non-adjustable and are nominally 50mm in length; the ideal space between their ends is 0.1mm to 0.5mm. The cups on Park dropout-aligning tools (illustrated in Figs. 13.5, 13.6, and 13.7) are adjustable in length, so that you can bring the faces up close to each other no matter what the

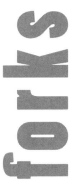

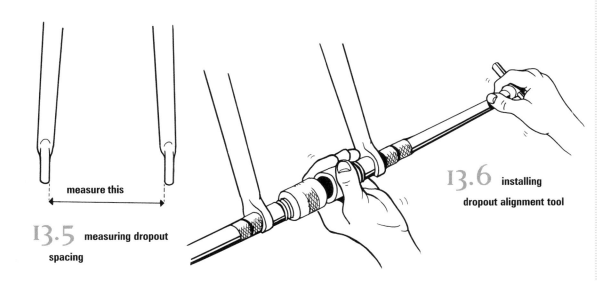

13.5 measuring dropout spacing

measure this

13.6 installing dropout alignment tool

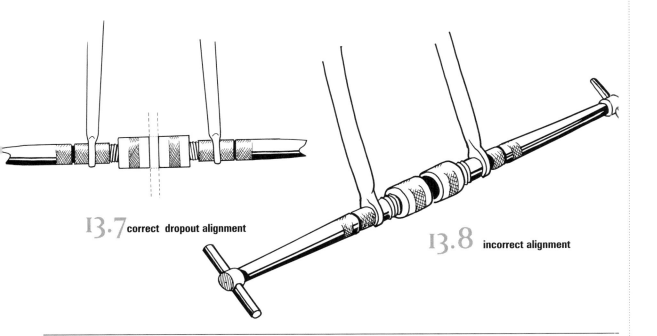

13.7 correct dropout alignment

13.8 incorrect alignment

checking
fork
alignment

dropout spacing. If they are lined up with each other, and the dropouts are spaced between 99mm and 102mm apart, continue on to step 5. If your steel rigid fork's dropouts are not lined up straight across with each other (Fig. 13.8), and the dropouts are within the 99-102mm spacing range, skip to Section XIII-5 to align them.

NOTE

It is very important that the fork dropout faces

are parallel before continuing with step 5, or the rest of the alignment procedures will be a waste of time. Clamping the hub into misaligned dropouts will force the fork legs to twist. If your dropouts are misaligned, any measurement of the side-to-side and fore-aft alignment of the fork legs will not be accurate.

5. Remove the tire from a front wheel. Make sure the wheel is true and properly dished

(Chapter 12, Sections XII-4 and XII-5).

6. Install the wheel in the fork. Make sure the axle is seated against the top of the dropout slot on either side, and make sure the quick-release skewer is tight. Lightly push the rim from side to side to make certain that there is no play in the front hub. If there is play, you first must adjust the hub (Chapter 6, Section VI-12D).

7. Look down the steering tube and through the valve hole to the bottom side of the rim (Fig. 13.9). The steering tube should be lined up with this line of sight through the wheel (Fig. 13.10). When you are sighting through the steering tube and the valve hole, you should see the same amount of space between either side of the rim and the sides of the steering tube. Turn the wheel around and install it again so that what

was the right end of the hub is now the left, and vice versa. Sight through the steering tube and the wheel valve hole again. Placing the wheel in the fork both ways corrects for deformation in the axle or any wobble in the wheel. If the wheel is true, properly dished and the axle is in good shape, the wheel should line up exactly as it did before. If it does not line up, but the wheel is off by the same amount to one side as it is to the opposite side when the wheel is turned around, the wheel is off and the fork is fine side-to-side.

If this test indicates the fork is up to 2mm to 3mm off to the side, that is close enough; continue on, please. If it is off by more than 3mm, get a new fork or have it aligned by a framebuilder (if it is steel ... because, by now you know that you should not try to realign suspension, titanium,

checking fork alignment

13.9 **sighting through steering tube to check fork alignment**

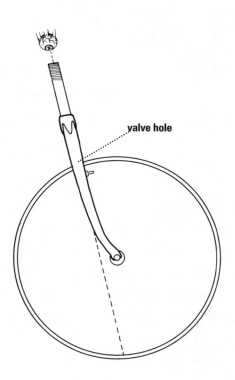

valve hole

13.10 **correct alignment of valve hole in a straight fork**

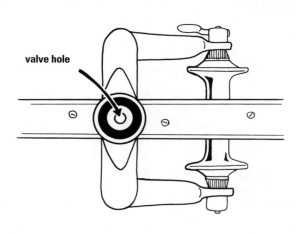

valve hole

carbon-fiber or aluminum forks).

<u>N O T E</u>

If you are sighting through the wheel in this way, and you cannot see the bottom side of the rim through the valve hole because the hub is in the way, your fork has big problems. In order for the bike to handle properly, the fork must have some forward offset from the front hub from the steering axis. This offset, or "rake," is usually around 4cm on a mountain bike. If you sight through the steering tube and see the front hub, the fork is bent backward so much that it has little or no offset! If this is the case, you need a new fork.

8. With the wheel in the fork, place a ruler on edge across the fork legs just below the fork crown (Fig. 13.11). Make sure the ruler is perpendicular to the steering tube.

9. Holding the ruler in place, lift the fork toward a light source so that you are sighting across the ruler and the front hub toward the light. The ruler's edge should line up parallel with the axle ends sticking out of either end of the hub (Fig. 13.11). This will tell you if one fork leg is bent back relative to the other one. If the two line up parallel or very close to that, your fork alignment has checked out completely, and you can put it back in the bike. If one fork leg is considerably behind the other, you need to get a new fork or have this one aligned.

XIII-5: ALIGN DROPOUTS ON RIGID STEEL FORK

You can only do this with a steel, non-suspension fork!

Dropouts are easy to tweak out of alignment; simply pulling the bike off of a roof rack and failing to lift it high enough to clear the rack

I3.II checking fork alignment with a ruler

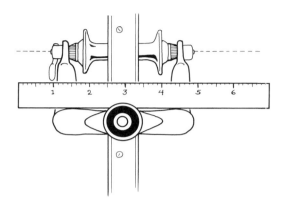

skewer will do it. Your forks may also have come with misaligned dropouts to start with.

If the dropout is bent more than 7 degrees or so, or if the paint is cracked at the dropout where it is bent, it is too dangerous to bend it back. Replace the fork.

1. Install dropout-alignment tools and check alignment as described in Step 3 and 4 under "Check fork alignment" two pages back.

2. If they are not lined up with each other, and the fork spacing is between 99mm and 102mm, you can align the dropouts. If the fork spacing is wider than 102mm or less than 99mm, there is no point in aligning the dropout faces, because you must bend the fork legs as well to correct the spacing. Without an alignment table or fork jig, you cannot do this accurately. You should get a new fork, or have a qualified mechanic or framebuilder align your rigid steel fork.

If your fork spacing is between 99mm and 102mm apart, clamp the crown or unicrown of the fork very tightly between two wood blocks in a well-anchored vise.

3. Grab the end of the dropout-alignment tool handle with one hand and the cup of the tool with the other. Bend each dropout until the open

XIII

forks

checking
fork
alignment

faces of the dropout-alignment tools are parallel, and the edges line straight up with each other (Fig. 13.7).

4. Remove the tools, and continue with "Check fork alignment", Section XIII-4, Step 5.

XIII-6: MAINTAINING SUSPENSION FORKS

maintaining
suspension
forks

Suspension forks (Fig. 13.2) are pretty much the standard on mountain bikes. They offer a significant performance advantage and increase the versatility of the bike. Rapid improvements in the science of bicycle suspension have resulted in a proliferation of numerous types of forks. Of course, with this rush of technology, older models quickly become obsolete. Because of that, you should remember that the details outlined here are applicable to forks commonly used in 1997 and prior years. As of this writing, the market is dominated by telescoping forks with a combination of coil- and elastomer-springs inside. Some also come equipped with hydraulic damping systems.

This chapter also outlines maintenance and adjustment procedures for air-sprung forks. You will be on your own if you have linkage-style forks or aftermarket upgrades retrofitted to forks; read your owner's manual carefully. Linkage-style forks rely on several pivot points, so there are plenty of places for things to go wrong. Be especially vigilant about inspecting these forks regularly. Since a lot of forks require snap-ring pliers for service, they are included on the tool list.

Elastomer, coil spring, and air-oil telescoping forks

Since these three types of forks operate on the same basic principle, many of the basic service steps apply to both.

XIII-7: REMOVE FORK LEGS FROM FORK CROWN

If you want to add or replace dust boots on your fork, you need to remove the inner legs from the crown, or pull the outer legs off of the inner legs (Section XIII-13).

When pulling the inner legs out of the crown, you can leave the fork brace and brakes on, and leave the fork in the bike when you do it. Removing the fork legs from the crown is not necessary to change coil springs or elastomers or to pump an air/oil fork.

N O T E

Some fork legs are pressed into the fork crown, rather than clamped in. These fork legs cannot be removed from the crown. Instead, installation and removal of dust boots on these forks requires the removal of the outer legs and fork brace structure. For example, 1996 and later Rock Shox Judy and Indy model forks use pressed-in crowns. (For instructions on how to remove the outer legs, see Section XIII-13).)

1. Disconnect the brake cable by removing the cable end from the brake lever (Chapter 7, the reverse of Section VII-6, Steps 8, 9 and 10).

2. Loosen the crown bolts (shown in Figs. 13.12 and 13.19) on both sides of the crown. If there are two on each side of your fork crown, do not completely undo one bolt while leaving the other fully tightened. Doing that places a great deal of clamping force on the remaining tight bolt and you can strip the head trying to get it loose. Instead, turn one bolt about a quarter of a turn and then do the same to the other. Then back to the first bolt and loosen by another quarter-turn. Repeat until the crown is loose enough to free the leg.

13.12 **1995 Rock Shox Judy fork exploded**

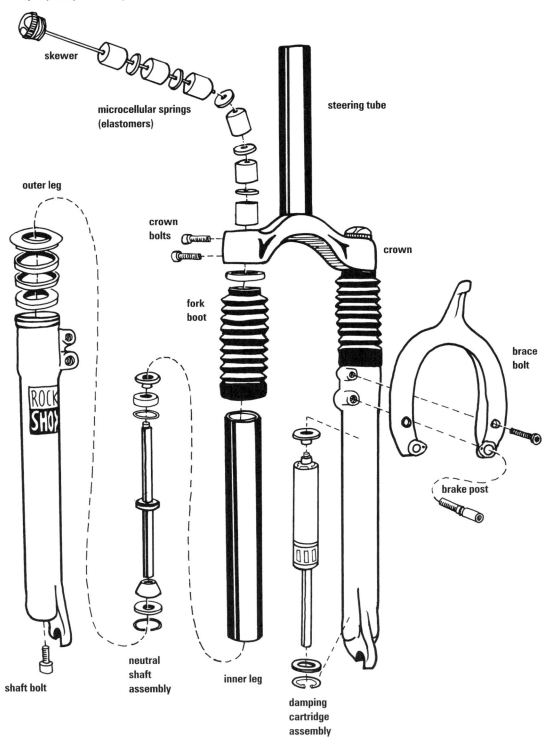

top cap and pre-load adjuster

skewer

microcellular springs
(elastomers)

steering tube

outer leg

crown
bolts

crown

fork
boot

brace
bolt

brake post

shaft bolt

neutral
shaft
assembly

inner leg

damping
cartridge
assembly

forks

suspension
fork exploded

3. Pull both fork legs out of the crown using a gentle rocking motion.

XIII-8: REMOVE AND INSTALL FORK BOOTS

With all telescoping forks, I recommend keeping fork boots on the inner legs (shown in Fig. 13.12) to keep them and the seals at the top of the outer legs clean and reduce maintenance and wear. You will need to remove the boots when you are checking your fork's travel.

1. Remove the fork legs from the crown (see Section XIII-7 above).

2. Pull the fork boots off.

3. To install boots, slide them on to the inner legs, with the large end down toward the outer legs. Make sure that you are using boots designed for your fork.

4. Pull the lip of each fork boot into the groove in the top of the outer leg. You may need to stretch the boot with a pair of needle-nose pliers to get it to slide over the outer leg behind the fork brace.

5. Replace the inner legs in the fork crown (see Section XIII-9 below).

NOTE

To replace fork boots on forks with pressed-in crowns, you need to pull the lower legs off to get at the boots; the procedure for this is included in Section XIII-13.

XIII-9: INSTALL INNER LEGS IN FORK CROWN

1. Wipe the inner legs clean, and make sure the fork crown bolts are loose. Install the fork boots (Section XIII-8 above).

2. Insert the inner legs into the fork crown. Some Manitou forks have a lip against which the

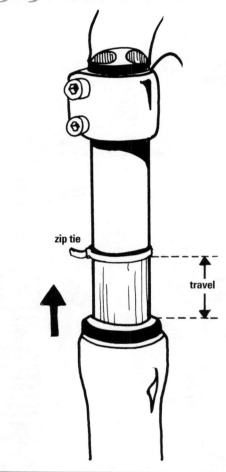

zip tie

travel

inner leg is supposed to rest. Slide the inner leg up into the crown until it hits the lip. Other Manitous and all Rock Shox forks slide all the way through the crown. Push the inner leg through the crown until the top of the leg sticks up no more than 2mm above the top of the crown.

3. Tighten the crown bolts, again alternately tightening each of the two bolts on each side. Pre-1997 Manitou single 6mm x 1 (tightened with 5mm hex key) crown bolts are to be tightened to a torque of 110 to 130 inch-pounds. Rock Shox's smaller, 5mm x 0.8 (tightened with 4mm hex key) paired crown bolts are to be tightened to 60 inch-pounds. 1997 Manitou forks use a small pair of bolts on each side, like Rock Shox (and tight-

ened to approximately the same torque). Use anti-seize compound on titanium bolts and medium thread-lock compound on steel bolts.

XIII-10: MEASURING FORK TRAVEL

A. Measure sag

"Sag" is the amount of fork compression that occurs when the rider sits on the bike without moving.

You'll need a friend to help you. Have your friend measure the distance from the top of the outer leg to the bottom of the fork crown when you are on the bike and when you are off of the bike. The difference between the two measurements is the sag.

The sag can also be measured using the trusty zip-tie method (Fig. 13.13):

1. After removing the fork boot (Section XIII-8 above), tighten a plastic zip tie around one inner leg, and slide it down against the top of the outer leg.

2. Get on your bike.

3. Get off your bike. When you are off your bike, measure the distance from the top of the outer leg to the zip tie (Fig. 13.13).

NOTE

If you want to measure the amount of travel you normally use while riding, go ride with the zip tie on. Hit bumps and check the travel after you stop.

B. Measure maximum possible travel

The fork's full travel can be measured by eliminating the spring from the fork. You can also go by the manufacturer's advertised travel for your fork, though I have often found that figure to be overstated.

1. Remove the springs from both fork legs.

With a coil spring and/or elastomer fork,

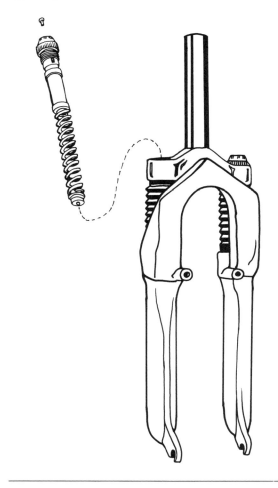

13.14 **removing spring stack from Manitou SX**

remove the top cap (Fig. 13.14) from both sides of the fork crown. Some forks have plastic knurled nuts (Figs. 13.12 and 13.14), while others need to be removed with a wrench (usually 22mm), like the top cap shown in Fig. 13.20. On some forks, loosening the crown bolts makes it easier to unscrew the cap.

With an air-oil fork, release the air from both legs. On older Rock Shox air-oil forks, remove either the Phillips screw (shown in Fig. 13.23) or the plastic snap-on cap covering the air hole, turn the compression damping adjustment to the highest setting, moisten the needle of a ball-pumping adapter, and stick it down into the hole to release the air. On Rock Shox SID forks, just insert the ball needle. On forks with Schrader valves, simply remove the valve cap and push down on the valve pin to let the air out.

2. Measure the distance from the bottom of the crown to the top of the outer leg when the fork is fully extended and when it is fully compressed. The difference between these numbers is the total available travel you have.

When riding with zip-ties on the inner legs, check if you are using up the total travel when you hit big bumps. This helps you determine the proper spring, pre-load, and damping to use. If the fork is adjusted properly for the course you are riding, it will bottom out (i.e. use the full travel) at least once on the course; otherwise, you are not using the fork's full potential.

XIII-11: MINOR MAINTENANCE OF TELESCOPING SUSPENSION FORKS

If you do this procedure frequently and keep the inner legs covered with fork boots, you can greatly increase the life of the seals as well as the time between fork overhauls. Stickiness in suspension forks is usually caused by a dry or dirty dust seal rubbing on a dry or dirty inner leg.

1. With the fork boots off or slid up, wipe off the outside of the seal on top of each outer leg and the length of the inner leg between the outer leg and crown.

2. Use a non-lithium grease (like Englund EDL or "Judy Butter") and put a thin coat of grease on the outside of the seals and inner legs.

3. If each of your fork boots has a foam donut at the bottom, keep the donut cleaned and greased with the same grease. The grease disappears quickly, so do this frequently; it protects the fork seals.

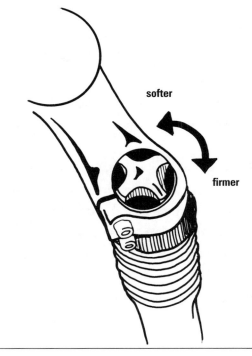

13.15 adjusting spring pre-load

softer

firmer

4. Pull the fork boots back into position. You may need to stretch the bottom of each fork boot with needle-nose pliers to get it in the groove around the top of the outer leg and behind the fork brace.

Coil spring and elastomer forks

Telescoping elastomer and coil spring suspension forks (Figs. 13.12 and 13.14) are beautiful in their simplicity. They have relatively few parts, are easy to tune to a rider's weight and riding style, and are really easy to maintain. They have very few things that can go wrong with them.

XIII-12: TUNING COIL SPRING/ ELASTOMER FORKS

A. Setting spring preload

Spring preload can be adjusted on most mid- to high-end coil spring/elastomer forks. Preload determines the way a spring responds to the forces applied to it. On a coil spring/elastomer fork, you can adjust the preload simply by turning the adjuster knobs on the top of the fork crown (Fig. 13.15). With most forks, you can adjust the preload while riding, as you encounter terrain variations.

Rotating the adjuster knobs clockwise gives a firmer ride by tightening down on (and thus shortening) the spring stack. Rotating the adjuster knobs counterclockwise softens the ride. Make sure the top cap surrounding the knob does not unscrew from the fork crown; you may need to hold it tight with one hand (or a wrench) when you loosen the adjuster knob. Check the top cap occasionally to make sure it is not unscrewed or being forced out due to stripped threads. If its threads seem to be stripped, get a new top cap right away, before you ride any more; if the top cap pops off, the spring can shoot up into your face at high velocity.

Preloading the springs does not limit the full travel for large bumps; it alters the force required to initially move the springs when you encounter smaller bumps. Varying the preload also changes the fork's sag.

B. Replacing elastomers and coil springs

To make major changes in the fork's spring rate, you must change the springs inside of the fork (Fig. 13.14). Manufacturers usually color-code the elastomers and coil springs for stiffness, though you can tell the difference between stiff and soft elastomer bumpers by squeezing them between your fingers (some manufacturers refer to the elastomers as "MCUs" for "Micro-Cellular Units," referring to small air voids trapped inside the elastomers). Extra springs usually come with the fork, or you can buy them from a dealer

The fork needs stiffer springs (or more spring pre-load) if it sags excessively when you sit on it.

Long-travel forks (those with more than 2 1/2-inches of travel) should sag around one-half inch. Short-travel forks should sag no more than a quarter-inch or so. The fork needs softer elastomers (or less compression damping — see the following section) if hard impacts with large bumps do not use the fork's full travel.

1. Unscrew the top caps (counterclockwise). Rock Shox recommends that you first loosen the crown bolts to relieve inward pressure on the fork legs before unscrewing the caps. On many high-end forks, like Manitou Mach 5, SX, SX-Ti and EFC and pre-1997 Rock Shox Judy, this can be done with your fingers. Many other forks use a wrench (22mm on Rock Shox Quadra, Indy and 1997 Judy) to unscrew the top cap.

2. Pull the springs out of the fork (Fig. 13.14). Oftentimes, they will come out attached to the top caps. Manitou SX and SX-Ti elastomers are held lightly inside of the top caps; sometimes they come out with the caps and sometimes not. Elastomer Rock Shox forks produced after mid-1995 hold the elastomers together with plastic spacers called "Judy Jax" with nubs on both faces. On many older forks, the top cap is connected to a rod (the "skewer"-see Fig. 13.12) that runs through each of the elastomer bumpers. If the springs do not come out with the top caps, turn the bike upside down or compress the fork to get them out.

3. Clean any old grease off of the coil springs, elastomers, skewers, Judy Jax and whatever else you found in the fork.

4. Choose the coil springs and/or elastomers that you intend to use. The manufacturers of combination coil spring/elastomer forks vary in approach. Rock Shox intends that you interchange only the coil and offer you only one MCU

choice, while Manitou offers selections of both coil springs and MCUs, often finding that riders can fine tune better for their needs by using the same coil and varying only the elastomers. Marzocchi Bombers interchange only the coil spring, as there are no elastomers inside.

Again, when choosing the springs, don't be afraid to bottom the fork; if you do not bottom it once on the course, you are not getting the full potential out of the fork.

If any of the elastomers are misshapen or look squished or worn in any way, replace them.

5. Apply a new coating of grease to the new parts and everything you just cleaned. Make sure you grease the outside of the coil springs to reduce the noise of the springs rubbing inside the legs.

The Marzocchi Bomber's cartridge swims in oil, which sloshes all around in the spring chamber, so there is no need to grease its coil spring. Make sure you don't let any dirt fall down into the leg.

6. Put the spring stack in the fork legs (Fig. 13.14), and screw the caps down. Be sure to re-tighten the crown bolts, if you loosened them. (Rock Shox recommends 60 inch-pounds).

C. Fine tuning damping

Some high-end elastomer forks have a hydraulic damping cartridge or cylinder (Figs. 13.12 and 13.19) inside one or both lower legs. Most elastomer forks do not have these (if there is no bolt at the bottom of the fork legs, it does not have one). Of those with damping cartridges, not all are adjustable (for example, the cartridges on the earliest Judy XCs were not adjustable). Manitou Mach 5, SX, SX-Ti and EFC and 1996 and later Rock Shox Judy forks (all models) have adjustable damping.

Rebound damping controls the speed at which

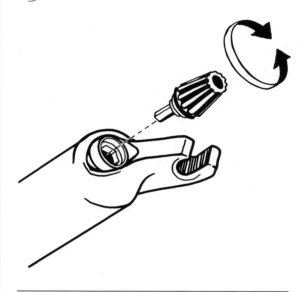

13.16 damping adjuster knob on Manitou

the fork returns to its original position after it has been compressed and released.

Compression damping controls the speed at which the spring compresses during the fork's downstroke.

On a Manitou Mach 5, SX, SX-Ti or EFC, the rebound damping is adjustable via a knob at the bottom of the left leg. The Mach 5/SX/SX-Ti rebound damping adjuster knob is tall and made of black plastic (Fig. 13.16); the EFC knob is flat and aluminum. Turning the knob clockwise increases rebound damping (and slows the return stroke), and counterclockwise decreases rebound damping. It is not recommended to ride with full damping, as it will almost prevent the fork from returning after compression. Compression damping in these Manitou forks can only be changed by varying the shim stack inside the damping unit; see your owner's manual.

On all pre-1997 adjustable Rock Shox Judy models, the compression damping is adjusted by inserting a 2mm hex key through the center of the hollow shaft bolt at the bottom of the

replacing
elastomers
and coil
springs
—
adjusting
damping

13.17 adjusting damping
on Rock Shox Judy fork

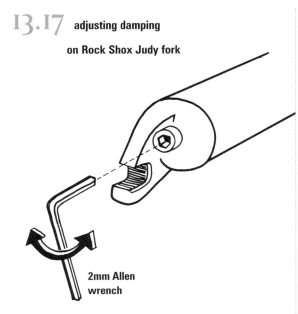

**2mm Allen
wrench**

left leg (the bolt is pictured in Fig. 13.17).
Clockwise rotation increases compression
damping. 1997 models have an optional
knurled aluminum knob inserted inside the
bottom leg bolt, like Manitou (Fig. 13.16); compression damping is adjusted by turning the
knob or, in the absence of the knob, by turning a 3mm Allen key inserted through the bottom bolt.

Only Judy DH and DHO forks (the red ones)
include an additional adjustable cartridge in
the right leg to control rebound damping. It
can also be adjusted with a 2mm hex key on a
DH through the center of the hollow shaft bolt
on the bottom of the right fork leg and on the
DHO with a 3mm Allen key or an optional knob.
Clockwise rotation increases rebound damping
(slows the return stroke). It is very important
that you do not turn this adjuster any more
than two full turns counterclockwise!

1998 Manitou forks will have no springs in
the left leg, only a "twin piston" damper
adjustable for compression damping at the top

and rebound damping at the bottom. All of the
springs will be in the right leg.

Marzocchi Bombers also have damping
adjusters on the bottom of the leg.

XIII-13: OVERHAULING FORK LEGS ON JUDY AND MACH 5/SX/SX-TI

level 3 This section only applies to Rock
Shox Judy and Manitou Mach 5, SX, and
SX-Ti forks. There are many other systems on the market, and each disas-
sembles in a different way. I could not include
all of them, so I opted to include those that are
most likely to be regularly overhauled. I am
assuming that someone with a high-end fork like
the Judy or the Mach 5/SX/SX-Ti will be the most
likely to regularly perform this task.

1. Disconnect the front brake cable (Chapter 7)
and remove the front wheel (Chapter 2, Section II-2).

2. Locate the shaft bolts on the bottoms of the
fork legs (Figs. 13.16 and 13.17). Before you
unscrew them, tighten the spring preload
adjuster on top of the crown (Fig. 13.15) all of the
way down (clockwise). This way, when you undo
the shaft bolts on the bottom of the fork leg, you
won't turn the dampers and the shafts along with
them. That done, unscrew the shaft bolts at the
bottom of both fork legs until there are only a
few threads still engaged.

NOTE

*A 5mm Allen wrench is required to turn these
bolts on a pre-1997 Judy. Both bolts on 1997
Judys require an 8mm hex key; you have to yank
the aluminum adjuster knob out of the left one
to get at it (this is easier said than done, so use a
pair of pliers padded with a rag). On a Mach 5,
SX, or SX-Ti, the right bolt takes a 4mm hex key,
and the large aluminum bolt on the left leg
requires an 8mm hex key. That 8mm hex is locat-*

forks

overhauling
fork legs

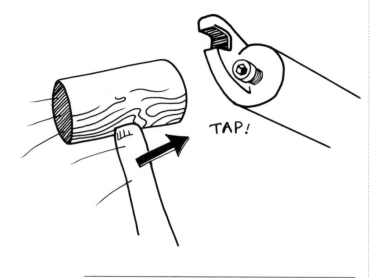

13.18 freeing inner legs from lower bushings

TAP!

**overhauling
fork legs**

ed beneath the plastic damper-adjustment knob, which must be pulled out by hand to get at the bolt (Fig. 13.16); it should come out easily.

WARNING

Do not unscrew the 5mm bolt in the center of the Mach 5's 8mm aluminum bolt. This is the damping adjuster, and if you unscrew it a bunch of turns, you will break it. This will create an oil spill all over your work area, and you will have to buy a new damping unit.

3. Before unscrewing the bolts completely (while they are still threaded in a few turns), tap the bolts with a mallet (Fig. 13.18) until the inner legs are free from the lower bushings. Remove the bolts. Pull the entire assembly that includes both lower legs and the fork brace off of the inner legs.

NOTE

Unless replacing it, there is no need to remove the fork brace; if you do remove it, be very careful not to overtighten the brace bolt or the brake post, as it is not hard to strip the threads in the aluminum or magnesium outer

legs. Do use Loctite on the threads. Late model Rock Shox and Manitou forks have integral fork braces that cannot be removed.

4. With a clean, lint-free rag, clean the inner legs.

NOTE

On the EFC, Mach 5 and later Manitou models, there is an elastomer around the damper shaft that extends from the left inner leg (Fig. 3.19). It is a good idea to clean and grease it, but, if you remove it, be ready to catch the steel ball that will fall out. This is the "detent" ball for the damper that puts the clicks in the damper adjustment!

5. Clean the wiper seals and bushings inside of the outer legs. There are two bushings in each outer leg: one at the top and one more way down at the bottom. You need to reach the bottom one with the rag wrapped around a long rod (Fig. 13.20).

6. Apply a thin layer of non-lithium grease (like "Judy Butter" or Englund "E.D.L." Lube) to the bushings and wipers in the outer legs. To grease the lower bushings, use a long rod (make sure it is clean), slather grease on the end of it, and reach down to the lower bushings with it (Fig. 13.21). With your (clean) hand, smear a thin layer of the same grease on the inner legs (Fig. 13.22).

7. Slide the outer legs gently over the inner legs. Take care not to damage the upper dust seals or the lower bushings. Push the outer legs on completely. It may help if you spread the outer tube and fork brace assembly slightly while you rock it side to side to engage the bushings on the inner legs.

8. Put a medium-strength Loctite on the shaft bolts (anti-seize on titanium ones). Put them back in the bottom of the outer legs, engaging the threads in the damper and neutral shaft. Push in the inner legs further, if the bolt threads

13.19 **1997 Manitou SX exploded**

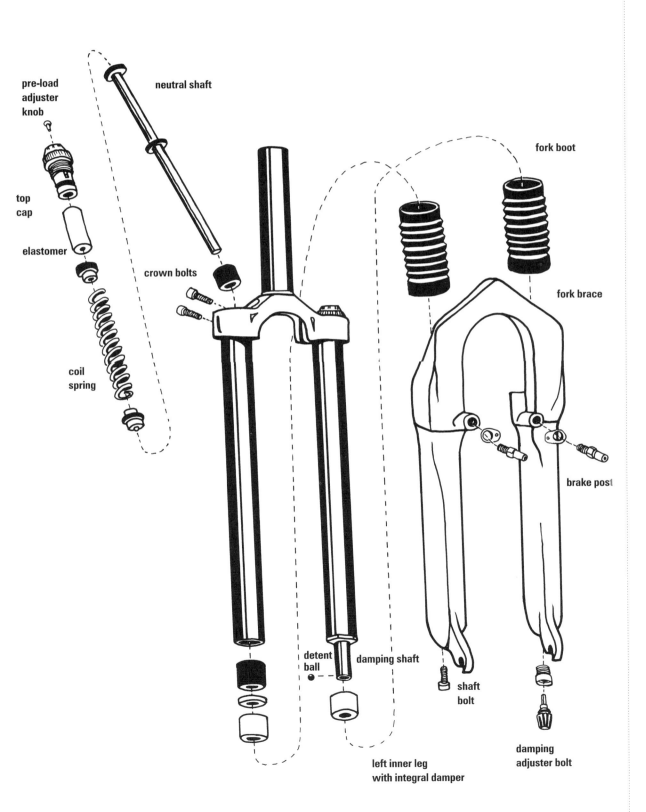

pre-load
adjuster
knob

neutral shaft

top
cap

elastomer

crown bolts

coil
spring

fork boot

fork brace

brake post

detent
ball

damping shaft

shaft
bolt

left inner leg
with integral damper

damping
adjuster bolt

forks

overhauling
fork legs

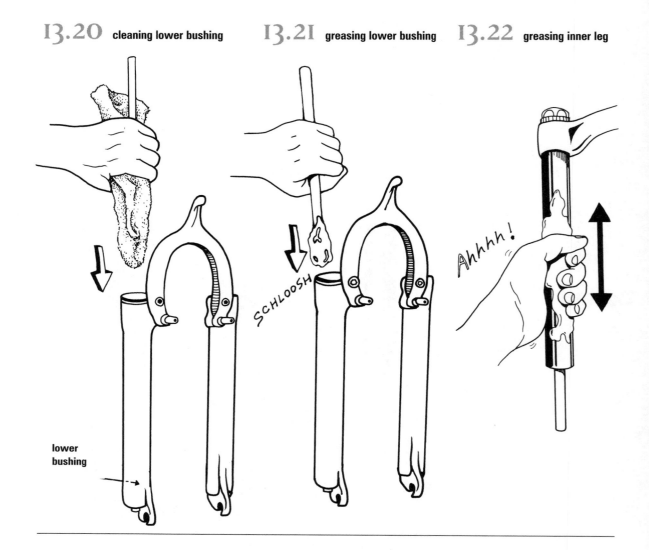

SCHLOOSH

Ahhhh!

lower
bushing

---

do not engage.

9. Tighten the bolts down (Fig. 13.17). Rock Shox recommends 60 in-lbs of torque; Manitou recommends 110 to 130 in-lbs.

XIII-14: CHANGING TRAVEL

The travel on many elastomer and coil spring forks can be changed. To increase travel, you require a longer cartridge, neutral shaft and spring stack (shown in Figs. 13.12 and 13.19), whether purchased from the fork manufacturer or an after-market supplier. Similarly, aftermarket springs and damping cartridges with the same travel

can be substituted for stock parts (for instance, aftermarket coil springs can be interchanged with the stock elastomer stack). Consult the owner's manual for instructions and required parts.

XIII-15: OVERHAUL HYDRAULIC DAMPING UNIT AND REPLACE 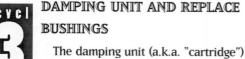 BUSHINGS

The damping unit (a.k.a. "cartridge") is overhaulable and the bushings are replaceable on Rock Shox Judy (Fig. 13.12) and Manitou Mach 5, SX, and SX-Ti (Fig. 13.19) and EFC, and many other brands of forks. Bushing replace-

ment and cartridge overhaul is beyond the scope of this book, mainly because of the special tools required and procedures specific to each fork. The Judy cartridge requires special Rock Shox seal installation tools and is a complex overhaul. Manitou dampers ("cartridge" is a misnomer with Manitou, as the built-in damper is not a separate unit) are overhaulable with standard tools. Consult your owner's manual.

XIII-16: ADJUSTING AIR/OIL FORKS

Because of the complex system of airtight seals and oil orifices, air/oil forks are much more difficult to work on than elastomer forks. Despite the complexity, air springs do offer a distinct weight advantage over other springs. It would, after all, be hard to come up with a spring lighter than one made of air!

1. Adjust air pressure

Compressed air acts as the spring in this type of fork. Greater air pressure means a stiffer fork, and vice versa. It is a good idea to pump your fork every couple of weeks, since all forks lose pressure over time.

Use the pump designed for your fork. Pump it up to the pressure recommended for your weight by your fork manufacturer. You might want to experiment with different pressures to find what you like best.

Do not use a tire pump on the fork; the large stroke volume puts too much air into the fork too quickly. The gauge won't tell you how much air is left in the fork, as you will lose so much of it when removing the pump head. You need either a shock pump for Schrader-valve forks, or the Rock Shox syringe pump (Fig. 1.2) for the ball valves on Rock Shox Mag 10 and up.

Rock Shox Mag 10, 20, 21, 21 SLTi: Rock Shox's

pump looks like a large syringe with a gauge on it (Fig. 1.2). The ball valve on each leg is located beneath either a Phillips screw or a plastic pry-off cap on top of the compression-damping adjusting knob (Fig. 13.23). Tighten down the compression-damping adjustment knob before inserting the pump needle. This will help you avoid pinching the rubber valve on the top of the adjuster rod inside, causing it to leak, a problem especially with some Mag 20 forks. Moisten the needle, and insert it into the valve hole (Fig. 13.23). Pump it up to the desired pressure. Forty pounds is a good starting point for a medium-weight rider.

2. Compression-damping adjustment

There is no damping adjustment on 1998 Rock Shox SID forks (other than interchanging damping cartridges). Compression damping on older air/oil forks can be adjusted by turning the knobs on top of the fork crown (Fig. 13.23). Doing so varies the size of orifices separating the oil-filled chambers. Turning the knob clockwise increases the compression damping, meaning that a larger bump (or pedaling force) is required to start the fork moving.

3. Other adjustments

You can make several other adjustments to some air/oil forks, including piston or oil height, oil viscosity, valve-spring preload, rebound bleed hole size, compression bleed hole size and travel.

On a Rock Shox SID, you can change the air volume by changing the piston height: increase volume by tightening the piston deeper into the fork; decrease it by unscrewing the piston or by pouring some oil in on top of the piston. You get at the piston by releasing the air with a ball needle and unscrewing the top nut with an

air/oil
fork
maintenance
—
adjusting
air/oil
forks

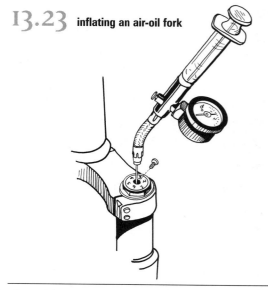

13.23 inflating an air-oil fork

adjustable wrench. Screw the piston in or out with an 8mm hex key. For instance, if you find an air pressure that works well, but you bottom the fork too often, you can decrease the air volume to stiffen the fork sooner with the same air pressure.

The following briefly describes how to determine if you wish to change your settings on any air-oil fork. I do not, however, go into the details of how to perform these adjustments with various forks. You will have to refer to your owner's manual for details.

Generally, heavier riders and heavier use (i.e., downhilling) will benefit from lower piston or oil height (which increases the volume of air), higher oil viscosity (to slow the compression and rebound of the fork), higher valve-spring preload, smaller rebound and compression bleed holes, and longer travel. The reverse is true for smaller riders and lighter use. The factory settings are usually for an average rider and average use.

XIII-17: MAINTAINING AIR/OIL FORKS

Other than the minor maintenance mentioned above in Section XIII-11 for all telescoping forks, maintenance of most air/oil forks involves considerable complexity and differs widely from brand to brand. If you ride your bike a lot, especially in dirty and rough conditions, it is a good idea to change the oil, replace the seals, and check wear on things like valve springs periodically. Consult your owner's manual for the details. If the forks get loose and sloppy, the bushings may need replacing; a shop equipped with the proper tools is required.

XIII-18: OTHER SUSPENSION SYSTEMS AND UPGRADES

There are a number of variations on suspension forks. If you have something other than those described in this chapter, you should consult the owner's manual for service requirements and procedures.

There are also a number of retrofit units designed to improve the performance of the forks covered above. So, you need not feel that you are stuck with a certain low level of performance from your fork. You can significantly upgrade a fork's performance without replacing it. Modern upgrades involve a lot more than just a few lightweight titanium fork bolts. Englund, for example, offers hydraulic damping units that install inside undamped elastomer forks. These improve performance by controlling compression and rebound speed. Englund also offers entire compressed-air units to replace the elastomer spring and the hydraulic damper in a high-end coil- or elastomer-sprung, fluid-damped fork. It is air sprung, and the damping is controlled by air flow through small orifices rather than by oil.

Many of the evolutionary improvements on newer Rock Shox and Manitou models will retrofit into the older models (i.e., you can make a Manitou Mach 5 into a Manitou SX-Ti, etc.).

air/oil fork
maintenance
—
other
suspension
systems and
upgrades

frames

> *"Come to kindly terms with your Ass for it bears you."*
> *— as quoted by JOHN MUIR*
> *in* HOW TO KEEP YOUR VOLKSWAGEN ALIVE

tools

ruler or caliper
string
bike stand
metric wrenches
 and hex keys

OPTIONAL
dropout-alignment
 tools
derailleur hanger-
 alignment tool
metric taps
English-thread
 bottom-bracket
 tap set
thread-cutting oil
drill and drill bits
16mm cone wrench

Your Volkswagen is not a donkey ... and your mountain bike is not a Volkswagen. Still, you'd be well served to follow the sage advice given above and stay on good terms with your bike. In doing so, pay close attention to the frame, because it is the most important part of your bike. It is the one part of your bike that is nearly impossible to fix on the trail, and when it fails, the consequences can be serious. So, get to know your bike. Come to kindly terms with it ... for it bears your ass ... or something like that.

XIV-1: FRAME DESIGN

The traditional "diamond," or "double-diamond," mountain-bike frame design evolved from a combination of postwar cruiser bikes and road racing bikes. The rigid design of a road bike relies on a "front triangle," and a "rear triangle" (Fig. 14.1); never mind that the front triangle is not actually a triangle — or much of a diamond, for that matter. While the basic concept is similar, there are some notable differences between road and mountain bike geometries. Mountain-bike frames feature a higher bottom bracket for more ground clearance; a longer and wider rear triangle for more tire clearance; a shorter seat tube for more standover clearance; brake bosses; and larger-diameter tubing. Another rigid-frame variation is the "elevated chainstay" design, in which the chainstays attach to the seat tube rather than to the bottom-bracket shell. This design enjoyed great popularity for a few years. Its primary benefit is the elimination of "chain suck," the jamming of the chain between the chainring

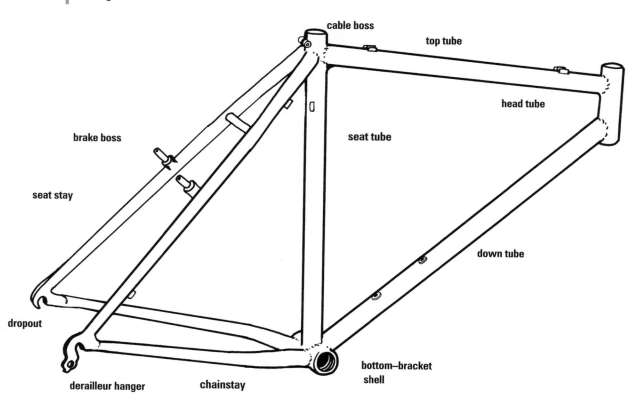

14.1 rigid frame

cable boss

top tube

head tube

seat tube

brake boss

seat stay

down tube

dropout

bottom–bracket
shell

derailleur hanger   chainstay

---

the frame

and the chainstay — and its primary drawback is added weight. When the chainstay-mounted roller-cam- and U-brake went out of fashion, many chain suck problems evaporated, and so did sales of elevated-chainstay rigid frames.

These and other modifications — sloping top tubes, large-diameter head tubes and the use of materials other than steel — are generally aimed at bringing a bike closer to the Holy Grail of bicycle design: low frame weight and price, coupled with high frame stiffness, strength and durability.

As a result of this pursuit, mountain-bike frame design has changed radically in the short time since the inception of the sport. Take a look at a modern mountain bike and compare it to the Marin County Repack-style bikes of the

late '70s or the Crested Butte off-road "cruisers" that popped onto the scene around the same time. The difference is amazing, even if you are just comparing modern design *without* suspension (Fig. I.2) to an early model. Start looking at full-suspension models (Figs. I.3 and 14.2), and you have a whole new breed of animal. As of this writing, most mountain bikes still use a rigid frame, but rear-suspension designs are rapidly working their way into lower and lower price-point bikes.

XIV-2: SUSPENSION FRAME DESIGN

Rear suspension (also called "full suspension," because it is usually combined with a suspension fork) involves a design totally different than the traditional double diamond. Most sus-

14.2 **rear-suspension frame**

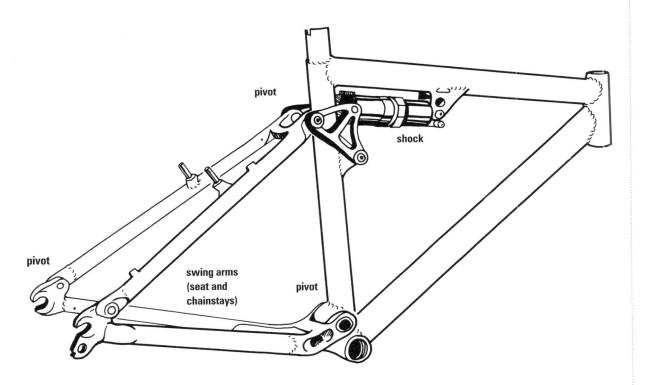

pivot

shock

pivot

swing arms
(seat and
chainstays)

pivot

pension frames have a front triangle and a "rear swingarm" (Fig. 14.2).

There are almost as many rear suspension designs (and names for them) as there are suspension frame designers. Over the past few years, the changes have been fast and furious, and I'd wager that within another few years there will be bring a whole new crop of popular designs with a whole new crop of hi-zoot names. It would be pointless to go on at length about specifics of current designs and their maintenance. This chapter will divide suspension frames into some very broad categories and give only general maintenance guidelines for them.

XIV-3: FRAME MATERIALS

The bicycle-frame-material revolution has

been going on since the birth of the bicycle. Wood was the material of choice for the first bicycles, but that was soon replaced by steel, aluminum, and even bamboo. Steel is still the material most commonly used to build mountain-bike frames, but aluminum, titanium, carbon composites, and metal matrix composites account for an ever-increasing share. Since the materials used in mountain-bike frames come in a variety of grades with varying costs and physical properties, assume that I am talking about the highest grades used in bicycles. For example, the aluminum used in window frames is a lot different than the 7000-series aluminum used in high-end bicycle frames.

Steel has the highest modulus of elasticity (a principal determiner of stiffness) as well as the

suspension
frame
design
—
frame
materials

highest density and tensile strength of any of the metals commonly used in frames. Aluminum has a much lower modulus, density or tensile strength than steel; and titanium has a modulus, density and tensile strength in between the two. With intelligent use of materials, long-lasting frames with comparable stiffness-to-weight and/or strength-to-weight ratios can be built out of any of these metals.

Carbon-fiber and similar composite frame materials consist of fibers embedded in a resin (plastic) matrix. These materials can be very light, very strong and very stiff. Bikes can be built by gluing carbon-fiber tubes into lugs (usually made of carbon fiber or aluminum), or they can be molded in a single piece ("monocoque" construction). The big advantage of composites is that they can be molded to be thicker where extra strength is needed. The real tricky part is holding them together in a frame that does not come apart.

Metal-matrix composite frame materials contain hard materials included into the metal to increase its mechanical properties (usually its tensile strength). These added materials are not alloying materials (i.e. they are not melted together with the metal), since that would usually contaminate the metal. Rather, pieces of sand-like materials (aluminum oxide, silicon oxide, etc.) are worked into the metal without melting them. The trick with these materials is making them weldable without weakening the frame at the joints.

Framebuilders have and will continue to experiment with all sorts of exotic materials that offer their own mechanical advantages. Beryllium, for example, was commonly used in the defense industry. Its light weight and low density coupled with high strength and stiffness made it an ideal material to use on the nose cones of nuclear missiles. Well, they're not making too many of those any more, so a few folks have tried building bikes out of the stuff. It works great, but has the drawback of being poisonous if ingested or inhaled; therefore I strongly recommend against trying to taste or snort a Beryllium frame.

XIV-4: FRAME INSPECTION

You can avoid potentially dangerous, or at least ride-shortening frame failures by inspecting your frame frequently. If you find damage, and you are not sure how dangerous the bike is to ride, take it to a bike shop for advice.

1. Clean your frame every few rides, so that you can spot problems early.

2. Inspect all tubes for cracks, bends, buckles, dents, and paint stretching or cracking, especially near the joints where stress is at its highest. If in doubt, take it to an expert for advice.

3. Inspect the rear dropouts and the welds around the brake bosses and cable hanger for cracks (see Fig. 14.1 for names and locations of frame parts). Check to be sure the dropouts, brake bosses and cable hangers are not bent. Some dropouts and brake bosses bolt on and are replaceable (some cable hangers are even glued in and replaceable). Otherwise, badly bent or broken dropouts, brake bosses and cable hangers need to be replaced; a framebuilder in your area may be able to do it.

4. Look for deeply rusted areas on steel frames. Remove the seatpost every few months and invert the bike to see if water pours out of the seat tube. Look and feel for deep rusted areas inside, or for rust falling out. I recom-

14.3 checking derailleur-hanger alignment

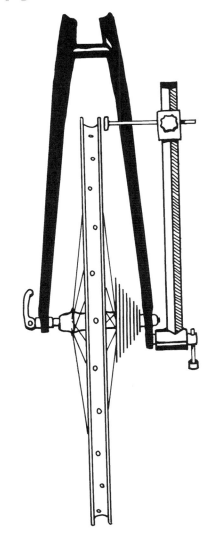

the pivots. Check the shock for leaking oil, cracks, a bent shaft or other damage.

6. Check that a true and properly dished wheel sits straight in the frame, centered between the chainstays and seatstays, and lined up in the same plane as the front triangle. Tightening the hub skewer should not result in chainstay or seatstay, bowing or twisting.

XIV-5: CHECK AND STRAIGHTEN REAR DERAILLEUR HANGER

1. If you have a derailleur-hanger-alignment tool (Fig. 1.5), thread it into the derailleur hanger on the right dropout (Fig. 14.3).

2. Install a true rear wheel without a tire on it.

3. Swing the tool around, measuring the spacing between its arm and the rim all of the way around. The arm of the tool should be the same distance from the rim at all points. Some tools have a set screw extending from the arm that you can adjust to check the spacing; others require you to measure it with a ruler or caliper.

4. If your tool has play in it, keep it pushed inward lightly as you perform all of the measurements, or you will get inconsistent data.

5. If the spacing between the tool arm and the rim is not consistent (within a millimeter or two all of the way around), carefully bend the hanger by pulling outward on the arm of the tool lightly where it is closest to the rim.

6. If the derailleur hanger is really bent, you may not be able to align it without breaking it (you may even have trouble threading the tool in, because the threaded hole will be ovalized). If you have a replaceable bolt-on dropout, replace it.

7. If the threads or the hanger itself are really screwed up, and you do not have a replaceable

frames

frame inspections

mend your squirting a rust-preventive spray for bicycle frames, WD-40 or oil inside your tubes periodically. Remember to grease both the seatpost and inside of the seat tube when you reinsert the seatpost. After sanding off the rust, touch up any external areas where the paint has come off with touch-up paint or nail polish (hey, it's available in lots of cool colors).

5. On suspension frames, disconnect the shock. Move the swingarm up and down, and flex it laterally, feeling for play or binding in

14.4 checking frame alignment with a string

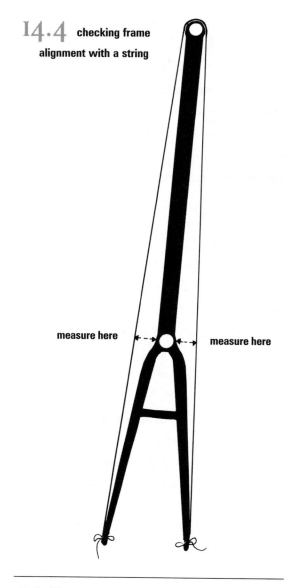

measure here → ← measure here

14.5 measuring dropout width

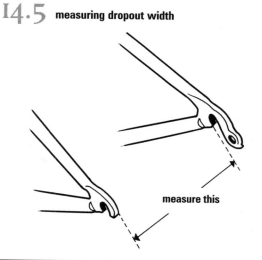

measure this

dropout, see "Fixing damaged threads," Section XIV-8C below for other derailleur hanger options.

XIV-6: CHECK FRAME ALIGNMENT AND ADJUST DROPOUT ALIGNMENT

level 2 These are inexact methods for determining frame alignment. If your alignment is way off, these methods will tell you. If you find alignment problems, other than perhaps moderately bent dropouts or derailleur hanger, do not attempt to correct them. Adjusting frame alignment, if it can be done at all, should only be performed with an accurate frame jig by someone who is practiced at its use.

1. With the frame clamped in a bike stand, tie the end of a string to one rear dropout. Stretch it tightly around the head tube, and tie it symmetrically to the other dropout (Fig. 14.4).

2. Measure from the string to the seat tube on either side (Fig. 14.4). The measurement should be at least within a millimeter of being the same on both sides.

3. Put a true and properly dished rear wheel in the frame and check that it lines up in the same plane as the front triangle. Make certain that the wheel is centered between the seatstays and chainstays (or swingarms). The hub should easily slide into the dropouts without requiring you to pull or push on the frame. Tightening the hub quick release should not result in bowing or twisting of frame members.

4. Remove the wheel and measure the spacing between the dropouts (Fig. 14.5). On most mountain bikes made since 1990, this spacing should be 135mm. Mountain bikes made between 1984 and 1990 or so should have a rear spacing of

14.6 using dropout alignment tools on rear dropouts

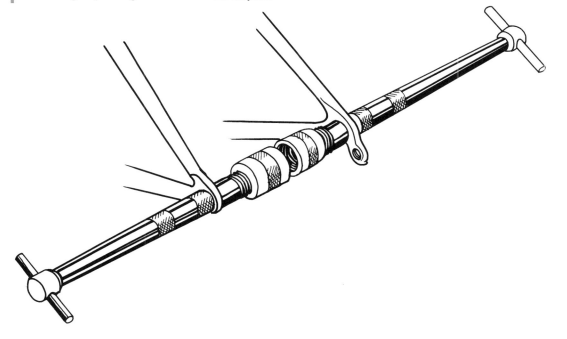

frames

130mm. Mountain bikes made prior to 1984 are likely to have a rear spacing of 125mm. Some high-end mountain bikes (older Manitous, for example) have custom rear hubs with wider spacing (like 150mm) to decrease wheel dish. Measure the width of the rear hub with a caliper to see what the rear-end spacing of the frame should be. No matter what the nominal measurement for your frame should be, if it is 1mm less or 1.5mm more than the nominal, it is acceptable. For instance, if you have a frame whose rear spacing should be 135mm, acceptable spacing is 134mm to 136.5mm.

5. If you have dropout alignment tools, put them in the dropouts so their shafts are fully seated into the dropouts (Fig. 14.6). Arrange the tool's spacers (and the cups, if they are adjustable) so that the faces of the cups are within a millimeter of each other. Tighten the handles on the tools. The tool's cups should line up straight across with each other, with their faces parallel.

If the tools do not line up with each other, one or both dropouts are bent. If you have replaceable bolt-on dropouts, go ahead and replace them. If you have a composite or bonded rear triangle of any kind, there is nothing you can do about it if your bike is not equipped with replaceable dropouts. If you have a steel rear triangle, you can align the dropouts by bending them carefully with the dropout alignment tools. Hold the cup of the tool with one hand and push or pull on the handle with the other. Aluminum or titanium rear dropouts can sometimes be aligned, but it is something you should have a shop do. Titanium is hard to bend since it keeps springing back, and you run a great risk of breaking aluminum by bending.

6. Suspension frames have one other alignment feature not shared with rigid frames. To

dropout
alignment

ensure proper swingarm movement, every separate link in the swingarm puzzle must be in perfect alignment with the next link, so that there are no side forces applied to the pivots. If, for example, the rear shock has to be forced into position between the two pivot points it connects, then there is unnecessary strain on the frame. These stresses will accelerate the rate of wear of the parts and compromise the linkage's ability to move smoothly.

XIV-7: CORRECTING FRAME DAMAGE

Other than alignment items covered above, the only frame problems you can correct are damaged threads, chipped paint, and small dents. Broken braze-ons and bent, broken or deeply dented tubes require a framebuilder to replace them, or a new frame is called for.

XIV-8: FIXING DAMAGED THREADS

level 3 A mountain-bike frame has threads in the bottom bracket shell, the brake bosses, the waterbottle bosses, the rear derailleur hanger. Some bikes have a threaded seat binder, and some also have a small threaded hole in the bottom of the bottom-bracket shell to which a plastic derailleur cable guide is bolted. Bikes equipped with new XTR front derailleurs have a threaded front derailleur mount.

1. If any threads on the frame are stripped or cross-threaded, try chasing through the threads with the appropriate-sized thread tap. Then replace the bolt or bottom bracket cup with a new one.

The following tap sizes are commonly found on most mountain bikes:

Waterbottle bosses and the hole
for a plastic shift cable guide: 5mm x 0.8
Seat binders and brake bosses: 6mm x 1

Derailleur hanger: 10mm x 1
Bottom-bracket shells: 1.37 inches x 24
(Remember, the chain-side bottom-bracket threads are left-hand threaded; the other side is right-hand threaded)

Whenever you re-tap any threads, use oil on the tap (canola vegetable oil with titanium threads). Specific thread-cutting oil is not necessary on old threads since they are already cut.

2. Turn the tap forward (clockwise) a bit, then turn it back, then forward (two steps forward and one back), etc. to prevent the tap from binding and possibly breaking. Be aware that taps are made of very hard, and brittle, steel. If you put any side or twisting forces on small taps, they can easily break off. So, be careful. If it breaks you'll have a real mess, since the broken tap in the hole is harder than the frame, so it's impossible to drill the broken tap out. If you break off a tap in your frame, do not try to get it out yourself. Take it to a bike shop, a machine shop, or a framebuilder before you break off what little is left sticking out. Unless you put the tap in crooked, breaking one should not be a problem when re-tapping damaged frame threads since these threads will be so worn; getting them to find any metal to bite into will probably be your biggest problem.

IMPORTANT NOTE

Tapping a bottom-bracket shell takes a good amount of expertise. You really need expert supervision, if you have never done it before and still want to do it yourself. In addition to making sure that you place the correct tap in the correct end of the shell, you must also be certain that the taps go in straight. Most bottom-bracket taps have a shaft between the two taps to keep them parallel to each other. They

frame
damage
—
thread
damage

must both be started at the same time from both ends.

If you mess it up, you can ruin your frame. So, if in doubt, ask an expert.

If tapping the threads and using a new bolt does not work, here are some specific remedies:

A. Brake bosses

Some brake posts are replaceable. Replaceable posts have wrench flats (usually 8mm) at the base, and they thread into a boss welded to the frame. If yours are not like this, you must take it to a framebuilder to get a new boss welded on.

B. Waterbottle bosses and threaded front derailleur braze-ons

Some bike shops have a tool that rivets bottle bosses into the frame. Check for this first, since you can avoid a new paint job that way although these riveted bosses tend to loosen up over time. Otherwise, take it to a framebuilder to get a new boss welded or brazed in.

C. Rear derailleur hanger threads

Some bikes have replaceable rear dropouts that bolt onto the frame. Another option is to use a "dropout saver" derailleur hanger backing nut (Fig. 14.7) made by Wheels Manufacturing and available at bike shops. The dropout saver is simply a sleeve threaded the same as your dropout *was*, with 16mm wrench flats. You drill out the hole in your damaged derailleur hanger with a 15/32-inch drill bit, push the dropout saver in from the back side, and screw in your derailleur. The dropout saver comes in two lengths, depending on the thickness of the dropout. Another option is to saw off the derailleur hanger with a hacksaw and use a separate derailleur hanger from a really cheap bike that fits flat against the outside of the dropout

and is held in by the hub axle bolts or quick release. The final options are to have the dropout replaced by a framebuilder ... or you could always get a new frame.

D. Seat binders

These can be drilled out and used with a quick release or a bolt and nut. Seat-binder threads rarely get stripped, however; it is usually the bolt that is the problem.

E. Bottom-bracket-shell threads

You can use an old Mavic bottom bracket (Chapter 8, Section VIII-9C, Fig. 8.14), if you can still find one, since it does not depend on the threads in the shell to anchor it. You must have a shop bevel the ends of your bottom-bracket shell with a special Mavic tool, and they will have the tools to install the bottom bracket as well.

F. Bottom-bracket cable-guide threads

A new hole in the bottom of the bottom bracket can be drilled and tapped, or the stripped hole can be tapped out with larger threads for a larger screw. Make sure the screw you use is short enough that it does not protrude into the inside of the bottom-bracket shell.

XIV-9: REPAIR CHIPPED PAINT AND SMALL DENTS

Fixing paint chips is simply a matter of cleaning the area and touching it up. Sand any chipped paint or rust completely away before touching up the spot. Use touch-up paint for your bike, model paint, or fingernail polish.

Small dents can be filled with body putty, but there is little point to filling them if you are only doing a touch up, since the area probably doesn't look that great anyway.

There are plenty of frame painters around the country who can fill dents, repaint frames, and

frames

repairing
paint
and
dents

14.7 inserting dropout saver

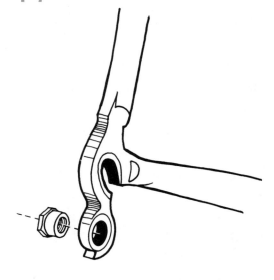

can even match original decals. Many of them advertise in bike magazines.

XIV-10: SUSPENSION FRAME SETUP AND MAINTENANCE

There are so many types of suspension frames, I will simply divide them into two primary categories: those with pivots, and those without.

XIV-11: REAR SUSPENSION TUNING

There are three variables to take into account when setting up the rear suspension system: sag, compression damping and rebound damping.

NOTE

These instructions do not apply to beam bikes, such as Softride.

The four main types of shocks are air/oil (Fig. 14.2), air/air, coil spring (or "coil over"), and elastomer (or "elastomer over"). In both air/oil and air/air shocks, compressed air acts as the spring. Air/oil shocks rely on the flow of oil

through a small opening separating two chambers to dampen the shock movement. Air/air shocks operate on the same basic principle, but rely on the movement of compressed air to damp the shock movement. "Coil over" and "elastomer over" shocks use either a coil spring or an elastomer spring surrounding an oil chamber or gas/oil chamber. The oil provides the damping, and the pressurized gas provides an additional spring. The most commonly used gas is nitrogen, since it is less likely to emulsify with the oil. This type of shock is not to be pumped by the consumer.

Air/oil and air/air shocks are tuned for spring rate by varying the air pressure. You must have a shock pump to pump these or to check the air pressure, since the air volume is so small and the air pressure is so high. Start with the pressure recommended by the bike manufacturer for your weight, and experiment from there. Since the location of the shock and pressure requirements vary from bike to bike, the recommendations will come from the bike manufacturer and not the shock manufacturer.

You can change the spring rate of most "coil over" and "elastomer over" shocks by turning a threaded collar around the shock body.

On rear shocks with hydraulic damping systems, damping is adjusted by varying the size of the orifices through which the oil (or compressed air) flows or by changing the viscosity of the oil. On many models, the damping orifices are adjusted with knobs, but the technique varies from shock to shock, so be sure to read the owner's manual that came with yours.

A. Setting sag

On a rear-suspension bike, "sag" represents the amount of shock compression that takes

tuning
rear
suspension

place when a rider gets on the saddle. As a general rule of thumb, sag should equal about one quarter of the total amount of travel available.

On some shocks, you can put a zip tie around the piston or piston shaft, slide it against the cylinder, and measure how much it moves with the suspension.

To measure the total travel available, deflate or disconnect the shock. Measure the height of the saddle above the ground with the swingarm fully compressed and fully extended. The difference between these two measurements is the total available travel. On some shocks, you can put a zip tie around the piston or piston shaft, slide it against the deflated cylinder, and measure how much it moves with the suspension (or bottom the shock out on a big bump when the spring is installed or inflated).

Adjust the sag by adjusting the air pressure in an air/oil shock and by adjusting the spring preload, and/or by changing the spring on either a "coil over" shock or an elastomer shock. The preload is usually set with both of these systems by turning a threaded collar surrounding the shock body that compresses the coil spring or the elastomers.

B. Compression damping

If adjustable, set the compression damping as light as possible without bottoming out the shock on the biggest bump you hit. Many shocks have a knob with which to adjust damping.

C. Rebound damping

If adjustable, set the rebound damping as light as you can get without causing the bike to "pogo" (bouncing repeatedly after a bump). Many shocks have a knob with which to set the rebound damping.

XIV-12: PIVOTLESS FRAME MAINTENANCE

Suspension frames without moving pivots fall into two categories: beam bikes, and bikes with a shock that depend on the flex of the chainstay, rather than on pivots.

The principal beam suspension used on mountain bikes is the Softride beam, and Softride, Breeze, Otis Guy and Ritchey are some of the frame brands that have used it. Installation and replacement of the beam is covered in Chapter 10. Inspect the beam-mounting points on the frame periodically for fatigue indications (stretched, bulged, or cracking metal or paint). There is not much else to say about Softride beams; they are fairly maintenance-free.

One of the simplest and lightest rear-suspension designs out there relies on a small shock behind the seat tube and flexing chainstays. The design was originally used in Moots frames and later adopted by Ritchey. Beyond checking the chainstays for indications of fatigue (stretched, bulged, or cracking metal or paint) all you really need to do with these is to keep the shock lubricated and tuned to your weight and riding style.

XIV-13: MAINTENANCE OF FRAMES WITH PIVOTS

The complexity of suspension frames varies, hence the ambiguity in the maintenance level. The maintenance to be performed, besides the regular inspections described early in this chapter, is on the shock and the pivots. Some systems, like the "unified rear triangle" — in which the bottom bracket and rear hub are both fixed to the swingarm — have a single pivot and a shock.

tuning rear
suspension

Others utilize numerous pivots.

A. Shock maintenance

Generally, other than shock tuning described above, any maintenance of internal parts and oil changing must be done by a shop with the proper tools.

B. Pivot maintenance

The pivots on any suspension frame require periodic attention. Pivots usually rely on cartridge bearings or bushings (usually steel on brass, but some are made of ceramic or plastic). They are held together by clamps with pinch bolts surrounding the pivot shaft or by bolts, pins, cotters or snaprings.

The shock also pivots on brass bushings on both ends of the shock body.

Pivot bushings must be cleaned and greased after about 40 hours of riding. You should inspect them for signs of wear whenever you perform regular service. With the shock deflated or removed, check for wear by feeling for lateral play and binding. Look at the bushings for scoring and ovalization, and listen for squeaks that indicate a need for lubrication. If the bushings are worn, replace them.

Pivot bearings must be replaced when they wear out. Check them for lateral play and for binding.

maintaining
pivotless
frames

appendices

This index is intended to assist you in finding and fixing problems. If you already know wherein the problem lies, consult the Table of Contents for the chapter covering that part of the bike. If you are not sure which part of the bike is affected, this index can be of assistance. It is organized alphabetically, but, since people's descriptions of the same problem vary, you may need to look through the entire list to find your symptom.

This index can assist you with a diagnosis and can recommend a course of action. Following each recommended action are listed chapter numbers to which you can refer for the repair procedure to fix the problem.

SYMPTOM	LIKELY CAUSES	ACTION	CHAPTER
bent wheel	1. misadjusted spokes	true wheel	6
	2. broken spoke	replace spoke	6
	3. bent rim	replace rim	12
bike pulls to one side	1. wheels not true	true wheels	6
	2. tight headset	adjust headset	11
	3. pitted headset	replace headset	11
	4. bent frame	replace or straighten	14
	5. bent fork	replace or straighten	13
	6. loose hub bearings	adjust hubs	6
	7. tire pressure really low	inflate tires	2, 6
bike shimmies at high speed	1. frame cracked	replace frame	14
	2. frame bent	replace or straighten	14
	3. wheels way out of true	true wheels	6
	4. loose hub bearings	adjust hubs	6
	5. headset too loose	tighten headset	11
	6. flexible frame/heavy rider	replace frame	14
bike vibrates when braking	see chattering and vibration when braking under "strange noises" below		
brake doesn't stop bike	1. misadjusted brake	adjust brake	7
	2. worn brake pads	replace pads	7
	3. greasy rims	clean rims	7
	4. sticky brake cable	lube or replace cable	7
	5. steel rims in wet weather	use aluminum rims	12
	6. brake damaged	replace brake	7
	7. sticky or bent brake lever	lube or replace lever	7
	8. air in hydraulic brake lines	bleed brake lines	7
	9. disc brake pads set wide	adjust disc brake	7

SYMPTOM	LIKELY CAUSES	ACTION	CHAPTER
chain falls off in front	1. misadjusted front derailleur	adjust front derailleur	5
	2. chain line off	adjust chain line	8
	3. chainring bent or loose	replace or tighten	8
chain jams in front between chainring and chainstay-called *chain suck*	1. dirty chain	clean chain	4
	2. bent chainring teeth	replace chainring	8
	3. chain too narrow	replace chain	4
	4. chain line off	adjust chain line	8
	5. stiff links in chain	free links, lube chain	4
chain jams in rear	1. misadjusted rear derailleur	adjust derailleur	5
	2. chain too wide	replace chain	4
	3. small cog not on spline	re-seat cogs	6
	4. poor frame clearance	return to dealer	14
chain skips	1. stretched chain	replace chain	4
	2. misadjusted derailleur	adjust derailleur	5
	3. worn rear cogs	replace cogs and chain	6, 4
	4. dirty or rusted chain	clean or replace chain	4
	5. tight chain link	loosen tight link	4
	6. bent rear derailleur	replace derailleur	5
	7. bent derailleur hanger	straighten hanger	14
	8. loose der. jockey wheels	tighten jockey wheels	5
	9. bent chain link	replace chain	4
	10. sticky rear shift cable	replace shift cable	5
chain slaps chainstay	1. chain too long	shorten chain	4
	2. weak rear derailleur spring	replace spring or derailleur	5
	3. terrain very bumpy	ignore noise	n/a
derailleur hits spokes	1. misadjusted rear derailleur	adjust derailleur	5
	2. broken spoke	replace spoke	6
	3. bent rear derailleur	replace derailleur	5
	4. bent derailleur hanger	straighten or replace	14
knee pain	1. poor shoe cleat position	reposition cleat	9
	2. saddle too low or high	adjust saddle	10
	3. foot rolled in or out	replace shoes or get orthotics	n/a
pain or fatigue when riding, particularly in the back, neck and arms	1. incorrect seat position	adjust seat position	10
	2. too much riding	build up miles gradually	
	3. incorrect stem length	replace stem	11
	4. poor frame fit	replace frame	14

SYMPTOM	LIKELY CAUSES	ACTION	CHAPTER
pedal(s) move laterally, clunk or twist while pedaling	1. loose crank arm	tighten crank bolt	8
	2. pedal loose in crank arm	tighten pedal to crank	9
	3. bent pedal axle	replace pedal or axle	9
	4. loose bottom bracket	adjust bottom bracket	8
	5. bent bottom-bracket axle	replace bottom bracket or axle	8
	6. bent crank arm	replace crank arm	8
	7. loose pedal bearings	adjust pedal bearings	9
pedal entry difficult (with clipless pedals)	1. release tension set high	reduce release tension	9
	2. shoe sole knobs too tall	trim knobs	9
	3. cleat guide loose or gone	tighten or replace	9
pedal release difficult (with clipless pedals)	1. release tension set high	reduce release tension	9
	2. loose cleat on shoe	tighten cleat	9
	3. dry pedal spring pivots	oil spring pivots	9
	4. dirty pedals	clean and lube pedals	9
	5. bent pedal clips	replace pedals or clips	9
	6. dirty cleats	clean, lube cleats	9
pedal release too easy (with clipless pedals)	1. release tension set too low	increase release tension	9
	2. cleats worn out	replace cleats	9
rear shifting working poorly	1. misadjusted derailleur	adjust derailleur	5
	2. sticky or damaged cable	replace cable	5
	3. loose rear cogs	seat and tighten cogs	6
	4. worn rear cogs	replace cogs	6
	5. stretched/damaged chain	replace chain	4
	6. see also *chain jams in rear* and *chain skips* above		
resistance *while coasting or pedaling*	1. tire rubs frame or fork	make axle adjustments or true wheel	2, 6
	2. brake drags on rim	adjust brake	7
	3. tire pressure really low	inflate tire	2, 6
	4. hub bearings too tight	adjust hubs	6
	5. hub bearings dirty/worn	overhaul hubs	6
	6. mud packed around tires	clean bike	2
resistance *while pedaling only*	1. bottom bracket too tight	adjust bottom bracket	8
	2. bottom bracket dirty/worn	overhaul bottom bracket	8
	3. chain dry/dirty/rusted	clean/lube or replace	4
	4. pedal bearings too tight	adjust pedal bearings	9
	5. pedal bearings dirty/worn	overhaul pedals	9
	6. bent chainring rubs frame	straighten or replace	8
	7. chainring rubs frame	adjust chain line	8

STRANGE NOISES

Weird noises can be hard to locate; use this to assist in locating them.

SYMPTOM	LIKELY CAUSES	ACTION	CHAPTER
creaking noise	1. dry handlebar/stem joint	put grease inside stem clamp	11
	2. loose seatpost	tighten seatpost	10
	3. loose shoe cleats	tighten cleats	9
	4. loose crank arm	tighten crank arm bolt	8
	5. cracked frame	replace frame	14
	6. dry, rusty seatpost	grease seatpost	10
	7. see *squeaking* below	see *squeaking* below	
clicking noise	1. cracked shoe cleats	replace cleats	9
	2. cracked shoe sole	replace shoes	9
	3. loose bottom bracket	tighten bottom bracket	8
	4. loose crank arm	tighten crank arm	8
	5. loose pedal	tighten pedal	9
chattering and vibration when braking	1. bent or dented rim	replace rim	12
	2. loose headset	adjust headset	11
	3. brake pads toed out	adjust brake pads	7
	4. wheel way out of round	true wheel	6
	5. greasy sections of rim	clean rim	6
	6. loose brake pivot bolts	tighten brake bolts	7
rubbing or scraping noise *when pedaling*	1. crossed chain	avoid extreme gears	5
	2. front derailleur rubbing	adjust front derailleur	5
	3. chainring rubs frame	longer bottom bracket	8
		or, move bottom bracket over	8
rubbing, squealing or scraping noise *when coasting or pedaling*	1. tire dragging on frame	straighten wheel	2, 6
	2. tire dragging on fork	straighten wheel	2, 6
	3. brake dragging on rim	adjust brake	7
	4. dry hub dust covers	clean and lube	6
squeaking noise	1. dry hub or BB bearings	overhaul hubs or BB	6, 8
	2. dry pedal bushings	overhaul pedals	9
	3. squeaky saddle	replace saddle	10
	4. dry suspension pivots	overhaul suspension	13, 14
	5. rusted or dry chain	lube or replace chain	4
	6. dry suspension fork	overhaul fork	13
	8. dry suspension seatpost	overhaul seatpost	10
squealing noise when braking	1. brake pads toed out	adjust brake pads	7
	2. greasy rims	clean rims and pads	7
	3. loose brake arms	tighten brake arms	7

The gear table on the following page is based on a 26-inch (66cm) tire diameter. Your gear development numbers may be slightly different if the diameter of your rear tire, at inflation, with your weight on it, is not 26 inches. Unless your bike has 24-inch wheels or some other non-standard size, these numbers will be very close.

If you want to have totally accurate gear development numbers for the tire you happen to have on at the time, at a certain inflation pressure, then you can measure the tire diameter very precisely with the procedure below. You can come up with your own gear chart by plugging your tire diameter into the following gear development formula, or by multiplying each number in this chart by the ratio of your tire diameter divided by 26 inches (the tire diameter we used).

MEASURE DIAMETER OF YOUR TIRE

1. Sit on the bike with your tire pumped to your desired pressure.

2. Mark the spot on the rear rim that is at the bottom, and mark the floor adjacent to that spot.

3. Roll forward one wheel revolution, and mark the floor again where the mark on the rim is again at the bottom.

4. Measure the distance between the marks on the floor; this is the tire circumference at pressure with your weight on it.

5. Divide this number by π (*pi*) — 3.14159 — to get the diameter.

NOTE

This roll-out procedure is also the method to measure the wheel size with which to calibrate your bike computer, except you do it on the front wheel with most computers.

rear hub cogs	20	22	24	26	28	30	32	34	36	38	39	40	
11	47	52	57	61	66	71	76	80	85	90	92	95	9
12	43	48	52	56	61	65	69	74	78	82	84	87	8
13	40	44	48	52	56	60	64	68	72	76	78	80	8
14	37	41	45	48	52	56	60	63	67	70	72	74	7
15	35	38	42	45	49	52	55	59	62	66	68	69	
16	33	36	39	42	45	49	52	55	58	61	63	65	6
17	31	34	37	40	43	46	49	52	55	58	60	61	6
18	29	32	35	38	40	43	46	49	52	55	56	58	5
19	27	30	33	36	38	41	44	47	49	52	53	55	5
20	26	29	31	34	36	39	42	44	47	49	51	52	5
21	25	27	30	32	35	37	40	42	45	47	48	50	5
22	24	26	28	31	33	35	38	40	43	45	46	47	4
23	23	25	27	29	32	34	36	38	41	43	44	45	4
24	22	24	26	28	30	32	35	37	39	41	42	43	4
25	21	23	25	27	29	31	33	35	37	39	41	42	4
26	20	22	24	26	28	30	32	34	36	38	39	40	4
27	19	21	23	25	27	29	31	33	35	37	38	39	3
28	18	20	22	24	26	28	30	32	33	35	36	37	3
30	17	19	21	23	24	26	28	29	31	33	34	35	3
32	16	18	20	21	23	24	26	28	29	31	32	33	3
34	15	17	18	20	21	23	24	26	28	29	30	31	3
38	14	16	16	18	19	21	22	23	25	26	27	27	2
	20	22	24	26	28	30	32	34	36	38	39	40	4

THE FORMULA IS:

Gear development = (number of teeth on chainring) x (wheel diameter) ÷ (number of teeth on rear cog)

To find out how far you get with each pedal stroke in a given gear,

multiply the gear development by 3.14159265 (π).

chainring gear teeth

42	43	44	45	46	47	48	49	50	51	52	53	
	102	104	106	109	111	113	116	118	121	123	125	11
	93	95	97	100	102	104	106	108	111	113	115	12
	86	88	90	92	94	96	98	100	102	104	106	13
	80	82	84	85	87	89	91	93	95	97	98	14
	75	76	78	80	81	83	85	87	88	90	92	15
	70	72	73	75	76	78	80	81	83	85	86	16
	66	67	69	70	72	73	75	76	78	80	81	17
	62	64	65	66	68	69	71	72	74	75	77	18
	59	60	62	63	64	66	67	68	70	71	73	19
	56	57	59	60	61	62	64	65	66	68	69	20
	53	54	56	57	58	59	61	62	63	64	66	21
	51	52	53	54	56	57	58	59	60	61	63	22
	49	50	51	52	53	54	55	57	58	59	60	23
	47	48	49	50	51	52	53	54	55	56	57	24
	45	46	47	48	49	50	51	52	53	54	55	25
	43	44	45	46	47	48	49	50	51	52	53	26
	41	42	43	44	45	46	47	48	49	50	51	27
	40	41	42	43	44	45	46	46	47	48	49	28
	37	38	39	40	41	42	42	43	44	45	46	30
	35	35	37	37	38	39	40	41	41	42	43	32
	33	33	34	35	36	37	37	38	39	40	41	34
	29	30	31	31	32	32	33	34	35	36	36	38
	43	44	45	46	47	48	49	50	51	52	53	

chainring gear teeth

gear development

MOUNTAIN BIKE FITTING

If you are getting a new bike, you might as well get one that fits you properly. Fit should be the primary consideration when selecting a bike; you can adapt to heavier bikes and bikes not painted your favorite color, but your body will soon protest on one that doesn't fit. The simple need to protect your more sensitive parts should keep you away from a bike without sufficient standover clearance (Fig. C.1), but there are a lot of other factors to consider as well. You need to make certain that your bike has enough reach to ensure that you don't bang your knees on the handle bar; you also need to check that your weight is properly distributed over the wheels so that you don't end up going over the handlebars on downhills or unweighting the front end on steep climbs. An improperly-sized bike will cause you to ride with less efficiency and more discomfort. So, take some time and find out how you can pick the properly-sized bike.

I've outlined two methods for finding your frame size. The first is a simple method of checking your fit to fully assembled bikes at your local bike shop. The second is a bit more elaborate, since it involves taking body measurements. This more detailed approach will allow you to calculate the proper frame dimensions whether the bike is assembled or not.

C.1

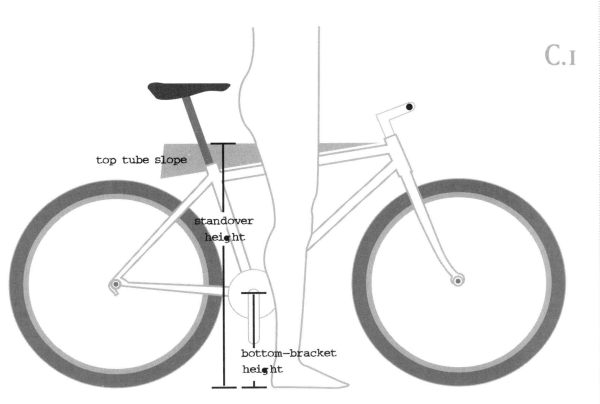

top tube slope

standover height

bottom-bracket height

C-11: SELECTING THE SIZE OF A BUILT-UP BIKE

1. Standover height

Stand over the bike's top tube and lift the bike straight up until the top tube hits your crotch. The wheels should be at least 2 inches off of the ground to ensure that you can jump off of the bike safely without hitting your crotch. There is no maximum dimension here. If you have 5 inches of standover height or more, that is fine, as long as the top tube is long enough for you, and the handlebar height can be set properly for you.

NOTE

If you have 2 inches of standover clearance over one bike, do not assume that another bike with the same listed frame size will also offer you the same standover clearance. Manufacturers measure frame size using a variety of methods. They also slope their top tubes differently and use different bottom bracket heights (Figs. C.1 & C.2), all of which affect the final standover height.

All manufacturers measure the frame size up the seat tube from the center of the bottom bracket, but the top of the measurement varies. Some manufacturers measure to the center of the top tube ("center-to-center" measurement), some measure to the top of the top tube ("center-to-top"), and others measure to the top of the seat tube (also called "center-to-top"), even though there is wide variation in the length of the seat post collar above the top tube. Obviously, each of these methods will give you a different "frame size" for the same frame.

No matter how the frame size is measured,

the standover height of a bike depends on the slope of the top tube (Figs. C.1 & C.2). Top tubes that slant up to the front are common, so standover clearance is obviously a function of where you are standing. With an up-angled top tube, stand over it a few inches forward of the nose of the saddle, and then lift the bike up into your crotch to measure standover clearance.

A bike with a suspension fork will have a higher front end than a bike with a rigid fork would, since the suspension fork has to allow for travel. This makes it difficult even to compare listed frame sizes from the same manufacturer to determine standover height.

Standover height is also a function of bottom bracket height above the ground. There is substantial variation here, especially with bikes with rear suspension whose bottom brackets are often very high so that ground clearance is still sufficient when the suspension is fully compressed.

Unless the manufacturer lists the standover height in their brochure and you know your inseam length, you need to actually stand over the bike.

ANOTHER NOTE

If you are short and cannot find a frame size small enough for you to get at least 2 inches of standover clearance, consider a bike with 24-inch wheels instead of 26-inch.

2. Knee to handlebar clearance

With one foot on the ground and one foot on the pedal, make sure your knee cannot hit the handlebar (Fig. C.2). Do this standing out of the saddle as well as seated and with the front wheel turned slightly, to make sure that the knee will not hit when you are in

C.2

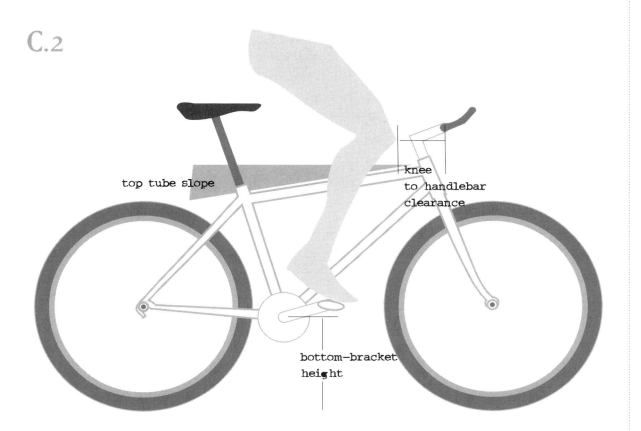

top tube slope

knee
to handlebar
clearance

bottom–bracket
height

the most awkward pedaling position you might use.

3. Handlebar reach and drop

Ride the bike. See if the reach feels comfortable to you when grabbing the bars or the bar ends. Make sure it is easy to grab the brake levers. Make sure your knees do not hit your elbows as you pedal. Make sure that the stem can be raised or lowered enough to achieve a comfortable handlebar height for you.

N O T E

Threadless headsets allow very limited adjustment of stem height. Large changes in height require a change in stems.

4. "Pedal overlap"

"Pedal overlap" is a misnomer, since you are actually interested in whether the toe, not the pedal, can hit the front tire when turning sharply at low speeds. Sitting on the bike with the crankarms horizontal and the foot on the pedal, turn the handlebars and check that your toe does not hit the front tire. Toe overlap is to be avoided for any kind of slow-speed, technical riding, since pedaling up rocky terrain slowly can often result in the front wheel turning sharply back and forth as the feet pass by. Toe overlap it is not an issue for most riding, since the speeds are high enough on the road that turning the bike does not require turning the front wheel at enough of an angle to hit the foot.

C-2: CHOOSING A FRAME SIZE FROM YOUR BODY MEASUREMENTS

You will need a second person to assist you.

By taking three easy measurements, most people can get a very good frame fit. When designing a custom frame, I go through a more complex procedure than this, involving more measurements. For picking an off-the-shelf bike, this method works well.

1. Measure your inseam

Spread your stocking feet about 2 inches apart, and measure up from the floor to a broomstick held level and lifted firmly up into your crotch. You can also use a large book and slide it up a wall to keep the top edge horizontal — as you pull it up as hard as you can — into your crotch. You can mark the top of the book on the wall and measure up from the floor to the mark.

2. Measure your inseam-plus-torso length

Hold a pencil horizontally in your sternal notch, the U-shaped bone depression just below your Adam's Apple. Standing up straight in front of a wall, mark the wall with the horizontal pencil. Measure up from the floor to the mark.

3. Measure your arm length

Hold your arm out from your side at a 45 degree angle with your elbow straight. Measure from the sharp bone point directly behind your shoulder joint to the wrist bone on your little finger side.

4. Find your frame seat tube length

Subtract 34 to 42cm (13.5 inches-16.5 inches) from your inseam length. This length is your frame size measured from the center of the bottom bracket to the top of a horizontal top tube. If the frame you are interested in has a sloping top tube, you need a bike with an even shorter seat tube length. With a sloping top tube bike, project a horizontal line back to the seat tube (or seat post) from the top of the top tube at the center of its length (Fig. C.3). Mark the seat tube or seat post at this line. Measure from the center of the bottom bracket to this mark; this length should be 34-42cm less than your inseam measurement.

Also, if the bike has a bottom bracket higher than 29cm (11-1/2 inches), subtract the additional bottom-bracket height from the seat tube length as well.

Generally, smaller riders will want to subtract close to 34cm from their inseam, while taller riders will subtract closer to 40cm. There is considerable range here. The top tube length is more important in a frame than any specific "frame size", and, if you have short torso and arms, you can use a small frame to get the right top tube length, as long as you can raise your bars as high as you need them.

You really want to make sure you have plenty of standover clearance, so do not subtract less than 34cm from your inseam for your seat-tube length; this should insure at least 2 inches (5cm) of standover clearance. If you are short and cannot find a bike small enough for you to get at least 2 inches of standover clearance, consider one with 24 inches wheels instead of 26 inches.

NOTE

A step-through frame (i.e., "women's" frame, "mixte frame", or "girl's bike") having a steeply up-angled top tube meeting near the bottom bracket shell makes seat tube length for standover clearance nearly irrelevant. With a step-through bike, the only considerations will be horizontal and

C.3

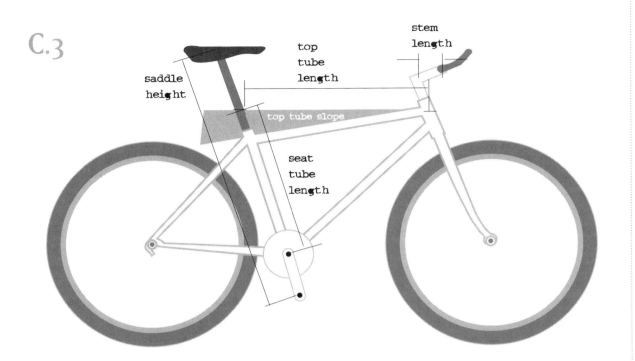

saddle height

top tube length

stem length

top tube slope

seat tube length

bike fit

vertical reach to the bars.

5. Find your top tube length

To find your torso length, subtract your inseam measurement (found in Step 1) from your inseam-plus-torso measurement (found in Step 2). Add this torso length to your arm length measurement (found in Step 3). To find the top tube length, multiply this arm-plus-torso measurement by a factor in the range between 0.47 and 0.5. If you are a casual rider, use 0.47; if you are a very aggressive rider, use 0.5, and, if you are in between, use a factor in between. This top-tube length is measured horizontally from the center of the seat tube to the center of the head tube (Fig. C.3). Obviously, the actual, horizontal top-tube length is less than the length found by measuring along the top tube on a sloping-top-tube bike.

6. Find your stem length

Multiply the arm-plus-torso length you

found in step 5 by 0.10 up to 0.14 to find the stem length. Again, a casual rider will multiply by 0.10 or so, while an aggressive rider will multiply by closer to 0.14. This is a starting stem length. Finalize the stem length once you are sitting on the bike and see what feels best.

C-3: POSITIONING OF YOUR SADDLE AND HANDLEBARS

The frame fit is only part of the equation. Except for the standover clearance, a good frame fit is relatively meaningless if the seat setback, seat height, handlebar height, and handlebar reach are not set correctly for you.

1. Saddle height

When your foot is at the bottom of the stroke, lock your knee without rocking your hips. Do this sitting on your bike on a trainer with someone else observing. Your foot should be level, or the heel should be

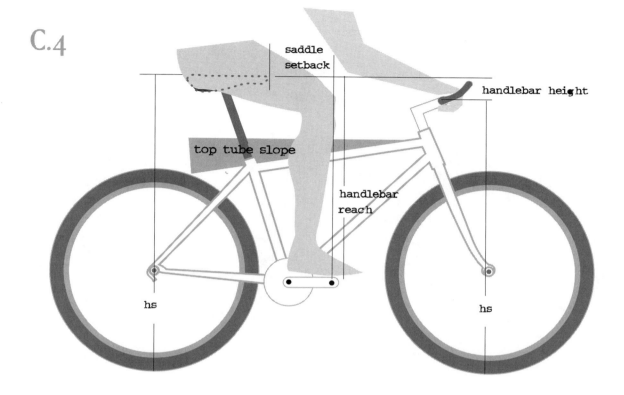

slightly higher than the ball of the foot. Another way to determine seat height is to take your inseam measurement (found in step 1 under "Choosing frame size from your body measurements", above) and multiply it by 1.09; this is the length from the center of the pedal spindle (when the pedal is down) to one of the points on the top of the saddle where your butt bones (ischial tuberosities) contact it (Fig. C.3). Adjust the seat height (Chapter 10) until you get it the proper height.

NOTE

These two methods yield similar results, although the measurement-multiplying method is dependent on shoe sole and pedal thicknesses. They yield a biomechanically efficient pedaling position, but if you do a lot of technical riding and descending, you may wish to have a lower saddle for better

bike-handling control.

2. Saddle setback

Sit on your bike on a stationary trainer with your cranks horizontal and your foot at the angle it is at that point when pedaling. Have a friend drop a plumb line from the front of your knee below your knee cap. You can use a heavy ring, washer, etc. tied to a string for the plumb line. The plumb line should bisect the pedal axle or pass up to two centimeters behind it (Fig. C.4); you will need to lean the knee out to get the string to hang clear. A saddle centered in this manner encourages smooth pedaling at high RPMs, while two centimeters behind the pedal spindle encourages powerful seated climbing.

Slide the saddle back and forth on the seatpost (Chapter 10), until you achieve the desired fore-aft saddle position. Set the

saddle level or very close to it. Re-check the seat height in Step 1 above, since fore-aft saddle movements affect seat-to-pedal distance as well.

3. Handlebar height

Measure the handlebar height relative to the saddle height by measuring the vertical distance of the saddle and bar up from the floor (Fig. C.4). How much higher the saddle is than your bar (or vice versa) depends on your flexibility, riding style, overall size, and type of riding you prefer.

Aggressive and/or tall cross-country riders will prefer to have their saddle 10 cm or more higher than the bars. Shorter riders will want proportionately less drop, as will less aggressive riders. Riders doing lots of downhills will want their bars higher; downhill racers often have 2-4 cm of drop from saddle to bar, and mountain bike slalom riders' bars are usually higher than their saddles. Generally, people beginning mountain bike riding will like their bars high and can lower them as they become more comfortable with the bike, with going fast, and with riding more technical terrain.

If in doubt, start with 4 cm of drop and vary it from there. The higher the bar, the greater the tendency is for the front wheel to pull up off of the ground when climbing, and the more wind resistance you can expect. Change the bar height by raising or lowering the stem (Chapter 11), or by switching stems and/or bars.

Again, threadless headsets allow only limited stem-height adjustment without substitution of a differently-angled stem.

4. Setting handlebar reach

The reach from the saddle to the handlebar is also very dependent on personal preference. More aggressive riders will want a more stretched out position than will casual riders. This length is subjective, and I find that I need to look at the rider on the bike and get a feel for how they would be comfortable and efficient.

A useful starting place is to drop a plumb line from the back of your elbow with your arms bent in a comfortable riding position. This plane determined by your elbows and the plumb line should be 2-4 cm horizontally ahead of each knee at the point in the pedal stroke when the crank arm is horizontal forward (Fig. C.4). The idea is to select a position you find comfortable and efficient; listen to what your body wants.

Vary the saddle-bar distance by changing stem length (Chapter 11), not by changing the seat fore-aft position, which is based on pedaling efficiency (Step 2 above) and not on reach.

N O T E

There is no single formula for determining handlebar reach and height. I can tell you that using the all-too-common method of placing your elbow against the saddle and seeing if your fingertips reach the handlebar is close to useless. Similarly, the oft-suggested method of seeing if the handlebar obscures your vision of the front hub is not worth the brief time it takes to look, being dependent on elbow bend and front end geometry. Another method involving dropping a plumb bob from the rider's nose

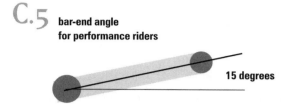

C.5 bar-end angle
for performance riders

15 degrees

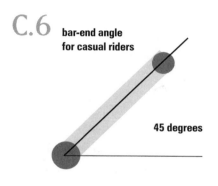

C.6 bar-end angle
for casual riders

45 degrees

while seated. Leave the bar end mounting bolts a bit loose, sit on the bike, and grab the bar ends comfortably. Tighten them down in that position.

Do not use the bar ends to raise your hand position by pointing them vertically up. If you want a higher hand position, get a taller or more up-angled stem, and/or a higher-rise handlebar. Bar ends are not meant to be stood straight up and held on to for cruising along sitting up high; that is the mountain bike equivalent of flipping a road drop bar upside down to lift the hands. As with the road bar equivalent, you cannot reach the brakes when you need them.

is dependent on the handlebar height and elbow bend and thus does not lend itself to a proscribed relationship for all riders.

5. Bar end position

Performance riders should position the bar ends in the range between horizontal and pointed up 15 degrees (Fig. C.5). Bar-end angles in this range allow powerful pulling on the bar ends when climbing out of the saddle, since the bar ends are perpendicular to the forearms when standing. This bar-end angle also makes for a lower, more extended position when seated and grabbing the hooks of the bar ends. Find the bar-end position you find comfortable for pulling on when climbing standing or seated, and for when pedaling seated for long stretches on paved roads.

Casual riders often prefer a higher angle to pull with a straight wrist and closed fist

adjustable cup: The non-drive side cup in the bottom bracket. This cup is removed for maintenance of the bottom-bracket spindle and bearings, and it adjusts the bearings. Term sometimes applied to top headset cup as well.

AheadSet: a style of headset that allows the use of a fork with a threadless steering tube.

Allen key (Allen wrench, hex key): a hexagonal wrench that fits inside the head of the bolt.

all-terrain bike (ATB): another term for mountain bike.

anchor bolt ("cable anchor", "cable-fixing bolt"): a bolt securing a cable to a component.

axle: the shaft about which a part turns, usually on bearings or bushings.

axle overlock dimension: the length of a hub axle from dropout to dropout, referring to the distance from locknut face to locknut face.

barrel adjuster: a threaded cable stop that allows for fine adjustment of cable tension. Barrel adjusters are commonly found on rear derailleurs, shifters and brake levers.

BB: (see "bottom bracket".)

binder bolt: a bolt clamping a seatpost in a frame, a bar end to a handlebar, a handlebar inside a stem, or a threadless steering tube inside a stem clamp.

bottom bracket (BB): the assembly that allows the crank to rotate. Generally the bottom bracket assembly includes bearings, an axle, a fixed cup, adjustable cup, and a lockring.

bottom-bracket shell: the cylindrical housing at the bottom of a bicycle frame through which the bottom-bracket axle passes.

brake boss (brake post or pivot; cantilever boss, post, or pivot): a fork- or frame-mounted pivot for a brake arm.

brake pad (brake block): a block of rubber or similar material used to slow the bike by creating friction on the rim or other braking surface.

brake post: (see "brake boss".)

brake shoe: the metal pad holder that holds the brake pad to the brake arm.

braze-on: a generic term for most metal frame attachments, even those welded or glued on.

brazing: a method commonly used to construct steel bicycle frames. Brazing involves the use of brass or silver solder to connect frame tubes and attach various "braze-on" items including brake bosses, cable guides and rack mounts to the frame.

bushing: a metal or plastic sleeve that acts as a simple bearing on pedals, suspension forks, suspension swing arms, and jockey wheels.

butted tubing: a common type of frame tubing with varying wall thicknesses. Butted tubing is designed to accommodate high stress points at the ends of the tube by being thicker there.

cable (inner wire): wound or braided wire strands used to operate brakes and derailleurs.

cable anchor: (see "anchor bolt".)

cable end: a cap on the end of a cable to keep it from fraying.

cable-fixing bolt: (see "anchor bolt".)

cable hanger: cable stop on a fork- or seatstay-arch used to stop the brake cable

housing for a cantilever or U-brake.

cable housing: a metal-reinforced exterior sheath through which a cable passes.

cable housing stop: (see "cable stop".)

cable-fixing bolt: an anchor bolt that attaches cables to brakes or derailleurs.

cable stop: a fitting on the frame, fork, or stem at which a cable housing segment terminates.

cage: two guiding plates through which the chain travels. Both the front and rear derailleurs have cages. The cage on the rear also holds the jockey pulleys.

cantilever boss: (see "brake boss".)

cantilever brake: a brake that relies on tension in a straddle cable to move two opposing arms, pivoting on frame- or fork-mounted posts, toward the braking surface of the rim. Cantilevers are probably the most common brake found on mountain bikes.

cantilever pivot: (see "brake boss".)

cantilever post: (see "brake boss".)

cartridge bearing: ball bearings encased in a cartridge consisting of steel inner and outer rings, ball retainers, and, sometimes, bearing covers.

cassette hub: a rear hub that has a built-in freewheel mechanism.

chain: a series of metal links held together by

pins and used to transmit energy from the crank to the rear wheel.

chain line: the imaginary line connecting the center of the middle chainring with the middle of the cogset. This line should in theory be straight and parallel with the vertical plane passing through the center of the bicycle. This is measured as the distance from the center of the seat tube to the center of the middle chainring (an easy way to measure this is to measure from the left side of the seat tube to the outside of the large chainring, measure the distance from the right side of the seat tube to the inside of the inner chainring, add these two measurements, and divide the sum by two).

chain link: a single unit of bicycle chain consisting of four plates with a roller on each end and in the center.

chainring: a multiple tooth sprocket attached to the right crankarm.

chainstays: the tubes leading from the bottom bracket shell to the rear hub axle.

chain suck: the dragging of the chain by the chainring past the release point at the bottom of the chainring. The chain can be dragged upward and until it is jammed between the chainring and the chainstay.

chainring-nut spanner: a tool used to secure the chainring nuts while tightening the chainring bolts.

chain whip (chain wrench): a flat piece of steel, usually attached to two lengths of chain. This tool is used to remove the rear cogs on a freehub.

chase, wild goose: (see "goose".)

circlip (snapring, Jesus clip): a c-shaped snapring that fits in a groove to hold parts together.

clip-in pedal (clipless pedal): a pedal that relies on spring-loaded clips to grip the rider's shoe, without the use of toe clips and straps.

clipless pedal: (see "clip-in pedal".)

cog: the sprockets located on the drive side of the rear hub.

compression damping: the deadening or diminishing of the speed of the compression of a spring on impact.

cone: a threaded conical nut that serves to hold a set of bearings in place and also provides a smooth surface upon which those bearings can roll.

crankarm: the lever attached at the bottom-bracket spindle used to transmit a rider's energy to the chain.

crankarm-fixing bolt: the bolt attaching the crank to the bottom-bracket spindle on a cotterless drive train.

crankset: the assembly that includes a

bottom bracket, two crankarms, chainring set and accompanying nuts and bolts.

cross three: a pattern used by wheel builders, that calls for each spoke to cross three others in its path from the hub to the rim.

cup: a cup-shaped bearing surface that surrounds the bearings in a bottom bracket, headset or hub.

damper: a mechanism in a suspension fork or shock that provides damping of the spring's oscillation.

damping: the deadening and diminishing of the oscillation of a spring, as in a suspension fork or shock.

derailleur: a gear-changing device that allows a rider to move the chain from one cog or chainring to another while the bicycle is in motion.

derailleur hanger: a metal extension of the right rear dropout through which the rear derailleur is mounted to the frame.

diamond frame: the traditional bicycle frame shape.

dish: a difference in spoke tension on the two sides of the rear wheel so that the wheel is centered.

disc brake: a brake that stops the bike by squeezing brake pads against a circular disc attached to the wheel.

double: a two-chainring drivetrain setup

(as opposed to a three-chainring, or "triple", one).

down tube: the tube that connects the head tube and bottom-bracket shell together.

drivetrain: the crankarms, chainrings, bottom bracket, front derailleur, chain, rear derailleur and freewheel (or cassette).

drop: the perpendicular distance between a horizontal line passing through the wheel hub centers and the center of the bottom bracket.

dropouts: the slots in the forks and rear triangle where the wheel axles attach.

dust cap: a protective cap keeping dirt away from a part.

elastomer: a urethane spring used in suspension forks and swing arms.

ferrule: a cap for the end of cable housing.

fixed cup: the non-adjustable cup of the bottom bracket located on the drive side of the bottom bracket.

flange: the largest diameter of the hub where the spoke heads are anchored.

fork: the part that attaches the front wheel to the frame.

fork crown: the cross piece connecting the fork legs to the steering tube.

fork ends: (see "dropouts".)

fork rake (rake): the perpendicular

offset distance of the front axle from an imaginary extension of the steering tube centerline (steering axis).

fork tips (fork ends): (see "dropouts".)

frame: the central structure of a bicycle to which all of the parts are attached.

freewheel: a removable cluster of cogs that allows a rider to stop pedaling as the bicycle is moving forward.

friction shifter: a traditional (non-indexed) shifter attached to the frame or handle bars. Cable tension is maintained by a combination of friction washers and bolts.

front triangle (main triangle): the head tube, top tube, down tube and seat tube of a bike frame.

"girl's" bike: (see "step-through frame".)

goose chase, wild: (see "wild".)

Grip Shift: a shifter that is integrated with the handlebar grip of a mountain bike. The rider shifts gears by twisting the grip. (see also "twist shifter".)

hex key: (see "Allen key".)

headset: the cup, lock ring, and bearings that hold the fork to the frame and allow the fork to turn in the frame.

head tube: the front tube of the frame through which the steering tube of the fork passes. The head tube is attached to the top tube and down tube and locates the headset.

hub: the central part of a wheel to which the spokes are anchored and through which the wheel axle passes.

hub brake: a disc, drum or coaster brake that stops the wheel with friction applied to a braking surface attached to the hub.

hydraulic brake: a type of brake that uses oil pressure to move the brake pads against the braking surface.

index shifter: a shifter that clicks into fixed positions as it moves the derailleur from gear to gear.

inner wire: see "cable".

Jesus clip: (see "circlip.")

jockey wheel or jockey pulley: a circular cog-shaped-pulley attached to the rear derailleur used to guide, apply tension to and laterally move the chain from rear cog to rear cog.

knobby tire: an all-terrain tire used on mountain bikes.

link: (1) a pivoting steel hook on a V-brake arm that the cable-guide "noodle" hooks into. (2) (see "chain link".)

locknut: a nut that serves to hold the bearing adjustment in a headset, hub or pedal.

lockring: the outer ring that tightens the adjustable cup of a bottom bracket against the face of the bottom-bracket shell.

lock washer: a notched or toothed washer

that serves to hold surrounding nuts and washers in position.

master link: a detachable link that holds the chain together. The master link can be opened by hand without a chain tool.

mixte frame: (see "step-through frame".)

mounting bolt: a bolt that mounts a part to a frame, fork, or component. (see also "pivot bolt.")

needle bearing: steel cylindrical cartridge with rod-shaped rollers arranged coaxially around the inside walls

noodle: curved cable-guide pipe on a V-brake arm which stops the cable housing and directs the cable to the cable anchor bolt on the opposite arm.

nipple: a small nut specially designed to receive the end of a spoke and fit the holes of a rim.

outer wire: (see "cable housing".)

outer wire stop: (see "cable stop".)

pin spanner: a V-shaped wrench with two tip-end pins that is used for tightening the adjustable cup of the bottom bracket.

pivot bolt: a fixing bolt that fastens the brake arm to the frame or fork.

preload: (see spring preload)

Presta valve: thin, metal tire valve that uses a locking nut to stop air flow from the tire.

quick release: (1) the tightening lever and shaft used to attach a wheel to the fork or rear dropouts without using axle nuts. (2) a quick-opening lever and shaft pinching the seatpost inside the seat tube, in lieu of a wrench-operated bolt. (3) a quick cable release on a brake. (4) a fixing mechanism that can be quickly opened and closed, as on a brake cable or wheel axle.

quill: the vertical tube of a stem that inserts into the fork steering tube. It has an expander wedge and bolt inside to secure the stem to the steering tube.

race: a ring-shaped surface on which the bearings roll freely.

Rapidfire shifter: an indexing shifter manufactured by Shimano for use on mountain bikes with two separate levers operating each shift cable.

rear triangle: the rear portion of the bicycle frame, including the seatstays, the chainstays and the seat tube.

rebound damping: the diminishing of speed of return of a spring after compression.

rim: the outer hoop of a wheel to which the tire is attached.

roller-cam brakes: a brake system using pulleys and a cam to force the brake pads against the rim surface.

saddle (seat): a platform made of leather and/or plastic upon which the rider sits.

Schrader valve: a high-pressure air valve with a spring-loaded air-release pin inside. Schrader valves are found on some bicycle tubes and air-sprung suspension forks as well as on adjustable rear shocks and automobile tires and tubes.

sealed bearing: a bearing enclosed in an attempt to keep contaminants out. (see also "cartridge bearing".)

seat cluster: the intersection of the seat tube, top tube, and seat stays.

seat: (see "saddle.")

seatpost: the post to which the saddle is secured.

skewer: a hub quick release or a shaft passing through a stack of elastomer bumpers in a suspension fork.

snapring: (see "circlip.")

spider: a star-shaped piece of metal that connects the right crank arm to the chainrings.

spokes: metal rods that connect the hub to the rim of a wheel.

spring: an elastic contrivance, which, when compressed, returns to its original shape by virtue of its elasticity. In bicycle suspension applications, the spring used is normally either an elastic polymer cylinder, a coil of steel or titanium wire, or compressed air.

spring preload: the initial loading of a spring so part of its compression range is taken up prior to impact.

sprocket: a circular, multiple-toothed piece of metal that engages a chain. (See also: cog and chainring.)

standover clearance ("standover height"): the distance between the top tube of the bike and the rider's crotch when standing over the bicycle.

star nut ("Star-fangled nut"): a pronged nut that is forced down into the steering tube and anchors the stem bolt of a threadless headset.

steering axis: the imaginary line about which the fork rotates.

steering tube: the vertical tube on a fork that is attached to the fork crown and fits inside the head tube.

step-through frame ("women's frame"; "girl's bike"; "mixte frame"): a bicycle frame with a steeply up-angled top tube connecting the bottom of the seat tube to the top of the head tube. The frame design is intended to provide ease of stepping over the frame and ample standover clearance.

straddle cable: short segment of cable connecting two brake arms together.

straddle-cable holder: (see "yoke.")

swingarm: the movable rear end of a rear-suspension frame.

threadless headset: (see "AheadSet".)

three cross: (see "cross three".)

thumb shifter: a thumb-operated shift lever attached on top of the handlebars.

top tube: the tube that connects to the seat tube to the head tube.

triple: a term used to describe the three-chainring combination attached to the right crankarm.

twist shifter: a cable-pulling derailleur control handle surrounding the handlebar adjacent to the hand grip; it is twisted forward or back to cause the derailleur to shift. (see also "Grip Shift".)

U-brake: a mountain-bike brake consisting of two arms shaped like inverted L's affixed to posts on the frame or fork.

V-brake: a cable-operated rim brake consisting of two vertical brake arms with a cable link and cable guide pipe on one arm and a cable anchor on the opposite arm.

wheel base: the horizontal distance between the two wheel axles.

wild goose chase: (see "chase".)

women's frame: (see "step-through frame".)

yoke: the part attaching the brake cable to the straddle cable on a cantilever or U-brake.

If you have a torque wrench, these are the standard tightnesses recommended by Shimano, Grip Shift, Rock Shox and Answer/Manitou for their products. Divide these numbers by 12 to convert them to foot-pounds.

torque table

brake assemblies	brake lever clamp bolt	.50-70 inch-pounds
		.(22-26 inch-pounds for slotted screw type)
	brake mounting bolt	.40-60 inch-pounds
	brake cable fixing bolt	.50-70 inch-pounds
	V-brake pad fixing nut	.50-70 inch-pounds
	canti brake pad fixing bolt	.70-80 inch-pounds
	straddle cable yoke fixing nut	.35-43 inch-pounds
	Shimano V-brake leverage adjuster bolt	.9-13 inch-pounds
	Avid Arch Supreme arch-mounting bolt	.35-40 inch-pounds
derailleur and shifting assemblies	front derailleur cable fixing bolt	.44-60 inch-pounds
	front derailleur clamp bolt	.44-60 inch-pounds
	rear derailleur cable fixing bolt	.35-52 inch-pounds
	rear derailleur dropout mounting bolt	.70-86 inch-pounds
	rear derailleur pulley center bolts	.27-34 inch-pounds
	shifter clamp bolt-hex key type	.53-69 inch-pounds
		.(22-26 inch-pounds for slotted screw type)
	shift lever parts fixing screw	.22-26 inch-pounds
	Gripshift lever mounting screw	.17 inch-pounds
hubs, cassettes, quick releases	hub quick release lever closing	.79-104 inch-pounds
	bolt-on steel skewer	.65 inch-pounds
	bolt-on titanium skewer	.85 inch-pounds
	quick release axle locknut	.87-217 inch-pounds
	freehub cassette body fixing bolt	.305-434 inch-pounds
	cassette cog lockring	.260-434 inch-pounds
crank, bottom bracket assemblies	crank arm fixing bolt	.300-435 inch-pounds
	chainring fixing bolt	.70-95 inch-pounds
	cartridge bottom bracket cups	.435-608 inch-pounds
	standard bottom bracket fixed cup	.609-695 inch-pounds
	standard bottom bracket lockring	.609-695 inch-pounds
	pedal axle	.307 inch-pounds or more
seats, stems	seat post clamp bolt	.174-347 inch-pounds
	stem handlebar clamping bolt	.174-260 inch-pounds
	stem expander bolt	.174-260 inch-pounds
	AheadSet stem clamp bolts	.130 inch-pounds
	Aheadset bearing preload	.22 inch-pounds
suspension forks	Rock Shox fork crown clamp bolt	.60 inch-pounds
	Rock Shox brake post	.60 inch-pounds
	Rock Shox fork brace bolt	.60 inch-pounds
	Rock Shox Judy cartridge shaft bolt	.60 inch-pounds
	Rock Shox Judy neutral shaft bolt	.60 inch-pounds
	Manitou 6mm single fork crown clamp bolt	.110-130 inch-pounds
	Manitou 5mm paired fork crown clamp bolt	.60 inch-pounds
	Manitou brake post	.90-110 inch-pounds
	Manitou fork brace bolt	.90-110 inch-pounds
	Manitou EFC/Mach 5/SX cartridge bolt	.10-30 inch-pounds
	Manitou neutral shaft bolt	.10-30 inch-pounds
	Manitou EFC/Mach 5/SX cartridge cap	.30-50 inch-pounds
shoes	shoe cleat fixing bolt	.44-51 inch-pounds
	shoe spike	.34 inch-pounds

It is the one part of the mountain-bike component market in which Shimano is not king. Since the introduction of the SPD (Shimano Pedaling Dynamics) mountain-bike pedal, there has been a flood of very successful competitors in a market once dominated by the Japanese component giant. Other manufacturers noticed an opening, and the number of SPD-compatible pedals available these days shows that they have taken advantage of it. But anyone who has tried more than one brand of pedals can attest to the fact that the phrase "compatibility" means different things to different people.

It is safe to assume that a manufacturer who sells an SPD-compatible system, produces cleats that are compatible with standard mountain-bike shoes (that have two slots in the sole). What "compatibility" *doesn't* guarantee is whether those cleats will work in other pedals. Indeed, no manufacturer we found will even mention whether its cleats work in other pedals, and vice-versa. So, I will.

Pedal/cleat compatibility is an issue on the dirt. Mountain bikes get traded around a lot. Riders want to try different suspension and tire designs over a variety of trail conditions.

In this chart, I included in addition to 1997 models, some old standbys, namely Shimano 737s and 525s, OnZa HOs, and 1996 Scott pedals (representa-tive of a number of Wellgo-made pedals currently in wide use). These 15 pedals, along with private-label models virtually identical to some of these, must represent more than 90 percent of the clip-in mountain-bike pedals on bikes and retail shelves.

To develop a compatibility chart, I simply tried every cleat in every pedal (with sometimes frightening results). When pedals had optional "multi-release" cleats designed to allow vertical release, I tested only the standard, higher-retention cleat. All pedals were set at mid-range spring tension. Pedals are graded according to how easy they are to enter and release, how well they retain the foot when pulling up hard or bouncing over rough terrain, and how much they allow the foot to float rotationally.

Float is a must: it makes cleat set-up much easier, can save your knees the agony of misadjusted cleats, and prevents premature release when wending one's way through twisty single track or bouncing down a bumpy descent on the verge of losing control. High retention is also a must, as it can be very disconcerting, if not dangerous, to come out of the pedal when not expecting it. Ease of entry and intentional exit is also a must for convenient and safe use. Two pedals not on the chart are Speedplay and Bebop. Both are free-floating, and neither are compatible with any other cleats.

CLEAT	VP 103	VP 104	ONZA H.O	TIME A.T.A.C.	WELLGO WPD-800	SHIMANO 747	SHIMANO 737	SHIMANO 636	RITCHEY LOGIC	CODA CO	SCOTT TWIN CAM '97	SCOTT TWIN CAM '96	TIOGA CLIPMAN	LOOK SL3	EXUS E-M2
Shimano 747/636 (SM-SH-51)	B	C	F	F	C	A	A-	A	D	C	C	B-	F	F	B+
Shimano 737 (SM-SH-50)	B	C	F	F	C	A	A-	A	D	C	C	B-	F	F	B+
Scott '96 (WP-98A)	B	C	F	F	C	A	A-	B	B-	C	C	B	F	F	B+
Scott '97/Coda/Wellgo (WP-97A)	B	C	F	F	C	A	A	B	A	C	C	C	F	F	B+
Look	F	F	F	F	F	F	F	F	F	F	F	F	F	A	F
OnZa	C	—	B+	F	C	D	D	D	C	C	C	C	F	F	—
Ritchey	D	—	F	F	C	B+	B+	B+	A	A	A	A-	F	F	—
Tioga	F	F	F	F	F	F	F	F	F	F	F	F	B+	F	F
Time	F	F	F	A+	F	F	F	F	F	F	F	F	F	F	F
VP (E-C01)	B	C	F	F	C	A	B	B	D+	C	C	C	F	F	B+

The grading scale is as follows:
A+ = very easy entry and release, abundant float, and very high retention
A = good entry, good release, good retention, good float
A- = good entry, good release, good retention, small float range.
B+ = good entry, retention and float; hard or intermittent release (or break-in required)
B = good entry, retention and release; no float
B- = same as B with hard or intermittent release (or requiring break-in)
C = good entry, release and float; poor retention (foot can be pulled straight up and out)
C- = same as **C**, and pedal is fixed (no float)
D+ = can clip in, but foot can only be released by twisting inward

(won't release outward)
D = can clip in but cannot release
F = cleat will not clip in

NOTE
COMBINATIONS GRADED **D+**, **D** OR **F** ARE NOT SAFE TO RIDE.

illustration index

Barnett, John. *Barnett's Manual: Analysis and Procedures for Bicycle Mechanics.* Boulder, CO: Velo Press, 1996, 3rd edition.

Brandt, Jobst. *The Bicycle Wheel.* Menlo Park, CA: Avocet, 1988

Dushan, Allan. *Surviving the Trail*, Tumbleweed Films, 1993.

Editors of *Bicycling* and *Mountain Bike* magazines. *Bicycling magazine's Complete Guide to Bicycle Maintenance and Repair.* Emmaus, PA: Rodale Press, 1994

Lindorf, W. *Mountain Bike Repair and Maintenance.* London: Ward Lock, 1995

Muir, John and Gregg, Tosh. *How to Keep Your Volkswagen Alive: a Manual of Step by Step Procedures for the Compleat Idiot.* Santa Fe, NM: John Muir Publications, 1969, 74, 75, 81, 85, 88, 90, 92, 94.

Pirsig, Robert. *Zen and the Art of Motorcycle Maintenance.* New York, NY: William Morrow & Co., 1974.

Stevenson, John, and Richards, Brant. *Mountain Bikes: Maintenance and Repair.* Mill Valley, CA: Bicycle Books, 1994

Taylor, Garrett, *Bicycle Wheelbuilding 101, a Video Lesson in the Art of Wheelbuilding.* Westwood, MA: Rexadog, 1994

Van der Plas, Robert. *The Bicycle Repair Book.*
Mill Valley, CA: Bicycle Books, 1993

Van der Plas, Robert. *Mountain Bike Maintenance.*
San Francisco, CA: Bicycle Books, 1994

bibliography

A-C

C-L

M-S

Frame	Serial Number	
	Size	Date of purchase
Fork	Serial Number	
	Steerer tube length	Date of purchase
Stem	Length/diameter	Date of purchase
Handlebars	Width	Date of purchase
Shifters		Date of purchase
Brakes		Date of purchase
Pedals		Date of purchase
Cranks	Length	Date of purchase
Chainrings	Size	Date of purchase
Bottom bracket	Width	Date of purchase
Saddle		Date of purchase
Seatpost	Length/diameter	Date of purchase
Wheels	Spokes	Date of purchase

Other

OTHER BOOKS FROM VELOPRESS

Cyclist's Training Bible *by Joe Friel*
Now in it's third printing! Hailed as a major breakthrough in training for competitive cycling, this book helps take cyclists from where they are to where they want to be — the podium. • 288 pp. • Photos, charts, diagrams • Paperback • 1-884737-21-8 • P-BIB $19.95

Single-Track Mind *by Paul Skilbeck*
This book represents a quantum leap in mountain bike training guides — the right combination of scientific training information, bike-handling skills, nutrition, mental training, and a proven year-round training plan. • 128 pp. • Photos, charts, diagrams • Paperback • 1-884737-10-2 • P-STM $19.95

Cyclo-cross *by Simon Burney*
A must read for anyone brave enough to ride their road bike downhill through the mud. Expanded from the original to include mountain bike conversion to cyclo-cross. • 200 pp. • Photos, charts, diagrams • Paperback • 1-884737-20-X • P-CRS $19.95

The Mountain Biker's Cookbook *by Jill Smith*
Healthy & delicious recipes from the world's best mountain bike racers. The ideal marriage between calories and the perfect way to burn them off. • 152 pp. • Paperback • 1-884737-23-4 • P-EAT $14.95

Off-Season Training for Cycling *by Edmund R. Burke, Ph.D.*
Get a jump on the competition with the newest training book from Ed Burke and VeloPress. Burke takes you through everything you need to know about winter training indoor workouts, weight training, cross-training, periodization and more. • 200 pp. • Paperback • 1-884737-40-4 • P-OFF $14.95

VeloNews Training Diary *by Joe Friel*
The world's most popular training diary for cyclists. Allows you to record every facet of training with plenty of room for notes. Non-dated, so you can start any time of the year. • 235 pp. • Spiral-bound • 1-884737-42-0 • P-DIA $12.95

Inside Triathlon **Training Diary** *by Joe Friel*
The best multisport diary available anywhere. Combines the best in quantitative and qualitative training notation. Designed to help you attain your best fitness ever. Non-dated, so you can start at any time of the year. • 235 pp. • Spiral-bound • 1-884737-41-2 • P-IDI $12.95

Barnett's Manual *by John Barnett*
The most expensive bicycle maintenance manual in the world ... and worth every penny. Regarded by professionals world-wide as the final word in bicycle maintenance. • 950 pp. • Illustrations, diagrams, charts • Five-ring loose-leaf binder. • 1-884737-16-1 • P-BNT $149.95

Bicycle Racing in the Modern Era *from the editors of VeloNews*
These 63 articles represent the best in cycling journalism over the past quarter century: the world championships (road and mountain), the Tour de France, technical innovations and much, much more. • 218 pp. • Paperback. • 1-884737-32-3 • P-MOD $19.95

Half-Wheel Hell *by Maynard Hershon*
This collection from writer Maynard Hershon gives a human view of cycling and the culture that surrounds it. Hershon explores our perception of ourselves and our sport with humor and sensitivity. • 134 pp. • Paperback • 1-884737-05-6 • P-HWH $13.95

Tour de France THE 75TH ANNIVERSARY BICYCLE RACE *by Robin Magowan*
A masterful account of the 1978 Tour de France, the Tour's 75th anniversary. Magowan's fluid prose style brings to life the most contested Tour de France as if it were yesterday. • 208 pp. • Photos & stage profiles • Hardbound • 1-884737-13-7 • P-MAG $24.95

Tales from the Toolbox *by Scott Parr and Rupert Guinness*
In his years as the Motorola team mechanic, Scott Parr saw it all. *Tales from the Toolbox* takes you inside the Motorola team van on the roads of Europe. Get the inside dirt on the pro peloton and the guys who really make it happen ... the mechanics, of course. • 168 pp. • Paperback • 1-884737-39-0 • P-TFT $14.95

Eddy Merckx *by Rik Vanwalleghem*
Discover the passion and fear that motivated the world's greatest cyclist. The man they called "the cannibal" is captured like never before in this lavish coffee-table book. • 216 pp. • 24 color & 165 B/W photos • Hardback • 1-884737-22-6 • P-EDY $49.95

Bobke *by Bob Roll*
If Hunter S. Thompson and Dennis Rodman had a boy, he would write like Bob Roll: rough-hewn, poetic gonzo. Roll's been there and has the T-shirts to prove it. If you like straight talk or cycling or both, this book is a must read. • 124 pp. • Photos • Paperback • 1-884737-12-9 • P-BOB $16.95

A Season in Turmoil *by Samuel Abt*
Samuel Abt traces the differing fortunes of American road racers Lance Armstrong and Greg LeMond through the 1994 season. With revealing, in-depth interviews, Abt examines the raw exuberance of Armstrong as he becomes the top U.S. road cycling star, while LeMond sinks toward an unwanted retirement. • 178 pp. • B/W photos • Paperback • 1-884737-09-9 • P-SIT $14.95

please mail to
VeloPress
1830 N 55th St
Boulder CO
80301

or fax to
303/444/6788

or call toll-free
800/234-8356

Your Name

Street Address

Phone ( )-   FAX ( ) -

City   State   Zip

☐ ☐   credit card number   expiration date

PLEASE ENCLOSE PAYMENT WITH ORDER

QUANTITY	PRODUCT #	PRODUCT TITLE	ISBN #	RETAIL	AMOUNT
	P-BNT	Barnett's Manual	1-884737-16-1	$ 149.95	
	P MOD	Bicycle Racing in the Modern Era	1-884737-32-3	19.95	
	P-BOB	Bobke	1-884737-12-9	16.95	
	P-BIB	Cyclist's Training Bible	1-884737-21-8	19.95	
	P-CRS	Cyclo-Cross	1-884737-20-X	19.95	
	P-HWH	Half Wheel Hell	1-884737-05-6	13.95	
	P-EDY	Eddy Merckx	1-884737-22-6	49.95	
	P-EAT	Mountain Biker's Cookbook	1-884737-23-4	14.95	
	P-OFF	Off-Season Training	1-884737-40-4	14.95	
	P-SIT	A Season in Turmoil	1-884737-09-9	14.95	
	P-STM	Single Track Mind	1-884737-10-2	19.95	
	P-BOX	Tales from the Tool Box	1-884737-39-0	14.95	
	P-MAG	Tour de France	1-884737-13-7	24.95	
	P-MTW	Two Wheels	1-884737-11-0	12.95	
	P-IDI	Inside Triathlon Training Diary	1-884737-41-2	12.95	
	P-DIA	VeloNews Training Diary	1-884737-42-0	12.95	

Total items ordered

PLEASE ADD $3.95 SHIPPING PER ITEM ORDERED

SUB-TOTAL
SHIPPING
TOTAL

ABOUT THE AUTHOR

Lennard Zinn is a bike framebuilder, technical writer, and bike lover who has written about cycling for enthusiasts' magazines since 1986. He grew up in Los Alamos, New Mexico, cycling, skiing, running rivers, and tinkering with mechanical devices. He earned a degree in physics from Colorado College in 1980. From 1980 to 1982, he was a member of the U.S. Olympic Development Cycling Team (road racing, since mountain bike racing was virtually nonexistent then). He worked as a mountain-bike framebuilder for Tom Ritchey at Ritchey Cycles in 1981, one of the principal pioneers of the mountain bike. He founded Zinn Cycles in 1982 and has been producing custom road and mountain frames and forks ever since. Starting in 1989, Zinn has written technical articles for *VeloNews*, the journal of record of bike racing, on a freelance basis. In 1993, he joined the staff and has served as the senior technical writer for both *VeloNews* and *Inside Triathlon* magazines ever since.

ABOUT THE ILLUSTRATOR

A former mechanic and bike racer, Todd Telander devotes most of his time now to artistic endeavors. In addition to drawing mountain-bike parts, he paints and draws wildlife for publishers, museums, design companies and individuals. Birds are his favorite subject, so he has included a little house sparrow.